SAILORS' TALES

Thanks mainly to the novels of C S Forester, Patrick O'Brian and Dudley Pope, there has been an upsurge of interest in the navy and sea life in the age of sail. This new series of contemporary memoirs and autobiographies fully supports the old notion that truth is stranger than fiction, since the best of the sailors' own tales are just as entertaining, informative and amusing, while they shed faithful light on the curious and outlandish world of the seaman. Avoiding the oft-reprinted or anthologised pieces, 'Sailors' Tales' offers only the rarest and most authentic accounts; but just as importantly they have been selected for their entertainment value.

AUGUSTUS HERVEY'S JOURNAL

The Adventures Afloat and Ashore of a Naval Casanova

Edited by
David Erskine

CHATHAM PUBLISHING
LONDON

Publisher's Note

This edition is a facsimile reprint of the first edition of 1953, which retains Hervey's sometimes idiosyncratic spelling of proper names.

Published in 2002 by
Chatham Publishing
99 High Street, Rochester,
Kent ME1 1LX

Chatham Publishing is distributed by Gerald Duckworth & Co Ltd

British Library Cataloguing in Publication Data
A catalogue record for this book is available from the British Library

ISBN 1 86176 123 6

Printed and bound in Great Britain by
The Cromwell Press, Trowbridge, Wilts

CONTENTS

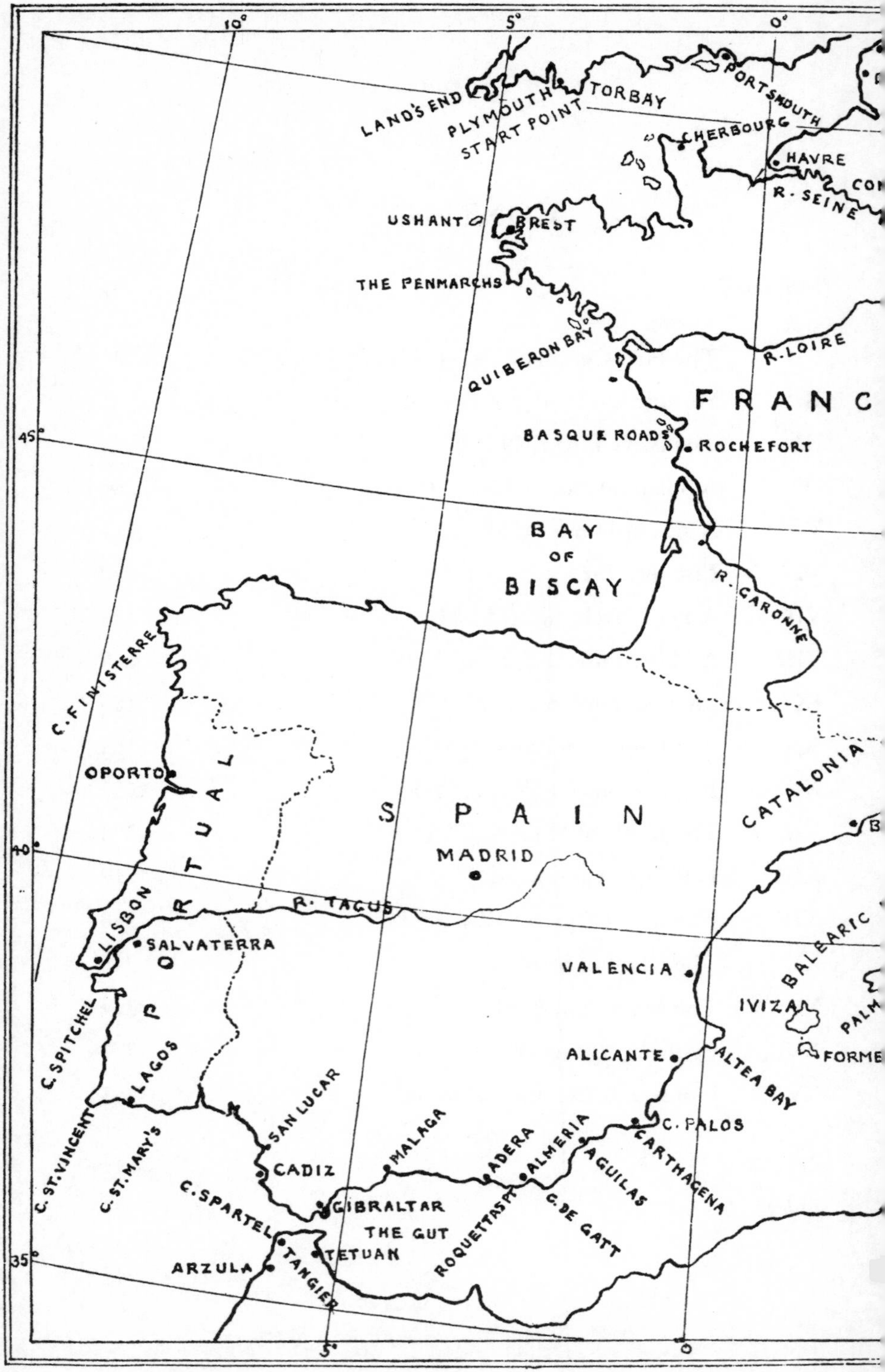
10°
5°
0°
LAND'S END
PLYMOUTH
START POINT
TORBAY
PORTSMOUTH
CHERBOURG
HAVRE
R. SEINE
USHANT
BREST
THE PENMARCHS
QUIBERON BAY
R. LOIRE
FRANC
BASQUE ROADS
ROCHEFORT
45°
BAY
OF
BISCAY
R. GARONNE
C. FINISTERRE
OPORTO
PORTUGAL
SPAIN
CATALONIA
MADRID
40°
R. TAGUS
LISBON
SALVATERRA
VALENCIA
BALEARIC
IVIZA
ALICANTE
ALTEA BAY
C. SPITCHEL
LAGOS
C. ST. VINCENT
C. ST. MARY'S
SAN LUCAR
CADIZ
MALAGA
ADERA
ALMERIA
AGUILAS
C. PALOS
CARTHAGENA
C. SPARTEL
GIBRALTAR
THE GUT
TETUAN
TANGIER
ARZULA
ROQUETTAS PT
C. DE GATT
35°
5°
0

WESTERN EUROPE
AND
THE MEDITERRANEAN
50 0 50 100 200
Scale of Miles
5°
10°
15°
45°
40°
35°
LAON
REIMS
AUXERRES
DIJON
R. RHÔNE
PROVENCE
PIEDMONT
TURIN
MILAN
VENICE
R. PO
SAVONA
GENOA
LA SEPZIA
LERICI
PISA
FLORENCE
R. ARNO
R. TIBER
LEGHORN
TUSCANY
MARSEILLES
TOULON
NICE
VADO BAY
C. de MELLE
MONACO
VILLA FRANCA
ANTIBES
HYERES BAY
C. CROISETTE
LACIOTAT
C. SICIE
CAPRAIA Is.
CORSICA
CIVITA VECCIA
ROME
NAPLES
TERRACINA
M. CIRCELLO
CASERTA
NAPLES
PONZA Is
SARDINIA
MAHON
ST. PIETRO Is
CAGLIARI
C. PULA
C. TEULADA
PALERMO
MARETTIMO Is
SICILY
GALITA
C. BONA
PANTELLERIA
TUNIS
C. PASSARO
GOZO
MALTA
LINOSA
RBARY

For Jean

ACKNOWLEDGEMENTS

ON BEHALF of the public and myself, I must first of all offer sincere thanks to my grandmother, Theodora, Marchioness of Bristol, for allowing this document to be published; it is her property and, like much other material at Ickworth, it would never have appeared in print but for the interest she has always taken in the Hervey family and its history.

I have consulted and troubled a great number of wise, learned and patient persons during the course of my labours. I thank them all for their help, and apologise to those whose advice I have been pig-headed enough not to follow.

First among those who have helped me I must mention the Earl of Ilchester, a good friend to all eighteenth- and twentieth-century Herveys. By his kindness I am able to reproduce Augustus Hervey's own drawings of the battle of Mahon, and also the letters quoted in Appendix C.

Those who have entertained me with lavish hospitality while I examined their papers are the Lady Elizabeth Byng and her son Mr. Julian Byng, the Earl of Albermarle and Viscount Hinchingbrooke, M.P.

To Mr. Marcus Cheke of the Foreign Office I am particularly indebted for advice on Portugal; may I say that his book *Dictator of Portugal* will be found to give an interesting picture of that land at the time Augustus Hervey visited it.

I must also mention Sir Lewis Namier, Mr. Brian Tunstall, and Dr. W. S. Lewis for advice on various points, and the Duke of Bedford for permission to quote from some of his unpublished papers.

For genealogical information I have consulted Mr. A. Colin Cole; Mr. Tom Barnard (on the Byng family); the Marchese Giancarlo Doria, of Genoa; the Achivio di Stato at Naples; and Capitaine de Frégate Vichot of the Musée de la Marine at Paris.

The acknowledgements for illustrations will be found under each plate.

I have to thank the staffs of several libraries and museums for their help; the British Museum, the National Maritime Museum, the Public Records Office, the Admiralty Library, the London Library, the Cullum Library at Bury St. Edmunds, and the Royal United Service Institution in Whitehall.

Mr. Tom Holland, assistant librarian of the R.U.S.I., deserves my special thanks for preparing the maps and plans.

I thank my cousin, Miss Flora Fraser, for her careful reading of my manuscript of the text.

For historical outline in naval matters I have relied mainly on Admiral H. Richmond's *The Navy in the War of 1739–48*, Sir Julian Corbett's *England in the Seven Years War*, Mr. Brian Tunstall's *Admiral Byng and the loss of Minorca*, and, for the biographies of minor naval personages, John Charnock's *Biographia Navalis*. I have consulted countless other historical, naval and genealogical works which I do not propose to list here.

DAVID ERSKINE

Ickworth
3rd August 1953

INTRODUCTION

THE memoirs which are here presented to the public for the first time were written by a member of one of the families which composed the Whig oligarchy which governed the England of George II. They cover the years from 1746 to 1759, and treat of the life of a naval captain in war and peace ; they deal equally with the perils of the deep as with the pleasures of the shore. The man who wrote them is usually noticed as "the lawful husband of the notorious Elizabeth Chudleigh, the bigamous Duchess of Kingston" ; the appearance of his memoirs should now enable him to take his rightful place among the characters of eighteenth-century England as a typical, haughty, aristocratic seaman and as the English Casanova.

The Honourable Augustus John Hervey, third Earl of Bristol and Vice-Admiral of the Blue, died of "gout in the stomach" at 6, St. James's Square on the 22nd December 1779, aged fifty-five. He was succeeded in the title and entailed estates by his brother Frederick, Bishop of Derry, from whom by his will he alienated all he could, even, it is said, the deer in the park of the family seat at Ickworth. The early but not unexpected departure of one of the leading actors in the most scandalous matrimonial farce of the age was, of course, noticed by Horace Walpole, for many years an intimate of the Herveys and the century's chief retailer of everybody else's business. On the 1st January 1780 Walpole wrote to the Countess of Upper Ossory:

> Lord Bristol has left a paper or narrative of the Lord knows what. that is to be padlocked till his son[1] is of age—nine years hence ; and then not to be published while *whom God long preserves*[2] is alive. This

[1] "Little" Augustus Hervey ; natural son of Captain Hervey and Kitty Hunter, born about 1764–5. Kitty Hunter had eloped to France with Hervey's friend, Lord Pembroke, in 1763 ; on her return she seems to have been "protected" by Hervey ; she was a daughter of one of the Lords of the Admiralty and ended her days as the wife of Field-Marshal Sir Alured Clarke. "Little" Augustus was killed in 1782, when the documents passed to his Uncle William.

[2] King George III.

was leaving the boy a fortune indeed if both live nine years! There too is another noble author—not for me but for a supplement. I had rather the Earl-Bishop would publish his father's memoirs.

Three days later he corrected himself:

My last intelligence was wrong; Lord Bristol's codicil, now printed, seems to relate entirely to his father's papers, to nothing of his own; nay it seems rather civilly than rudely meant as to the hour of publication and to prevent disagreeable truths appearing with regard to the late Prince of Wales.[1]

The work to which the codicil referred was indeed Lord Hervey's celebrated *Memoirs of the Court of George II*; the effect of the prohibition was to conceal this prime historical source until 1848. But, unknown to Walpole, Augustus Hervey did leave writings of his own. By his will he left all his naval papers to his nephew, the second Lord Mulgrave, a seaman and parliamentarian who was reputed to possess the finest maritime library in London.[2] The ultimate fate of these papers is not known; one item which could properly be expected to be found among them is in the British Museum,[3] but the rest are not to be traced. Of all Augustus Hervey's writings there now remain but two volumes, both of which are with the family's archives at Ickworth, but the date and manner of their return is known to no-one. The larger volume comprises over a thousand folio pages of speeches, manuscripts of pamphlets, broadsides and newspaper articles written between the years 1746 and 1779. The second volume consists of 380 closely written folio pages in which Augustus Hervey has retold the main events of his life between the years 1746 and 1759. This latter volume is the work here printed.

The reader will readily understand from the contents of the memoirs why family feeling has not previously allowed this document to be exposed to the public eye.[4] But now an interval of two hundred years has elapsed since the events described; the public are indebted to my grandmother, Theodora, Marchioness of Bristol, the present owner of the manuscript, who has allowed

[1] Frederick, Prince of Wales, who had died in 1751; George III's father.

[2] See note on p. 309.

[3] His midshipman's logs and an account of his part in the attack on Carthagena in 1741. *Add. MSS.* 12, 129.

[4] A few brief extracts appeared in Miss D. M. Stuart's work on Augustus Hervey's mother; *Molly Lepell* (Harrap, 1936).

it to be published at a time when it can cause embarrassment to no-one.

A word must first be said of the remarkable family into which Augustus Hervey was born on 19th May 1724. His father was John, Lord Hervey, Vice-Chamberlain to Queen Caroline and the " Lord Fanny " and " Sporus " of Pope's bitter attacks. His mother had been one of the brightest jewels among the circlet of Caroline's maids of honour, and the marriage of the Herveys had been celebrated by Lord Chesterfield and William Pulteney in the " Ballad of Molly Lepell ", one of the printable verses of which ran:—

Bright Venus yet never saw bedded
  So perfect a beau and a belle
As when Hervey the handsome was wedded
  To the beautiful Molly Lepell.

Augustus was the third child and second son of this union; among his sponsors at his christening was the Prince of Wales, the future George II.

The family owed its prominence to Lord Hervey's father, John, 1st Earl of Bristol, who described himself as " an old Whigg and for ever freeborn Englishman "; he was indebted for his barony to the influence of Sarah, Duchess of Marlborough and for his earldom to his support of the Protestant succession in 1714. By two judicious marriages with " worthy, wealthy " heiresses the Earl had added broad acres to the Hervey domain at Ickworth. At the time of Augustus's birth Lord Bristol had long been retired from public life to the rural simplicity of Suffolk, from which " center of rest, sweet Ickworth " he attempted to control the wild and profligate lives of his younger sons. These scapegraces, the children of his second wife Elizabeth Felton, who was dead before these memoirs open, composed that generation of the family which gave rise to the saying that the Herveys were a third category of humankind, to be numbered apart from men and women; " Men, women and Herveys ". Constantly squabbling over the pittances their frugal parent allowed them, at each parliamentary election scheming against each other for his nomination to the family seat at Bury St. Edmunds, and incessantly imploring him to use his influence to procure them places, benefices and commissions, Lord Bristol's sons drew from him a succession of letters, which would have cowed all but the most brazen rascals;

it would indeed be a harassed parent who could not find among Lord Bristol's answers a precedent suitable to rebuke every imaginable filial misdemeanour.[1]

Four of these " wicked uncles " make brief appearances in Augustus's story. To describe them as wicked is perhaps unfair, for there is no doubt that the Felton lands were not the sole dowery their mother brought to the Hervey family, which previous to her advent had been sane and healthy. All her children suffered from some physical or mental disability. Her eldest son, Lord Hervey, was an epileptic, and many of his eleven brothers and sisters who grew to maturity showed similar symptoms and suffered from her hereditary gout; and three of the sons, to put it at the lowest, were mentally unstable.

The wildest and wickedest were Tom and Harry. Tom must be for ever memorable for eloping with his godfather's young wife and subsequently carrying on a debate in pamphlet form with the injured husband, in the course of which he described the lady as " our wife—for, in heaven, whose wife shall she be ? " Harry's youthful scrapes and extravagances had cost his father dearly, until he followed the advice and practice of the " good old Lord ", married an heiress and changed his name to Aston. Formerly a cornet of dragoons he ended his days in Holy Orders; even the Duke of Newcastle, who was the recipient of so many and varied extraordinary requests for preferment, must have lifted an eyebrow when Harry's petition for the see of Chester came to his hands.[2] However Tom and Harry have some claim to the gratitude of posterity, for it was they who protected young Samuel Johnson when he first came to London, friendless and in need; he at least was grateful to them, saying that though they were both vicious men, Tom was one of the genteelest that ever lived, and that Harry was " very kind to me; if you call a dog Hervey I shall love him." Help for the distressed is their redeeming feature; Augustus Hervey benefited from it when an impecunious Lieutenant, but in later life this kindness was forgotten. In 1766 Tom wrote in a raving pamphlet that the hatred he bore his nephews George and Augustus was " utterly inexpressable ", which provoked Augustus to reply that Uncle Tom was " the most detestable and daring monster that ever ventured to insult mankind so openly."

The most respectable of the uncles we shall meet was Felton

[1] *The Letter-books of John, 1st Earl of Bristol*, ed. by S. H. A. Hervey; three volumes, 1894.

[2] *Add. MSS.* 32, 714, folio 309.

Hervey, who led an exemplary, if dull, life after the two early disasters of being sacked from Eton and dismissed for misconduct as one of Queen Caroline's pages. Thereafter he is remarkable for never troubling his father.

Uncle William is the most important of the brothers in the history of Augustus Hervey, for it was with him that the author of these memoirs was sent to sea to learn the naval officer's trade. Unfortunately William was the most barbaric of them all. In 1716 Lord Bristol had sent him into the Navy under the protection of Sir John Norris, an old friend and contemporary of the golden days of the Glorious Revolution. A naval career was a novel venture for a member of the Hervey family; it was attractive to Lord Bristol in that the meagre pay and half-pay provided a useful supplement in time of peace to the £100 a year he allowed his unmarried sons, and there was always the chance that rich prizes would make a seaman's fortune in time of war. In 1729 Lord Bristol brought his peculiar skill at match-making to the aid of his sailor son, by then a captain of two years' standing. After an exchange of notes reminiscent of the ultimatums which precede the outbreak of hostilities between nations, he procured for William a wife and a settlement of £8,000. Both these treasures had been in the gift of Thomas Ridge, a rich brewer of Portsmouth, and since the first departed this life in childbirth within a year, the second was wholly devoted to the support and comfort of the bereaved captain and his infant daughter.

In May 1735 Augustus Hervey, then aged eleven, joined William Hervey's ship the *Pembroke* and was rated " Captain's servant ", which description conceals the true nature of his position in the ship, which was to all intents and purposes that of cadet. From a professional point of view, Uncle William was a suitable patron for a budding officer, for he is spoken of as a fine seaman and competent commander. But his brutality over-shadowed these qualities. John Charnock, the century's most rewarding naval biographer, passes this severe judgement upon him:

> This gentleman, though so nobly descended and honourably educated, appears to have been very ill-qualified for a naval command; austere in his disposition, even to a degree of cruelty, he became at once an object both of terror and hatred to his people.[1]

In 1742 this sea-monster was cashiered by court-martial for his brutality; his nephew, then a lieutenant of two years' seniority,

[1] *Biographia Navalis*, IV, 181.

had to seek out another patron. Augustus always retained an affectionate regard for his uncle; he does not seem to have been a brutal officer himself, but he was sufficiently indifferent to his uncle's vices to be able to describe that officer's fate as "his misfortune of being dismissed the service". It was a brutal age, and the Royal Navy was one of the most brutal features of it.

Augustus Hervey was his mother's favourite son. When these memoirs open she had been a widow for three years. For her another twenty-two years of entertaining life lay ahead. The days when Nicholas Rowe had described her as "laughing Chloe" were past, and she was rapidly adapting herself to her role of one of Horace Walpole's devoted old ladies. Her delight in all things French made it difficult for her to rejoice unreservedly in the triumphs which her "poor dear boy" scored over them at sea. But, however much she might quarrel with her other seven children, with her hot-blooded, passionate, and imprudent second son she was always on the best of terms. Conscious of his defects, she attempted to warn and protect him against the dangers into which his impetuosity lead him. Their attachment was never broken, and he was with her when she died.

Augustus's relations with his brothers and sisters were not so invariably cordial. The three youngest, William a soldier, and Emily and Caroline do not enter into this story; a brief word must be said of the two elder brothers and the two elder sisters.

The eldest was George. When these memoirs open he was styled Lord Hervey and had a seat in the Lords; in 1751 he succeeded his grandfather in the family honours and estates, thereafter being referred to as "Brother Bristol". He was of a delicate constitution and of an overbearing pride; he filled two diplomatic posts abroad and several offices of state at home; his two ambitions were a Dukedom and the Garter. His most valuable service to his country was given when Ambassador to Spain at the outbreak of war in 1761; his most useful service to his family was during his tenure of the Lord-Lieutenancy of Ireland in 1766. Although he never crossed St. George's Channel and resigned the office within six months, he found time, after the custom of the age, to appoint Brother Augustus to be his Chief Secretary (at £4,000 per annum), procure for Brother Frederick the Bishopric of Cloyne, and advise the creation of his brother-in-law Constantine Phipps as Baron Mulgrave in Ireland.

Augustus and George were inconstant in their friendship; this was rendered more precarious by George's frequent tiffs with his mother. But the factor which was of greatest importance to the younger brother was George's bad health; unmarried and childless, his death meant that Augustus would succeed to the family estates. When George was ill, interested parties ordered their conduct with this eventuality in view.

The younger brother Frederick features prominently in the latter half of the century, when as "Earl-Bishop" he lived mostly on the continent, travelling about, and leaving there as his permanent memorial a string of Hotels Bristol. What the origin of the implacable feud between him and Augustus was, we do not know; as the years went by all hope of ending it vanished, for they took opposing sides in politics, the Bishop supporting Catholic emancipation in Ireland and independence in America, while the Admiral voted against the repeal of the Stamp Act and was a member of Lord North's administration.

The eldest sister, Lepell, married Constantine Phipps, later Lord Mulgrave, the wealthy heir of the last Duchess of Buckingham. We catch a brief glimpse of them as hosts at Mulgrave Castle in 1752, where they were rearing a family with whom all the Herveys, irrespective of their internal feuds, appear to have been on the most friendly terms.

Sister Mary, eighteen months younger than Augustus, was his favourite. She had been married in 1747 to a turbulent Irishman, George Fitzgerald, and by 1754 the union had ended in a legal separation. Thereafter she seems to have enjoyed herself among her brother's circle of friends, and for a time she was an intimate of the notorious Earl of Sandwich.[1] She lived to the age of eighty-nine, and, before her tragic death in a fire in 1815, she had found consolation in Lady Huntingdon's Methodist congregation.

These were the most prominent members of the Hervey family in the mid-eighteenth century.

What were the main characteristics of the Royal Navy in Augustus Hervey's day?

The officer corps was very different from the closely-knit, unpolitical and financially disinterested body we know today. When Hervey went on board the *Pembroke* in 1735 he was entering a service riddled with politics, in which influence, or "interest" as it was called, counted far more than merit or ability (though these qualities were not completely disregarded). It was also a service in which large fortunes could be made.

[1] See *A bit of Eighteenth Century Romance*, by H. C. Marillier.

The main reason for political interference was that in order to rule the country ministers had found it necessary to have a majority of votes in the House of Commons. To achieve this end members and electors must be influenced, and the most satisfactory and inexpensive way of doing this was at the public charge. Sir Robert Walpole had perfected the system by which patronage was made the handmaid of government in an age when every man was prepared to admit that he had his price; the Duke of Newcastle was an apt pupil and worthy successor. The Navy, among the other public services, provided an excellent field in which to find bribes and rewards. A commission or a warrant for some hesitant elector's near relation, a post in a dockyard or a hospital for some troublesome dependant, or, richest plum of all, the appointment of some borough-monger (or his brother) to the command of a lucrative station abroad, were all favours which would ingratiate the recipients and their patrons to the ministers in whose gift they had been. The disastrous result was to divide the sea-officers into political factions, and the strongest evidence of this is the long succession of discreditable courts-martial which bedevilled the Georgian navy. Not until the turn of the century did politics begin to play a less important part in a naval career; until then it was customary to wash the service's dirty political linen in public; the trials of Mathews and Lestock in the '40's, of John Byng in 1757, and of Keppel and Palliser in 1778 are the symptoms of this condition. But what else could be expected of a profession in which it was the exception to find an admiral who had *not* got a seat in Parliament? The political character of the Navy stands out clearly in Hervey's account—nowhere more clearly than when he describes the opposition to the passage of the Navy Bill in 1749.

The financial attractions of the naval service were not to be found in lavish pay or secure pensions. They were prize-money, head-money and freight.

Prize-money, the fruits of war carried on against the enemy's merchantmen, was the chief source of naval wealth; every officer hoped and schemed to be appointed to a lucrative station in time of war. It had become customary at the outbreak of hostilities to issue a proclamation by which the Crown granted to the captors its rights in enemy property taken at sea. King's ships and privateers all benefited by this strange legalised looting, for which there was no parallel in the laws of war by land.

Strict rules were laid down to regulate the distribution of the spoils. The captain of the successful ship received no less than three-eighths of the proceeds of sale, of which he might have to surrender one-eighth to the flag officers who commanded on the station. The lieutenants and the master had an eighth to share out amongst them, as did the warrant and petty officers respectively. The remaining two-eighths went to the lower deck. Thus if a prize taken by a small ship of the line was sold for £800, after deducting the fat commissions and fees which agents and lawyers manage to extort from such transactions, the captain would receive £300, each lieutenant £20, a warrant or petty officer £5 or so, while a seaman or marine would be lucky if he was entitled to ten shillings—and luckier still if he survived the rigours of the service to enjoy it. Such distribution was clearly inequitable. It provided the senior officer with a gold mine and the seaman with a penny dip.

The system was the cause of much jealousy between commanders as they jockeyed for the most rewarding "cruising" stations. Legal disputes were frequent; during the period of which Hervey writes they seem mostly to have been settled by arbitrators drawn from among the officer corps, but as the century progressed suits became more and more frequent in the courts. Prize-money brought great wealth into England; many handsome country houses are witnesses to the truth of this statement. Probably it was the only way to inject the required stimulus into naval officers in the most cynical of all ages, but it certainly led to bitterness and hard feelings, Hervey shows us how service under an indulgent admiral could make a young officer's fortune; within a year, at the age of twenty-four, his circumstances were so changed that, whereas in 1747 he could not raise a hundred pounds to fit out his new command, by the end of 1748 his friend Byng had put him in the way of £9,000.

The attractions of pursuing fat merchantmen were so strong that the Admiralty was forced to bribe its servants to attack the less valuable men-of-war. In Stuart days a reward had been paid of £10 for every gun carried by the captured enemy warship; by Hervey's day this had been replaced by a grant of £5 for every member of the enemy crew alive at the beginning of the action. This sum was distributed in like proportion to prize-money, except that the flag officers got nothing. "Head-money", as this payment was called, seems to have been regarded as a fortuitous tip; prize-money was a business.

The third source of revenue, reserved exclusively for flag officers and captains, was freight money. This had the added advantage of being paid both in war and peace. Whenever a man-of-war carried bullion or coin on a voyage, whether on the public or on private account, the captain was entitled to a fee, of which the flag officer took one-third. The rate was fixed by agreement between the merchants and all the captains on the station, and naturally this varied with the risks of the voyage. For instance, to convey coin from Lisbon to London was less hazardous than to run it from Lisbon to Genoa, past the lairs of the Barbary pirates; in war still higher freights could be demanded. One and one-half per cent seems to have been the highest rate that Hervey ever received, and one-half of one per cent the lowest.

Lord Macaulay, by implication, would have us believe that this was one of the evils of the Stuart navy which the Glorious Revolution put a stop to. Hervey reveals that the Whig navy was still revelling in the profits of this trade nearly a century later. In the years of peace between 1752 and 1756 while commanding the *Phoenix* on the Mediterranean station he seems to have earned about £1,000 a year on this account; his pay as captain of that ship was £110 a year. We find him delaying his departure from Lisbon in the hopes of picking up a sizeable cargo of coin; we find him and Howe engaged in an unseemly squabble at Cadiz over the rate at which freight should be charged; and we find him and Keppel going to arbitration over the latter's entitlement to a flag officer's share. In fact this source of wealth was as disruptive to discipline and good fellowship as was prize, and unless all the captains on a station were agreed and remained good friends, a squadron could easily degenerate into a pack of bickering brokers.

The chief figure in naval administration during the years covered by Hervey was George, Lord Anson. In 1744 this silent but formidable officer had returned in the *Centurion* from his celebrated voyage round the world. Wealthy and well-connected (he was Lord Chancellor Hardwicke's son-in-law) in the same year he was appointed to the Board as a junior member; he did not become its titular head until 1751, but before that date the two First Lords, the Duke of Bedford and the Earl of Sandwich, left the details of administration in his capable hands. He remained at the head of naval affairs until his death in 1762, save for a break of six months in 1756–7.

The debt which the Navy owed to Lord Anson was large. The war which had broken out in 1739 had revealed many defects in the organisation, discipline and tactics of the fleet; it was Anson who righted many of these failings. Hervey gives him no credit for his reforms in the dockyards, for the new designs and ratings of the ships, for the new Fighting Instructions, for the establishment of the Marines on a permanent footing, for the introduction of the officer's uniform; in fact, he gives him no credit for any of the steps which he took to make the naval service an efficient machine to be tended by competent professionals. To Hervey Anson is the prejudiced party tool of Newcastle, Hardwicke and Fox; the treatment accorded to Byng served to blind him further to the good qualities the First Lord undoubtedly possessed.

Hervey repeats the familiar accusation that Lord Anson favoured with lush commands only those who had accompanied him on his great voyage. No doubt these officers were his favourites; but then the *Centurion's* little band was a deserving one. We find among them Keppel, Saunders, Brett, Denis, Hyde Parker, Saumarez and Byron, officers who proved themselves worthy of the advancement which their patron secured for them. The truth is that the sea officers of this date saw the shadow of nepotism and interest lurking behind every appointment, so Hervey's strictures must not be given too much weight. Patronage was the prevailing system; Hervey's turn came when he was a junior Lord of the Admiralty from 1771 to 1775; no doubt he furthered the careers of a few friends!

In fact, Anson has the reputation of having refused many of the Duke of Newcastle's pressing requests. As his prestige and authority grew, he was daily more able to resist the prostitution of the service to political ends. Despite all Hervey's complaints, it should be observed that Anson commissioned him to command the *Phoenix* in the Mediterranean in time of peace, when there were many other more senior and more distinguished officers worthier of his attention; Hervey's appointment is itself one example of Lord Anson's concern for the good of the service.

Many other officers distinguished in the great maritime wars with France and Spain are mentioned by Hervey. Care must be taken not to accept his strong comments on them as if they were the result of impartial judgement. Hervey held strong views coloured by political connections, and his opinions are without doubt biased. Apart from what he tells us about Anson and Byng, perhaps the most interesting light he sheds is on Edward, Lord Hawke. This admiral had a high regard for Hervey's professional qualities, as will be seen from what he wrote when Hervey left his squadron before the victory of Quiberon in 1759.[1] Hervey's

[1] p. 304.

judgement of him, when writing of the failure of the Rochefort expedition of 1757, was that he was an officer who had not "a head to conduct an expedition, however he might and certainly had a heart to gain an engagement."[1] Hervey's description of Hawke's command in the Mediterranean in 1756 after Byng's fiasco bears out this uncomplimentary opinion.

The admiral of whom Hervey tells us most is John Byng. This officer was the central figure in the most famous of all naval courts-martial; his execution was an act of gross injustice and political cowardice.

Their association started fortuitously. In March 1742 Augustus Hervey, aged seventeen, was given leave to come to London from Plymouth; he had just returned from the West Indies in his uncle's hell-ship *Superb*, and he was the happy claimant to a lieutenant's share in a rich prize, the *Constant of Tenerife*—valued by the newspapers at £200,000[2]—which luck, but not deserts, had put in the way of the home-coming ship. There were two pressing reasons why he should return to sea at once. First, he could not afford to remain idle in time of war, both on account of expected promotion and hoped-for prize; secondly, if he stayed in the kingdom, he would be called as a witness at his uncle's forthcoming court-martial. His "interest" was in the ascendant at this moment. His father was enjoying his last office, that of Lord Privy Seal, and the new First Lord, the Earl of Winchelsea, was a family friend. H.M.S. *Sutherland* was lying at Plymouth about to sail for Newfoundland to inspect the fisheries there and then to bring home the trade by way of Lisbon; her captain was John Byng, and to him on the 5th May Augustus was sent, with instructions that he was to do duty as an acting lieutenant should there be no vacancy among the lieutenancies in the ship. By the time the *Sutherland* returned home nine months later a firm friendship seems to have grown up between Hervey and Byng; Hervey was immediately commissioned as fourth lieutenant in Byng's next ship, the *Captain*, and in her he served on the profitable cruising station of Ushant. In October 1743 Byng left the *Captain*, but Hervey stayed on in her.

The reason for this separation was clear. Hervey had reached the age of nineteen and a half, and, as the scion of a prominent Whig family, he could reasonably expect to receive his first

[1] p. 262.

[2] There is no reason to suppose that newspapers then were any more accurate on such subjects than are their counterparts today.

independent command at about the age of twenty—regardless of what the regulations laid down about minimum ages. His father had died during his absence in the Channel, but his grandfather provided the usual, though in this case ineffective, letter suitable to the occasion. It was written on the 5th October to Thomas Davers, a captain about to receive his flag; he was a member of a family of West Indian planters who had settled at Rushbrooke in Suffolk; he himself had his home at Little Horringer Hall which touched on the pale of Ickworth Park.

> As I hope the time has now come which has been long wished for by all your friends and particularly myself, when justice will be done to your rank and merit in the service of your country by giving you a flag, and the bearer my grandson Augustus being more ambitious of being your Captain (in that event) than of any other present preferment, if you would be so good as a neighbour and relation to think him worthy of that honour, the obligation would be too great ever to be forgot by, sir, your most affectionate friend and humble servant, Bristol.[1]

Thus began the thoroughly unprofitable association between Admiral Davers and Augustus Hervey. When Davers got his flag in December 1743 he did not make Hervey his captain, and the Duke of Newcastle prevented the First Lord giving him the *Grampus* sloop, as at that moment the Duke was uncertain of George Lord Hervey's attachment to the government in parliament.[2] In June 1744 Davers took Hervey on board his flagship the *Cornwall* as second lieutenant, and in that appointment he served in the West Indies until June 1746. No promotion came his way, either to commander of a sloop or to the rank of captain; it is at that moment of disenchantment that the memoirs open.

To return to Byng. He was born in 1704 and had early entered the service under the auspices of his distinguished father George, Lord Torrington, the victor of the battle of Cape Passaro in 1718. His career was made easy for him by his father's prestige; his rise was reasonably rapid; he became a captain at the age of twenty-three—not a late age in time of peace. He was continuously employed afloat, but he managed to avoid service in the unhealthy West Indies; it is said he deliberately refused appointments which might take him there. This supports the view that he was an easy-going individual, possessing little ambition, since family

[1] *Lord Bristol's Letter Books*, Vol. III, No. 1184.

[2] p. 39.

influence and prestige could get him the advancement he required without troubling himself with unpleasant and hazardous stations. It would be wrong to think of him, however, as a man not well versed in the mysteries of his profession ; Hervey had an admiration for his knowledge of sea affairs, and an examination of his library and papers preserved at Wrotham Park supports this favourable view of his qualifications. He had all the learning necessary to make an expert admiral ; but he had not the graces to endear him to others nor the spirit to make him an effective commander.

Outside the immediate circle of his relations and dependants it is impossible to name any naval officer who was an intimate friend of Byng ; Hervey is perhaps the only one. This was very noticeable after the indecisive battle of Mahon. Hervey tells us practically nothing new about the events of that fateful day ; what he does reveal—and this has never before been revealed—is how the rear-admiral and captains of the fleet behaved towards the commander-in-chief in the days which followed. At first there was not a word to be heard against the Admiral's conduct, but by the time the fleet had returned to Gibraltar the captains had realised the full import of the fleet's failure. To be associated with the Admiral in his disgrace would mean unemployment ; he became a pariah, shunned by all ambitious men. Eventually there remained only three to support him ; they had all served under him as lieutenants ; Arthur Gardiner his flag captain, John Amherst, and Augustus Hervey. It was a sad sight, and a shaming example of what fear of political disfavour could do to the unity of a fleet.

It is in his conduct towards Byng that Lord Anson's record is hardest to defend. Byng was an officer of a different political connection. He was in large measure the victim of those circumstances which are so frequently the lot of British commanders at the outset of their country's wars. He was sent with a barely adequate force to succour an isolated garrison ; the force was inadequate because the ministry and its professional advisers, the chief of whom was Anson, had been misled as to the intentions of the enemy ; they had, wrongly, plumped for home defence in preference to strength in the Mediterranean. The rage and chagrin to which the nation gave vent when the news of Byng's failure arrived thoroughly frightened the ministers and their friends. They realised that only the sacrifice of Byng would be effective to assuage and divert the fury of the King and the populace : this sacrifice they were prepared to make at the expense of an admiral who had been put in a perilous position by their own error of judgement. It should be remembered that the court which tried Byng acquitted him of cowardice and disaffection, but found he had neglected to do certain things in the heat of battle which, they thought, (on quiet reflection) he ought to have done. For that he was shot. It is only fair to point out that Anson was out of office at the date of the execution, but there is no doubt that he took no step to prevent an injustice which served to cover up the mistaken appreciation he had made of the enemy's designs on Minorca.

Augustus Hervey was Byng's warmest defender—too warm, perhaps. Given to overstatement to the point of absurdity, he tended to be too noisy to be able to present a case with dignity; but probably Byng's fate would have been the same however the paper war in his defence had been conducted. The ministers were adamant that the sacrifice should be his and not theirs. When the immediate bitterness had worn off, the result of Byng's judicial murder was no doubt as Voltaire would have it; it served "pour encourager les autres". The thought that one may be shot for a negligent error of judgement in battle tends wonderfully to concentrate the mind on the matter in hand.

On the naval side, there now remains only the task of assessing Augustus Hervey's character as an officer. We have seen that he was typical of the aristocratic Whig sailor, with all that type's usual defects; we must now point out his better qualities. Leaving aside his factiousness, it is clear that he was a highly competent seaman; Hawke was not one to bestow praise lightly, and the tributes which he paid Hervey after the blockade of Brest in 1759 were genuine. As a staff officer he was clearly above the level of his day, as will be seen from his account of his management of Admiral Henry Osborn's squadron in the Mediterranean in 1757 and 1758. As a strategist he can claim credit from the same period, as well as from the time of Byng's command in 1756. It is interesting to note that he alone, of all the members of the council of war summoned by Byng after the battle of Mahon, was for keeping at sea off Minorca and against returning to Gibraltar; this course is the one recommended as correct by the war's chief historian, Sir Julian Corbett, writing one hundred and fifty years later.[1]

We learn nothing of Hervey's treatment of his officers and crew; he rarely mentions the lower deck, and then only to tell us that they were restive at the scarcity of prize-money or the

[1] *England in the Seven Years War*, Vol. I, p. 126.

absence of leave. His ships' logs show no more than the usual amount of brutal punishments with which the Navy used to discipline the strange mixture of seamen and landmen which the press gangs and the hope of glory flung together in the muster-books of the King's ships. Probably he was an average commander of men—harsh, as befitted the age, but not a tyrant.

His active service career after the conclusion of these memoirs was not long. In 1760 he served under Boscawen off the French coast, and in November 1761 he sailed in the *Dragon* for the West Indies in the last great venture of the war. This resulted in the capture of Havanah, a blow which broke Spanish power in America. Hervey played a most distinguished part in this famous siege, particularly in the bombardment of the Moro Castle at the entrance to the harbour. As a reward for his services he was sent home with the despatches announcing the capture. Peace was concluded, and he never held a sea command again. He was, however, most active in naval debates in both Houses of Parliament. He was considered one of the foremost speakers on maritime matters, and his interest in the service never flagged. From 1771 to 1775 he was a member of the Board of Admiralty; in that latter year he succeeded to the peerage and left the administration. It is said that he fell out with his erstwhile friend Lord Sandwich owing to his desire to supplant that nobleman as First Lord; there is nothing to contradict this assertion, and I fear it must be taken as the true reason for his changing sides in politics. By the time Admiral Keppel's court-martial came on in 1778 he was whole-heartedly committed to the opposition; perhaps a fear that an injustice similar to that suffered by Byng was in store for Keppel was among the motives which inspired his ardent efforts to defend his former political and service rival; but, from what we learn of him in these pages, it is likely that he rushed into that final controversy in the same impetuous, heedless spirit with which he had entered his earlier disputes with Admiral Davers in 1746, the Board of Admiralty over the Navy Bill of 1749, and the whole government of England on behalf of Admiral Byng in 1756.

In 1779 the gout which had troubled him for nearly thirty years ended his life.

The other main subject of which Augustus Hervey treats is women.

First we must dispose of his wife; not because she makes frequent appearances in his memoirs, but because she is " the clog . . . which will not let me remain in England with any satisfaction to myself ",[1] and also because it is through her notoriety that his name has previously been known.

On the 4th August 1744, before sailing with Admiral Davers in the *Cornwall* for the West Indies, Lieutenant Augustus Hervey, aged twenty, had married Miss Elizabeth Chudleigh, probably four years his senior, one of the Princess of Wales's maids of honour, renowned for her gay beauty and easy virtue. It is said that they first met at the Winchester Races that June. The match was engineered by Miss Chudleigh's aunt, Mrs. Hanmer, who thought she saw in the alliance good financial prospects for her niece—for at that moment George Lord Hervey was paying one of his periodic visits to Death's door. They were married in secret in the tiny church in the grounds of Lainston House, near Salisbury; the ceremony took place at dead of night by the light of a candle standing in the upturned hat of one of the witnesses; the newly wedded pair were formally put to bed. A few days later the Lieutenant had to rise early in the morning to repair on board the *Cornwall* at Spithead; the maid Ann, who called him, said " they were very sorry to take leave ".[2] Hervey's ship lay at Spithead all summer, but we do not know if he saw her again before he sailed for the West Indies on the 18th November; perhaps she had to return to her duty about the Princess in London, for she had to retain her appointment in order to support herself, a burden her husband could not afford to undertake. Their next meeting is described in these memoirs.[3]

If ever there was a marriage which was enterprised unadvisedly, lightly or wantonly, with an utter disregard for the causes for which matrimony was ordained, it was this one. It was the work of a third party, who had procured the union of a bride of promiscuous habits with an impecunious youth about to spend the next two years abroad.

Miss Chudleigh was the daughter of Colonel Thomas Chudleigh, one time Lieutenant-Governor of Chelsea Hospital, who died while she was still a girl. After his death she had passed a few years in the West Country, whence she is said to have been brought to London by William Pulteney, later Earl of Bath. When he tired of her, he paid her off by having her appointed maid of honour

[1] p. 93.
[2] See *The Trial of the Duchess of Kingston*, in the Famous Trials Series and also *The Amazing Duchess* by C. E. Pearce.
[3] p. 44.

to the Princess of Wales at Leicester House; the pension was £400 a year. Who were her successive lovers we know not; but it is reasonably certain that, about the time of her marriage with Hervey, James 6th Duke of Hamilton was an ardent suitor and had already offered her his hand. We shall never know what it was that made Mrs. Hanmer reject the Duke's offer to her niece. What is certain is that Miss Chudleigh continued to receive the Duke after her marriage, even when her husband was at home. The birth of a short-lived child to the "Herveys" in 1747 did nothing to make their attachment stronger; when Hervey departed for another eighteen months abroad, this time to the Mediterranean, Miss Chudleigh continued to support herself by the means to which she had been accustomed. Her husband's remittances to pay her debts confirmed that his desire was still to please her if he could;[1] but on his return in December 1748, he "was very much displeased with many things I heard of Miss Chudleigh's conduct, especially from her own relations, too, which put me out of humour and made me mind several little circumstances that perhaps would otherwise have passed with me as nothing."[2] On the 25th January 1749, after "some *éclaircissments*" with her, he "took a resolution from this afternoon of going abroad and never having any more to do in that affair".[3] On the 2nd June Miss Chudleigh besought him to change his mind; "but I was deaf to all the siren's voice".[4] On the 3rd he crossed to France.

The Duke of Hamilton did not press his suit with Miss Chudleigh; he consoled himself with one of the Misses Gunning. The Duke of Ancaster made a brief appearance on the scene, but very early in the '50's he had been displaced by Evelyn, 2nd Duke of Kingston. With this nobleman Miss Chudleigh kept company, on and off, until the day of his death. Rumour naturally linked her name with those of countless others; even the aged George II was said to have a passing infatuation for her.

In 1759 her wifely status suddenly took on a new significance. George Lord Bristol was again *in extremis*; if he died, Augustus would come into his own. On the 12th February Miss Chudleigh hurried down to Lainston and there and then got the old parson who had married her to enter the details of the ceremony in the register. She said, in triumph, that "it might be a hundred thousand pounds in her pocket". Then George recovered.

Nine years later Augustus Hervey took a fancy to a Miss Moysey, daughter of a fashionable Bath physician, and was minded to be

[1] pp. 56, 68 and 76. [2] p. 76. [3] p. 77. [4] p. 84.

rid of Miss Chudleigh and to marry again. He therefore threatened steps which would establish his marriage with her, in order that he might bring proceedings against her on the grounds of her adultery and have the marriage dissolved. But things turned out differently. Bribed, it is said, with £16,000 as the price of his silence, Hervey was the respondent to a manifestly collusive suit in the Ecclesiastical Court, which resulted in a declaration that Miss Chudleigh had never been his wife and enjoined him to stop asserting that she was.

This declaration set her free—she thought; on the 8th March 1769 she married the Duke of Kingston at St. George's, Hanover Square. It has been said (almost certainly wrongly) that Augustus was present, and said that he had come to take a last look at his widow. He himself seems to have had scruples about contracting another marriage; or, more likely, to use his own phrase, "the passions cooled, or new ones succeeded".

Elizabeth Chudleigh enjoyed her Duke until 1773, when he died; she had induced him to leave her all his personal estate and a life interest in his realty, after which it was to pass to his younger nephew Charles Meadows; the Duke entirely disinherited his elder nephew Evelyn Meadows. This latter was responsible for what followed. If he could prove the Duchess's marriage bigamous, he would be a beneficiary under the Duke's will.

At Evelyn Meadows's instigation, the Duchess was indicted, tried and convicted of bigamy before the House of Lords in April 1776; her marriage was proved by the register she had herself completed in 1759, and by the sole surviving witness of the ceremony, the maid Ann, who in 1752 had married Hervey's steward William Cradock. Fortunately for Elizabeth, a year before the trial came on in Westminster Hall, Brother George had at last died; that meant, that though she was no longer a Duchess, she was certainly *de jure* Countess of Bristol; her husband's peerage saved her from the penalties of her felony—which included branding on the hand—and she was discharged on the payment of her fees. To escape the vengeance of Evelyn Meadows she fled abroad, where she remained, leading a dissolute and demented life all over the continent until a timely death removed her in 1788.

These, then, are the barest bones of the most notorious matrimonial scandal of the age. A pair of scissors, wielded by the same prudish hand[1] which mutilated Lord Hervey's *Memoirs*,

[1] Traditionally supposed to be that of Frederick, 5th Earl and 1st Marquis of Bristol (d. 1859), son of the Earl-Bishop.

has excised a few of the short passages referring to Miss Chudleigh in Augustus's manuscript; in consequence we learn little more from him of this fantastic affair beyond what is already known. There is no credit for either party to the marriage to be found in the story. By his youthful indiscretion Hervey was for ever prevented from getting himself a legitimate heir. From about 1771 he found solace in the arms of a Mrs. Mary Nesbit, who in her youth had been among Sir Joshua Reynolds's galaxy of beautiful models. With this *de facto* Lady Bristol he lived out his last years faithfully; it was a striking contrast to the promiscuity of his youth.

Little need be said in this introduction of Hervey's many conquests. Who was the first we do not know; Mrs. Nesbit was probably the last; how many came between we shall never learn—but they were legion.

From what he says in his memoirs[1] we learn that at the age of sixteen a beautiful Italian singer, Ellena Paghetti, admitted his attentions at Lisbon in the winter of 1740–1. By deduction it appears that a Mrs. Artis of Yarmouth was equally accommodating in the spring of 1743 when he was commanding a pressing tender—incongruously named the *Charming Joan*—at that port. He had been sent up the East coast by Byng to secure men for the newly commissioned *Captain*; the aged post-master at Yarmouth, Samuel Artis, had a pretty young wife—a likely girl to take the Lieutenant's fancy![2]

Thereafter a succession of ladies are paraded before us, and Hervey's experiences with them are described with a nostalgic gusto. I have made no attempt to count their number; suffice it to say that they were drawn from every stratum of society; princesses, duchesses, marchesas, countesses, the wife of a Doge, artists' models, publicans' daughters, nuns, actresses, singers, dancers. The portals of every salon were open to him by his birth and breeding; some personal qualities which are now lost to us—and which are not revealed by his portraits—opened to him those smaller doors which lead into more intimate rooms.

Readers will delight in his three principal *affaires*; at Paris with Madame de Caze, who later was to receive the great Kaunitz; at Genoa with Pellinetta Brignole-Sale, unattained object of the Duc de Richelieu's designs; at Lisbon with the Duchess of Cadaval,

[1] p. 74.
[2] See *The Perlustration of Great Yarmouth*, by C. J. Palmer, Vol. I, pp. 232 and 312.

then the only lady of that rank in the Portugese peerage, who had him kidnapped to satisfy her desire. But there is nothing permanent in these attachments; the exigencies of the service come to his rescue and he is free to hunt in pastures new.

In describing his gallantries he has the ability to laugh at himself when things go wrong and to kick himself for having been duped as he looks back across the years. In this he is vastly superior to his contemporary and competitor, Casanova, who seems to have been blessed with little sense of humour. Hervey also scores over his rival by virtue of the fact that his stories are certainly true; they are so circumstantial and the main characters are so easily identifiable that we can accept them with confidence. On the other hand Casanova is an unmasked liar. It is interesting to note that Casanova claims to have met "Lord Augustus Hervey" in London in 1763; this meeting could well have taken place; our only regret must be that they confined their discussion to politics, and did not branch out on a subject which both would have found most congenial.

Is the way of life which Hervey says he led in the Mediterranean very different to that led there by the other famous rakes of the eighteenth century? If "Old Q" or Lord Sandwich had written their intimate memoirs, would they have been very much different to these? Probably not; we must be thankful to Augustus Hervey for opening up to us a view previously hidden and obscure; the rakes can thank him, too, for he shows that an uninhibited and dissolute private life was not irreconcilable with distinguished service to his country.

I have not thought it necessary to describe here the state of France and Italy at this period. Hervey gives an intimate account of society at Paris, Genoa, Leghorn, Florence and Naples; we see the brilliant and the brittle, which was swept away for ever in the violent revolutions of the closing years of the century. But a word of explanation is needed about a third land.

Portugal was a country in which Augustus Hervey found himself peculiarly at ease. There are many accounts written by Englishmen of travel on the continent and life in other foreign countries at this epoch, but Hervey's account of Lisbon before the catastrophic earthquake of 1755 and the harsh reforms of the Marquis de Pombal is unique.

Portugal in the first half of the eighteenth century was in a state of torpor and decay. There were two main reasons for this;

first, the national will to work had been sapped by the demoralising influence of vast imports of bullion from the mines of the New World; secondly, the priesthood had gained a stranglehold over the life of the people and a totally disproportionate amount of wealth and man-power was devoted to the maintenance of the external magnificence of the Church.

The import of silver and gold from America brought immense riches to the country, but Portuguese trade had passed almost completely into the hands of the foreign merchant communities of Lisbon and Oporto. Of these "Factories", as they were called, the English at Lisbon was by far the most powerful and numerous. A series of advantageous treaties concluded since Cromwell's day between the two countries had given to the English merchants a virtual monopoly in the cloth and grain trades; they were allowed many special immunities from Portuguese law, they had their own commercial court presided over by their own judge, and they enjoyed very valuable privileges in the Customs House. In return for this most favoured treatment, Whigs at home drank port wine. The Factory was a close, "purse-proud" community; Hervey naturally did not go much among these tradespeople—except when he sought the rich freights which were in their gift!

During the long reign of King João V (1707–50) the Church in Portugal had grown immensely in power. That king lavished wealth upon it. He presented vast quantities of plate and jewels, he set up the Archbishop of Lisbon as a local pontiff, styled the Patriarch, complete with a Sacred College, and he built magnificent convents, in the greatest of which, Odivellas, he disported himself as if he was an oriental potentate in a well-stocked harem. Voltaire said of him "This monarch's gaieties were religious processions; when he took to building he built monasteries; and when he wanted a mistress, he chose a nun."[1] In return for his devotion and munificence the King extracted from the Pope the title of "Most Faithful", so that he could vie with his Most Catholic Majesty of Spain and his Most Christian Majesty of France. It is

[1] It should be pointed out that when Hervey describes his escapades with the nuns at the grates of the convents, it is very probable that the ladies were not under vows. In the large unreformed communities, like the Bernadines at Odivellas, there was a large floating population of lodgers and pensioners—ladies whose husbands were overseas and wished to be chaperoned, wards in chancery waiting till they came of age, and ladies who had been sentenced to a period of reclusion in a convent for moral escapades. The choir sisters, too, were probably selected more with an eye to their vocal than to their virtuous qualities.

estimated that over a tenth of the whole population of two million people were in Holy Orders or attached to some religious establishment. Constant religious holidays brought what work there was to a frequent halt; processions and feast days were so numerous that the shops were hardly able to keep open three days together. Every other department languished. The aristocracy was a small, idle, licentious and closely inter-married body, with nothing to do but make love and duel. Every public office stank of corruption. The country was ripe for a reformer, and it got one.

Sebastian Joseph de Carvalho e Mello, better known as the Marquis de Pombal, began his attempt to rejuvenate the country after the death of King João V. He was for twenty years the chief minister of the new monarch, José I, who did not inherit his father's all-consuming religious zeal, but who was happier in the company of his hounds, in his riding-school or at the opera.

The earliest and most popular reforms which Pombal instituted were directed against the foreign Factories—in particular against the English. During the years 1750–55, when Hervey was a frequent visitor to Lisbon, the chief minister was gradually whittling away the privileges which the merchants had acquired, and attempting to enforce more strictly the reciprocal benefits which England had granted to the Portuguese, and which, over the years, had become dead letters. It need hardly be said that the Factory bitterly resented this invasion of their favoured status, but their position was indefensible, and, complain they ever so loud, no amount of protest by the British Minister at Lisbon or the government at home could stem the tide of nationalist reform. Pombal also set about the Church. Although the Jesuits were banished, he could make little permanent impression on an institution so much to the liking of the Portuguese mind. The aristocracy, too, did not escape his attention. A mysterious attempt to assassinate the King, of which the true facts will never be known and which is a "King Charles's head" in Portuguese history, provided the occasion for Pombal to stage a frightful holocaust of two whole families. The Tavora conspiracy of 1758 occurred after Hervey had left Lisbon, so we hear nothing of its details from him; but as early as 1753 he gives hints that lend support to the view that the plot was in origin the result of the King's desire for the young Marchesa de Tavora;[1] this may well have been so, and the attempt by her family on the monarch's life gave Pombal the chance to strike a blow at some of the aristocrats he had hated from his youth.

[1] pp. 153 and 179.

B

The Lisbon which Hervey knew was totally destroyed in a violent earthquake on All Saints' Day 1755. The news was a severe blow to him;[1] he had certainly enjoyed himself there after the manner of King João V.

The style of Augustus Hervey's memoirs is colloquial. He makes no attempt at the precise, polished and formal English in which his father's work is written. In fact there appears little in common between them—save that they each illumine a particular facet of their century. Lord Hervey took care to keep himself in the background, to observe and to comment on events and people as they passed him by. His son is not so modest. Augustus relates his own exploits and experiences. Not for him is his father's self-effacing habit of referring to himself in the third person; he is the chief actor, and he is essentially egoistical.

It is doubtful if he meant his account for publication. He was capable of writing in a far more finished style, as his pamphlets and newspaper articles show. The narrative breaks off in the middle of a sentence in the middle of a page; there is no clue to tell us why he gave up. From internal evidence[2] it seems that it was written between 1767 and 1770—that is at least eight years after the last event herein described; but for whom it was written we shall never know.

He reveals that he kept a private journal. Speaking of his life at Paris in 1749 he says " . . . as I write this over purely for my own satisfaction of recalling to my memory most of the events of all kinds of my life, I pursue the thread of it, just as I had set it down every day of my life as it happened, only not quite all the very particular circumstances attending it."[3] Some passages he seems to have copied verbatim out of these journals, without changing the future and present tenses in which they are cast; the consequence is a break in the correct sequence of tenses. He also kept professional journals, which is fortunate, as in consequence minor naval technicalities are kept to a minimum.

In editing the manuscript I have attempted to standardise spelling both of words and names. I have left the French in

[1] p. 189.

[2] He refers to his sister Lepell on p. 297 as Lady Mulgrave—the peerage was conferred on her husband in 1767; he refers on p. 296 to "Colonel (John) Campbell who will be Duke of Argyll"—he succeeded in 1770. There is nothing inconsistent with the work having been written between these two dates.

[3] p. 91.

Hervey's original. I have expanded the many contractions and conventional signs he uses for words, and I have adopted the modern system of punctuation and capital letters.

Someone before me has cut out several short passages from the manuscript; these are indicated by asterisks. I have deleted nothing on the grounds of indecency, only a little on the grounds of dullness. I have left out a few long lists of dinner guests, arrivals and sailings of ships, details of boring voyages, some lengthy lists of pictures in galleries, and a long diplomatic correspondence with the Moors. These deletions are indicated by a series of dots immediately following the word preceding the passage removed. I doubt if the amount deleted by me is more than one twentieth of the whole.

Hervey wrote a few phrases in shorthand. These I have had translated, and I do not indicate which they were. One phrase only I have not seen fit to transcribe for reasons of taste; this is my sole prudery. Hervey himself left one particular word in the form of a dash; I have left it so.

It is I who have presumed to divide the text into chapters. To some of these I have added brief head-notes, which will, I hope, assist those not familiar with the general history of the period; those who consider these passages unwarranted intrusions on my part can ignore them.

I have resisted as much as I have been able the temptation to add foot-notes. Some seven hundred people are mentioned in the text, and it would have been impossible to give them each a separate notice. I trust the index will make clear their identities.

I must confess to having inserted into the text some dates; this I have done because quite a few of Hervey's dates are written in the margin of the original. Where he has done this he frequently writes in the text "This day I did so-and-so;" in such cases I have replaced "this day" by the appropriate date, and have *not* put the inserted date in square brackets. All other insertions by me have been put in square brackets.

Among the items I have relegated to appendices will be found a previously unidentified broadside by Horace Walpole.

I

THE FIRST COMMAND

1746–47

The war which was in progress in 1746 was that popularly known as the "War of Jenkins' Ear," which had its origins in the rivalry between England and Spain in West Indian trade. By 1744 hostilities had become general, with France allied to Spain, and the Empire and Piedmont to England. In the sickly West Indies both sides were too weak to do anything other than protect their own commerce. Hervey was aged twenty-two when the Journal opens.

'TWAS now near two years I had been at Jamaica as Second Lieutenant of the *Cornwall* with Admiral Davers,[1] where we remained as idle in the harbour, as inactive as to the fleet, as had it been a profound peace, and only so many ships stationed there for their amusement. Few captures were made either on France or Spain, and no depredations comitted on the enemy. I think only one sorti we made (of about fourteen days) whilst I was there, in which time I was landed with a small party to burn some poor cottages in the Bay of Leogane and take away some canoes. As to the rest, the Admiral employed himself in promoting contentions and divisions in the island amongst the Assembly people, only to give uneasiness and trouble to one of the best of men who was then Governor, Mr. Trelawny.[2] In this the Admiral for a time succeeded but too well, but as the people he had to work with were a mean blundering kind of wretches, he very soon lost sight of his wishes, as well as of his character. He had wanted to employ me in all this, but had so often deceived me and made me give assurances to Mr. Trelawny that he eternally broke, that I at last was drove to the necessity of desiring the Admiral to let me no more be employed on these occasions, but only to pursue my duty on board. This he took so heinously ill that he in a manner confined me constantly to all the duty aboard, till wore out with those crosses, and seeing no prospect of any

[1] Introduction, p. xxiii.

[2] Edward Trelawny, Governor of Jamaica, 1738–52.

promotion for me, nor indeed for anyone he had brought with him, I at length was ill, and desired leave to go on shore for my health, which with difficulty I obtained; nor did I ever return on board but to get my things away, having determined to resign my commission of Second Lieutenant of the *Cornwall* and go home passenger in the *Sea-horse*.

I had met with so many extraordinary civilities in this island from Mr. Trelawny, in particular from Mr. Ord and his lady,[1] from Mr. Manning and from most of the principal gentlemen of the island, being so long amongst them, that indeed it was with regret I left the island, very great regret. I was particularly attached (though in the most virtuous sense) to Mrs. Ord for her kindness and partiality for me and the civilities I had received from all her family, the Elletsons, at Hope, their plantation. The 22nd June, then, Mr. Manning had invited Mr. Trelawny, the Speaker of the Assembly Mr. Price, Mr. Ord, Mr. Harry Moore, and Mr. Prevost with several others, to dine at his penn[2] by Kingston to take leave of me, as I was to embark on board the *Sea-horse*, Captain Denis, that evening, who was to sail with a convoy the next day for England. This day was passed with many of us in reciprocal promises of friendship, which at the distance we were soon to be separated at could only be kept up by letter. I received a very kind and melencholy letter in the evening from Mrs. Ord, and gave an answer to it to her husband to deliver to her. The Governor would carry me down to the waterside, and most of those gentlemen accompanied me thither and there took our leaves. Early in the morning we sailed from Jamaica with a great convoy, without my ever taking leave of that very worthless character Admiral Davers, whom Lord Winchelsea once to me very characterisingly called " that Insignificant Significancy ".

There was Captain David Hamilton, who had been long Governor of Fort-Royal, on board of the *Falmouth* who was in company with us, and who in the passage used frequently to visit one another and other people in the ships. I employed myself most of the passage in writing a pamphlet entitled *A Letter from a Friend at Jamaica to a Friend in London*, which was " to describe the faction in that island, give an account of their rise and pursuits; to show the progress they had made, and how nobly and sensibly

[1] James Ord was one of the principal merchants of the island; his wife was Anne-Petronilla, daughter of Roger Elletson, and sister of Sir Roger Hope Elletson, Lieutenant-Governor 1766–71.

[2] A farm, plantation, country house or park.

they were always defeated by the superior conduct and judgement of the Governor."[1]

We had a very good passage to the Downs, excepting one accident of the ship I was in being afire in the sailroom in the night, but which we extinguished without great damage or even disturbing the passengers on board, among whom was the Captain's wife, a very pretty woman who was with child far gone. . . . The 19th August Captain Hamilton and I landed at Dover and took coach for Canterbury that night, where we lay. We there learnt the news of the death of the King of Spain and of the King of Denmark, the defeat of the Spanish army in Italy by the King of Sardinia, and many other accounts new to us. The next day we set out early, and got to London about 2 in the afternoon, enjoying ourselves with all the pleasing scenes of harvest &ca. that surrounded us in our journey, and thinking everything was new to us. We dined together at the Star & Garter as I had none of my family either in Town or that kept house for me to dine at. I took lodgings at the Golden Ball in Pall Mall, my tailor, Mr. Volls.

As I had letters very pressing from Mr. Trelawny to the Duke of Newcastle and his brother Mr. Pelham, the then ministers of this country, the one First Lord of the Treasury, the other his Chancellor of the Exchequer, I went after dinner to the Duke of Grafton's, where I found the Duke of Newcastle dined at a wedding dinner for Lady Caroline Fitzroy,[2] married to Lord Petersham, Lord Harrington's eldest son. The Duke received me with all that civility ministers can put on, and with all that falseness natural to his Grace, and seemed astonished I was not a Captain, when he was the very person in the year 1744 who prevented Lord Winchelsea giving me the *Grampus* sloop to go out with Mr. Davers because, he said, my brother set out with being a protesting Lord. I received the Duke's carresses and flatteries as if I believed them good current coin, soon took my leave, and, as I found Mr. Pelham was at his house at Greenwich, I went down to him, delivered him my letters who kept me many hours there talking of the situation of Jamaica and things there, and making me many promises on the recommendations Mr. Trelawny had given of me, but which promises were of as little use as the carresses of his brother the

[1] I can find no printed copy of this pamphlet; the MS. is at Ickworth. In it the Lieutenant says of the Admiral "His public carriage in his public office tallys with his private conduct in his private life; for they were both oppressive, cruel, unjust, scandalous, mean and selfish."

[2] A celebrated flirt and beauty, later notorious as the Countess of Harrington.

Duke. Mr. Pelham told me that with great difficulty he had obtained the King's leave for Mr. Trelawny to come home, and that Mr. Price was (as Mr. Trelawny had desired) to remain Lieutenant-Governor in order to carry on Mr. Trelawny's plan in everything.

I returned to Town rather late and went to my brother Lord Hervey, who was waiting for me, and had my brother William with him, who soon after went away. My brother told me both Lord Bristol and himself had been told I was married[1] to Miss ——,[2] still Maid of Honour to the Princess of Wales, and desired to know if it was so, for that, if I owned her, he had got Lord Bristol to consent to the receiving her. However, I evaded the question by saying the world always advanced more than they knew of. Yet my brother told me she herself did not deny it. However the conversation there dropped, having so many other things to talk of, and he perceiving I was unwilling to keep up that topic, which indeed I had no reason to continue till I knew how things were and were likely to be, not ever having had that assistance from the family, either in point of interest or fortune, which could prompt me at once to dip myself in a scene so totally new, and for which I was so totally incapable of supporting, not being worth then above three hundred pounds in the world, and at that time only £50 a year left me by my father till my grandfather's death, then equal with the rest £200 a year annuity.

I went and supped at White's with my Uncle Hervey[3] and others, the club being then open (as Parliament not sitting) for every member to carry his friend, and I was not then of it. The day after, I delivered all my letters, and particularly took care to write and send one to Mr. Elletson (Mrs. Ord's brother)[4] who was then at Cambridge. The next day, the 22nd, I went to Lady Townshend[5] who had always (on Mr. Winnington's account) been very kind to me, as he loved me very much, and Lady

[1] In the MS. the word "engaged" has been written over the original "married".

[2] Elizabeth Chudleigh; Hervey calls her "Miss C——" or "Miss ——" throughout, but hereafter her name is printed in full.

[3] Thomas; see Introduction, p. xiv.

[4] See note on p. 38.

[5] Audrey Harrison, wife of Charles 3rd Viscount Townshend, and mother of the 1st Marquess and of the brilliant Charles. She had corresponded with three generations of the Hervey family, and was for fifty years a centre of intrigues and gallantries. Thomas Winnington was a friend of Lord Hervey, and had been Paymaster-General from 1743 until his death early in 1746.

Townshend gave me in about two hours the history and state of everything in my own family, as well as of other things of concern to me, with some small entertaining embellishments of her Ladyship's, and some inuendos that were sufficient to ground some sort of suspicions in me that Miss Chudleigh's conduct was not altogether as Vestal-like as I might have wished from her connections. However, as she was out of Town when I arrived, I determined to wait and see how all that stood myself, and not take alarm too quick, knowing how ready people in general are to censure others or to endeavour to level them with themselves whenever they are fallen rather beneath the standard of proof.

The Sunday following Lord Vere Beauclerk[1] came to see me in the morning, who was then one of the Lords of the Admiralty, and said the Duke of Bedford (then First Lord) had intended to give me a sloop immediately, and that if I pleased I should be stationed with my friend Harry Legge[2] at Barbados. I went to Court at Kensington and was presented to the King by Lord Waldegrave. His Majesty rather rumped me and looked sour. I dined with Colonel Frazier and Mr. and Mrs. Tom Hervey who I found were married. In the evening I went to the Duchess of Richmond's assembly, and everyone seemed very glad to see me. I played cards with her Grace and Madame Capella, the Venetian Ambassadress, who was beautiful. Several days were taken up in paying and receiving visits of friendship, and some of ceremony. My old friend Fermor[3] I found a Captain, tho' I was at sea two years before him. My good friend and former kind Captain, Mr. Byng, I found an Admiral and glad to see me again, tho' vexed I had gone to the West Indies for nothing.

After several of these useless visits &c, my brother took me down to Ickworth the 26th to make a visit to my grandfather and mother. In our way we must necessarily go visit that old stately pile of building at Audly Inn of some of our ancestors. In the evening we all met at Ickworth, Sister Phipps and Sister Mary were there also, and the next day being my grandfather's birthday, we were all (according to ancient custom) to dance—Lords, Ladies, gentlemen, servants, maids, kitchen-maids, &ca; and this we did

[1] A son of the 1st Duke of St. Albans and grandson of Charles II; created Lord Vere of Hanworth in 1750; a member of the Board 1738–42 and 1744–49, he was cordially disliked by Anson.

[2] Edward Legge, a son of the 5th Earl of Dartmouth; died in the West Indies in September 1747.

[3] William Fermor, second son of 1st Earl of Pomfret.

in a little room enough to stew us all to celebrate the good old Lord's natal day. I remained a few days here only, as it was thought necessary I should go up and endeavour to forward my preferment. I therefore set out Monday 1st September carrying with me a letter from my brother Lord Hervey to the Duke of Bedford and one from my mother to Mr. George Grenville, a Lord of the Admiralty, and *eight* guineas my grandfather gave me after two years absence from him—with his blessing![1]

When I got there the Duke of Bedford was not in Town; Mr. Grenville was very civil and told me he would promote my promotion all he could. In short the town was very empty, I was very poor, and knew not what to do with myself, and therefore went Wednesday the 3rd to Rickmansworth to see my Uncle William Hervey, who I found in a manner retired from the world since his misfortune of being dismissed the service.[2] He was so good to take care of what little money I had scraped up before, and answer my bills for me when abroad. I therefore settled accounts with him now, and gave him my note for £68 : 12 : 7 which was due on a balance to him. I returned to London about the 6th with my Uncle Aston,[3] who was very kind to me in this distress. As I found on my return I should soon be commissioned for a sloop, I also found I should want money to fit me out. My Uncle Aston carried me to Sir Francis Gosling's, the family banker, but I could raise none there. At length Mr. Layton, an attorney, got me some (about £120) on tickets which I had for different ships. This helped me a little, and having got *The letter* published which I had wrote, and seen my friend Mr. Elletson, I set out again for my Uncle William's, where I stayed merely to keep out of Town. . . . I received here a letter from my old acquaintance Mrs. Artis, but was not in a humour or situation to renew that old connection.[4] I was amazed in all this time not to have heard from Miss Chudleigh, and that she did not come to Town, being in the West at this time, which rather made me suspect there might be something in the reports I had heard of her conduct.

I returned to London the 15th, as I found by Lord Vere, who came and breakfasted with me, that I was that day commissioned for the *Porcupine* sloop, and which I afterwards found was the

[1] Lord Bristol entered ten guineas in his account-book.
[2] Introduction, p. xv.
[3] Henry Hervey-Aston; Introduction, p. xiv.
[4] See Introduction, p. xxx.

Duke of Bedford's absolute orders, and not Lord Vere's undertaking, as he had insinuated to my brother.[1] I was sworn in the 17th, tho' she was not then launched and was building in Taylor's yard. I was told by Mr. Grenville I might either be stationed at home or go abroad. I preferred the latter, having had sufficient experience of the effects of promises at home with regard to preferment, and having now the mortification of finding most of my contemporaries and many, too, that went to sea after me had got post over me, which was irrecoverable.

In the midst of this preparation for going to sea and fit myself out, I was not unmindful of my friends at Jamaica. I sent a number of things to my friend the Governor, and to Mr. Needham and Mrs. Ord, and to her a very pretty onyx toothpick-case with an enamelled picture of me in the top.

The 20th the *Porcupine* was launched, and a number of people went down with me to it. I was so distressed for money to fit myself out I was obliged to write to my grandfather, who, after much work and making me send him an inventory of everything wanted and the prices of each article, he sent me one hundred pounds.[2] As this was not sufficient by a third, I went to Mr. Henshaw to take up some money on interest, but like an old usurer

[1] This is unfair: " . . . I am told your grace has been writ to by my Lord Hervey to beg your favour to his brother who is come home from Admiral Davers, and has been six year a Lieutenant, and if your grace should incline to do it, there is a sloop will be ready here in the river the latter end of the month. I am told, if he has faults, it is not want of spirit nor knowledge in his profession." Beauclerk to Bedford, 9th September 1746; *unpublished Bedford papers*.

[2] Unfortunately the inventory has not survived: but Lord Bristol's letter has (Vol. III, No. 1216): " I . . . am much concerned to find that you are still in want, tho' upon your own stating of your case, I must own you ought to have lived upon much less; for what would you have done if fortune as you call it (but I more justly term it Providence) had not thrown upward of fifteen hundred pounds (*) into your lap? one thousand whereof I would have saved had I been you, for future exigencies, one whereof it seems is now arrived, but what that is you do not at all explain, but I must in the mean time so far to do so as to let you know that my finances were never lower, nor taxes and my expenses never higher than at this time, and therefore if your present demands will not be suitable to my circumstances, I must not think of concerning myself at all with yours; therefore for your own sake let your next demands not exceed whatever is absolutely necessary, which I should think might well be contrived to come within the compass of one hundred pounds more to that already given you by your affectionate grandfather, Bristol."

* His share as a lieutenant in the prize money of the *Constant of Teneriffe*, taken by his uncle's ship *Superb* in 1741; Introduction, p. xxii.

of an agent as he was, he would extort so much that my Uncle Aston would not let me take it, and I got some more money of Mr. Layton.

I was in Town a great while, as my sloop was fitting at Deptford, in most of which time I never heard from Miss Chudleigh, tho' I did of her. Being young and much about it was not surprising I got hold of some things; the Galli[1] and the Campioni, both famous in their way on the stage, admitted my attentions. The latter was beautiful, and as she would accept of nothing from me, being kept by the Count Hasslang,[2] I found it most suitable, as well as most agreeable, to stick to her; which I did, and only when I went away gave her a diamond ring.

About the 16th October Miss Chudleigh came to Town, and sent to me to meet her at Mrs. Hanmer her aunt's, which I did, and it passed in mutual reproaches. She thought I should have gone down to Devonshire to see her, and I that she might have come up to attend her duty on the Princess if she had any inclination to see me. However being both very young, this little quarrel passed off, nor did we let it break in on our pleasures. We often met at Mrs. Hanmer's (who was not in Town) about midnight, and passed together quite uninterrupted till 4 or 5 in the morning, and this continued whilst I remained in Town. I very seldom met her at any public place, as I avoided it, having been told some secrets by many people. I found her much more taken up with her pleasures, with the Court and with particular connections than she was with our attachment, which naturally chilled mine at my age, and after having heard many things, which she denied. However I was weak enough to run in debt to satisfy her vanity and to gratify my own inclinations, which were still to please her if I could. I gave her money to pay her debts whilst I was contracting my own for it. I gave her an onyx watch set with diamonds, and, in short, whatever people would trust me with, trusting to the chance of war and success of prizes to be able to repay it all.

About the latter end of the month just as I was preparing to go out of the river with the sloop, being tired of London life, and especially as I was cometimes prevented going to Miss Chudleigh of an evening, tho' I knew her at home, there came accounts to me from Jamaica of the shameful conduct of Captain

[1] Signora Galli sang in London between the years 1743 and 1797. She became the confidante of Lord Sandwich's mistress, Martha Raye, and was with her when she was murdered in 1779. The Galli died in 1804.

[2] The Imperial Ambassador.

Mitchell who commanded a small detachment of Admiral Davers' fleet and who met an inferior one of the enemy's and suffered them to escape almost unattacked. These letters, as the Town was full of it, I shewed at White's.[1] The 1st November many of the Admiralty came on board the sloop and dined with me out of of compliment to me, and returned all drunk at 2 in the morning.

It was now determined I should go out to the Barbados station with Captain Legge, my old friend, who was Commodore there, and that he was to give me post. But my very good friend Admiral Byng had a different and more kind plan for me, which will be mentioned in its place.

I was surprised the 10th in the evening at my lodgings in Pall Mall, as I was to go away in a day or two * * on * * 5 in the Morning and then * * * where she had left her * * *

The 17th I went down with the sloop to Galleon's Reach and the next day to the Nore, and the 27th whilst the sloop was paying, I slipped up for a day to London and returned the next to the Nore. I carried a very large convoy round with me to the Downs, where I was to meet Captain Pigot in the *Centaur* of 20 guns, put myself under his orders and proceed to Spithead, then to Ireland to take the convoy for the Leeward Islands. My people grew sickly very fast owing to the timber being new with which the sloop was built, which was a great misfortune in general, and a great neglect of the surveyors when they contracted for ships that they did not particularly watch that the wood with which the shipping was built was with well-seasoned timber. There was here a Captain Huish who told me a great deal about his correspondence with Mrs. Artis, a former very intimate acquaintance of mine at Yarmouth. Whilst I lay here, I had letters from Mrs. Hanmer telling me that all she could do, Miss Chudleigh would receive the Duke of Hamilton,[2] and that they were very often together. I wrote to her on this subject, but in vain.

We were detained here with the convoy by contrary winds, and the 10th December I received the account of Admiral Davers' death at Jamaica; in his grave I buried all my resentments to him for his irreparable ill-treatment and * * * * *
The 13th December I received a letter from Admiral Byng, who was then at Brook (Mrs. Master's)[3] about twenty miles off, to tell

[1] Captain Cornelius Mitchell was dismissed the Service by a court-martial for his supine conduct in this action against Conflans.

[2] James, 6th Duke, who later married Elizabeth Gunning.

[3] The Admiral's aunt (his mother's sister) widow of Streynsham Master,

me he was going to command in the Mediterranean and if I pleased I should be his Captain. I accepted it with most grateful thanks, and wrote to the Duke of Bedford and all my friends for their assistance if requisite to obtain that rank. Mr. Byng very kindly made it a point; Lord Vere opposed it, and as it was then intended Admiral Byng should go by land and his ships follow him, Lord Vere very impertinently asked him if he would carry his Captain in his pocket, which Mr. Byng answered with the contempt it deserved.[1]

In the interim the wind sprung up at N.E. and the 18th we sailed with the convoy to the westward, ninety-three sail. The 21st, having baffling winds, in the morning early a French privateer had got about the trade.[2] I chased him, and after seven hours' chase I run her on shore on the coast of Boulogne, she having throwed everything overboard to get clear of me. The next day I got sight of the trade going into Portsmouth, and Captain Frankland of the *Dragon* told me Captain Pigot was gone on, so I followed him, altho' I was near in at Spithead and expected letters of very great consequence there as to my promotion.

The next morning the 23rd I was off Peverel Point and saw a sail that I perceived was chasing me. I concluded him a French privateer, and therefore judged it was best to decoy him. I therefore made from him, and threw many things overboard to stop my sloop's way, which succeeded; I hoisted a Dutch jack, and he answered me with a Danish one; I then spread a French ensign and pennant and fired a gun to leeward; I then hoisted a jack at my gaff-end and a weft in the French ensign;[3] he then bore down right to me, and as soon as ever I had him under my guns I spread my English colours; he then fired at me his broadside, but soon

---

who had been Captain of the *Superb* at the battle of Cape Passaro, where he had taken the Spanish flag-ship *Real San Felipe*; John Byng, then aged 14, took part in the boarding.

[1] Byng wrote of Hervey on this occasion that he "never saw a more complete exact officer since I have had the honour of being in His Majesty's sea-service". *P.R.O. In-letters.*

Lord Bristol (Vol. III, No. 1232) was impressed; "I am very glad you are at last promoted to such a post as you desired and in so very honourable a way for you as Admiral Bing's insisting on your being his Captain, a strain of friendship unknown among the moderns, and which I now know you well enough to assure myself you will never forget."

[2] "The trade" meant the convoy; also used to denote merchant ships collectively.

[3] i.e. knotted in the centre; usually a distress signal.

after mine he struck and surrendered, and proved a very famous one, the *Bacquencourt*, Captain de la Mer, come out only this morning from Cherbourg, 65 men, and had formerly taken many, many prizes. I bore in for Plymouth with him, and glad of the excuse. It blew so hard I had near been cop'd on the Dead Man,[1] but the 25th I got in with my prize, and found Mr. Boscawen, Mr. Edgcumbe and others there. I appointed Mr. Morsehead my agent and was for selling her at once in order to follow Captain Pigot. She was sold the next day; Mr Morsehead came off and paid the people; my share £149 for her, each man had just £1 : 1 : 0.[2]

Just as I was getting under weigh the Commissioner's yacht came off to me with an express from the Admiralty to leave the command of the sloop to my Lieutenant with all my orders for her proceeding, and go myself to Town to take the command of the *Princessa* of 74 guns to go to the Mediterranean with her after Admiral Byng, who was going in the *Superb*. I was not long getting clear of the sloop and dispatching her. I lay ashore that evening at Mr. Morsehead's, and the next day sent away the *Porcupine*. It was the fourth day of January before I could set off for London which I did on horseback, no post-chaises in those days. I lay at Ashburton, and the next day at Exeter, the next at Dorchester, where I bespoke all my strong beer to be sent me of one Purcell. The next I dined at Blandford and lay at Salisbury, the next at Basingstoke, and the next day the 9th I got to London at 6 in the morning, going all night on horseback, having no chaises in those days to travel with, and the roads very bad all that western way.

I had heard it strongly reported and in the news that —— was dead of a dose of laudanum that had been given by mistake, and very near indeed it had killed; however that evening I got to Town and I met that person, and found them [*sic*] very much alive.

The 16th I was to my great joy sworn in Captain of the *Princessa*. She was at Portsmouth, and a glorious ship she was, but rather too large for my wishes of cruising.[3] Every evening whilst I was

[1] Dodman Point, 15 miles E.N.E. of Falmouth.

[2] Hervey's £149 should be $\frac{3}{8}$ of the proceeds of sale, which probably amounted to £400, to which should be added a considerable sum for the agent. Later the Treasury would pay "head-money": £5 for every member of the crew of the *Bacquencourt*, which £325 would be distributed in like proportion to the prize money.

[3] The *Princessa* (properly *Princesa*) was a Spanish prize taken in 1740. She is spoken of as a magnificent ship.

in Town I met Miss Chudleigh, but still found there was some underhand game going on that I did not comprehend. I found great mysteries, great falseness, and every mark of what I wholly disapproved. However I determined to shut my eyes and ears as much as I could to it all, as I was so very shortly to go abroad.[1] But the *Princessa* took up a great while fitting, tho' I knew not why, as she had been for a flagship before.

I was quite tired of London, tho' I made several excursions about to see my friends, as also several to Portsmouth to forward all in my power the fitting of that ship, as I was very impatient to get out, and I was also very ill most of April and May with a rheumatic pleurisy that was very painful. Dr. Dawson and Dr. Monsey[2] attended me, but at last I was persuaded to try Ward's Drop, which I did, but without any other effect than reducing me very low, so that I left it off, and believe only my own constitution helped me at last.

The news came to Town the 16th day of Admiral Anson and Admiral Warren having defeated a French squadron and taken six sail of men-of-war, four Indiamen, and several merchant ships, all outward bound. The Tower guns were fired, and at night illuminations; but we have since found this glorious acquisition was more owing to Admiral Warren's courage and conduct than to that of Admiral Anson, who might have taken them all had he not chased in a line so long, and who would not have taken one had he not agreed to Admiral Warren's intercessions of pursuing the enemy without the line. We lost in this action a most gallant and amiable officer in Captain Grenville, who was shot.[3]

The 23rd May I went down again to Portsmouth to spur them up in fitting the ship, and to see all these prizes that were brought in, which drew conquests of people down, and great fun we had here. My Captain of Marines, Captain Foulks, was a very old West-India companion when I was at the siege of Carthagena with Admiral Vernon, and with different parties that now flocked down to Portsmouth we made ourselves very merry . . . Admiral Warren came in and dined with me the 1st June on board the

[1] These meetings resulted in the birth of Augustus Henry Hervey, who was baptised at Chelsea on 2nd Nov. 1747, and died shortly afterwards.

[2] Physicians of St. George's and Chelsea Hospitals respectively.

[3] Thomas Grenville, killed in this action against de la Jonquière, was a brother of Earl Temple and George Grenville; Sir Peter Warren, K.B., was the captor of Cape Breton in 1745.

Princessa, as did my Brother Frederick and Mr. Morris[1] from Southampton. Lord Darnly and others came and dined with me; and another day another party, Mrs. East and Admiral Norris[2] and daughters.

The 11th I was on shore to settle all my affairs, and dined with Norris,[3] Foulks and others. We supped also at the King's Arms, and at half past 11 at night the drawer came up to me and told me there was one wanted me. I went down (imagining it was someone wanted a convoy) without hat, sword or cane, and when down I saw behind the door Mr. Blankley (this was a clerk in the dockyard) whom three days ago had been very impertinent, and who I had threatened to beat, yet he never took any notice of it then. I perceived he was very drunk, and he said I had used him very ill and he was come to ask me satisfaction. I told him it was a very odd time of night and as I saw his condition and had been these two days about the town, I would certainly give it him in the morning in any way he pleased. So as I turned to go up I perceived he made a blow at me with his stick, which I caught and immediately seized him and gave him a very good drubbing with it. As he was drunk I easily threw him down. This made a great bustle, and people came about us; so I returned to my company. We all agreed he was a great scoundrel and a bully, but I determined to see what he was made of the next morning and to thrash him again if he did not give me satisfaction with his sword. At 6 in the morning I went with Norris to Blankley's house and asked for him. His father came out and assured me he was not at home. I told him I was sure he was. At last I spoke to one of the servants who told me he was in bed. I sent for him, and he came down stairs all undressed. I told him to make no noise but dress himself, fetch his sword and pistol and follow me; I would wait till he came. He seemed greatly surprised. I stayed an hour, sent two or three times, and he not coming, I rung the bell. The servant gave me a very rude answer, and at last a boy told me he was gone out at the back-door. I then called out in the house that he was a scoundrel and a villain, and that wherever I met him I would treat

[1] The Rev. Edmund Morris, then rector of Nursling, was tutor to Brothers Frederick and William; Lady Hervey corresponded with him for many years.

[2] Admiral of the Fleet Sir John Norris, a friend and contemporary of Lord Bristol's, nicknamed by seamen "Foulweather Jack" from his consistent ill-fortune with the weather.

[3] Harry Norris, youngest son of the Admiral of the Fleet, a member of Byng's court-martial, and later Vice-Admiral.

him like one.[1] I told every mortal I met of this, and so did Harry Norris. Every one said he was a villain and the only thing I could do was to treat him as such wherever I met him. I went again about noon, but he was not to be found. In the afternoon (tho' my ship was at St. Helen's under Captain Hill's orders for sailing immediately) yet I went on shore again, but could not find the dog. I told the Commissioner of it, that, as I was obliged to sail, he might know it all. In the morning early the 13th we had the signal for sailing. I wrote to Captain Robinson of Colonel Frazier's Regiment the whole story that he might tell every one what a villain this was, from whom I received a very pretty and satisfactory letter in return.

We sailed with above fifty sail under convoy, having orders myself to obey Captain Hill till he was off Lisbon, then I was to proceed with the storeship and Mediterranean trade to Gibraltar, and thence to Mahon and put myself under Admiral Medley's command.

[1] See p. 129.

II

FORTUNE UNDER BYNG

1747–48

The strategic task of the British fleet in the Mediterranean was to command that sea by preventing the concentration of the inferior enemy squadrons which lay in varying states of readiness at Toulon, Cadiz and Carthagena. Keeping this object constantly in mind, Vice-Admiral Henry Medley was under orders to give all help in his power to the seaward flank of the Imperial and Piedmontese armies. When in the summer of 1746 the Allies had driven the French and Spaniards westward along the Riviera, the fleet had assisted both with its guns and with supply. But in November fortunes on land had changed. Genoa rose against her Austrian occupiers, and strength had to be diverted to invest that port. The French, in their turn, expelled the Allies from Provence.

During the eastward retreat a weak squadron had successfully defended the small Lerin Islands off Antibes, the limit of the Allied advance. So advantageous a post did these islands present from which to harry French coastal traffic, that in April 1747 Hervey's friend Byng, newly arrived as Medley's Rear-Admiral, was entrusted with their defence. He failed badly. He had approached his task with neither confidence nor energy, and it was not surprising that the islands fell to a small force which slipped across from the mainland in foul weather on the 15th May. For those who were to select the commanders for the next war here was evidence of Byng's unsuitability for ventures requiring boldness, resolution, and imagination.

When Hervey, now aged 23, arrived at the end of July, the task of the fleet off the Ligurian shore was reduced to the interception of French coasters attempting the supply not only of their Provencal army, but also, with surprising success, that of the beleaguered Republic of Genoa, where the Duc de Richelieu was established at the head of a substantial army. These small vessels with their military stores were but poor prizes compared with the rich merchantmen sailing to and from Marseilles, Naples, and the Levant. It was on these latter routes that the impecunious Hervey longed to cruise. His friend did what he could for him, though the chronic lack of small craft suitable for inshore work prevented him sending the *Princessa* away more often.

Nevertheless, before the Peace of Aix-la-Chapelle brought business to a close, Hervey records remittances home of £6,850. If to that figure is added a sum to cover the expenses of his way of life, and also £800 for the freight he carried home from Lisbon, a conservative estimate of Hervey's share of the spoils would be £9,000, a fortune adequate to support him through the next three years of unemployment and pleasure.

WE MADE the Rock of Lisbon on the 24th June in the morning early, and I separated from Captain Hill and the 27th got into Gibraltar where I met Captain Donkely with the *Spence* sloop, who told me the Spanish fleet was out of Carthagena and ours up the Mediterranean. I therefore moored for other intelligence, as I would not risk the storeships and victuallers, but finding the next day by General Hargrove that he had certain accounts that the Spanish fleet were not out, and I knowing how much the stores &ca were wanted, weighed that evening, taking the *Spence* with me to look out. I had a very good passage, having sent away the *Spence* from off Cape Palos. I got into Mahon harbour 12th July, where I found Commissioner Trefusis as Superintendant to command in the absence of the Admiral, Lt-General Wynyard Lt-Governor, but no orders for me.

Admiral Byng was going to cruise with part of the fleet off Toulon, whilst Admiral Medley lay at Savona to cover the seige of Genoa, which was reported to be raised. I heard strange accounts of Admiral Medley's conduct, who was totally devoted to a Piedmontese mistress he had, who was wife to an officer in the army, and, it was thought, was left there purposely to command him and give accounts of everything he did. She was an artful, insinuating, interested woman. I continued some days at Mahon that I might carry up the storeship with me. . . . I diverted myself very well here till the 21st I sailed with the storeship for to join Admiral Medley, but determined I would try to fall in with Mr. Byng in my way, which I did the 27th, having first spoke to the *Revenge*, Captain Murray.

I dined with Mr. Byng, who after dinner took me aside and told me the situation of affairs here, and I found he was much hurt at being left off this place, where he could be of no service to the public or himself, and where he had been since April, and with one letter from Mr. Medley in this time, tho' Mr. Byng had wrote several to him which required answers. The Admiral sent Captain Murray with the storeship to join Mr. Medley and kept me cruising with him. In Toulon all seemed quiet and nothing stirring. We found the chief view Admiral Medley had in keeping this squadron here was to get rid of the Captains he did not like, and to keep them out of Fortune's way.

Our squadron were :—

Princess Carolina	80	Rear-Admiral the Hon. John Byng Captain John Lovet
Bedford	70	Hon. George Townshend
Revenge	70	Hon. George Murray
Superb	60	Thorpe Fowke
Essex	70	Richard Hughes
Princessa	74	Myself
Dartmouth	50	James Hamilton
Colchester	50	Lucius O'Brien

The next day all the Captains came to see me and to hear what news, and, in short, I collected but very disagreeable things from them of the situation of affairs here, the neglect of everything under Mr. Medley, no captures made but by some few favourite frigates. The ships here now and then took a small vessel or two inshore. We run inshore every day and stood off at night, for there was not the least appearance of the French moving or arming.

The 12th August we were joined by the

Nassau	70	Essex Holcombe
Dunkirk	60	James Young
Revenge	70	Hon. George Murray
Phoenix	20	Hugh Forbes
Terrible	bomb	William Martin

with an account of Admiral Medley's death, so that the command in the Mediterranean devolved on Mr. Byng. He sent for me late in the evening to look over all the public orders and letters brought here, several I had brought out not opened by the Admiral's illness. Mr. Byng told me he would hoist his flag in the *Boyne* to leave me in the *Princessa* to cruise. The next day we all went away for Vado Bay, and the *Dartmouth* was sent to Lisbon. The 16th, as we were turning into Vado Bay, the *Burford*, Captain Strange, got under sail and came out to meet us. Admiral Byng hoisted the blue flag at the foretopmasthead, and we all saluted going into Vado.

In the afternoon General Paterson, a Scotch man in the King of Sardinia's service many years, who was now commandant of the King's gallies, came on board the Admiral with all his officers. This was a gallant and very worthy man, a very good officer, a great friend to the English in every respect, and yet a most excellent and faithful servant of the King of Sardinia's. In the afternoon I went with some of the Captains to walk about Vado and found it a miserable looking country, the people as poor as rats, and all the ravages of war were to be seen throughout the country about Savona. But the climate made up for all.

In the morning at daylight the Admiral made my signal, and I assisted him in sorting all Admiral Medley's papers, and had then an opportunity of judging of that officer's incapacity, and how unfit for a great command. We found all his orders and letters from England were continual reprimands and reproofs for some neglect or misconduct, many that he never answered and even some not opened, several that had come in my ship. The 19th the Admiral and Captains all dined with me, and after dinner we attended Mr. Byng in our barges to Savona to wait of the Governor, le Chevalier de Sforza, and afterwards to General Paterson. The forts and gallies all saluted the Admiral as he landed. Savona is but a small town, with a very good port for gallies and small craft. The streets are very narrow, the citadel very strong, and would be a most convenient place for the King of Sardinia if at the Peace he is allowed to keep it, and with Finale he will soon rival most of the trading ports of Italy. But the Genoese, if they can avoid it, will never admit of it. The bay of Vado just by it is convenient in war-time for any number of ships, and tho' open, yet the wind from the sea never blows home; there comes a great swell, and from all westerly, northerly and easterly winds you are well sheltered. You may anchor in 20 fathoms close in, and shut in by the little island of the West point with Cape Vado. The 21st Admiral Byng hoisted his flag into the *Boyne*, and my officers were all put on board her, and the *Boyne's* into me. I wanted sadly to get into a smaller ship for the advantage of cruising, as I could much better be spared when in a small ship than in so large a one, and one not the best for sailing.

The 22nd, having little to do, and the Admiral having arranged all his ships, I went as far with Mr. Duncomb in their way to Turin as Millesimo. This is a village in which there is a fine old house belonging to the counts of that name, and as the Countess of Millesimo was there, who is a very amiable sensible lady,

Captain Foulks and I went there to pay our respects to the Count and Countess. They would not suffer us to lay anywhere else and were very civil to us. She is daughter to the Marquis of Pallavicino at Turin; he is one of the King of Sardinia's chamberlains. She played and sung to us and was very agreeable, rather pretty, very gallant, as was said, and I know had attached Captain Latham, Admiral Medley's Captain, to her, as they had a house in Savona. The next day the Count would accompany me back to Savona, and we got to General Paterson's house about 11. The roads thither was abominable, very romantic, but the country destroyed by the armies. The vinyards and olive groves, the only produce of that country, were totally demolished by the different parties of the war that had traversed all this country; the people miserable, the women in general very ugly, altho' the children were mostly pretty and good features, which I can only account for by the women very early carrying such great burthens on their heads and travelling all the day in the sun.

We met the Admiral at dinner here the 23rd. He there offered me a cruise with the *Essex*, Captain Hughes, which I was glad of. The next day the Admiral, Governor and General Paterson, Count Millesimo, Count Arrignan and several Captains dined with me, and in the evening next day the *Essex* and I sailed to cruise off Cape Bona, having had some company to dinner with an officer and his lady, Madame de la Osa, who was very pretty, and with whom I had made an intimacy.

All these days the *Essex* and I were cruising off Cape Bona and nothing remarkable occurred. The 8th September I fell in with a Maltese man-of-war, the *St. Antonia* of 64 guns, 480 men. He refused to let my boat go on board him, and as we had repeated intelligence that the Maltese were constantly carrying cannon to Toulon, I insisted on searching him, as he was bound thither. He refused it at first, but finding I was determined to fire into him and had ordered my boat away, he consented; and tho' we found nothing, I found afterwards we had occasioned the gentlemen forty days quarantine when they arrived at Toulon. The 20th we were more successful, for we took two outward bound Turkey-men from Marseilles. They were rich and we chose Mr. Goldsworthy, Mr. Birtles, and Mr. Howe[1] for our agents at Leghorn, and Captain Hughes determined to go see them safe into Leghorn, and I returned to the Admiral as I wanted to go a cruise off Cadiz.

[1] Burrington Goldsworthy was for nearly twenty years consul at Leghorn; John Birtles, in peace time, was consul at Genoa; James Howe was a merchant.

Before I left Captain Hughes my first care was to write by way of Leghorn to Miss Chudleigh of my success, and ordered by Uncle Aston to pay her £200 immediately, which I remitted to Mr. Henshaw to repay him. At the same time I remitted about £350 more to pay all my debts. The 28th the *Essex* and I parted off the island of Caberera; she stood away for Leghorn and I for Vado, where I arrived the next day and gave the Admiral, with whom I dined, the good news of our success.

After dinner the Admiral told me that he had taken a resolution to send an officer up to Turin to wait of the King of Sardinia, and that he had pitched on me for that service; that he thought it was proper on his coming to the command, and he was sure it was expedient from the correspondence which was going on between Mr. Villettes,[1] the King's Minister at Turin, and himself, and General Wentworth and himself. General Wentworth was sent out to Turin and to Vienna to see those Courts provided their quota of men which the Allies had reciprocally complained off, but which neither did comply with; nor was General Wentworth of more use to the Allies here than he had been in the year 1740–1 to his King and Country when he commanded in the West-Indies at Carthagena and on the island of Cuba.[2] However Mr. Villettes began a correspondence with Admiral Byng in the same style he had continued one with Admiral Medley, which was that of dictating and finding fault, as if the Commander-in-chief in those seas had been immediately to act under his orders and directions, and so used to make the King of Sardinia imagine they were so. Mr. Byng knew his duty too well to need such instructions, and had his Master's service too much at heart to let that ill-behaviour of Mr. Villettes' *éclaté*. Therefore the intent of sending me up was under the pretence of paying the compliment of the Admiral to the King of Sardinia, and assuring his Majesty that the fleet should be ever active in the common cause and that the Admiral only desired to know where it could best serve that purpose to execute it, but I was to state to Mr. Villettes the offence the Admiral took at his late letters and that if he did not alter that method he should keep an officer himself at Turin to convey the King of Sardinia's wishes to him, and should in that case have no communication with Mr. Villettes. The next was to consult with General Wentworth what was the steps to be taken by the

[1] Arthur Villettes was at Turin as Secretary 1734–41, as Resident 1741–49; later at Berne.

[2] Where he had fallen foul of Admiral Vernon.

general council of war for distressing the Republic of Genoa, endeavouring to take Porto-Specia,[1] and by that means cut off all communication between the eastern coast of Italy and Genoa. These were the principal points I was to attend to, and others with regard to the exchange of French prisoners which were easily to be settled. I stayed four or five days diverting myself here after the cruise, and Mr. Bathurst arriving from Leghorn, he and I set out together for Turin the 8th October, lay at Carask[2], a filthy inn, and got the next day at noon to Turin.

I went in the afternoon to Mr. Villettes, who I found a very sensible and very artful man. He was very polite, but soon found I was on an errand that might prove very disagreeable and detrimental to him if he did not alter his tone. We went together to General Wentworth, who told me he supposed I knew the purpose of the Admiral's letter. I said " Undoubtedly, sir, or I have no business here." We remained most of the evening together, and I found Mr. Wentworth was to go in a few days to Milan to consult with Count Browne[3] about the operations of next campaign. At night I went with Mr. Villettes to Madame Pallavicino's, to whom I had a letter from her daughter Madame de Millesimo, then we went to Madame d'Entraives, then to the Count Thaon, Governor of Turin. That night I came home and wrote a short letter to the Admiral of my arrival.

The next day after dinner, which was at Mr. Villettes', General Wentworth came in, who was going that night to Milan. We sat about four hours together, settled entirely about the French prisoners, also about mortars for the fleet, and several other points. I took that opportunity of telling them both the Admiral only wished to know where and when he could best serve the common cause, and where the King of Sardinia wished the assistance of the fleet for that purpose ; but that, after that was expressed, the Admiral looked upon himself as the sole judge there whether the King's ships could co-operate or not, and that as he alone was responsible for the conduct of the fleet, he was in hopes not to be dictated to in that style which he found his predecessor had suffered himself to be, which was begun with him, but which he was determined not to admit of, and that as he knew how dangerous it was for the King's service that anything of the kind should continue or that anything of it should transpire, he had chose to send me there

[1] The modern La Spezia.
[2] Cherasco.
[3] Austrian Commander in northern Italy.

with these assurances to them rather than trust to letters by any courriers whatever, and hoped it would end here. In short I had reason to be very well satisfied with this consultation, as many things were explained, many prejudices removed, and all in a fair way of being set to rights.

At night I went and refreshed myself after all this political stuff at Madame Cavalleri's assembly, where was collected all the pretty women of Turin. I was presented to the Marchesa d'Ozar, Barrone Gamba, Marchesa Sensan, and many other too tedious to mention. I thought them all very polite, very affable and very attentive to please.

The next day, the 11th, was fixed for my audience with his Sardinian Majesty,[1] to which I was introduced by Mr. Villettes in the King's little cabinet, where the King was sitting at a writing-table, who immediately rose, and I made him the following compliment.

" Sire, Monsieur l'admiral m'a commandé de lui mettre aux pieds D : V : M : et de lui assuré qu'il ne manque que l'occasion de témoigner a V : M : les preuves essentielles de son zèle pour le service de V : M : et la cause commune, et que, l'instant que les affaires de la flotte actuellement sous ses orders lui permettra, il aura l'honneur de venir en personne assurer sa M : de la même, et que d'abord que j'aurai les ordres de S : M : je doit repartir pour lui les communiquer ".

The King made me a very gracious answer and asked me many questions about the Admiral and the situation of the fleet ; then of the enemy and their situation at Toulon when we was off there. The King was very gracious and affable and seemed to know a great deal about us all. He joked with Mr. Villettes about many matters ; in short all together took up near an hour, when we retired and then went to the Duke of Savoy's[2] apartment, who received me very carressingly indeed. He asked me many questions about the fleet too, and of several Captains he had seen at Nice, particular after Hamilton of the *Dartmouth*. Afterwards we walked before him, as the custom is, to the King's apartment, and from thence before the King to chapel. I just looked into it during the time of service ; it was melancholyly fine, being all of a black marble and gold, but excessive fine music during Mass. When the King returned we all walked before till the anti-chamber of his closet, where a lane was made for him. He went in, and then gave

[1] Charles Emmanuel III, ascended the throne in 1730.

[2] The King's son, who in 1773 succeeded him as Victor Amadeus III.

audience to all of the rank of Lieutenant-General and the foreign ministers. We remained talking in the apartments, which are very fine indeed, and then dined with General Wentworth who put off his journey to Milan for a few days. Count Richecourt, the Imperial envoy, dined with us.

In the afternoon Captain Foulks arrived from the Admiral with letters from him to me. I went from there on to Mr. Villettes and we sent for General Wentworth and talked over the contents, as the Admiral wanted to attack Porto-Specia very early in the spring, and by making ourselves masters of that fine gulf and harbour, which is a place of security for the fleet and as a constant guard on the eastern riviera of Genoa, so that with Vado on one side, and Porto-Specia on the other, we must soon reduce Genoa to terms. General Wentworth answered by saying he would propose this from the Admiral to Count Browne, but he was apprehensive the Austrians could not be spared so low down in the spring. We looked over several plans of the coast and where the fleet could best act, but it all ended in this conference and this proposal. The evening I went to several assemblies; I played with Madame Sola, la Barrone Prone and Madame de Verdin, all pretty and amiable.

The next day having little to do in the morning, I sat for my picture to the Clementina[1] for Mr. Byng.

Villettes shewed me in the afternoon all his correspondence with Medley and with Mr. Byng. I told him fairly I had seen all, for having the perusal of Mr. Medley's papers to put us *en fête* of what was going on, I saw them all, and Mr. Byng kept no letters from me. However after much conversation he thanked me for the kind part I was taking, and hoped I should be able to keep them well together.

In the afternoon, too, I went with the Marquis de Frabrose to see the palace, which, as I do not write these Memoirs to describe those kind of places so much better done by others and so generally known to all travellers, I shall only say I was struck with the regularity of all of it, the richness of the furniture, of which they have three sets, I found, for the different seasons; but that all

[1] Maria Giovanna Clementi, a fashionable miniaturist, who had studied under Meytens.

There was a second portrait as well; " I am extremely glad Captain Hervey's pictures are got safe to your hands, as I know one of them is designed for you; and I would not by any means have Mr. Hervey be disappointed of the pleasure he proposes in the contemplation of his fair one." Villettes to Byng, 7th December 1747; *unpublished Byng papers.*

the offices, the Opera-House, and everything should be in it, I thought very well planned, as by that means business was carried on with the Crown and for the public with much more dispatch and facility. The evening I passed at Barrone Gamba's. The next day, the 13th, I went all over the town, which is very regular, clean and pretty. I dined with General Wentworth, where we had a mixture of company and consequently no great conversation. The afternoon I was presented to the Prince and Princess de Carignan. He was very polite, and she very affable and sweetly pretty.[1] The 14th I had a conference after Court with General Wentworth and Mr. Villettes, and settled that we should all meet early at Savona, that the correspondence should from this time be begun in a different style and the past buried in oblivion, and the most friendly confidence began with the Admiral. This was agreed to, and I sent an express to Mr. Byng to desire leave to return, as I thought I had completed all his business here and as I found nothing could be determined here with regard to the operations of the spring, and so many of the Allies that must be consulted. I therefore wished to be at sea cruising on the enemy.

I passed my time here very agreeably, everyone shewing me civilities. The Duke of Savoy did me the honour of having me often with his Royal Highness and shewed me several fine plans of all the coast of Italy. I had several English to dine with me one day, and the 18th, receiving the Admiral's leave to come away in the night, I went to Court and took my leave in the morning, and of the Duke of Savoy, and went my rounds in the afternoon. The evening I set out with Captain Foulks and lay at the first post, where Peter Bathurst and several English were so obliging to go with me. The next day I got on horseback at Mondovi and after passing sad mountainous country I got to Vado about 6 in the afternoon, where the Admiral seemed very glad and pleased with my success, the letters I carried him being in a style to confirm all I had said to him. Next day I was at Savona.

The 22nd I found Mr. Birtles with the Admiral, who had been consul at Genoa and was now fixed as a merchant at Leghorn during the war and one of our agents. He brought about 3,532 zecchini,[2] part of the prize money, to pay the people. I passed

[1] Louis-Victor-Amadeus, Prince of Carignan, of the House of Savoy, married in 1740 to Christine-Henriette, daughter of the Landgrave of Hesse-Rheinfels.

[2] A zecchino was worth 9 shillings.

my time as well as I could here till the Admiral could spare my ship to cruise, which was not till the 28th of this month, and seeing the inconvenience of so large a ship, I offered Captain Horne of the *Superb* £400 to change with me, as he had little chance of cruising; but he would not. So the 28th in the evening, the Admiral bidding me write out my own orders, he signed them, and I went that evening to sea in order to cruise off Malta, Cape Bona and Pantalleria, all of these being the best situations to interrupt any of the enemy's ships bound to or from the Levant.

There was nothing remarkable during all the first fourteen or fifteen days of my cruise but chasing neutral vessels and exercising my men, till the 13th November when I took a vessel without a living creature on board; found her floating. The 14th I fell in with a French ship called the *St. James* belonging to and come from Marseilles bound to Smyrna. As soon as I had shifted my people, I saw a French ship that appeared like a frigate to me, and which I had reason to think was the *Flora* of 26 guns. I chased him that day and night twenty-two leagues till he run me close in with the sands off Gozo and Linosa. I was obliged to leave off and stand away in the night. When I got clear of those sands I began to calculate how he would steer to get away from the coast, and so shaped my course accordingly, and in the morning I fell in with him, but had very little wind, and so I continued three days and three nights, losing sight every night and altering my course, and yet always saw him in the morning. The 19th I had my course interrupted by a Neapolitan pollacre[1] that threw himself in my way, and would never shew me colours nor bring to, tho' I fired into his several times; on which, as soon as I came near him, I run on board him. His people took to their boat and made for Malta, and the vessel sank, I suppose, some time after. The 21st in the morning I was within gunshot of the *Flora*, but it fell calm, and he towed and rowed away from me. The Lieutenant of the Watch, Mr. Rogers, having in the middle watch shortened sail for the prize, or I should have been at daylight almost on board the *Flora*, at noon I could see no more of her, she stole away from me so quick. I stood up to Cape Matapan, and to the entrance of the Archipelago,[2] where we knew she was bound, in hopes of seeing him again, but we did not.

I took a French pollacre, which I ransomed, having many

[1] A pollacre was a three-masted ship, generally furnished with square sails upon the mainmast, and lateen sails on the fore and mizen.

[2] The Aegean Sea, sometimes referred to as The Arches.

The Eastern Mediterranean.

Turks on board. I met with no other vessel all the time I cruised about, till 9th December I made Sicily, and the 11th I saw the *Antelope* in chase of a pollacre which he took when I joined him, being the *Ciprion* from Marseilles to Smyrna. I took her with me to Leghorn where I determined to go to see my prize safe in, my ship being foul and my provisions out. I arrived at Leghorn the 22nd, and took up my abode at Mr. Birtles', tho' Mr. Goldsworthy would have had me gone there.

I remained till the 28th, and amused myself extremely well the whole time. The ladies there are gallant and pretty. There was the Bonfiglio and the Bonaini, two merchants wives, principal people there, that I escorted about. The Governor, the Marquis de Ginori, who was a Senator of Florence and a very principal nobleman in Tuscany, was particularly kind to me, and Count Bellrusst, the Colonel of the Austrian Regiment there. It was with regret I left the place, but I knew Mr. Byng would want me or my ship at Vado, so I sailed the 28th from Leghorn at night, and on 3rd January I anchored at Vado where I found Admiral Byng, with only the *Boyne* 80, *Burford* 70, *Royal Oak* 70, and a bomb vessel.

I was sorry to find the Admiral established on shore at Vado, where he had a good neat house, but only a guard for his person of twenty Piedmontese soldiers and a few marines, as I thought a bold attempt might be made in the night to carry him off. The Admiral was pleased with the success of my cruise. I received many letters from Town that were of an old date. I remained here refitting the ship till the 12th, in which time I amused myself on shore and on board, with ladies often to dinner, and, for the novelty, I gave them a masquerade on board which was singularly pretty, by the whole ship being so illuminated that she was as pretty a sight to those on shore as those within her, and all the officers of the fleet had dressed themselves in some characters, and the whole ship's company had contrived to mask themselves.

I sailed on another cruise the 12th taking the *Conqueror* fireship as far as Toulon with me, that we might look in and send the Admiral whatever intelligence or observations I could from thence. I got off Toulon the 16th; as I could not get so near in with my ship as I wished, I went on board the *Conqueror* and there had a full and satisfactory view of all that was passing in the road and part of the basin at Toulon. I took three different views, and saw three men-of-war rigged seemingly ready for sea, five unrigged, and some in the basin without masts. I dispatched Captain Edwards in the *Conqueror* to the Admiral with this account, and proceeded on my cruise off the South end of Sardinia, and so to Cape Bona.

I had no success and very dull work, till the 29th I fell in with and took a French pollacre from Candia to Marseilles and sent her into the port of Cagliari. The port of Cagliari on the South end of Sardinia was a very good safe bay for our prizes to continue in whilst we cruised, and so take them up at the end of our cruise, and send or carry them to Leghorn which was always my plan. The 3rd February I took another French ship from Damietta bound to Marseilles; I sent her to Cagliari, and landed all the prisoners at Tunis that I might not shorten my provisions, and took a receipt from the Captains for their number which would account in the exchange of prisoners. The 7th proved more successful to me; I took a French ship from Alexandretta bound to Marseilles called the *St. Joseph*, and very rich she was. I sent the prisoners into Tunis, and determined then to go away and carry my prizes to Leghorn. I stood into Cagliari the 15th, but I would not go on shore; sent my first Lieutenant, Mr. Foulks,[1] to the Viceroy with compliments &c, and sailed away with my three prizes for Leghorn. In my passage I wrote several letters to England and Jamaica to be ready to dispatch from Leghorn. The 20th I anchored in Leghorn Road, and tho' my prizes were made to lay quarantine, yet I was admitted to pratiqua,[2] which was a great indulgence to me. I found all my friends there well, and Mrs. Goldsworthy just brought to bed of a boy, to which I afterwards stood godfather and named Augustus.[3] The 28th of this month, and all the principal people of Leghorn invited to it, I gave a very fine ball and music on the canals.

I continued amusing myself every day and evening there, till the 6th March as I was coming from the ship of a Sunday morning in my barge I perceived a fire break out on board of a large

[1] Peter Foulks received his first appointment as Lieutenant in 1745; he was First Lieutenant in several of Hervey's ships; in 1777 he became a Commander, and probably died in 1782–3 when his name disappears from the Sea-Officers' List. Do not confuse him with Captain John Foulks of the Marines.

[2] Given a clean bill of health; the pratiqua system was designed to prevent the plague spreading from North Africa, but influence and bribery rendered it unscientific.

[3] On 25th March 1753 Godfather Hervey entered Augustus Goldsworthy, then aged five, on the books of H.M.S. *Phoenix*, rating him midshipman. This is a good example of a "false muster". The child appears on the books of all Hervey's ships until the end of 1758, but he does not seem to have continued in the service.

merchant ship in the mold, and she was in the middle of a second tier of ships, and as she was known to have a great quantity of powder on board no one would go near her, and every one deserted the mold where there were three hundred sail of ships. She was called the *Calidonia*. I went towards her immediately, and ordered another boat to direct the ships in the road to send boats and assistance to help to tow her out of the tier, which was all I could wish to do to save the mold, storehouses, ships, and, perhaps, the town. I found no one would go near her, so I went on board her and cut her cables with my own hand that was fast on shore, and towed her out, having my coat burnt almost all the skirts off. As soon as I had towed her clear, she blew up, and hurt none of our boats, but made a most violent blast. I went on shore and found the town all in alarm, but all the people followed me for my services done them with huzzas and blessings, and I was not let alone the whole day as I was at dinner at the Consul's. The next morning the different consuls at the head of their factories came in form to me to thank me for so signal a service. The Governor and the chief magistrates came to me, and thanked me (as they were pleased to say) for saving the Emperor's mold. I passed that evening at the Bonaini's, where a great number of people flocked to see me.[1]

The next day I was obliged to sail and arrived at Vado the 10th following, where I found the Admiral. I lay that night at General Paterson's at Savona, as there was to be a council of war next morning there which the Admiral would have me attend.

The 14th also I was on shore at the same place with the Admiral, having attended another council, and at daylight in the morning the Admiral and myself got up as was our custom and intended to walk thro' the town of Savona, and there take his calash[2] to go to Vado. As we were going over the eastern bridge from the mold we perceived a great number of boats off Celle,[3] and was scarce got from that eminence but the town was attacked by the French, who had arrived late, having come from Genoa the night before

[1] This exploit drew a laudatory letter from old Lord Bristol, addressed to "my Gallant Grandson", but which had had to be prompted by Brother George, Lord Hervey; "I have sent you, since you desired it of me, a letter to your brother Augustus, tho' I found it a little against the grain as a parent to be paying where I owed nothing, having never heard from him but when he wanted money; but his late behaviour on this last lucky occasion shall cancel all former prejudices." Vol. III, No. 1288.

[2] A light carriage, with low wheels and a removable, folding hood.

[3] Five miles east of Savona.

too late, or they had surprised the town and mold. However they fired very briskly, the Admiral and myself made what haste we could to Vado and there secured all the sick and hospital, lest they should succeed and come round. The *Essex* and *Nassau* was ordered immediately to go and cover the town, but whilst this was doing, Lord Roche,[1] who was now Governor, wrote the Admiral word that the French were in possession of the Capucin convent which commanded a part of the town and overlooked the mold. The *Revenge* was ordered to slip and go lay off the town and these ships to batter the Capucin convent. Another letter arrived that the enemy had now surrounded the town and had taken their advanced guards, that Count Arrignan, Major-General, was wounded in endeavouring to check the progress of the enemy, that Lord Roche was retired to the citadel and determined to defend it to the last. The Admiral sent to desire they would get the gallies out of the mold. He dined on board my ship, and then we went together on board the *Essex* off Savona mold, which was now firing on the enemy's lodgements at the Capucin convent. I went into the mold to order the gallies out. They fired at me on all sides and killed two of my bargemen, but I got on board the gallies, and they were preparing for coming out that night. In the evening the town by order of Lord Roche was illuminated as light as day, as he suspected the inhabitants to be in concert with the French and Genoese, and had on pain of death commanded every house to be lighted up and not an inhabitant to stir out of their houses. The enemy's fire slackened very much by midnight, and all ours revived. The enemy made no approaches more, and on finding the enemy had retired before daylight, the Admiral returned to his ship and I to mine.

We found the next morning the enemy had lost many men, and from the information of prisoners and deserters we found that 6,000 men under the Duke de Richelieu's nephew had undertaken this expedition which had failed in this manner, and was a lucky circumstance for the King of Sardinia's affairs in the beginning of the spring. Lord Roche fined the town, as he found the enemy's

[1] John (or Raymond) Roche of Ballydangan, who had wrongfully assumed the title on the death of his cousin Ulick, 10th Viscount Roche of Fermoy. Villettes told Byng that Roche had " been in the service of this crown from his most tender youth and for these fourty years past and upwards; laying aside his party prejudices and his bigoted zeal for the Steward family and the pretended issue of it now at Rome (even in which he is very discrete and reserved) he is a very good natured honest man and a very gallant gentleman;" *Unpublished Byng papers.*

designs of this attack were known to several eight days before. 50,000 livres was therefore levied immediately on the inhabitants to be paid in two hours, and all other necessary regulations pursued. I went with the Admiral to congratulate Lord Roche, and afterwards to see the Count Arrignan who we found badly wounded but not dangerously. The 18th I wrote an account of this for the Admiral to send home to the Secretary of State. The *Revenge* was ordered for the future to lay to the eastward of Savona, tho' the French army had come in feluccas[1] from Genoa as far as Celle, and then marched along shore.

The 25th the *Postilion* xebeque[2] came in from Leghorn and brought me letters from Mr. Mann[3] our Resident there, which enclosed me some from the Regency of Florence with thanks for my behaviour at Leghorn at the fire of the *Calidonia*. I received orders to go to Leghorn and convoy some provision vessels for the Imperialists. At my arrival at Leghorn the 27th in the morning I found Captain Noel there in the *Severn*, to whom I gave verbal orders to join the Admiral at Vado.

I remained several days to get these vessels ready, and had nothing to do but to divert myself, which I did very much, as every one studied to contribute to my amusement, and I was no less solicitous to amuse them. For which reason on the 5th I made a very great entertainment on board for the Governor and his cicisbee,[4] the Marana, a Genoese lady not of the first class, about twenty-eight of the nobility from Florence and other places, Pisa, Pisa Baths, and Lucca, and some from Milan that had come down to see Leghorn. I had a very fine concert of music on board, and in the evening when dark all the bridges upon the many various canals in that town were illuminated by my orders; boats with different sets of music, others with cold collations were placed at proper distances on the canals for us; whilst we all went about the night with our boats and music too, and passed the night on the canal, with thousands of spectators who accompanied us all along the streets of the canals and all the people at their windows made it a delightful show, and a most calm, delightful night we had. The Bonfiglio was not at it, as she would not go on my giving

[1] Small coasting vessels, propelled by oars and sails.

[2] Xebeques were very similar to pollacres (see p. 61) but with better lines and more suitable to warlike purposes.

[3] Horace Mann, later K.B. and 1st Baronet, Horace Walpole's correspondent; at Florence until his death in 1786, when he was succeeded in that post by Hervey's nephew, John Augustus, Lord Hervey.

[4] For Hervey's description of the relationship of *cicisbea* to *cicisbeo* see p. 133.

a preference to the Bonaini. All that stuff subsisted more among the Livornese women than anywhere. The 23rd however I got the vessels ready, and did not let my pleasures retard my duty, for I sailed the instant they were so, seventeen of them, with a pollacre I bought for Mr. Byng for a tender. I arrived at Vado the 26th, and to my great surprise found there Admiral Forbes from England by land, with his flag on board the *Burford*, but intending to hoist it on board my ship and I was to go into the *Phoenix*, which a relation of Admiral Forbes, and of his name, commanded. I liked the exchange very well, for as there was a talk of peace I was in hopes by getting into a frigate I might be continued on the Mediterranean station. The 29th the *Phoenix* arrived, and I changed into her, removed all my people and things and got Mr. Foulks with me for my Lieutenant, and in three or four days afterwards the 4th May came an express from Lord Sandwich from the Hague that the preliminaries were signed with France. The Admirals, General Paterson and all the Captains dined with me that day, and a melancholy one it was, as we all disliked the peace, especially the King of Sardinia's friends, and we found the Empress would not accede to them.

The 10th I got orders for a suspension of arms at such a day, and to sail up the Archipelago to cruise the six weeks that were allowed. I therefore sailed that night. Captain Foulks set out the same evening to go by land to England and carried all my letters;[1] with one for Miss Chudleigh and a remittance and that I would pay all her debts if she would let me know what they were. I ordered Mr. Henshaw to pay her £500 immediately, and remitted him the money.

The 17th I chased and came up with an old vessel laden with corn, but no living soul on board, or papers. I took possession of her,[2] and the 22nd I met the *Seaford*, Captain Wilson, and gave him the Admiral's packet. The 26th in the Archipelago I spoke with a large French ship who was hired by the Grand Signior and had a Turkish Basha on board with twenty-six of his women, wives and others, and many Turks on board going to Candia. I sent them presents, and as it was calm and I wanted to see if I could get the women to the windows, I sent my music in boats

[1] Including one to Lady Townshend (*Hist. MSS. Comm. Townshend*, 369) which said ". . . Except (from) my mother I have received no letter from any relation; I have had only one from my uncle Aston ever since I have been out of England."

[2] See p. 146.

under her stern, by which means I saw several of them with my glass. The 31st I joined my old friend Captain Gardiner[1] in the *Faversham* who I had not seen for six years. The 7th June I left the *Faversham* and *Seaford* going to water at Modon[2] and I made the best of my way to Leghorn. The six weeks being over and no success, the 24th I came in and surprised Mr. and Mrs. Goldsworthy at dinner.

In the evening Captain de Hearce, the Captain of the Port, came to me at the consul's in the name of the Emperor and presented me with a letter from Count Richecourt and a very fine gold box set with diamonds with the Emperor's and Empress's picture, and with the kindest expressions to me for my services.[3]

The 25th, Mr. and Mrs. Goldsworthy, Mr. Birtles and I set out for Florence, where I had a mind to go before I left the Mediterranean, in seven stages with very good roads and a charming country. We arrived early the 26th, and having refreshed ourselves with laying down for three or four hours, we went to Mr. Mann our Resident, who received us with his usual politeness and hospitality. We dined there with a Mr. St. Leger of Ireland, who was here on his travels and who I had heard of at Turin ; General Saline and his lady dined here, and we went to a *burletto*[4] afterwards.

We remained at Florence to the 1st July, amusing ourselves with all the various curiosities that were collected there by the great family of the Medici, no longer anything in Tuscany now. I dined twice with Count Richecourt, who lives in the palace, is head of the Regency and Governor of Tuscany,[5] and by whom we were magnificently entertained the 28th at dinner with about eighty people. The bridge La Trinita struck me the instant I saw it for its lightness and beauty ; three arches carries it over the

[1] Arthur Gardiner had been Byng's First Lieutenant in several ships, among them the *Sutherland* and *Captain*, in which Hervey served. He was flag-captain in the *Ramillies* at the Battle of Mahon, and was killed in 1758 commanding the *Monmouth* in the Moonlight Battle ; see p. 272.

[2] Modoni, ten miles South of Navarino.

[3] Hervey left the box to his illegitimate son Augustus (d. 1782) who left it to General William Hervey (d. 1814), but it does not appear in the latter's very detailed will.

[4] A musical farce.

[5] When in 1737 Francis II, Duke of Lorraine, was about to marry the future Empress Maria-Theresa, France, fearing a Lorraine under Austrian domination, insisted on his taking Tuscany in exchange for his proper dukedom ; hence the presence at Florence of the Lorrainers, led by Emmanuel de Richecourt, whose chief Tuscan rival was Carlo Lorenzo, Marquis di Ginori.

Arno; there are other bridges, but not to be named with this. The Arno runs thro' the town but is a dirty coloured water. There are a number of statues and fountains all over this city, but one particular bronze boar which the Electress made a present of to the city, and which supplies the market-place with water, is very fine. The gallery of the Great Duke is the most famous in the world for the collection it contains, and as it has been so often described I shall only speak of what struck me; a statue of a Roman consul speaking in the Senate; a Tuscan king haranguing the people; an Agrippina in her chair is very fine, with several others not inferior. The pictures that are done of all the different masters, each one by himself, are very curious and pleasing, and the only collection of the kind in Europe. The collection of pictures here are very fine indeed, and very numerous. The famous Venus, of which there are so many copies, is here, and the statue of the Venus of Medici, the finest I ever saw. The quantity of out-of-the-way riches that are amassed here from antiquity is very extraordinary of all kinds, in jewels, plate, bronzes, pictures, statues, and, in short, all kind of things. We went to see the workers in hard stone, and from thence to the famous chapel of St. Lawrence, which is built of the finest marble and hard stones intermixed with precious stones, but it never will be finished, I believe. The arms of all the Tuscan towns is here in precious stones. The Great Duke Cosmus, who was the last of the Medici family,[1] his noble tomb is here. One would wonder where one family ever so powerful now in Europe could have collected such riches, which, according to the modern estimation of them, all the Princes in Europe together could not purchase them; but in dipping into the history and private life of that family our wonder is taken off, as we find they stuck at nothing to gratify their ambition and their pride and every passion that human frailty is subject to.

We visited the Palazzo Pitti, built by a simple particular[2] of that name; it is a very magnificent building and most richly furnished, but was much more so before the House of Lorraine came to Tuscany. There is a bed of gold tissue very richly embroidered with pearls, and a great fringe all round it of pearls; the tables and chairs, frames of the glasses and everything else is all silver in the apartment throughout. There was besides this a great collection of medals in it, but I am told they are no more,

[1] Cosimo III, died 1723; in fact the last was Giangastone, died 1737.
[2] i.e. a private individual.

and since I was at Florence I believe the silver was all melted down and sent to Vienna.

The dinners given us here were very agreeable and entertaining. The conversations were equally so, as the ladies are the most gallant of Italy and the husbands the least jealous in my opinion. At night we used to go to the bridge of La Trinita where there was all the coaches of the town, and for ever music that someone or other was entertaining his mistress with. The ease of this diversion or amusement has something so singular in it, that I must just drop a word of it. You generally go there undressed with a little silk *bagnian*, or nightgown, and a straw hat; and the ladies all conveniently at their ease. You go either to meet or else with your cicisbee; no one else takes the least notice of each other, 'tis reckoned rude to know anyone there that you are not in company with or go to. You remain as late as you please and as you find amusement. Before I left Florence Mr. Mann would give us a conversationi in his gardens which he had illuminated in the nature of Vauxhall, and very pretty it was, and very convenient. But at last the intrigues that was carried on there became so notorious and so general and so open that Mr. Mann was obliged to suppress it a little and light up his dark walks and recesses.[1]

During the whole time I was here the Marchesa de Pecori and the Marchesa Acciaioli was my intimates. I used now and then to go sup with the Parigi, who was the first opera-woman, kept by the Baron il Nero.

Having seen all we could at Florence, and my time being short and wanting to be at Leghorn where I was mostly attached, we set out the 1st July, and in our way stopped at the Convent St. Bernardo of nuns at Pisa, where Mrs. Goldsworthy had several acquaintances of the Battachi family. There were three sisters of them, Donna Clarcia, Donna Francesca, and Donna Josepha that were remarkably pretty. We arrived later at Leghorn, and I supped at the Bonaini's.

Whilst I remained here my time was taken up with the Bonfiglio and Bonaini. The first I had every enjoyment with I could wish, and she was very pretty as well as entertaining. The other pretended to be in love, but I could not obtain but silly favours in com-

[1] Some double Windsor chairs (copied from a present of Horace Walpole's) whereon two persons could sit, were essential equipment for this entertainment. They were much approved by the Florentines, more so after Mann had the central arm removed; he nicknamed them "*cicisbeatoji*"; *Mann and Manners* I, 90–3 and 185–7.

parison of the other, tho' I tried her jealousy every way.[1] We had concerts and opera almost every night, and the Genoese families that had retired here from the seige of Genoa made it very lively and agreeable. I cannot omit here a most magnificent entertainment given me by the Bonaini; a dinner, concert, ball and supper to which everyone of distinction in the town and all my officers were invited, and we sat up till 8 the next morning. There was no expense spared for everything that was rare to be had here.

I paid all my bills the 8th July, remitted £5,800 home, and prepared for going, when the Governor insisted on my staying to supper with him, having the Marchese and Marchesa de Grigoria, going to Palermo, to sup with him, She was divinely handsome, and he the ugliest old fellow I ever saw. He had been commissary with the army, and in coming from Nice had been on board Admiral Byng's ship at Vado. I supped and stayed late, and the 9th at 4 in the morning left Leghorn with much regret.

The 13th the Admiral received orders to suspend all hostilities, on which he directed me to go immediately to Genoa with compliments to the Doge and Senate and to the Duke de Richelieu who was there, and to open the communication between the Republic and us. Then I was to proceed to Leghorn on other business of a private nature.

I got off Genoa the 15th, sent an officer on shore to acquaint them of my arrival and business. Immediately an officer was sent from the Duke de Richelieu and the Captain of the Port with two nobles from the Doge. They carried me on shore, and conducted me up to the Doges's palace thro' a multitude of people, who were very civil and seemed excessively pleased to have an English man-of-war once more off their port as friends. The Doge was Brignole;[2] he received me with great civility, and told me he hoped this would be a lasting and firm peace. After many ceremonies and compliments, he got off his chair and came to the window, and asked me several questions in French, and was very polite. I took my leave, as I wanted to see the Duke de Richelieu, and having then no acquaintance at Genoa, to get to Leghorn as soon as I could. I found the Duke de Richelieu[3] at a house a little way

[1] On 2nd May 1773 Brother William, at Perugia, saw "La Signora Maddelena Boldrini Bonaini, who was acquainted with Augustus." *Journals of the Hon. William Hervey* 1755–1814, edited by S. H. A. Hervey, p. 236.

[2] Gian Francesco Brignole-Sale, hero of the rising against the Austrians in 1746.

[3] The gallant, soldier, politician, and memoir writer, who commanded the attack on Minorca in 1756; Horace Walpole wrote: "His first campaign was

out of town of Rodolpho Brignole's, brother to the Doge. He was extremely civil to me, talked much of my mother, that he knew her in France with the Duchess of Richmond.

I took my leave of him soon, and sailed for Leghorn immediately, where I arrived about 4 in the morning of a Sunday, after as providential an escape from being cast away as ever man had, being obliged from being surprised by a sudden gale of wind right on the shore (which split most of my sails in the night) just at dawn of day to run thro' a very narrow passage called the Swash, off Pisa bar, which the gallies only make use of, and only finding it out by the distance between the breakers of the sea, having no pilot for it, nor no knowledge of the marks for it. I had near five feet of water in my hold the sea was so great. On my arrival I sent an express after the Captains who were at Florence to order them down and to join the Admiral.

I remained at Leghorn doing the business I was sent on, and amusing myself with entertainments for the ladies that came from Florence. The Bonfiglio gave me her picture in a ring set with diamonds . . . I got to Vado to dinner the 30th, and found Mr. Byng was ordered home with almost all the fleet, and Admiral Forbes to be left to settle all about the prisoners and other affairs, which was to be just after the Peace. Mr. Villettes arrived from Turin and brought Admiral Byng from the King of Sardinia that King's picture set with diamonds, valued about £3,000, as a testimony of His Majesty's approbation of his services. We had nothing but feasting and taking leave of our friends at Savona, till the 8th August when Admiral Byng (now Vice-Admiral of the Red) sailed for Minorca with the *Boyne*, *Burford*, *Essex*, *Princessa*, *Rupert*, *Leopard*, *Phoenix*, *Lowstoft*, two fireships and two tenders. We left with Rear-Admiral Forbes the *Superb*, *Severn* and *Lyme*, and that evening I was despatched to the Maréchal de Belle-Isle[1] to settle with him about some prisoners, who was at Nice and then commanded the French army in Provence with the Marquis de las Minas, the Spanish General.

I arrived early and landed at Nice with my boat. As I landed the Maréchal saluted me with the same number of guns I had saluted on my arrival. I dined with him and was very magnificently entertained. We dined in a church close to his house. His son

---

hiding himself at fourteen under the Duchess of Burgundy's bed, from whence he was led to the Bastille." At this date he was supposed to be *cicisbeo* to Pellinetta Brignole, the Doge's sister-in-law, of whom anon.

[1] He had been in command since 1746; Minister of War 1757–60.

the Count de Gisors, who was a very amiable young man, carried me all about the town where there was nothing to be seen but officers and soldiers. There was the Marquis de la Chetardie in this army, who had been famous by his embassy in Russia in 1740, a Monsieur d'Asscher, Lieutenant General, all Cordon Bleus. We all walked over the ramparts, and had a comedy at night which the Maréchal ordered should be, tho' the company had packed up everything for their march. We supped at the Maréchal's very late, and several accompanied me on board about 4 in the morning, when I sailed for Mahon and had the good fortune to overtake the Admiral again in his passage thither the 13th, and got into Mahon harbour the 17th.

We were all preparing our ships for sailing for England, and I was disappointed of my wishes to remain on this station: I found Lord Anson had allotted the command to Mr. Keppel[1] and a few favourite Captains chosen by him. We sailed the 30th, and September 13th, when we made Gibraltar Hill, the Admiral sent me away for Lisbon and the *Nonsuch*, Captain Martin, that we might get good freights home. I therefore took leave here of Mr. Byng, who had been better than a father to me in everything, and had the war continued would undoubtedly have made my fortune; he had ever been so since first I knew him, and scarce ever gave me time to ask a favour.

The 22nd I got off Lisbon late, and led the *Nonsuch* in over the bar at night. In the morning we found here Captain O'Brien, Captain Edgcumbe, Captain Jelfe, and Captain Gambier, all for freights home. Mr. Keene,[2] who had been envoy in Spain, was the envoy here, ready to return to Spain, and Monsieur de Chavigny was French Ambassador, who had been so in England some years ago, and then very intimate with my father and mother, and who shewed me many civilities here. I here found my old acquaintance, the Signora Ellena Paghetti, a very famous Italian singer, and not less so for her beauty. There had been a sister here; the Marquis d'Abrantes, the King's Lord Chamberlain,

[1] Augustus Keppel was a year younger than Hervey, but two years senior to him as a captain. He owed his rapid advance to Anson's patronage and his family's connection with the Duke of Cumberland—as well as to his undoubted professional merit. After being enemies all their lives (except during the attack on the Havannah in 1762), Hervey and Keppel were at last united in friendship at the time of the latter's court-martial in 1778–9; Hervey was one of his most active defenders.

[2] Sir Benjamin Keene; at Lisbon 1746–48, at Madrid 1727–39 and 1748–57. Hervey's elder brother George, 2nd Earl of Bristol, succeeded him at Madrid.

kept this lady some years, and now had made a noble provision for her. I had formerly been very intimate with her when I was here a Lieutenant in the *Superb*,[1] and now renewed it, as she was still very handsome, and besides, had all the conversationis every evening at her house, which was at Junqueira, a little way from Lisbon by the river-side, and there I passed most of my evenings, and many of my nights.

There was a Duke de Bagnos here, a young lively Spanish grandee, who had a lawsuit with the Marquis de Gouvea[2] for the Aviero estate, who I lived much with, and used to frequent the famous nunnery of Odivellas with. This convent is about five miles from Lisbon, has 700 professed nuns in it, and as many novices, servants and others. Most of the ladies are of quality, of the order of Bernardines. The late King had two mistresses in this convent, and a child by each, Donna Magdalena Maxina (a great friend of mine afterwards) and Donna — — ; and what was most astonishing, that the children were afterwards both acknowledged by the King, and both very high in the Church and Law, tho' acknowledged by these nuns.[3] Don Juan de Bemposto (the late Infant Don Francisco's son),[4] who is cousin to this King, was ever very kind to me and made his palace as my own. I used to dine there, lay there, and use his equipages just as I pleased. I used, too, to go out to my friend Mr. Mayne and Barn's quinta,[5] where I was very much at ease. I had also several dinners on board for the French ambassador, for Don Juan and for several of the Portuguese nobility.

We had a great ball at Mr. Levius's, a merchant, at which Francisca Brezio sung, who is a very pretty Portuguese woman. I found she had a friend in the Conde de Cantanheira, who is son to the Marquis de Marialva, General of the Horse ; the Conde was a great favourite of the King and Queen's, a great musician, and

[1] In the winter of 1740–41, when he was aged 16.

[2] Don José de Mascarhenas, later 8th Duke of Aviero, barbarically executed in 1759 for his complicity in the Tavora plot.

[3] Donna Magdalena Maxina de Miranda, Madre Paula, and a French nun were the respective mothers of Gaspar, Archbishop of Braga, Don José, Grand Inquisitor, and Don Antonio. In 1787 William Beckford visited these two latter " Palhava princes " in their palace of that name.

[4] Don Francisco, King João V's brother, had two sons by Donna Mariana de Sousa ; the younger was Don João de Bemposta who was legitimated in 1750, and was later Captain-General of the Navy and Great Chamberlain to the Queen.

[5] A country house, or villa.

a very good kind of man.[1] However I was not acquainted with him, and therefore did not check myself in my wishes for being so with Signora Brezio, who I attacked in the Portuguese manner by going in my great Portuguese cloak constantly under her window, by which means I shewed my inclinations and soon got myself introduced to the house. I cannot omit one morning's work the Duke de Bagnos and myself had with Monsieur de Vergennes.[2] We went in cloaks to upwards of, I verily believe, thirty ladies houses—ladies of pleasure, I mean.

I got a very good freight, about 80,000 Moydores,[3] and then sailed for England the 21st, and got in the Downs the 2nd December. I was soon ordered to the river to be paid off, and as I went by Sheerness found Mr. Keppel fitting in the *Centurion* to go Commodore to the Mediterranean. I was paid off the 27th December. Admiral Byng carried me to Lord Anson who expressed his approbation of my conduct and that the Admiralty would always be glad to oblige me, tho' they had just refused me to remain on the Mediterranean station.

In this time I had seen Miss Chudleigh at Mrs. Aston's and gave her £500 to pay her debts, a list of which she gave me, and in a few days afterwards gave her £200 more. I was employed now in renewing my acquaintances. I lived at Mrs. Aston's, finding my uncle was dead just before I arrived. I was presented to the King, who took no notice of me. The 30th, I gave Miss Chudleigh £100 more. This was a very idle time now, and I was very much displeased with many things I heard of Miss Chudleigh's conduct, especially from her own relations, too, which put me out of humour and made me mind several little circumstances that perhaps would otherwise have passed with me as nothing.

I was so tired of London that I went and stayed four or five days at Finchly with Admiral Byng, who was very busy there building.[4]

[1] Don Diego de Noronha, 3rd Marquis of Marialva (d. 1761) was the father of Don Pedro d'Alcantara de Menezes, 6th Conde de Cantanheira and 4th Marquis (d. 1803); this latter was William Beckford's host in Portugal in the year 1787.

[2] Charles Gravier, Comte de Vergennes, later Foreign Minister under Louis XVI; he was Chavigny's nephew.

[3] Worth £110,000; the normal peace-time freight was one per cent, so Hervey would have £1,100, whereof Byng was entitled to one-third.

[4] He was building the present house in Wrotham Park. He had written to the Duke of Bedford " the little fortune I have been able to pick up since having the command of His Majesty's Fleet in these seas I shall ever gratefully attribute to your Grace " *Bedford Papers*, I, 518.

On my return I carried it very cool with Miss Chudleigh wherever I met her. The 25th January I had come *éclaircissments* as to Miss Chudleigh's conduct with her, which she did not approve, and Mrs. Aston was present the whole time. In short, I took a resolution from this afternoon of going abroad and never having any more to do in that affair.

III

THE NAVY BILL

1749

The end of the war saw a great reduction in the active fleet, and consequently there were many fewer posts for officers who wished to be employed. Following the usual eighteenth-century practice, commissions went to the favourites of those in power; the remainder had to rest content on their meagre half-pay, which for Hervey was four shillings a day. Like many of the unemployed, in contemplation of the next reign he hitched his chariot to that uncertain star, Frederick, Prince of Wales, his father's old enemy, and this ensured no favours would come his way during the lifetime of his present sovereign.

In this situation, the attempt by the Admiralty to include in the Navy Bill[1] a new Article, the 34th, designed to subject officers on half-pay to trial by Court Martial, was represented by the Opposition as a dangerous infringement of the liberties of Englishmen. The opponents of the bill argued that half-pay was granted as a reward for past services, and not as a retainer for the future. They feared that a vindictive Board might persecute political and service rivals by appointing them to posts unacceptable by reason of rank and seniority, and then have them broken by court-martial for refusing to assume them. By all means let the Admiralty order half-pay officers to their duty, they said, but let the punishment for their disobedience be no more than the stopping of their half-pay. In view of the political system of Hanoverian England, they were fully justified in their successful stand, as a result of which officers of the Royal Navy on half-pay were never subject to trial by court-martial.[2]

Several other amendments (notably to the 18th and 33rd Articles) were forced upon the Board by the sea-officers, who had the good fortune to prevail upon the Admiral of the Fleet, Sir John Norris, now in his ninetieth year, to lend his name and authority to their campaign, thus cloaking with respectability a body no doubt largely factious.

An important change was made by this bill to the 12th Article, which in its new form prescribed no punishment alternative to death

[1] 22 Geo. II cap 33, repealing, amending and codifying the previous acts.
[2] Half-pay was abolished in 1938.

for an officer convicted of negligence in the face of the enemy ; it was under this harsh provision that Byng was to suffer in 1757. It is interesting to note that the House of Commons (according to Temple West, the bill's most skilful naval opponent) understood the Article to mean negligence arising only from cowardice or disaffection, and not from incapacity or want of judgement, " for which reason no alternative was left in that article, as otherwise there would have been."[1]

That Anson was vindictive towards the organizers of the Board's rebuff is neither surprising nor out of keeping with the times, though it would be inexcusable in a modern First Sea Lord. John Charnock, the mid-eighteenth-century's naval biographer, provides examples of his inordinate preference for his friends to the exclusion of his enemies.[2] Even nine years later Rodney, who no doubt would have acted a similar part had he been in Anson's shoes, wrote to George Grenville " You know him ; you remember the Navy Bill ; you know his resentment."[3]

Hervey's narrative of this important event in the evolution of the naval profession is the only one which survives. It confirms fully Horace Walpole, who says, writing of the Army's Mutiny Bill of the same year, " My Lord Anson, who governed at the Admiralty Board, was struck with so amiable a pattern, and would have chained down his tars to a like oar ; but it raised such a ferment in that boisterous profession, that the Ministry was forced to drop several of the strongest articles, to quiet the tempest that this innovation had caused."[4] In his *Life of Anson*[5] Sir John Barrow casts ridicule on Walpole's suggestion that there was anything in the nature of a " tempest " or a " ferment in that boisterous profession " ; but even in 1839 when he was writing, Sir John, who was secretary to the Admiralty, could have examined the Board's Minutes for the 20th and 21st February 1749, where he would have found Walpole's description officially confirmed.

THE 2nd February the Peace was proclaimed with a very silly ceremony. I passed my time stupidly enough. I went to the House of Commons the 7th and heard Lord Egmont's motion for addressing the King to lay all the papers before the House relative to the late Treaty of Peace, which passed in the negative by a great majority. I was at this time a good deal with

[1] West to Lord Temple, Jan. 27th, 1757 ; Charnock, Vol. IV, p. 422.
[2] Charnock, Vol. V, p. 352.
[3] *Grenville Papers*, I, p. 231.
[4] *Memoirs of the Reign of George II*, Vol. I, p. 38.
[5] *Life of Anson*, p. 217.

the Opposition set, of which Lord Egmont was the leader and mostly in the Prince of Wales's confidence and favour.[1]

About the 16th there grew up a bill wherein the sea-officers was much concerned. 'Twas a bill the Duke of Cumberland with Lord Anson and Lord Barrington[2] and others had been concerting to alter the 34th Article of War, in order to oblige all the officers on half-pay to be subject to the same discipline and liable to the same orders as if on whole, so that by this means the whole corps of officers may be kept in the utmost subjection and sent where the Admiralty please, even if in Parliament. A great number of Admirals, Captains and others determined to oppose this with every means in their power. I was applied to, and entered the lists willingly, and by attending the meetings at which Sir Peter Warren, Admiral Lee,[3] Sir John Norris and others headed, I was soon chose a manager with Mr. West[4] and Mr. Dut.

I wrote a pamphlet first entitled *A Letter from a friend to Will's Coffee House*;[5] the intent of this was to spirit up all the officers, to set before them what was intended against them.

At this time the King's Arms Club chose me of them, Lord Egmont, Lord Doneraile, Lord Gage, Mr. Nugent, Colonel Lyttleton, Sir Edmond Thomas, Mr. Thomas Pitt, Mr. Boone, Mr. Bathurst, Sir John Cust, Lord Baltimore, and many others.[6] Mr. Nugent was with me one morning about this Bill, but having had some reason to mistrust him from what he said in the House, I refused to let him see all our reasons against it. I dined the 19th with Lord Doneraile and others, and in the evening I went with

[1] Frederick, Prince of Wales, bitter enemy of Lord Hervey, and detested by his father George II, who preferred his younger brother William, Duke of Cumberland. John Perceval, 2nd Earl of Egmont, was First Lord of the Admiralty 1763–66, and a prolific pamphleteer.

[2] William Wildman, 2nd Viscount Barrington was Secretary at War during the early years of the American War; he, too, was an active pamphleteer.

[3] Vice-Admiral Fitzroy Lee (a grandson of Charles II) is said to have been the original of Smollett's "Commodore Trunnion".

[4] Temple West (to be Byng's Rear-Admiral off Mahon in 1756) had been dismissed the service in 1746 for his conduct in the battle of Toulon; a member of the Pitt-Grenville "cousinhood", he was soon reinstated. Horace Mann found West's intelligence a welcome relief from the boorishness of other "sea-monsters".

[5] MS. at Ickworth; see Appendix A.

[6] Among these members of the Prince's Household are the future Robert, Earl Nugent; George, 1st Lord Lyttleton; Chatham's elder brother Thomas Pitt of Boconnoc; and Sir John Cust, Speaker of the House of Commons 1761–70.

him to Carlton House, where the Prince came about half an hour afterwards. He was mighty gracious to me, talked to me a great while about this Bill, desired to see my list of all the officers who had signed against it, spoke of the hardship of it, and sent for a Navy-list to compare who was for it. The Prince said it was "shameful for Lord Anson and Lord Sandwich to make so many brave men slaves"—those were his words. He told me he would certainly serve me when in his power and said he knew more of me than I imagined. I went away at 6, and left Lord Doneraile and Lord Baltimore with his Royal Highness.

The 21st I went to the Admiralty, where there were a number of Admirals and Captains assembled by desire of the Admiralty on our having signed an address to the Admiralty desiring them to protect us from the severity of that Article of War, and not let us lay under more heavier and weightier severities in time of peace than in time of war. We were called into the Board, where Lord Sandwich as First Lord presided and who desired to know our objections to it. Sir Peter Warren, Admiral Lee, Admiral Smith, Mr. Rowley[1] and Mr. West spoke against the Article, and only Mr. Mostyn for it.[2] Lord Barrington said that had any of three or four gentlemen come to him and talked over the Bill and given these gentlemen's reasons for being so averse to it, he would have set them right. Lord Sandwich made use of several harsh expressions against the assemblies and meetings that had been; that they were mutinous, seditious, and not to be paralleled in a civilized country, and that for his part, he knew what light to look upon it in, and he believed the Board had no favourable opinion of them. On which I could not help saying what follows.

"My Lord, unqualified as I am both by my inabilities and my rank in the service either to speak to your Lordships or before this numerous attendance of officers, yet I cannot help claiming some few minutes of that indulgence your Lordship seems so ready to grant to those who are desirous of making known to you their sentiments on this occasion.

"I hope, my Lord, what I'm going to say will neither prompt

[1] Thomas Smyth was to be president of Byng's court-martial in 1756; William Rowley, later Admiral of the Fleet and K.B., had been summarily removed from his command in the Mediterranean in 1745 for his conduct at the court-martial of Sir John Norris' eldest son, Captain Richard Norris, whom he had placed on half-pay and thus put out of the power of the court. No doubt the Board was trying to avoid a repetition of this sort of scandal.

[2] Savage Mostyn was rewarded on the 22nd March with the Controllership of the Navy.

anyone to imagine I'm either induced to it from a vain and very hopeless desire of being thought an orator, or from a disposition to censure and find fault with whatever my superiors are pleased to think requisite. No, my Lord. I little thought when I came here to have either met this body of officers, or indeed to have appeared myself at this Board; you will not doubt the truth of this assertion when you look at my dress, which would have prevented my appearing before your Board had I not been absolutely sent for.[1] It may appear to your Lordship and this Board very extraordinary in me to tell you that tho' I shall endeavour to justify the gentlemen who delivered this petition and are here present, yet I would not be thought to be an advocate for them from having been one of those assemblies and advertisers (which I confess, had I known of, I should have been) and not even the harsh epitaphs and disguised threats uttered by your Lordship would have awed me into a fear of doing what I thought and shall endeavour to prove was right.

"I never, my Lord, saw this petition now before you till about two hours before it was delivered to your Lordships; I read it, considered it, approved and signed it, and so far am I from repenting, that I esteem it an honour my having been permitted to do either. For you must give me leave to say that I think this body of Admirals and Captains here before you have paid your Board the greatest compliment in their power. They think themselves grieved, they think themselves in danger of being fettered by such new regulations as are now in agitation, and which if passed into law are such, as they think, make it impossible (for those who are born to breath the air of liberty) to survive under. In this emergency what do they do? Why, they fly to your Lordships' banner for redress, for protection from this expected injury. By that do they not show that they expect you to be their benefactors and their protectors? What greater compliment, my Lord, what stronger proofs could they give you? Surely they all know they have the right of every subject, that of petitioning the Parliament, nay, the King's own majesty? And had they done this at once who could have blamed them for having gone immediately to the very fountain of Justice; and, indeed, still more excusable had these Petitioners been, from your Lordships being the composers of and advocates for the Bill, and I fear I must confess that the reception these gentlemen have met

[1] The first uniform regulations for naval officers had been issued in the previous year.

with here proves still stronger that they would have had at least a more favourable one from the Crown itself.

" What Lord Barrington was pleased to say that had any two or three gentlemen waited of him to have given the opinions of these Petitioners makes it necessary for me to take up a little more of your time.

" Your Lordship sees this body of officers. I would be glad to know, my Lord, what two or three would have dared to declare the sentiments of all these gentlemen without having known them, or even having been authorised by any lesser number of them to do so. I am sure I would not have been one, could I have read the heart of a dozen of the ablest and most approved of them ; and how were they to know these gentlemen's sentiments without meeting and confering with each other ? And pray, my Lord, may I ask which way (supposing them inclined to this seemingly approved gentle means) were all these gentlemen to meet when so scattered about the town, nay about the Kingdom, without an advertisement, (which your Lordship lays such stress on) ? That is the ancient and indeed only method of calling people together, nay which your Lordships' very Board is often obliged to have recourse to. This is a fact which I hope will make these public advertisements appear more excusable, these general meetings less criminal than your Lordship would point them."

Here Lord Sandwich interrupted me, saying he could not answer this, 'twas not for him, 'twas not to the purpose, and proposed our withdrawing ; and so the Board broke up without hearing the rest which I would have said.[1]

However, when we were dismissed, and pretty abruptly, I went to a meeting at the King's Arms, and was appointed to draw up a petition to Parliament and one of the five to conduct the whole. Several things were printed pro and con on these Articles of War.[2] However we carried our point, and they were obliged to desist from it. The Duke of Cumberland and Lord Anson was very angry with me. The lst March Sir Peter Warren came to me and wanted us to mitigate our resentment to this Article and to let some other Article of the kind be put in, but I would never give way.

[1] His peroration would have threatened strong parliamentary opposition by the Prince's party, and ended by suggesting that " the Petitioners have rather paid you a compliment deserving your applause than done you an outrage meriting your revenge "; MS. at Ickworth.

[2] See Appendix A.

I wrote a pamphlet entitled *A Detection of the Navy Bill*,[1] also one entitled *Objections to the 34th Article of the Navy Bill* (a copy of it among my papers).

Having carried our point, and I being tired of London, I went down to Wrattins to Sir Robert Smyth[2] for a few days, and then to Ickworth, where my mother was with Lord Bristol. The 2nd April I went to the Newmarket meeting, but it was chiefly with a design of meeting Mrs. Artis who had wrote to me from Norwich that if I did not meet her somewhere, she would come to Ickworth to see me; so we stayed on the road two days together, and I returned to Ickworth.

I grew so tired of the country life that was stupidly led here, and yet so horridly vexed to go to London to see all that was going on there, that I determined to go abroad, and thro' France and Italy and visit all the ports of France that they would let me. So I wrote to the Admiralty for leave the 3rd May, which I obtained the next post.[3] I went therefore the 6th to Town, taking leave of my grandfather, brother and mother. The 19th I placed £1,000 pounds in my banker's hands to serve me whilst abroad.

As I was packing up my things the 2nd June to set out next day, tho' in all this time I had never heard from Miss Chudleigh, yet she suddenly came in upon me at Mrs. Aston's, which I impute to their having sent to her and told her of my design. But I was deaf to all the siren's voice.

[1] In which he described the Board of Admiralty as "a medley of Court nobility, broken squires, and now and then a solitary nominal Sea-officer or two, who sit there and sleep for their salaries".

[2] Sir Robert Smyth, 2nd Baronet, had married Lord Bristol's fifth daughter Louisa in 1731; he lived at West Wratting, near Newmarket.

[3] Lord Bristol was shocked (Vol. III, No. 1338): "I must begin by taking notice it is not only my opinion, but will undoubtedly be the judgment of the public, that your wise and able masters of the a——y ought instead of giving you leave to travel to have prevented that request by appointing you to some beneficial station, as was so much your due, in ye Mediterranean, or some other post equal to the timely and voluntary service and honour you had done your country and our allies in saving all the ships from being destroyed by fire at the port of Leghorn. . . . I think after what has passed tis now too late to complain where only we could hope for any redress, which, had it been refused, I would have petitioned His Majesty that he would give you leave to serve any state or prince but that of his most Christian Majesty or the Turk."

Lord Bristol would have been even more shocked had he known that their Lordships stopped Hervey's half-pay when he went abroad; for, they said, the warrant granting it did not cover those gone out of the Kingdom.

IV

A SPLENDID COURT

1749–1750

"Il y a ici souvent les mardis des presentations d'étrangers. Nous vîmes hier un jeune homme qui vient d'être présenté. C'est un Anglois, âgé seulement de vingt-quatre ans ; il s'appelle milord Harwey. Sa mère, qui étoit une belle femme, est venue en France ; il est petit-fils du Comte de Bristol, pair d'Angleterre. Il a déjà fait quatorze campagnes. Il faut qu'il ait commencé de bonne heure ; il a même commandé une escadre de douze vaisseaux ; il montait un vaisseau de 74 canons."

Memoirs of the Duc de Luynes, June 1749.
(Vol. IX, p. 432.)

I SET off the 3rd June with Mr. Skreen, we were agreed to go together.[1] Colonel Townshend and Lord George Manners went with us to Dover to see us embark, which we did the 5th, and landed at Boulogne early in the morning, hired two Italian chaises and set off. This town was a most beggarly place indeed. We lay at Montreuil, and not a very good inn, the roads good and the country very well cultivated, but very few people seen anywhere but in the villages, and these mostly very old men, women and children. We set out early the next morning and got that night to Breteuil, where we lay, having passed by Abbeville and Amiens, and a very fine forest of the King's just at the entrance of Picardy, an old house of the Duke de Chaulnes that seemed quite a ruin, as also one of the Marquis de Cardon. We got about noon to Chantilly, a palace of the Prince de Condé, truly magnificent indeed, the stables very grand and more modern than the house. The apartments are numerous, but did not answer

[1] His companion was William Skrine, a collateral of the Skrines of Warleigh. He went on to Italy where Mann reports him entertaining lavishly. From 1771–82 he was M.P. for Callington, Cornwall, and in 1783 he shot himself in a tavern in Newgate ; play debts contracted at Brooke's are said to have been the reason ; E. W. Ainley Walker, *Skrine of Warleigh*, p. 102.

my expectation from the outside, the park pretty and wild. We went all over it, and got to Paris about 8. The roads about Paris are very magnificent.

I went to an hotel dans la rue des petits Augustins that Monsieur de Chavigny, who was at Paris, had prepared for me, and where he and Monsieur de Vergennes were so obliging to come that night. In the morning Mr. Skreen and I went and returned that visit. I went to Madame de Bukby, and Madame Monconseil[1] for whom with others I had letters from my mother. I went and waited of Colonel Yorke,[2] who was secretary to Lord Albermarle's Embassy, but at present Minister till his arrival. With him I soon after went to Versailles and was introduced to the King,[3] who just said one word to me as he passed by, for 'twas just after his dressing and his prayers, which is in his own bedchamber immediately after he is dressed.

I went to see the Tuileries and Palais Royal, and all those fine collections of pictures which the Regent had collected. Lord Cornbury[4] was here, and we were often together with his nephew Lord Charles Douglas.[5] I went to see the Palais de Bourbon which was built for the Duchess Dowager; there are but four rooms of the apartment, but magnificent they are, and finely finished and ornamented. But the Palais Royal exceeded all, which was built by Cardinal Richelieu and by him given to Lewis the 13th, and by Lewis the 14th to the Duke of Orleans. I shall not describe this Palais nor the great collection of pictures in it; as I lived so much in it afterwards during my long stay at Paris, I may have occasion to throw in often something or other of its apartments. There is the finest set of originals by Guido, Corregio, Titian, Paul Veronese, Raphael, Rubens and several others that can be, many out of that noble collection of the Queen of Sweden's. There are seven pictures of the Sacrament by Raphael that cost 40,000

[1] "Bukby", I suggest, should be Bulkeley. Perhaps the sister of General Mahony at Naples (see p. 138) and wife of James Bulkeley, a Lieutenant-General in the French service.

Madame de Monconseil was Claire-Cécile-Thérèse-Pauline de Rioult Douilly who in 1725 had married Étienne, Marquis de Monconseil. She was now aged 43, and had long been an intimate of Stanislas, the exiled King of Poland and Duke of Lorraine and Barr.

[2] Joseph, later Lord Dover.

[3] Louis XV, now aged forty.

[4] See p. 108.

[5] Later Earl of Drumlanrig, d. 1756, second son of the 3rd Duke of Queensbury.

crowns. Lord Sussex and Lord Cathcart were here as hostages for the restoration of Cape Breton, which were most infamously granted by the Treaty of Aix-la-Chapelle. They had great allowances here, and lived very splendidly at the Government's expence. I often returned to examine the pictures at the Palais Royal. I went again to pay my court at Versailles and to see that pile of magnificence and grandeur. I went to see Monsieur de Puisieulx, who was the Ministre des Affairs Étrangères, with whom I dined, and was by him presented to several ladies. In the afternoon I took a walk thro' the long gallery to observe it at my leisure, where is that remarkable piece of vanity of Lewis the 14th on the ceiling, where he is represented as looking on a map of Holland and the expression is, "Lewis dont des ordres pour chatier les Hollandois". The Dutch at the Peace of Ryswick sent expressly that they would not make peace till those words were altered, and now they are "Lewis dont des ordres pour attaquer les villes des Hollandois".

The next day I was presented to the Queen,[1] she spoke to none of us; afterwards to the Dauphin in his apartment, then to the Dauphiness in hers.[2] Then we went up to Madame Pompadour's apartment. She was at her toilette, and the handsomest creature I think I ever saw, and looked like a rock of diamonds. Then we went to Madame L'Infanta de Parma,[3] and Mesdames. The Infanta of Parma spoke to me directly and asked me how I liked Paris, and how Italy. I was the only one spoke to that was presented, and that only by her Royal Highness and Madame Pompadour, who had all France round her toilette and seemed to have much more court paid to her than to the Queen. In the evening I was presented to Madame Flavacourt,[4] the Duchess de Luynes, and the Maréchale de Belle-Isle. I went home late to Paris and dined, but received such an idea of the grandeur of the French Court that I had a very pitiful opinion of our own at St. James's, nor have I ever altered my opinion, tho' lately so much in it and so long of it. . . .

[1] Marie Leczinska, daughter of Stanislas, the exiled King of Poland. Louis XV had long ago deserted her for a succession of mistresses.

[2] Louis de France and his second wife Marie-Josephe de Saxe, the parents of Louis XVI, Louis XVIII and Charles X.

[3] The King's eldest daughter, Louise-Elisabeth married in 1739 to Philip, Infant of Spain and Duke of Parma.

[4] One of the de Nesle sisters, three of whom (Madame de Mailly, Madame de Vintimille, and Madame de Châteauroux) were successively mistresses of the King, for which position Madame de Flavacourt had also competed.

I dined often with Colonel Yorke, Lord Cathcart and Lord Sussex. The 18th I went with Lord Cathcart to see Meudon, a house of the King's about three miles from Paris, and which has a beautiful prospect of Paris and the environs, with the River Seine in several branches. From thence we went to see that famous house, or rather enchanted palace, of Bellevue, built by the present King for Madame Pompadour, and indeed, by torchlight as well as sunshine, it is altogether the finest thing and the completest I ever saw, and nothing can exceed its situation and command of prospect. It beats St. Cloud greatly. There we went immediately afterwards; the furniture of this house is beyond description for magnificence, taste and elegance. The next day we went to see the water-works play at Versailles, which was ordered for the two hostages. They are very fine and very numerous, but cost Lewis the 14th such immense sums that one rather regrets the loss of the publick in them. We went about in gondolas on the water, to see the menagerie, Trianon, etc, and all spoke the greatness of the Prince whose they are.

The 21st I went to the Hotel Luxembourg, rue des petits Augustins for 16 louis[1] a month, but very fine apartments.

I went about now to several villas, a pretty one of Colombes of Marquis Courtenveaux, one of the Duke de Gesvres, one of Madame Monconseil called Bagatelle. In the evening of the 23rd I went to the Italian comedy, where I made up to the Corrolina, a famous actress kept by the Prince de Monaco, and who, whilst I was at Paris, I offered one thousand louis d'ors in gold[2] for her, but was refused *nette*. I speak of it as a most astonishing circumstance.

I now begun to *pour me plaire* at Paris, and Skreen could not get me away. I had a great deal of company to dinner constantly, and musick twice a week. I began to establish myself here for some time. The Duke of Chartres' house was opened to me in town and at St. Cloud, so was the Prince of Conti's and the Duke de Penthièvre's. Marshal Coigny[3] grew very fond of me, and made me be often with him. I also now took to the Court, and was so well received every where that it was impossible for me not to like to be here, tho' I found I was spending all my money very fast. About the beginning of July I took to the eldest Bellno, one of the Opera dancers, who was very handsome and kept by the old

[1] A louis was equivalent to seventeen shillings.

[2] About £850.

[3] François, Duc de Coigny, was then aged 79.

Great Chamberlain de Pologne; the Duke of Chartres kept the other sister. But I did not stick faithfully here, for I soon took to the Lani, another dancer, but famous in her kind, and she played upon me for a virgin, and I paid her and her mother accordingly—like a fool as I was, I suppose. But this did not last neither. The 3rd Lord and Lady Rochford dined with me in his way to Turin, where he was going Envoy. The next day I gave her supper with about twenty people, by way of getting her acquaintance. With all this I got up very early of a morning, rode three times a week, I fenced an hour of a morning three times a week, danced every morning half an hour, and kept on my harpsichord constantly after dinner two hours if I dined at home. The ladies I soon found out were very gallant, and had no aversion to little gallantries being sent them. I had an opposite neighbour that was pretty, and I got acquainted with a strange fellow, a Marquis de Ganis, who I found was acquainted with her, in order to get introduced, which I was soon after, but it did not answer, the distance deceived me. I now generally passed my nights with the Bellno and the Lani.

Lord Albermarle arrived here the 15th as Ambassador and was expected to make a great figure, but I shall only say here he made none, except for his mistress Mademoiselle Lolotte, who had been an actress at Brussels, and formerly had gone thro' the whole French army. 'Twas thought the French paid their account in this cunning girl's being so much mistress of Lord Albermarle. He kept a great table for the English, but hardly ever a Frenchman dined with him, nor was he either liked or esteemed at Paris. It was imagined all this strange conduct was to pay his court to the Duke of Cumberland, who openly professed his dislike to the French.[1]

About this time Monsieur de Ganis, not succeeding by his other lady, introduced me to two ladies, Madame de Bellveau and Madame de la Motte, but it would not do, I did not bite; nor was the dupe of his plan there, as I found he wanted me to throw away some money there to pay for his work.

The 16th, as the Court was now at Compiègne a-hunting. I followed it there. I arrived at 2, and met the King just going out to hunt, and very grand it was indeed, the number of equipages and

[1] William Anne, 2nd Earl of Albermarle, K.G., was the father of Admiral Augustus Keppel. He died in Paris in 1754; Mademoiselle Lolotte (Louise Gaucher) then married the Comte de Héronville, and died in 1765. Marmontel speaks well of both Lord Albermarle and his mistress, but D'Argenson and Walpole agree with Hervey.

horses and led horses with very rich furniture was prodigious. Here is nothing but a continual scene of dining, supping, hunting, walking, and court without any restraint on your dress, and, as this charming place is more collected, your acquaintances are sooner made, and you see one another oftener. Lord Albermarle had his first audience here, and in it forgot to carry the King his Master's letter—*pour dêbut*! I was introduced to the Duke d'Aumont, Governor of Compiègne and one of the four Lords of the Bedchamber to the King. He is a very obliging magnificent nobleman. I supped there often, and played at Madame de Luynes', where the Queen played three times a week at *cavagnole*. Madame Pompadour had always her toilette filled here too. The King supped at his *grand couvert* generally three times a week, where there was an opportunity of paying our court to him, which I never missed whilst I remained there, and found I was not the worse received for it, either at Court or anywhere else. I went a-hunting constantly, and had every time three horses for relays of the King's. I supped often with the Duchess of Modena and the Prince of Conti. The Duke de Richelieu was very civil to me here, and remembered me at Genoa. I mostly went a-hunting with the Duke de Penthièvre[1], for we went to the rendezvous sometimes four or five, sometimes seven miles. The 20th I dined with Monsieur de Puisieulx, a dinner for Lord Albermarle; we were sixty-eight at table, and my Lord left Compiègne almost immediately after dinner. As I was at the Duchess de Luynes Madame de Brignole[2] came in, a sister-in-law of the beautiful Pellinetta Brignole who was at Genoa.

The 23rd I left Compiègne for Paris, and that night went to Bagatelle to see Madame Monconseil, who I found alone there, and who I stayed and supped with. She shewed me the prettiest little boudoire that could be—nor did I lose my time in it; but the next day I went and lay at Bellno's, who I still liked very much.

The 2nd August I went to see the tapestry manufactory at the Savonnerie, which is very curious and very fine. I think I

[1] Louis-Jean-Marie de Bourbon, grandson of Louis XIV, and titular Admiral of France.

[2] Annetta, wife of the Marquis de Brignole. Soulavie's *Vie privée du Maréchal de Richelieu* (Vol. II, 135) says: "Annetta n'étoit peut-être pas aussi séduisante que sa sœur; mais elle étoit aussi belle. Avec une cœur aussi tendre, elle avoit moins de principes et de craintes pour l'avenir. . . . [Richelieu] vit bien qu'elle seroit moins cruelle que Pellinetta. . . . Elle passa six mois dans son hôtel avec sa fille . . .; ce temps fut plus que suffisant pour mettre le maréchal dans le cas de ne plus rien desirer."

never saw such fine colours and shades in my life. I got a carpet made for my mother, which cost me a great deal of money.

The Duke and Duchess of Chartres being come to St. Cloud and having invited me there, I went with Lord Cathcart first and supped there. She was charmingly entertaining and droll, very pretty, tho' she had then a breaking out in her face, for which she had taken something of a pomatum that very much disfigured her, yet she was very pretty, her only fault was bad teeth.[1] However I supped there, and all her ladies were delightfully agreeable, Madame de Boufflers, Madame de Mortyn, Madame de Blot, Madame de Polignac, Madame de Rochambeau.[2] In short 'twas a splendid Court, with all the magnificence of one without the form and disagreeable part of one. I was pressed to lie here this night, but they insisted I should come as often as I pleased and have an apartment there allotted me to come to when I would. I returned to town very late.

The 6th I was at the French comedy and Mademoiselle Romainville, one of the principal actresses, kept by Monsieur Maison-Rouge, a *fermier-général*, had some mind for a slice of me I found, which I had no scruples about, tho' she was not very pretty, but had another very good quality of being very sweet and very fond. I went and supped with her once or twice, and there I think it ended.[3] I am obliged to recount all these different little uninteresting scenes, as my whole time at Paris was scarce anything else, and as I write this over purely for my own satisfaction of recalling to my memory most of the events of all kinds of my life, I pursue the thread of it, just as I had set it down every day of my life as it happened, only not quite all the very particular

[1] Louis-Philippe de Bourbon, grandson of the Regent Orleans, and Louise-Henriette de Bourbon-Conti were the parents of Philippe-Égalité. The Duke, who was the same age as Hervey, had greatly distinguished himself in the battles of the late war, particularly at Dettingen, but he took little part in public life, being indolent and nicknamed " the Fat ". The Duchess was a by-word for licentiousness. In 1752 they became Duke and Duchess of Orleans.

[2] The Duchess's ladies were: Marie-Louise de Campet de Saujeon, wife of Edouard, Marquis de Boufflers-Rouverel; Madame de " Mortyn " was Alison de Clermont-Tonnerre, Marquise de Montoison, a sickly girl who died of smallpox in November 1752, aged 27 (see p. 142); Madame de Blot was Madame de Monconseil's niece; Madame de Polignac was the wife of François, Chamberlain to Stanislas, King of Poland; and Madame de Rochambeau (née Bégon) was governess to the Duchess' children, and the mother of the general famous in the American Revolution.

[3] In February 1752, two months after the death of his wife and to the horror of his family, M. Masson de Maison-Rouge married La Romainville.

circumstances attending it. These little flighty suppers broke into my appointments often at Bagatelle, where I still continued to go as often as I could, and stayed as late as I could, tho' not always as late as the Countess would have me. . . .

The 15th was St. Louis' Day, a great gala day. I made a very magnificent suit of clothes, and went to Versailles where I was very well received, and as I was almost the only Englishman there except the Ambassador, I was not the worse off for it. I supped at the Duchess of Modena's with the Duke and Duchess of Penthièvre, the Sardinian Ambassador, and many others. I returned late to town and went to the masquerade with the Marquis de St. Germain. There I accosted the Duchess of Chartres, pretending not to know her, and I found the next day she was delighted with it, as Lord Cathcart told me. The next night I had a great concert and supper for Madame de Brignole and the Prince de Wirtemburgh, with a great many others. I walked in the Palais Royal the next day, and there Madame Coupé of the opera accosted me. As I had no objection to vanity, was young and healthy enough to bear it all, I agreed to go see her the next day, which I did, and a most luscious *jouissance* she was. But I was told she was at all, so that I had done with her after about seven or eight nights keeping to her. The Bellno was my most constant night companion of all these sort for the present, tho' I soon found I should have better game, but then not quite so much at my devotion, and where I must be more upon my guard. Lord Sussex and his girl (the Beaufort) came and supped with the Bellno and me. The Duke of Wirtemburgh, Lord Albermarle, the Sardinian Ambassador, Duke d'Antin, Colonel Yorke, Lord Charles Douglas and the Count Bernstorff[1] came and dined with me.

The 28th being the festival of St. Cloud I went there, and there was the water-works, and the gardens full of millions of people. I lay there that night and returned to town next day after dinner, which was taken very civil. I dined the 30th at Monsieur de Challions, a Captain of a man-of-war, with whom was a Madame Deshorns, a very pretty woman. They all dined with me the next day. The next day I went with Lord Cathcart to the Palais Marchand, where we saw Madame de Geeche, natural daughter of monsieur le duc,[2] who was beautiful. After the Comedy a Mademoiselle Blotin came with her mother to me and supped with

[1] The Danish Ambassador.

[2] Henriette, daughter of Louis, Prince de Condé, formerly Duc de Bourbon; she was legitimated in 1739, and the next year married Jean, Comte de la Guiche.

me, and whilst the mother lay on a couch in the antechamber, the daughter went to bed with me, and returned home that morning.

I went to see Choisy, a pleasure house of the King's, of which the young Count de Coigny was Governor, as his father had been before, who was a great favourite of the King's and killed in a duel, tho' it was said his chaise was overturned in the night down a precipice. There are fine apartments and pretty gardens here. The King generally passes three or four days here with Madame de Pompadour when he has a mind to be quite retired. In the gallery are all his battles painted, and the Battle of Fontenoy, with all his Court about him, is so exactly done that I knew every one of them that I had ever seen before. I lay at the Maréchal Coigny's that night, and went a-shooting the next day, and then returned to Paris the day after. The 5th Mademoiselle Blotin came to see me, and I went to see the Duke of Richmond, who was just come from England, and the next day dined at Lord Albemarle's with his Grace, and went to the Comedy with him. He told me 'twas time for me to go on or return home. I said I knew it was, but that there was a clog which prevented me leaving Paris for Italy, and one that would not let me remain in England with any satisfaction to myself. I knew I was immerged in pleasures here, and could not get away.

The 8th I went to St. Cloud and stayed there four days. The Duchess had very little company there at present. The 13th I went to dinner with Monsieur de Courtenvaux; we went to the Opera, Madame la Mare and several others, and afterwards they persuaded me to go out of town with them to Colombes, which I did and returned next morning after shooting with the Marquis de Castries. I was very much heated and drank cold water when I came in, so that I was blooded at night. In the morning I was not very well, but thought it would go off, and went to St. Cloud as I had promised to dine there. I was persuaded to stay to supper, which I did, and afterwards, being in the drawing-room with the Duchess, only Madame de Boufflers, Madame de Polignac, Madame Mortyn, and Madame de Rochambeau there, I was all of a sudden taken with a violent pain in my side. It increased so much that I could scarce breathe or speak. They all undressed me, sent for the household surgeon, and I was blooded and put to bed. I was bled three times before morning. My servant was sent for a

---

This is a good example of Hervey's phonetic spelling of foreign names, which makes identification difficult.

physician. Never was anything so kind, so attentive as the Duchess and her ladies. They stayed with me till near 4 o'clock that morning. At last Monsieur de Chenay,[1] a very good physician, came to me. In short I continued to the 30th very ill, with three physicians, blooded constantly, purging and sweating. The Duke and Duchess came almost every other day to see me. They were obliged to go to Fontainebleau, and yet left every thing established for me, and the Duke got a litter of the King's to be ready to carry me to town when I pleased. I grew better about the 3rd October, when the Irish physician I had would carry me to air in another room. I got a relapse by it, and was very ill again of my side, worse than before, and so continued till the 20th when I grew stronger. Madame de Rochambeau used to come and sit with me almost the whole day. I prepared to return to Paris, which I did the 18th, and made a number of presents to the different officers left in the palace for me. I grew better next day, tho' very weak. The 19th Lord Cathcart and Lord Sussex came from Fontainebleau to me and shewed me the boxes the King gave them with his picture set with diamonds as they had taken leave of the court, having received the news of Cape Breton being restored. The next day little Bellno came and dined with me. I gave her a diamond ring of 50 louis. Monsieur de Vergennes was very good in sitting often with me.

The 24th I was so well to go airing a good way, and as the Duke was returned to St. Cloud I went that day to his court to thank his Royal Highness for his great goodness to me. The 26th Captain Arbuthnot came to see me, who was going out by land to command poor Fermor's ship, who died in the Mediterranean, my old acquaintance and school-fellow.[2] To the 31st I only kept continually airing, and saw everyone that came to me. That day I found the Duchess was arriced at St. Cloud. I went there to express my gratitude for all her Royal Highness's goodness and condescension to me. She took me aside and spoke to me about a picture Lord Cathcart had asked the Duke and Duchess for. I took care not to say anything that could make the Duchess think that the world could imagine there was any impropriety in it. Madame de Forcalquier was there.[3] Madame de Mortyn talked to me a great while about Monsieur de Melfort, who was reckoned the Duchess's favourite, and whom the Duke began to have an

[1] Perhaps Quesnay, Madame de Pompadour's household physician.

[2] See p. 41.

[3] La Belle Comtesse, la Bellissima.

aversion to.[1] I was very weak and unable to ramble about all these days, so that I used to stay a great deal at home and had company chiefly there. The 5th November Madame Bukby sent me word she was going to England. Afterwards I went to take my leave of her, and then to the Opera to the Duchess of Chartres' box, and supped there afterwards.

I continued this kind of same round of pleasure till the 12th November that I went with the Duchess of Chartres to the masquerade, and there it opened a new scene to me, as I fell in love with the most beautiful woman in France, Madame Caze, a *fermier-général's* wife. Her name was Lescarmotier, she had ever been brought up and intended to have been mistress to the King with her beauty, but the Duke de Richelieu succeeded for Madame de Pompadour, then Madame d'Etoiles only, and wife also to a *fermier-général*.[2] However as I was with the Duchess, who I never left the whole night, it was not easy for me to show Madame Caze much of my solicitude about her, yet I did contrive it in part by pulling her gown once or twice when my mask was off and her's on.

The 15th one Monsieur St. Olas, a good drole *débauché* dined with me with others. It come into our heads to write to many of the Opera people (principals) and so direct the letters of one to another, which made strange confusion and was a good scene to us at the Opera the next night. The 17th I went with the Duchess of Chartres to the Prince de Condé's ball, a masked one he gave, and very well entertained I was, except that Madame Caze was not there, and I could not continue to see her or let her know my situation. I went to Versailles the 20th, and after court dined with the Duke de Gesvres. The Prince of Hesse was there. I returned to St. Cloud and supped there, and came to Paris next morning. This was mostly my way of life, and too uninteresting to dwell upon the particulars, but that I write it for my own amusement

[1] Louis Drummond, Comte de Melfort, a grandson of the Jacobite Duke of Perth. He was a Lieutenant-General in the French army, and was eventually dismissed from court for his liaison with the Duchess of Chartres. Madame de Oberkirch wrote that he was " dans sa jennesse un des hommes les plus brillants et les plus seduisants".

[2] She was Susanne-Felix Lescarmotier, who in 1747 had married, as his second wife, Anne-Nicolas-Robert de Caze. The Duc de Luynes (XIV, p. 189) says " Madame Caze . . . est connue depuis longtemps par sa grande beauté ; elle est fille d'un secretaire de M. le premier président Pelletier. Madame Lescarmotier étoit encore plus belle que sa fille". Unfortunately none of the portraits of her by Liotard can now be identified.

and recollection. The Duke of Hamilton and Lord March[1] arrived. I carried them to St. Cloud the 30th and they set out for Toulouse the 3rd December, where the Duke went for his health. I got them many letters of recommendation from the Présidente de Nicquet and others, but they could not persuade me to go with them. I went in the morning the 9th with Monsieur de Vergennes to a Madame de Pleneuf, which I did to get acquainted with Madame Caze who often went there. The 14th I went and spent some days at St. Cloud a-hunting with the Duke, being tired of Paris and yet not able to leave it. The 16th I was at Madame de Boufflers'[2] magnificent ball, for which I made a pair of diamond buckles, that cost 225 louis. I danced with the Princess de Robecque and Madame de Villeroy. At 6 in the morning I returned home. The 22nd I was introduced at Mr. Haye's to a Baronne Blanche, with whom the next day I could not avoid being more intimate with than I had an inclination for; she was a great, black, lewd woman about 30, that was at all, and amused herself in that style with whom she took a fancy to. She was rich and lived in this way. The Prince of Monaco frequented her, and at her house met many ladies of this stamp and degree.

I was at the masquerade the 25th with the Duchess of Chartres, but did not see Madame Caze there. I supped the 28th with a Mr. Johnson who has a sweet house, and most elegantly he lives. Madame de Monconseil carried me there. He is a famous sharper concerned in cheating the Duke of Bedford, but never plays here.[3] I did not like the company however, and deteremined to go there no more. I lived now mostly at the Palais Royal, where every one was most extremely kind to me. I was at the masquerade the 30th, and brought home from thence a Madame de Mirancourt who pretended to be a very modest lady, yet she stayed with me till near daylight. We returned to the masquerade in order to separate. The 3rd January I supped with the old Duchess of Maine and her two sons, the Count d'Eu and [the Prince de Dombes].[4] She is a curious frightful old woman. She has her toilette at 10, and then

[1] Later 4th Duke of Queensbury, notorious for his rakish life; "Old Q".

[2] This Madame de Boufflers was the widow of the Duc de Boufflers, who died at Genoa during the siege of 1747; in June 1750 she married secondly the Maréchal-Duc de Luxembourg.

[3] Henry Janssen, who succeeded his brother as 3rd Baronet in 1765 and died at Paris the following year. Pope refers to the incident mentioned by Hervey: "Or when a Duke to Janssen punts at White's"; *2nd Satire*, 88.

[4] Louise-Anne de Bourbon, daughter of the Prince of Condé, and widow of the Duc de Maine, son of Louis XIV and Madame de Montespan. She was

again at 12 at night, at which every one assists that is there. I went and sat for my picture to Liotard, a famous Genevan painter, who had been long in Turkey, and by wearing their dress and having a long beard he was very much followed as a great artist. But tho' he took likeness well, yet I think him no painter. However his price was high, and he sometimes did extremely well. I gave 16 louis for a small picture of me. [1]

The 6th I received a letter from Lord Doneraile to press me home, and urging that the Prince had spoke about it. But it was too late, I was engrossed with all these voluptuous pleasures, and was now in pursuit of Madame Caze, which I could not leave. The 12th Madame de Monconseil and I had a terrible *éclaircissement* on my going there so seldom now, and never but when there was company. However I got off it pretty well, for I found she was grown cool too, and I knew myself to blame, so I said little, but I could not tell her the reason " that others pleased me more ". I blessed the moment that people came in, which was my good old friend the Marshal de Coigny.

Sunday evening I supped with the Duchess of Chartres, and with her, Madame de l'Hôpital, Madame d'Estrées and Madame de la Mare I went to the masquerade; there I saw Madame Caze again, who I determined to accost, and did so, and was as resolved to sup where she told me she should on Tuesday the 16th. The 14th I went to a great ball of the Maréchale de Belle-Isle's, where was 700 people and the most splendid entertainment I had ever seen there in every respect, the house so magnificent and so finely illuminated. The next day I supped at Madame Pleneuf's, where Madame Caze came, who was lovely indeed. I was placed luckily next to her at supper, and was invited to sup at her house Sunday next and to go to the masquerade with her. The 17th I went with Monsieur de Vergennes to see Madame Caze, and Monsieur came in, who appeared the most coxcomical little *fade*[2] I ever saw, full of himself, and therefore did not imagine his wife could ever like any one but himself. They insisted however for me to stay to supper, which I did, tho' engaged to Madame Pleneuf's.

---

an arch plotter during the Regency. It was the Prince de Dombes who slew the Comte de Coigny, see p. 93.

[1] Jean-Étienne Liotard (1702–89) probably painted the heads of the six figures in the picture illustrated opposite p. 96. He was more accomplished in pastels than in oils.

[2] An insipid man; a " wet "; the Comte de Cheverny (I, 89) says he was nicknamed " le beau danseur ".

There were two coquettish sisters of his, Madame de Calvisson and Madame de Forbin, who I found soon which way to gain them, and fed them accordingly. Thursday I went to sup with Madame Caze, and this now seemed to take up all my attention. I dined next day with the Marquis St. Germain, who I got to engage the Lani to dance at Turin at the opera to be given on the Duke of Savoy's wedding, but which means I got rid of her and provided for her in her own way. I gave her £200 in louis to fit her out. The 20th I supped at Madame Caze's with a great many pretty women of the *financiers*. The next day I went to the masquerade with Madame Caze, and so continued this sort of life on, but never gave up St. Cloud and the Palais Royal where I continued as assiduous as ever.

The Prince of Hesse[1] teased me a good deal here, for tho' his Royal Highness did me a great deal of honour by insisting so much on my being with him, yet 'twas a *gêne* and very *ennuyant*, which I had no view in. I went to the Palais Marchand and bought several New Year's gifts, which is greatly the vogue here, and where indeed one may be much tempted to ruin oneself. The 2nd February I dined with the Marquis de St. Germain and Count Marmora, us three only, and we fell into a political discourse after dinner on the match the Duke of Savoy was going to make with the Infanta of Spain. I said he ought to have married one of Portugal and got a good sum of money with her, which would have made amends to the Sardinian Treasury for the expences of last war, and given no jealousy to either France or Spain. He said that would be filling the pockets, and not looking upon the map. " Oh, Oh," says I, " then the King did give a look on the map, and the coast of Genoa too, perhaps," said I, " when he made this match."

The next day I went a party with Monsieur and Madame Caze to a villa of their's at Torcy about five leagues from Paris by Vincennes. Madame d'Orfeuille (his sister), a Monsieur de Croissy and a l'abbé (Monsieur le Grange) went with us. We did not dine, but supped very splendidly. It is a sweet pretty villa, and he is making a magnificent terrace to it, finely furnished but not yet finished. We stayed three days here fishing, riding and diverting ourselves, and after supper the 6th returned to Paris where we arrived about 4 in the morning. I lost no time to persuade Madame Caze of my devotion to her.

[1] Frederick, Hereditary Prince of Hesse-Cassel, who in 1740 had married Princess Mary, daughter of George II.

The next day I went to Palais Royal and to the hotel de Toulouse. The Duke of Penthièvre shewed me many projects for ships, etc. Whilst I was there an officer came in with a plan of a ship he had projected that was to go without masts or sails, and be rowed under water about three foot, with a place a pilot is to be in to steer, all covered with leather. The intention of this is to go into a harbour and sink ships in the night by running an iron beak into them. I never heard of so wild and mad and absurd a project. I argued with the projector, but could get no lights from him, and asked him when this iron beak or prow was stuck in the ship, what was to become of the one under water and the people who were to row it. In short we concluded him mad.[1]

I supped at the Palais Royal, where I found my tour to Torcy had not pleased. I settled my account with my bankers and found my money run away fast. The 10th I was at St. Cloud where the Duke and Duchess, Madame la comtesse de Boufflers, Madame de Mortyn and several others of the nobility of that Court played the comedy of *La Cotti Imaginaire* and *La Magnifique*. The dancers were by Lord Aboyne, Monsieur Melfort and many others. There were above sixty ladies in the little theatre. I got Madame Caze a box. The 12th I went to Versailles and paid my court the whole tour, came to St. Cloud in the evening, where the same illustrious set acted the *Philosophe Marié* and the *Dépit* for *petit pièce*.[2] There were 114 persons at supper at three tables in three different rooms, all served with three courses and a dessert at the same time, the finest entertainment I had ever seen. I played at *cornet*[3] with the Duchess after supper, we sat up till 4 in the morning.

The 16th Lord Albermarle went to Palais Royal for his audience of the Duke and Duchess. The Duchess made me laugh telling me how, the instant Lord Albermarle came in, she said "*votre excellency*", and then the Ambassador, according to the etiquette, may go away as soon as he pleases, and 'tis reckoned to token

[1] There had been many unsuccessful experiments with underwater craft by this date, though it is not possible to identify the particular project here referred to. The vessel described is not unlike Simon's submarine of 1747. Hervey must have been confirmed in his scepticism in 1774 when one Day of Yarmouth was lost during an experiment in Plymouth Sound, but during his lifetime, in 1776, Ezra Lee in Bushnell's first submarine was to make an unsuccessful attack with explosives on H.M.S. *Eagle* lying in New York harbour.

[2] Presumably Hervey means Molière's *Sganarelle ou le cocu imaginaire*, *Les Amants magnifiques*, and *Le Dépit amoureux*, and Destouches' *Le philosophe marié*.

[3] Dice.

that the Prince or Princess wants to get rid of them when they do. She had a great contempt for Lord Albermarle, and therefore shewed it that moment as the only opportunity she had, and she was always apt to speak her mind to everyone and of everything. She said once (speaking of the King of Prussia's coming to Paris) " Ah, mon Dieu, que je serai bien aise de voir un roy ", by which one may judge her opinion of her own. She gave me a very fine sword knot the 21st to go to Court in.

I was now wholly taken up with this new pursuit after Madame Caze, who gave me all the encouragement I could wish, and I was as attentive as could be. I dropped all my *filles d'opera* and all other pursuits, as well as I could cleverly. There was one which on every account I could not drop, and which I was obliged to have some consideration for. However, I set out the 6th for another tour to Torcy with Madame Caze, a Madame Chaumanette and her daughter and husband, good sort of poor and convenient people. We amused ourselves as usual, went to Champs to the Duke de la Vallière and about to several places. At last we found an opportunity to open our minds to each other and found our inclination mutual, but that we were obliged to have much management. In short she was everything I could wish, all that was lovely, but would not grant me the last proofs of her assertions to me. We returned to Paris the 15th and I supped at Madame Caze's. The next day by a long engagement I dined at St. Ouen, the Duke de Gesvres', with a great number of people, and a great entertainment it was. I supped at Madame Monconseil's that evening. I went to St. Cloud the next day, and supped there but returned to Paris afterwards, and found a note from dear Madame Caze telling me she went out of town in a day or two again, and insisted on my going, which I did the 19th, and carried Monsieur de Vergennes in my chariot with me. We now, in these days which we spent together here, became very strongly attached to each other, and which could not be hid, as we were imprudent enough to be inseparable. The 26th we went all to St. Maur, a house of the Prince of Condé's, who gave a masquerade there on his coming to take possession of that palace which was built by Francis the 1st, King of France. 'Tis not very fine, tho' the situation is delightful, and the gardens very fine. Madame Caze gave me a little ring to-day, with a motto *L'Union en est la passe*. We came away from St. Maur early as she was not well. The 30th Monsieur, Madame and I went to town together, and very sorry I was. We went to the opera immediately and I gave her a little ruby set with diamonds, *un seul me suffit*. We returned to Torcy *en famille* only. I gave him a very fine horse that I gave Lord Cornbury 45 guineas for. The 2nd April we returned to Paris, as she was not well.

I lent Lord Charles Douglas £150 to pay some play debt or other which he was in distress about. I went to St. Cloud immediately on getting to town, and lay there, but returned to Paris next day, being making visits etc, but ever employed how to see and be with Madame Caze, which we contrived very well almost every day. I gave her a pair of gaters [*sic*], white and gold in the middle; it had a long flourish embroidered with my own hair. I was still much at the Palais Royal, Versailles sometimes, and often at the Hotel de Toulouse. The Maréchal Coigny I supped with often, had company to dine and sup with me often, and contrived to meet Madame Caze when I could, not at her own house from prudence, but at Madame de Pleneuf's or Madame Chaumanette's. At the painter Liotard we met for three hours almost every morning and had our pictures done over and over again for each other, so that that rascal Liotard got many a score louis of me. The 15th I went to see the Venetian Ambassador's publick entry, which was only a fine show of coaches and led horses. Almost all my evenings were now devoted to that only object, who gained such an ascendancy over me and who persuaded me that she was equally devoted to me, tho' I could never yet obtain the last proof. I gave her the 26th a gold medal, representing on one side the ocean with a ship in it and the sun shining upon it, on the other side a tree bearing fruit, supported by two Cupids, and two more gathering it. The case that held the medal had a secret spring in, and contained my picture. She gave me her's by Liotard for a pocket-book.

The 30th I went after dining at St. Cloud to Madame Caze and stayed very late with her, and do believe I should have obtained all had her mother not come in. They kept me to supper, and she vowed I should not always be refused, that she was no longer her own mistress, that she was solely mine, and, indeed, as her husband went to his father's at La Bôve the 4th, she sent to me to come early to her that afternoon. 'Twas of a Thursday, and we remained together all that afternoon and evening till midnight, giving and receiving the last charming proofs of an unbounded love, and I never tasted such most exquisite delight, nor was I ever more fit for the scene. We were then to be sure the happiest of mortals, and only planned how we should ever see each other without giving jealousy to him. We knew that everyone remarked our attachment and always put us together. That was nothing; we had only to contrive to give no scandal. I received the 6th several things from England which I gave her, bawbles, and some Irish stuffs, and English tabbies.[1]

The 8th I went to Versailles and lay at St. Cloud, where I supped and dined the 9th, and then returned to Paris. All this time was equally employed. The 25th was her birthday, on which I gave her a most beautiful box, emblematical, done on purpose for her. The 28th after seeing the Fête de Dieu, which was nothing equal to that kept in Portugal, I went out to Torcy to join Monsieur and Madame Caze, where were many people. Here we spent many days delightfully. He going away to Choisy, I used to go to her room then, and lay there with her in bed four or five hours together, and so get away again. The 31st at High Mass I went into the *chapelle*, and I am afraid at the elevation of the Host she took that time to swear fidelity to me. I say I fear it, because for her it was so sacred a moment and I fear she has not kept it since my leaving France. I found out that he now grew jealous and had spoke to his wife of it. However we went on notwithstanding, remaining at this sweet retreat till the 10th June, when we all returned to Paris, to the great grief of Madame Caze and me.

I went to St. Cloud now, determined to stay some days to make up for all those I had been without seeing them. I returned from St. Cloud the 17th, where I had passed my time very dully in comparison of Torcy because I could only be pleased in her company, and supped that night at Madame Caze, where there was much company. I went to see a house of the King's called La Muette just at the entrance of the Bois de Boulogne. 'Tis very pretty and richly furnished. I went the next day to hunt with the Duke of Chartres at St. Cloud and supped there. I returned to Paris to meet Madame Caze at her father's, Monsieur de Lescarmotier. After dinner we walked in the garden, she and I, where she vowed to me if ever her husband treated her ill, she would fly away with me to England. We were very melancholy, as she was to set out with her husband soon to the provinces as he was to go his journey; but I had determined I would soon meet them there.

The 23rd they set out for Compiègne where the Court was in their way. The same day I set out and got to Senlis, half-way between Paris and Compiègne. She had left Fanny up to tell me by all means to lay there that night, which I did, and in the morning

[1] Watered silks.

they were all up, and Mademoiselle Bazière who went with them. We stayed and dined all together there, and went to see a convent of nuns called La Presentation. We all set out together for Compiègne, where I arrived at 6 and had taken my lodgings directly opposite to Monsieur Fournaon, where Madame Caze and all of them were to lodge. Lord Albermarle came to see me directly. I supped at the Duke de Gesvres and went to the *grand couvert* that night. The next day Madame Caze presented me to la comtesse de Baschi,[1] who was the lady of the house of Monsieur Fournaon's. I was at Madame Caze's toilette and by accident found her purse on it laying empty, and I thought she might want money and put 100 louis in it, as I happened to have brought a good sum with me in cash. She was very angry with me at night, but however I found means of pacifying her, and told her 'twas to pay for any extraordinary expresses she might have occasion to send for me and which her husband was not to know of. At night I went to the comedy, and Madame de Pompadour being in the box, I went and made my bow to her. I supped at Monsieur le Premier's.

The next day she told me she was with child, and that it was the 24th May that I lay almost all night with her at Torcy. The 18th Madame Caze set out early. I wrote and received a letter from her, early as it was. I dined at the Spanish Ambassador's and went to Court. In the afternoon and evening I took my leave of every one at Compiègne and set out for Senlis, where I got about 2 in the morning and lay in the same room and bed which Madame Caze did going down. I was distractedly in love with her and was wretched at this separation. I got to Paris the next day and employed myself chiefly going to her relations, once or twice a week to Torcy to see her two children left there, and so to write them word about them.

I however went and stayed at St. Cloud some days, as it was near the Duchess's being brought to bed. Whilst I was at St. Cloud I was so impatient Madame Caze should hear from me, to whom I wrote every day, tho' as yet I could not send it, that I dispatched my servant L'Allemand on horseback to Baukenville (the village of the Château de la Bôve) with orders to wait there hid and send for La Jeunesse her servant and wait for him, deliver that letter and wait an answer. This I did up in an embroidered sack. It was 90 miles off by Soissons and Laon. I remained at St. Cloud to make the Duchess's party of an evening,

[1] Whom Hervey met later in Portugal when her husband was French Minister there. She was sister-in-law to Madame de Pompadour.

and a great deal of company came constantly there. The next day 25th came back L'Allemand with letters in answer to mine that made me as happy as I could be in her absence.

There was now all the world assembled here to wait the Duchess's lying in, the Prince and Princess of Conti, Madame de Sens, Comte de la Marche, Madame de Luxembourg, Madame de la Vallière, Princess de Robecque, Monsieur Forcalquier and many others, Madame Tallard, Madame de l'Hôpital, Princess de Lynn—*une absente m'étoit plus chère que tout l'univers ensemble*. The 29th June (8th July new style) the Duchess was delivered of a daughter 25 minutes after 8 in the evening.[1] Maréchal Noailles was sent from the King to be present. Numbers of the nobility above were in the room the whole time, where there was a little bed placed in the middle of the room. The Duke held her the whole time. The Duke went to the King to Compiègne the next morning, and all the nobility of Paris came here to enquire after the Princess. The 2nd July the Marquis de Souvré came with a compliment from the King. The Duke would always have me with him now at all his *petits soupés*, which I would rather have been excused. The 3rd the Duchess began to see some of us every afternoon and was rather chatty. The Duke carried me to shoot pheasants that morning, and great sport we had. I went to see Madame Pleneuf at a little villa of her's called Chatou and supped there with a great deal of company, and then returned to St. Cloud. The 5th I went a-hunting with the Duke. We run three stags and took ne'er a one. We had many ladies out in chaises. The 6th I went to sup with Mrs. Greville at Passy who was here, and a Madame Tiron with her who was pretty.

I kept writing every day to Madame Caze. The 7th in the morning Monsieur de Vergennes, my friend, set out for Coblentz where he was Minister from the King. He was to stop at Dijon in his way, and I gave him straw hats for Madame Caze and Madame Bazière who were to be at Dijon, and a letter of 33 pages for Madame Caze. I was sorry to part with Monsieur de Vergennes, our acquaintance was an old and uninterrupted one, our friendship very sincere and disinterested, but I knew he would make a figure one day in the political world. I went the 8th to dine with the Maréchal Coigny at Orly, and then returned to St. Cloud. The

[1] The child was Louise-Marie-Thérèse-Bathilde, who in 1770 married Louis-Henri-Joseph, Duc de Bourbon. They were the parents of the Duc d'Enghien, last of the House of Condé, who was shot by order of Napoleon in 1804.

12th I was invited by the Prévost des Marchands to a great dinner at St. Ouen given the Duke de Gesvres, and where there were thirty people. The next day I had a letter from Madame Caze by L'Allemand, who I had sent the 9th to Reims, 158 miles off, and if he did not find there, to go to Challons-sur-la-Marne. I was happy to find her well. The 14th I went with the Duke to Paris and found my own coach and six at the Palais Royal, in which I set out for Torcy, found the children all well. Madame d'Orfeuille, Monsieur Croissy and I returned at 5 in the morning. The 15th I settled accounts with Mr. Selwyn, and a dreadful one again it was, drew for £580 more. I went and made all my visits of leave, determining to go home and see how things were and then return again as soon as possible, as my mother gave me hopes of coming back with me. I found since I had been at Paris I had spent a great sum of money.

I set out the 17th at 3 in the morning, and after going all over Chantilly again and being overturned between Laigneville and Clermont, I got to Amiens early in the morning and went to see the Cathedral, which was very fine and built by the English in the 15th century. I got to Dover the 19th and set out for London, where I found my mother in her house at St. James's Place that was not quite finished. Most of my time was spent with my mother. The 26th I went to see my Uncle William at Rickmansworth, where several of my relations were, from whom I heard the whole state and situation of this shattered family. The 28th my Brother Hervey being come to town, I went to him. He began with telling me my mother had acted a most shameful part by my youngest sisters,[1] that she had made them rank Jacobites and taught them to reverence the Pretender, and even to ridicule and censure the present King, that he had been obliged to take my sisters from under her tuition, and determined himself to have as little to say to her the rest of his life as possible. He was extremely warm in his language of her, and I had heard of this before from Sir Robert and Lady Louisa.[2] I said I had nothing to do with it all, that my mother was very kind to me, and I should not enter into any quarrels, but live as well as I could with them all. The 29th I set out for Ickworth to see Lord Bristol, where I found my sister Phipps and Mr. Phipps who had a house at Bury. The 1st August I returned to London, and the 3rd went to Muffetts in Hampshire to see my dear friend Mrs. Ord and him, where I

[1] Caroline and Emily.
[2] Smyth; see p. 84.

stayed three or four days, and very happy they were to see me and I the same by them. I returned to town the 8th, and the 13th my mother and Brother and Sister Phipps set out with me from Dover for Paris, after I had cleared all accounts and paid all bills in London. We could not get to Boulogne, and therefore put for Calais, and arrived there about 2 o'clock in the afternoon. We set out directly and got to Boulogne at midnight, where we lay, and I found letters there. The next morning we set out late and lay at Abbeville, the next day at Clermont. The 16th we went all over Chantilly and met my coach at Ecouen, and got to Paris early to Madame le Blanc's, Rue de Condé, the first floor, at 500 livres a month, the second at 150.[1]

That evening I went to pay my court at St. Cloud, where the Duke and Duchess were very glad to see me. Some days were taken up shopping with my mother and sister. The 19th I went to Versailles and the whole tour there. I was now taken up by a thousand visits I was necessarily obliged to make, but nevertheless determined to go to Dijon if I heard from Madame Caze when she arrived there and that I had a chance of seeing her alone. I presented my mother, brother and sister at St. Cloud, and very well received they were.

The 23rd, having had letters that suited me, I set out at midnight without saying a word to anyone for Dijon. I only took Allemand in my chaise, and half-a-dozen shirts. I passed Fontainebleau the next morning early, without ever going to see that magnificent palace, Sens and Auxerres, and in a fine road the whole day along the charming River Saône. In short I did not stop, for at 8 in the morning the 25th I got to Dijon without ever getting out of my chaise the whole 72 leagues, or 36 posts. I went to bed immediately at the hotel de Condé on the left hand coming into town at the gate of Paris. I gave my name "Joseph Stradi", a travelling gentleman, wrote a line to la Jeunesse to give his lady, and had an answer at noon to go there at night, which I did at midnight to the house of the Marquis de Beau-pré where they lodged and he was gone to Besançon. I lay there all night, and she pretended to be ill the next day, so that I lay in bed all the next, and till 4 o'clock next morning, only La Jeunesse and her maid Fanny knowing of my being there. I set out immediately again for Paris, without seeing anything of Dijon but by moonlight as I passed, and it seemed a small, clean, regular built town, with a pretty *place* in it where Lewis the 14th's statue was. I got to

[1] Twenty-five livres were approximately one pound.

Paris about 6 o'clock the 28th, where my mother and sister were surprised at my diligence. I was afterwards vexed I had not turned short and so made as had I just arrived at Dijon when he returned, and stayed there some days. But he grew so jealous that it was best not. She was however soon to return to Paris.

My mother and sister diverted ourselves with going about to see everything and everybody worth seeing or knowing, and in short 'twas one continued scene of pleasure, for my mother had numbers of acquaintances there. The 8th September my dear friend Monsieur de Chavigny went from Paris for Dijon in his way to his Embassy to Venice, having been disappointed of the great office he had reason to expect in the administration here, but they were afraid of his abilities and his intrigues. We all went to Versailles the 13th and shewed my mother and sister everything, and the Court paid them great attentions and they were delighted with the place and their reception there, as we saw the excessive fine fireworks the King gave to the Dauphiness, being placed in the great gallery at Versailles, where Madame Pompadour came and spoke to my mother and sister, the Duke de Richelieu and several others. We had now such a scene of uninterrupted pleasures there is no describing all the particulars of them, as they were too much of a sameness in all this time. The Duke and Duchess of Chartres shewed all the attention possible to my mother and Mr. and Mrs. Phipps. We were at St. Cloud and the Palais Royal as often as they pleased, and to operas and plays etc. When the 3rd October Mr. and Mrs. Fitzgerald arrived here, we were all charmed to see dearest Mary, who was the delight of us all. I gave her my picture in a bracelet that day set with diamonds, and soon after a fine pair of diamond ear-rings, and the next day the 4th I had the happiness to receive a letter by La Jeunesse that Madame Caze was arrived at Torcy and would be in town this evening. I went with Sister Phipps to meet her just out of the town. She and Madame Bazière got out of their coach and I carried them home, where my sister went in and stayed about half an hour, and then came away to sup with Lord and Lady Bath[1] at Lord Cornbury's, for we were now a perfect colony of English here.

I went now every day early to Liotard's to meet Madame Caze. I supped there often and spent my afternoon mostly there, till we were a little disturbed by his jealousies, tho' his vanity got the better and he would be always entertaining most splendidly

[1] Lord Hervey's old antagonist and Miss Chudleigh's first "protector", formerly William Pulteney, now retired from politics.

my mother and sisters. I passed my time almost eternally with her now at some place or other, and in short we neither of us could be easy without the other was present. I carried her often in the country to her father's or wherever we were engaged. Madame de Nicquet helped us out very often, she was a good friendly lady, tho' I was obliged to be grateful to her too, for she understood all that very well. An unlucky accident had ne'er overturned all these joyous scenes, indeed nothing could be nearer. For the 4th November of a Sunday evening I went with my sisters to take leave of her. I remained, and as we had just finished some very tender caresses, the husband came in. A large muff of mine slung to a girdle luckily screened what I had not time to set well to rights, but he perceived our confusions and thought we had been only kissing, I suppose, and went out in a great huff to his library. I went soon after to Madame de Chaumanette where I waited to hear from Madame Caze what had passed with her husband. I found it went off very well, he kept his suspicions to himself.

The 9th Mr. and Mrs. Phipps left us, being obliged to return to London. The 10th Mademoiselle de la Roche-sur-Yon died of the small-pox, a Princess much regretted for her hospitality, and to whom many had great obligations to.[1] The 13th I carried Mr. and Mrs. Fitzgerald to St. Cloud, where they were extremely well received. The 18th, Lord Cornbury, in great confidence, shewed me a letter he was going the next day to send his friend Lord Foley, acquainting him that he was going to be called up to the House of Lords and with the reasons which had made him desire it and recommending him the Oxford election, and a very pretty letter it was, giving an account of his transactions for years past.[2] I gave Madame Caze a pretty knot ring of rubies and diamonds. The 19th we had news of the death of that great General, the Maréchal de Saxe, at Chambord, just after he had been magnificently entertaining the whole Court, and much lamented he was. He called to his nephew just before he died (the Count de Frise) and told him: "Ah, mon neveu, voilà la fin d'un beau songe".[3]

[1] Louise-Adelaide de Bourbon-Conti, aged 54; D'Argenson wrote "cette une bonne princesse et qui laisse beaucoup de bâtards".

[2] Henry Hyde, Viscount Cornbury, was being called up as Baron Hyde, after having sat as M.P. for Oxford University in the Jacobite interest since 1732; he died in Paris in 1753 following a fall from his horse.

[3] The victor of Fontenoy, Rocoux and Lawfeldt was hastened to his grave by his dissolute life. D'Argenson reports the same dying speech as Hervey,

I now began to go every evening late to Madame Caze, and was let in by the stables and staid till 2 or 3 in the morning, as he went now often to lay at Versailles, being *secretaire du cabinet*, which gives them the *entré* at night when the King is going to bed, and which he would not miss for all the women in the world. I got of L'Abbé Pomponne[1] an original picture of Madame de Sévigné, in order to have it copied for Mr. Selwyn. My time was wholly taken up with being with Madame Caze and going everywhere that I could to be in her company and she was the same with me, and yet I endeavoured never to be wanting in my attentions at St. Cloud and every other place I had received civilities from. The 4th December the Duchess of Chartres carried me, with Madame de Boufflers only, to La Vivienne, about five leagues from Paris and close to St. Germain, a very pretty situation, to dine with her mother, the Princess of Conti. She was delightful gay the whole day. The 6th I went with Monsieur Sorba, the Genoese Minister, to make my first visit to the Count de Kaunitz, the Emperor's Ambassador here, who was lodged in the beautiful Palais de Bourbon, and I never saw such a coxcombe in all my life.[2] I was almost every night let in to Madame Caze by either La Jeunesse or Fanny.

The 11th my mother, sister and myself rose very early and went to the Palais with Madame de Boufflers to see the Duke of Chartres received as Peer of France, also the Archbishop of Paris as Duke and Peer. The room where the Parliament is held is a very poor one, the ceremony a very trivial one, and there was only to see the Duke of Chartres going from his own palace to the Palais with all his coaches, fourteen of his own in his own liveries preceeded his state one, in which he went, and four or five servants in his liveries behind each, and twenty-five pages before his coach, and a number of all the nobility following. This day I gave Sister Mary a pair of diamond earrings cost me 260 louis. The 13th we went to Versailles to hear the musick Christmas Eve.

I now began to think of returning to England, as I found my money go very fast here and my interest decline there, and besides

---

but says it was spoken to Docteur Sénac. The more usual version is "Docteur, la vie n'est qu'un songe. La mien a été beau, mais il est court".

[1] Charles-Henri Arnauld, last of the famous Jansenist family. He died in 1756.

[2] Maria-Theresa's brilliant Chancellor was in Paris 1751–54. He was the chief inspiration of the "Diplomatic Revolution" which allied France to Austria at the outbreak of the Seven Years War in 1756; see p. 132.

I should have been very sorry to have wanted money here, or to have contracted any debts. I found also Monsieur Caze very jealous of me and giving her great uneasiness on my account, and as much as possible preventing our being together. All these things made me determine to go home as soon as I could bring myself to it, but I was more uneasy as she was now eight months gone with child, and I loved her more now than the first hour of our happiness, tho' her husband threw such difficulties in our way. The 17th I was let in by Jeunesse, and spent the whole night with her till 6 in the morning, her husband being gone to Versailles. I gave Madame Caze several little presents for the *jour de l'an*, and my mother also two pretty poperies of blue chinay prettily set with bronze, as also a candlestick for her bed. The 21st being their *jour de l'an* every one went to Versailles, but I did not go. I supped at the Princess de Conti's. I went to Versailles the 3rd and took my leave of the Court. The Queen was very civil, and Madame Pompadour also upon the occasion. I returned and supped at the Palais Royal where I was reproached for my fondness for Madame Caze. In the evening I was going as usual to be let in to Madame Caze, when before I got out of my *fiacca*, La Jeunesse came and told me that Monsieur was supposed to be at Versailles, when not ten minutes ago, all of a sudden, he returned and pretended he had left his *porte-feuille*, and searched all over the house and under her bed etc, which they imagined was on some pretence to find me. So I did not venture that evening. I put off my journey a few days to be longer with her, but at last the fatal day came when I was obliged to leave her the 3rd, after all the vows of mutual attachment in the world. I left Allemand to receive and forward my letters thro' Mr. Selwyn till she was brought to bed, and at 10 I set out, leaving my mother and Mr. and Mrs. Fitzgerald, and lay at Clermont that night. Friday I was kept six hours at the gate of Amiens, the sentinel not going to the Commandant. I got to Boulogne that evening and Saturday evening landed at Dover, hired a coach and got to Canterbury by the worst weather and roads in the world. I got to London Sunday, being much tired went to Mrs. Aston's, and before I went to bed, sent off a letter for Dover by express for Madame Caze.

V

A YEAR AT HOME

1751

MONDAY 7th January I was presented to the King by Lord Harcourt, who took not the least notice of me. I then heard all about a certain lady[1] being made House-keeper of Windsor Castle, at which I was much displeased, but said nothing. I was very well received at Leicester House by the Prince and Princess of Wales the 8th.

The 10th I went to Ickworth, being sick of London. I found my grandfather very ill with a fit of the stranguary. My brother was there, Mr. and Mrs. Phipps at Bury. I passed my time very well here, dining sometimes at Bury and sometimes at Ickworth. My brother was laying out all he intended to do, as there was little hopes of my grandfather's recovery. He continued sleeping in a manner for four or five days till the 20th that he expired about a quarter after 8. My brother and I now talked over much business that must ensue. . . . My brother told me he now intended to join the Duke of Grafton's interest at Bury, which I expressed my sorrow for; in short, I saw my brother was totally inclined to go to the Court. The 22nd my brother and I saw him put in his coffin, and all his first wife's letters placed in the coffin with him as he desired on his left cheek, a blue Turkeystone ring she gave him put on his finger, and his bracelet of her hair on, which he ever wore. The 27th my grandfather was buried in Ickworth Church between his two wives, and there ended the very thoughts about the poor old Lord of this place, to whom this family is so much indebted. The 29th my uncle, Will and I went to Town, and met Mr. and Mrs. Phipps on the road.

Whilst I was in Town I went often to Leicester House, but seldom to St. James's. I found by Sister Phipps the Princess

[1] Mrs. Chudleigh, Elizabeth's mother; the appointment is said to have been the result of a passing infatuation of the old King's for the "Married Maid"!

Caroline[1] told her how every one laughed at my brother's having thrown himself into the Duke of Dorset's[2] hands, and that the King was only persuaded to speak to him when he was presented but by the Duke of Dorset's making a point of it. I heard a great deal, too, of my mother's silly work about the Pretender. These things hurt me very much, tho' I could not help them.

Nothing passed extraordinarily with me, till the 20th February I received a letter from Fanny with the news of Madame Caze's being brought to bed of a son the 12|23 February at 11 at night, and her now being very well.[3] I grew very tired of London life, it was all visiting and going to operas, plays and assemblies. I must not omit here given an account of an extraordinary entertainment Mr. Delaval gave the Town in order to exhibit his person in the character of Othello. He hired Drury Lane playhouse for that night, the 7th March. There was such a crowd of nobility and gentry as is not to be conceived; pit-boxes in one, and galleries, upper galleries and all was just as people could get to them. A Mrs. Quamon acted Desdemona.[4] About this time came about the two famous beauties, Miss Gunnings,[5] that Lord Harrington had protected when in Ireland. I used to be very much with them with Lord Coventry, who was in love with one of them.

The 21st of this month coming from the Oratorio I was told of a great loss the Kingdom in general had suffered, and myself in particular, in the Prince of Wales's death; he died of a mortification having got a cold at tennis. I found my brother had wrote to my Sister Phipps a note to tell her of it, in which he put a postscript at the bottom, saying "I suppose this will stagger, tho' not fix, your Brother Augustus". I was this evening late with Lord Egmont who was inconsolable, as well he might be, losing such a master and such a friend. I found the next day various countenances upon this occasion according to people's interest.

[1] George II's third daughter, who had been Lord Hervey's favourite member of the Royal Family.

[2] Lionel Sackville, 1st Duke, at this time Lord-Lieutenant of Ireland.

[3] He was Alexandre-Louis de Caze, "maitres des requets aux conseils du roi", who married Madeleine-Hyacinthe de Guillandeu, who bore him three daughters.

[4] The manner in which Othello (Sir Francis Blake Delaval, Bt.) embraced Desdemona (Mrs. Quon) "set many a fair heart among the audience a-longing"; see *The Gentleman's Magazine* 1751, p. 119 for an amusing critique.

[5] The daughters of John Gunning of Castle Coote; Maria, Countess of Coventry; and Elizabeth, married in 1752 to James, 6th Duke of Hamilton, and secondly in 1759 to John Campbell, later 5th Duke of Argyll.

The prince left no will and was vastly in debt. The young Prince was to have a family,[1] but most of his father's friends were to be kept from him. I confess I felt this much in my own particular; I knew it was a stroke to me, to whom he had promised to be very kind, and I was sure Lord Egmont and all that set would not let him forget me. However he was soon buried, and as soon forgot, and named no more than if he had never been.

Mr. and Mrs. Phipps and I passed a great deal of our time together. I kept up with all our old club of the Prince's friends, and Lord Egmont, General Townshend and I met very often. I had constant accounts how dear Madame Caze went on, and was very happy to find her well. I was persuaded to go to Newmarket this meeting by Townshend and Norris, which I did, tho' I did not care for any one diversion at it. I stayed most of the week there, and hunted very often, but, what was worse, I lost my money, for there was no resource here—one must play or drink, and I chose the first rather than the last. I lost a good deal on a horse called Trimmer, of Mr. Prentice's, who had 2 to 1 in his favour at starting, but by a supposed trick was distanced and led in. Mr. Prentice was suspected in this and was excluded Newmarket on this account. . . . I returned to Town the 16th.

My brother told me he had been offered to be a Lord of the Bedchamber to the young Prince but had refused it, on which plan I knew not, as it was plain he was quite what the Duke of Dorset and that set pleased to make him. Lord Harcourt was declared Governor to the Prince of Wales; his family was settling also.

The life I led at London and about the country is too uninteresting to recapitulate here. I was in constant scenes of dissipation, parties of pleasure in the country, and about a great deal with Lord Coventry and the Gunnings, with my sister Mary, with Lord Egmont and that set. Mr. and Mrs. Ord and Mrs. Inglis I saw often, and made parties to Twickenham with them and Lord Sandwich,[2] Mr. Dent having a house there and a very pretty wife. I heard often from and wrote constantly to Paris, and regretted my affairs would not let me go over any more yet, tho' I determined to do so whenever my finances would let me. I attended the Parliament whilst the Regency Bill was debating there, but all opposition seemed now very lank and depressed

[1] i.e. Household.

[2] This is the first sign of Hervey's close friendship with Lord Sandwich which lasted twenty-five years to the American War.

having lost its chief supporter. Mr. and Mrs. Fitzgerald were returned from Paris and was at Mr. Phipps's house, and I found they were frequently quarrelling and that he began to use her very ill, which I one day being a witness to, expostulated with him upon it, and we had near quarrelled. I was the 7th June chose of White's Club by Lord Coventry's putting me up. I was at this time very much taken up by Mr. Phipps's appeal to the House of Lords about his cause with Lord Anglesey, and endeavouring to be of all the use to them I could in it;[1] they were so kind and affectionate to every individual of our family.

I was quite wore out with this sort of life and vexed I could not get to Paris, so I determined to go out to sea. I therefore endeavoured to get the Newfoundland station, but could not. I then applied for a 40-gun ship in the Mediterranean, but could not get it, no more than one of the frigates, which made me very indifferent about it, especially as I began now to pass my time with Madame de Richecourt, the Imperial Minister's lady, who was very pretty, and with whom I made a party to go to Tonbridge with Monsieur and Madame de Vernicheff, the Russian Ambassador and Ambassadress. We remained thirteen days at Tonbridge with that sort of life, and when I returned to Town I was obliged to look out to be employed as I was quite sick of this idle, inactive way of living without any view, and I found my Brother Bristol could be of no use to me, the King frequently rumped him when he went to Court. I went with the Richecourts and more foreigners to see Sir Hans Sloane's cabinet at Chelsea, which is very rare; there are 49,600 volumes, 370 manuscripts, and 32,000 medals; there is something in his collection of every kind, and very valuable it is, since left to the Museum and deposited there, which was once Montagu House.[2] The 25th we left off mourning for the late Prince of Wales, and 'twas observed the King left off deep mourning and second mourning a week each sooner than usual, which was a weakness the poor proud King could not help to show his detestation of his son.

My brother and I went down to make Phipps's a visit at this time at Mulgrave in Yorkshire. We passed by Burleigh, and went to see it, being a very magnificent palace in the style of Audley Inn, built by the Treasurer Burleigh about a mile from Stamford. The great apartments are not finished, the ceiling finely painted;

[1] A cause relating to the legitimacy of Richard Annesley, 6th Earl of Anglesey, on which depended much of the late Duchess of Buckingham's property.

[2] This collection formed the nucleus of the British Museum.

the other apartments are very good and very well laid out, but not well furnished. The gardens are not extensive. There are good pictures in this house, the most remarkable I thought was one of Our Savour with a loaf in his hand by Carlo Dolu, which is in Lady Exeter's cabinet. There is a picture of Lady Betty Cecil that is extremely handsome. I just saw Lady Exeter and Lady Betty walking at a distance in the gardens. In our way we saw Belvoir, a seat of the Duke of Rutland's, seven miles from Grantham, and Belton, a seat of Lord Tyrconnell's. We drank tea with Lord and Lady Tyrconnell, who were extremely pressing for our staying there. We went to Sleaford, a chief place among my brother's estates in Lincolnshire. I left my brother there, and went on to Doncaster, and had like to been lost in the forest as my chaise broke down in the night and very dark it was. I passed thro' York the 12th September, and a very fine city it was, saw Castle Howard in my way to Malton, a seat of Lord Carlisle's, and a magnificent one too. I was obliged to lay at Saltersgate, a wretched hut, the moors were so bad, and at breakfast next morning was at Mulgrave, where was my two young sisters, Frederick and Mrs. Goate, and very merry we all were in this very hospitable house, which was built by the Duke of Buckingham.

The house was not large, but the situation delightful, the garden and terrace commanding all the sea of the harbour of Whitby, and seeing every ship and vessel that passes and repasses to the Northern Seas. 'Tis a delightful situation, but the great distance from the capital and the bad roads rather make the journey unpleasant. We went shooting here, riding, fishing, and in short every amusement that we liked, without being any restraint to each other. My sister here let me into a secret about Frederick, which was that he intended to marry Miss Betty Davers,[1] and I thought her friendship to Miss Betty Davers had encouraged this. Mr. Phipps's allum works here are very large; he has fourteen large boiling cisterns all in a row regularly built, in which seventeen chaldrons of coals are consumed a day, and make two tons of allum; he employs about 140 men, and farms this to a Mr. Prissick for £2,000 a year clear of all charges. My Brother Bristol arrived the 2nd October, and we were here very merry a long time. My brother told me one morning he had asked to go Envoy to Portugal, and that the Duke of Newcastle had hinted the Embassy to Spain

[1] She was the daughter of Sir Jermyn Davers, 4th Bt., and niece of Admiral Thomas Davers. Her marriage in 1752 to the future Earl-Bishop was to prove an unhappy one.

one day or other. I said I believed the Duke of Newcastle meant him nor his family no good, and that I really thought he ought to keep house, that it had an odd appearance his living always with others in this manner. In short he partly agreed with me upon it, and we stayed here till the 19th and then prepared for setting out for Town. I saw my brother was tired and wanted to be in Town; we therefore set out and lay at Malton. For my part I left Mulgrave with regret, as they were the most pleasing and obliging people to live with that were possible, and did everything for their company with an ease and an exactness that left no one unwatched, whilst they appeared without the least care upon them.

I had whilst here an opportunity of penetrating into my Brother Frederick's disposition *au fond*, and an accident which led me to look into a book he had been reading, called La Bruyère's *Caractères, Ou Moeurs de ce Siecle*, wherein he had marked some XI Chapter 53 Page 2nd Volume—XI—59 Page, fixed me with regard to him.[1]

Next day we went to see the Cathedral at York, a magnificent pile of Gothic building, and with very fine painted glass, in it several curious tombs, particularly that of Constantine the 1st,[2] the Black Prince's brother, several bishops and others. There are rings and challices that had been buried with the bishops and found afterwards in the vaults. The Assembly Room, which was built by Lord Burlington, is very fine; there are forty windows and forty pillars in it, and therefore rather cold, I should think, yet convenient. Next day the 22nd we lay at Grantham. In our way, talking of the Duke of Newcastle, I desired him to let me go with him one day to wait of him, as he had been very civil always to me. He said that was impossible because he always went privately to him. I thought this a very poor excuse indeed. We drank tea with Lady John Sackville and her daughter who was retired in this town. Passing thro' Hatfield we went to see that fine house of Lord Salisbury's which was going to ruin. It had been chiefly built by Queen Elizabeth when Princess and in a sort of banishment there, but we could not see many of the apartments, my Lord

[1] Chapter XI of the *Caractères* is entitled "de l'Homme". The book is unfortunately no longer in the library at Mulgrave, so the marks which damned Brother Frederick are lost to us.

[2] Presumably meant to be Flavius Valerius Constantinius I, father of Constantine the Great, said to have been buried at York in A.D. 306. The tradition is now dead.

was just gone to dinner, they said. He is a strange man, and lives out of the world, his great joy is building and driving coaches along the road like stage ones.[1] We went to see the chapel, where there is a fine tomb of the Treasurer Burleigh. We got to London early the 24th, where I found many letters from France.

London grew soon very disagreeable to me from many considerations; I therefore went to Mr. Byng's at Kitts Inn,[2] and my Uncle William at Rickmansworth as often as I could, and to Mr. Ord's at Muffetts I went.

I remember one night in Town poor Sir John Bland came up to me, I suppose out of peek, having lost much money at faro at a famous bank in which I was told many were concerned, and said that he could tell me who had a sixth share in that bank. As I knew who he meant, and as he said it with that sneer which those young gentlemen are apt to have, I was very quick in my reply, by saying that, upon my word, I did not care who had, that if I had any interest in it I would freely forgive him the sum I had heard he owed it. He made no answer, looked very silly, and walked away.[3]

I went to Ickworth with my brother the 20th November; the waters were so much out at Chelmsford we were obliged to return to Newmarket and lay there, and the next day went home. In this excursion in the country we went and stayed three days at Euston with the Duke of Grafton. 'Tis a very good habitable house, but not a magnificent one. He has above a hundred horses under cover, keeps a very hospitable house, making fifty beds for gentlemen in it. Lord Arlington built it who was Chamberlain to King Charles II, and there lay three nights in this house the following splendid company; King Charles, the Duke of York, the Prince of Orange, the Great Duke of Tuscany, the Duchess of Cleveland, seven Knights of the Garter besides, and a number of the Court, and were entertained equal to their rank. The park is pretty, but not equal to Ickworth Park, tho' the river is beautiful that runs thro' the grounds by the house. We had a great deal of company here; my brother and I stayed three days and returned to Ickworth. We visited all the neighbouring gentlemen whilst here. Mr. and Mrs. Phipps being at Bury made it very agreeable

[1] James, 6th Earl of Salisbury.

[2] Probably meaning Wrotham Park, near Kitt's End, Hertfordshire.

[3] Of Sir John Bland, 6th Bt., *The Complete Baronetage* says: "By his wild dissipation and his unconquerable disposition to play, he squandered immense estates—the whole of Manchester and its environs—and left little more at his death [in 1755] than the family patrimony of Kippax."

to us. We amused ourselves in reading over many papers of my grandfather's—particularly all his letters to his wives, in which were curious and entertaining anecdotes.[1]

The 21st December I received a letter from the Board to take the command of the *Phoenix* for the Mediterranean station. I was much surprised at this, as I had asked a 40-gun ship, and this was only a 20. I therefore went to Town to refuse her, but when I came to the Admiralty, Lord Anson assured me he had commissioned me purely to oblige me, as there was no 40-gun ships went there, and that he wished I would be employed, that I should have what officers I pleased with me. So I accepted, and got Mr. Foulks my Lieutenant and all my other officers, and I put the ship in commission the 3rd January at Deptford and begun to fit her for the Mediterranean.

I made several trips to my ship whilst fitting. Among the rest the Marquis de Bellegarde who was travelling here, and who I met among the foreigners, had an inclination to go see my ship, and he went with me one day. In the chaise, talking of Italy and Italian ladies, he told me a long story of Pellinetta Brignole of Genoa, which I remembered some years afterwards when she and I was intimate for three or four years.

I wrote to Madame Caze to tell her of my having this ship to go abroad, that I did it to dissipate me, as I could not bear being in England and not being able to make any excursions to France. I found she was given up to devotion, and had said often lately to me that she should always like to see me as a friend, but that since her mother's death she had confessed herself and received pardon, and was determined never to injure her husband again.[2]

I now wanted to raise some money for this voyage, and easily obtained it of my agent, Henshaw, at 5 per cent. I now went to Bury to take my leave of the Corporation, as my brother was at Ickworth, and before I left him I did all I could to reconcile him to my mother, but in vain; I found too many people had encouraged his little opinion of and affection for her, and who found it their interest to keep her from having any hold of my brother. I left Ickworth the 6th February, and my brother came

[1] Now to be read in *The Letter-books of John Hervey, first Earl of Bristol* (three vols.), edited by the Rev. S. H. A. Hervey, 1894; in 1775 Hervey wrote in them, after the end of the last letter, "Here ends the correspondence of my most dearly beloved grandfather, whose loss I shall ever regret, and whose memory I shall ever honour, and maxims endeavour to follow."

[2] But see p. 132.

as far as Hockerill[1] with me, and there we parted. The 12th I carried dear Mrs. Ord all the letters I had ever received from her, as I was going abroad, and begged she would destroy mine. I went very often whilst in Town to dine with them. The 14th my mother returned from France, and she talked to me much about her situation with my brother and mentioned having had several letters from England acquainting her that my Sister Phipps had not played her fair there, but I always said I could not believe that. The 16th I went to wish Mrs. Gunning joy of her daughter's marriage with the Duke of Hamilton, and I hoped soon of the other's with Lord Coventry, as I knew that was long intended.

I was now much pressed to get my ship round to Portsmouth in order to carry Lord Tyrawly[2] to Lisbon in a great hurry on a representation the merchants of that factory had made of some heavy grievances they laboured under, particularly with regard to shipping their money. It was the 2nd March before the wind admitted my mooring, and then I got surprising quick round to Spithead the 3rd in the evening. Lord Tyrawly arrived with Mr. Castres[3] the present Envoy to Lisbon the 8th. I was amusing myself at Portsmouth with my old acquaintances, poor pastime compared to all I had had at Paris etc, but I learnt to make myself easy in all situations.

[1] A parish at Bishop's Stortford, Essex, in which was the Crown Inn, " well known to all frequenters of Newmarket ".

[2] James O'Hara, 2nd Baron Tyrawly was being sent to assuage the murmurings against the beginnings of the Marquis de Pombal's reforms ; he had been there previously 1728–41, and was " singularly licentious even for the courts of Russia and Spain " (Walpole, *George III*) ; he is said to have left Lisbon with three wives and fourteen children. In 1787 the Grand Inquisitor told William Beckford he had heard Tyrawly was an archbishop in England !

[3] Abraham Castres, consul at Lisbon 1742–49, then minister until his death in 1757.

VI

LISBON

April to September 1752

THE wind was quite contrary till the 20th, when we all embarked, and had a very good passage to Lisbon, where we arrived the 29th March. We were all very merry and happy on board in this passage with Lord Tyrawly and Mr. Castres. Among many things, they told me that when the Spanish fleet turned out of Cadiz Bay for the expedition of Don Carlos, that the people were so ignorant what ropes they were to go to, having been put on board in such a hurry, that they put cards to all the different ropes, and so were ordered to " Pull away the Ace of Spades ", " Make fast the King of Hearts ", and so on.[1] The 30th I landed and saluted Lord Tyrawly. The captains we found here were Captain Shuldham, bound home, and Captain Arbuthnot, bound up the Straits.[2]

I went directly to see my dear friend Don João de Bemposto, with whom when young I had been so much with, and who was now acknowledged by the King of Portugal[3] for his nephew and was a great favourite. He was delighted to see me and carried me to the Marquis d'Abrantes who was then very ill. Don João came on board the next day to breakfast with me. We went together to see Lord Tyrawly. I dined at Don João's palace at Bemposto, where he desired I would use his house and equipages as my own whenever I came in here. The day after I came in I went to Court with Don João; both the King and Queen[4] were

[1] In 1731, when the future King of Naples and the Two Sicilies and Carlos III of Spain set out from Cadiz to Leghorn to take possession of his Duchies of Parma and Piacenza.

[2] " The Straits " were those of Gibraltar, but the term was commonly used to denote the whole of the western Mediterranean up to the north Italian ports.

[3] José I, who had succeeded his father in 1750.

[4] Marianna Victoria (1718–81) daughter of Phillip V of Spain.

very gracious to me. I was with the Duke de Sotto Major (the Spanish Ambassador) a good deal.

Lord Tyrawly talked to me a good deal about the affairs here, and I found his tone very much altered with regard to the Portuguese from what it was in the voyage. He now condemned the Factory as a set of dissatisfied, restless, proud and extravagant fellows, and I had reason to think his old friends here had got some ascendancy over him. In short at last he grew outrageous with the Factory and abused them all. He obtained the redress to the complaints he was sent to enquire into, and was not long after recalled, going away with the contempt and the curses of all the English, who I think are in general very unreasonable in their demands, and yet think, in some things, the Portuguese are endeavouring to prejudice the trade with them, but not more so to us than other nations; and who can blame them for wanting to save a very great part of the balance of that trade that is against them, if they do not favour any other country to our prejudice? But our merchants here live much more expensive than their principals in London; they game very much and very high, and no wonder the trade cannot support their extravagance. There was a very good substantial house here of Messieurs Mayne and Barn, which went on in the old way that I remember in 1737 when I was here with my uncle in Sir John Norris's fleet. I lived a great deal at their house, tho' I lodged at Guards at Bairro Alto, and was very seldom with any other of the merchants, liking none of them, being purse-proud people and ever envious of those who were from their birth intitled, and received among the Portuguese nobility, who rarely admitted any of them, the Portuguese being very proud themselves.

I used to go frequently to Odivellas convent and renew my old acquaintance there, and to the English nuns sometimes, where Mrs. Hill was again Lady-Abbess. Don João's mother[1] made a great party to Odivellas purposely to carry me there and show me all the handsome women that could be brought to the grate. This we had 18th May, and a most delightful evening it was. I got an old woman that had been very usefull to the late King, called Ellena, that Don João recommended to me. She promised to give a letter for me to the Condessa d'Atougia,[2]

[1] Donna Marianna de Sousa, killed in St. Anne's Convent by the earthquake of 1755.

[2] Marianna, daughter of 3rd Marquis de Tavora, and wife of the 9th Conde d'Atougia; shut up in the convent of Marvila after the Tavora conspiracy of 1758.

but tho' she told me she had, I met no success from it; but she carried me to see a very fine woman at her window that was daughter to the Guarda Mor,[1] and that if I liked her she would contrive to get us together. In the evening of the 30th I received a letter from a beautifull creature, sister to Antonio Saltara de Mendoza, and was appointed where to meet her. In this intriguing manner did I spend all my time, having nothing more to do with myself.

The 1st May I went up in one of Don João's barges nine leagues up the river to St. Mora, a palace of his. He received me with near twenty horsemen at the water-side and carried me a-boar-hunting that day, and we had all kinds of diversions whilst here. The 4th we came down in barges the river to Lisbon. I had frequently much company on board to dinner of the Portuguese and the Foreign Ministers. The 7th I was invited to Odivellas again to a great grate by Virgolino, a friend of mine, the late King's favourite's son. There were many most beautiful nuns came this evening, and we had music. Signora Donna Juacquena Clara de Virgolina did the honours. Donna Magdalena Maxina and Mercia de Mello were there, Donna Anna Barddona, Donna Maria Antonia de Miranda, niece to Madame Maxina, but supposed daughter of her's by the late King, and many others. We stayed late, making love in the *frereatica* [*sic*] way (as they call it).[2] A Signora Maria de Almera, Donna Anna Felice, Donna Euphemia de Rita d'Ouseo were all beautifull; this last I made much up to, which I could perceive the jealousy and envy of Donna Madame Maxina did not like, because of her niece whom she thought had pretensions superior. The 17th being a great holiday at La Trinidada, I went in my *capota*[3] to that church with Virgolino, where were many fine women at Mass, and a great deal of musick. There I saw a very fine country-girl called Vincennes, whom I had followed and got Magdalena to get her for me some days afterwards, and a most lovely piece she was. I went out to Mr. Burn's quinta at Brasio de Plato for two or three days to cool myself in the country, as all this time I was waiting for to get the money of the Rio fleet to carry up to Italy, and the garrisons of Gibraltar and Minorca's money.

[1] A court official.

[2] "*Freiratico*," as a noun, means "one who is given too much to the love of nuns" or "one who goes often to nunneries". Perhaps "nunnish" is the best English equivalent.

[3] A cloak.

Don João, who with his mother was ever intent to oblige me, got me a window in the Rua do Escudeiro to go see the procession of Corpus Domine, which was very fine and where the King with his whole Court and every religious Order attends the Sacrament in procession, the streets all covered, the windows dressed and ornamented, and all the ladies at them. The preceding and following nights are very good ones, as everyone walks the streets, which are much illuminated, and there sees their lovers. Soon after this I went with Don João to another convent out of town, called Chillies,[1] where we carried musick, and I think I never heard so fine a voice as one of the ladies who was a secular there who came to the grate and sung to us, called Donna Marguerita Tomasia de Sylvera ; her aunt, Donna Francissca Antonia de Sylvera, came with her. She was the daughter of Don Lewis de Teixeira, afterwards an intimate family of mine, where I went very often, and as often to this nunnery—but for the sake of another nun called Donna Anna Peregrinia de Gloria with whom I afterwards got in correspondence and frequently visited.

June 6th being the King of Portugal's birthday, I dressed my ship with colours, fired twenty-one guns, and went to Court in great gala, all the nobility being there, and made a compliment to the King, and the Queen afterwards, who were very civil to me. This is a very tedious ceremony indeed, especially to the Queen and Infantas, being in a very long room with twenty ladies of each side whom you pass singly, making three bows to the Queen and Infantas on their thrones, and the same retiring. I told the Queen " que je ne pouvais rien desirer de plus flatant que d'avoir l'honneur de me jetter aux pieds de sa Majesté au jour qui lui étoit si cher, et que n'éstoit pas moins acceptable à l'Europe qu'à Portugal ". She was very affable and spoke a great deal to me and said she heard I diverted myself very much here. . . .

I went often sailing up the river with Don João, and to nunneries, and that way passed my time, and making love to someone of the Portuguese ladies or other, as they are all very amourous and very intent at never losing an opportunity of amusing themselves, their husbands being very jealous and very watchful of them, which makes the strictest of them have their wives and daughters chiefly fall a sacrifice to their upper servants, but 'tis no strange event here for brothers and sisters, uncles and nieces etc : etc : , in a family way to partake of those joys which the rigidness of their parents

[1] Probably meaning the Grillo convent.

and their husbands refuses them, and which the climate and their constitutions induce them to, and their no education in general does not restrain them from.

Mr. Keppel[1] came in in the *Centurion* from the Mediterranean, and I went on board him and Proby in the *Lyme*. This last was obliged to be sent out again, as they were afraid he would be taken up on a former affair of his boat's crew with regard to money. Lord Tyrawly and Mr. Castres both pressed Mr. Keppel on this subject, and he was sent away, as the King had even mentioned this affair, and said he would not suffer it. I carried Mr. Bristow to Lord Tyrawly and Mr. Castres and reconciled them all together. In the evening I went to Signora Niccolini's, a very pretty woman, wife to an Italian merchant. Keppel and I were often together here, but he did not like to go much among the Portuguese, nor I amongst the English. The 15th I made a great entertainment on board with music for the Niccolini, Madame Galli and her daughter and several ladies, and went on the river all night and had a number of boats after us. The 18th Lord Tyrawly left Lisbon, but I think had not obtained any one point for the merchants. I was not very well having a great boil on my side which was very painful to me; it broke in two or three days, and threw out much matter. Whilst I was confined Signor Don João came almost every day, and the Infant Don Pedro[2] sent constantly to me. I was quite well by the 5th August. The 7th Mr. Keppel sailed, and I went with him almost over the bar. He gave me orders to put myself under his command and to take in the money for the garrison, but I told him then I thought he could have no right to my freight, as he had no business with me and would be paid off probably before I might sail, and more so as I had let his ships both go with great freights, because I would have nothing to do with them, nor interfere.[3] I went to Don Louis de Teixiera's that evening who had a good pretty family of women at home, and was very well received in that family.

[1] Augustus Keppel was about to hand over the command of the Mediterranean station to the Hon. George Edgcumbe, later 1st Earl of Mount Edgcumbe. Edgcumbe was three years older than Hervey, and two and a half years senior to him on the Captain's list. His family's extensive influence in the elections for the Cornish boroughs ensured him a steady advance in the service. He does not appear to have been a very forceful commander.

[2] King José's brother; in 1760 he married his niece, the Princess of Brazil; in 1777 they ascended the throne as Maria I and Pedro III.

[3] See p. 237.

The 23rd Don João, who was for ever carrying me about everywhere and making me acquainted with every one, insisted I should go to make a visit with him to the Patriarch,[1] who he said was a good kind of man that lived well and wanted to be acquainted with me. So I went and he received us in great form, sitting under a canopy, and the triple Cross held by him the whole time. In a little time he got up and carried us into another apartment, where we had sweetmeats, chocolate etc: and then carried us over his house, which is very fine. The next day I went to the bull-feast where I had a box, and carried Lord Robert Manners and Mr. Crowle the consul with me. Here I saw and got acquainted with the Princess of Holstein,[2] married to Don João de Calhariz, Captain of the Queen's Guard, and a very fine woman she was and I soon perceive she was game, which I thought would do when I returned, as I was now going soon away.

The 25th a man, one Jean-François Captain Cocquelain, a Frenchman, came to me with a letter and offered to discover a scheme of Monsieur de la Bourdonaise against all the East-India Companies in general but the French, and which was carrying on here thro' Monsieur Greinier (a French merchant) with the interest and protection of Diogo de Mendonca, Secretary of State, for establishing a Custom-House General at Goa, that no goods may come out of or go into the Indies without paying their customs, which will be extravagant, and should the French adopt this it would greatly affect all the trade of other nations with the East-Indians. I told it to Castres, who frankly owned he knew nothing of this but that he had heard many little things drop, which confirmed to him there was some truth in this plan.

The 27th being the Queen Mother's birthday and the present King's Proclamation Day, I went to Court *en gala*. The 31st I was at the opera of *Cyrus* by David Peres[3] in the King's theatre, which was magnificent. It was built at an immense expense in his own palace, and was the finest theatre of the size in Europe, supported by marble pillars which had conveyances about each for water in case of fire. The King's box took up all the front and was most magnificently ornamented, as was the whole, for every-

[1] Head of the Church in Portugal, who kept state similar to that of the Pope.

[2] Marie-Anne-Leopoldine, daughter of the Duke of Holstein, was married to Manoel de Sousa de Calhariz; they were the grandparents of the celebrated nineteenth-century statesman, the Duke of Palmella.

[3] *Il Siroe*, by David Peres, who had come from Italy to be the chief composer to Don José's court.

thing was at the King's expense. The ladies were all in boxes, and boxes for the Foreign Ministers; the nobility (men) were in the pit, but there were only men (as at Rome) that sung and danced here. The orchestra were about seventy people in rich scarlet and silver clothes, and each side of the theatre was a tribune for French horns, clarinets etc, who played between the acts. The tickets were difficult to get as the King had it purely for his own amusement, but there was a disagreeable ceremony for the men, for as you came in under the King's box, before you sat down you were to turn about and make a low bow to the Royal Family and another to the ladies, and this every time that you had occasion to go out or come in, which prevented people stirring if they could avoid it. There was no changing your places, or visiting the ladies, all was form and silence, but magnificent and noble.

The 2nd September having taken leave of every one, I had Don João on board and was sailing down the river to prepare for going over the bar. The castle had no colours out, which I told Don João was a slight to the King of England's ships going out, and that if it was not for his Excellency, I would take mine down. "Pray do, then," says he, "it will be a good reproof to them." I immediately did, leaving my pendant flying which my instructions say is a sufficient mark of distinction. The castle fired a shot at me; I came to an anchor, immediately went to the Secretary of State and complained, knowing it was to no purpose to go to poor old Castres, and after having the matter well explained and examined, I had the officer in the fort put in arrest, and then asked his relief, and obtained orders never to fire at the King's ships again. But these castles had no soldiers in them, only eight or ten fellows hired for the time to do duty of those who were paid to be in them.

I stayed a day or two at a country house of Don João by Paço d'Arcos a-shooting and hunting. This day, 14th September, the Old Style was changed according to Act of Parliament, which was brought about by the Earl of Chesterfield who saw the absurdity of our being different from all other nations, and which made great confusion in many places and business. And the next day I sailed for Gibraltar and Italy with about 30,000 Moydores[1] freight, but determined to call at Cadiz to see what I could pick up there. Don João with several of the nobility went over the bar with me, accompanied with his yachts. I carried Lord Robert

[1] £41,250 at one per cent.

Manners with me, who was going to Gibraltar, and a Captain Lynn to Port Mahon. I left Lisbon with some regret from the great attentions that had been shewn me there, and my intimacy with several Portuguese families, which are not easy for strangers to obtain there.

VII

A YEAR'S YACHTING

September 1752 to September 1753

THE 18th September I was off St. Lucar, which at a distance looked like the land of Cadiz, and I soon found my master was ignorant of the whole coast, and, indeed, so he proved to be all the way up. The 19th I got off Cadiz and anchored off there that evening. I missed of the *Fuerto* and another man-of-war two rich ships from the Havannah having on board fourteen millions of dollars and much unregistered money, which would have been put on board my ship had I gone down to them. The next day I went to wait of the governor (Don João De Villielva) then to the Admiral and Intendant of the Marine, Don Navarro, he who commanded the fleet against Admiral Matthews and was created Marquis de la Victoria for that battle. I did not much like Cadiz from its appearance, the Spaniards being shy of strangers, but the French factory there lived elegantly and well and delighted in strangers. I dined next day with the Spanish Admiral, whose apartment was all done with his own drawings, and there were some very fine ones of the battle of Toulon. . . .

As I went on board that evening 25th September I sent an express to Madrid for the King's money to go to Naples, and diverted myself very well now, as the Spanish officers got me acquainted with several ladies, and the French houses were all open to me. I lay often at Monsieur Solier's, a very worthy good man, and his wife a good old woman, Protestants all of them. Don Ventura de Ossio, Administrator, was very civil to me and gave me a great dinner. I dined also with Don Manuel Guirier, Major-General, where was Don Francisco de Luna, Don Lewis de Velasco,[1] Don Pedro de Moro, Don Joseph Solano, Don Diego de Fuentes and all these very pretty, well-behaved gentlemen. I was delighted with their Guarda Marines[2] to see them so decently

[1] In 1762 mortally wounded defending the Moro Castle at the Havannah, in the attack on which Hervey took a leading part.

[2] Cadets.

behaved and so well educated and on such a good establishment. This Marine Corps in Spain only wanted practice; they had all the theory of the service requisite. The 5th October I had 500,000 dollars[1] of the King's put on board me without any trouble, in 167 chests, for which I was to have one per cent, and sailed that evening, having received a great many civilities from all the people at Cadiz, particularly at my friend Solier's house, where I lay and lived.

The 10th I got into Gibraltar, and having long resolved whereever I met Mr. Blankley (who was Naval officer here now) to call him to an account for his behaviour at Portsmouth in the year 1746 which I related before,[2] I desired Captain Morgan, a friend of mine and an officer of the garrison, to go to that fellow and tell him that to avoid any intercourse with him I desired he would immediately give me satisfaction for his conduct and that we must meet with sword and pistol at 4 o'clock on the Neutral Ground. He sent me word by Captain Morgan he desired to ask my pardon publickly in any manner I pleased, upon which Captain Morgan and Lord Robert Manners, whom I sent too, told me, surely it was sufficient, let his offence have been what it would. And so he came with his friend, and asked me pardon before these gentlemen, all in the humblest manner. I asked then these gentlemen before him if they thought this was publick enough; on their saying surely so, I turned to him and told him I should think no more of it. Everyone said I had done wrong had I done more.

I stayed here but three days, as it was a wretched place to be at and as I had such great sums on board for Italy that I was uneasy to get it landed. I had a very tedious passage indeed with only Easterly winds, as my journals will produce particular accounts of, which I keep at sea as regularly and much more particular than this, every four hours being productive of something which I mark.

The 8th November I got off Mahon harbour and was obliged to anchor in the evening off the mouth of the harbour, the wind being right out, in order to send in the garrison's money, which I did at 4 the next morning. In the meantime the wind shifted at once and blew very hard from sea, so that my situation with the land of Cape Mola (which I was too near, by my anchors coming home) became a very dangerous one. Captain Proby came out to see me, but was glad to get in again. As soon as my boat

[1] £112,500. [2] p. 49.

returned from landing the money I slipped my cable with a spring upon it to cast the ship the right way, and made sail off, just getting the other way, so that the 12th November I was obliged to put away before the wind for Villa-Franca, being then off Monaco, and got into that safe harbour of the King of Sardinia's about noon, and got pratiqua the next day, which was a favour to the English men-of-war, and almost the only port in the Mediterranean that will admit the English men-of-war from Mahon and Gibraltar so soon to communication, on account of those garrisons trading with the Africans who are so liable to have the plague among them. . . .

I went to Nice, which is about two miles from it, where my old friend General Paterson now commanded as Governor of that province and Lieutenant-General, Monsieur Gibair[1] being Commandant of the gallies. I dined at Nice, and afterwards went with the General to see the mold the King was building on the East side of the town at an immense expense, but which I do not imagine, from the great seas it is exposed to, will ever come to anything material or beyond small barks. The plan is a very great and expensive one, the cases they sink are enormous. In the evening I returned to Villa-Franca and lay on board, as my ship was close to the shore.

The next day, the 14th, the wind continuing and having blown very hard that night, I went over to a little house that Peter Reboult (the Lieutenant of the port) had in St. Soupirs Bay to see him and his daughters who I had known at Savona in the war. There I saw a felucca that had put in in the night with very bad weather, and I saw several gentlemen and ladies who seemed to me in distress and was at breakfast on the shore by a little dirty cottage, where, it seems, they had landed and lain that night. I went up to them to see if I could be of any use to them. I found it was the Marquis de Bernis, brother to the Abbé, afterwards Cardinal, de Bernis, now Ambassador at Venice, and his lady, who had come from Antibes going to Genoa in their way to Venice. She was very handsome indeed; I insisted on their coming on board my ship to dinner and to remain there, and I would carry them all, baggage and all, to Genoa.[2] They accepted of it, and General Paterson with the Intendant and his lady and others dined with me. In the morning the next day all these people came aboard of me, with a

[1] His real name was Guibert.

[2] Philippe-Charles, elder brother of the Cardinal de Bernis, and his wife Renée d'Arnaud, Barrone de la Cassagne, whom he had married in 1746.

priest, a physician, a maid, an officer who was with them, and four servants. The 15th I put to sea, and was in a fair way to get in a day or two to Genoa, when the wind came again as hard as ever from the Eastward, and after passing a most dreadful stormy night I was obliged to put again into Villa-Franca. The 18th we lay thirteen hours under a mainsail with a very violent gale of wind indeed, these people all sick and frightened to death. Most of my own servants were sick too, and I was night and day attending this poor Madame de Bernis, even to giving her the chamber-pot and holding her head and the basin eternally whilst she was sick. We got into the harbour again, and I took lodgings for them all at the late Commissary for the gallies, Madame de Bonfis, whilst I caulked and refitted my ship, which took me some days, in which time they recruited themselves and we diverted ourselves very well with entertainments on board and on shore. We had balls, and the 22nd I stood godfather and Madame de Bernis godmother to a child of Monsieur Gibair's, and dined all at the Chevalier de Bellona, Captain of one of the gallies, and we towed out of Villa-Franca with the gallies' boats the 23rd. Madame de Bernis was charming the whole passage, elle avait tant de politesse avec tant d'esprit, tant de bonté au millieu de tant de souffrance, et tants de sentimens de virtue avec tant des traits d'un paraître beauté, qui est rare d'encontre dans une personne si jeunne, et avec toutes ces perfections une simplicité et une modestie qui faisait voir qu'elle ne connaissait point posséder toutes ces qualities. We had such fine weather the latter end of our passage that we all dined at table on the deck under a close awning, and, as I had a good deal of musick on board, it was very delightful.

The 27th I anchored off Genoa and the next day I got into the mold, where I met with many letters, not very pleasing, as I heard of the prosecution going on with my Sister Fitzgerald and her husband to be separated, and Frederick's marriage with Miss Betty Davers, who I was afraid had not fortune enough to make him easy.

I was taken up with landing my company who went to Monsieur de Chauvelin's the French Envoy to this Republick,[1] and who received them most nobly, and sent off an officer to me to invite me to dinner the next day. Madame de Bernis was indeed amiable, and seemed fully satisfied with all the attentions I had for her, but her husband, who was a very surly, jealous fellow, restrained her from showing all the effects of her sensibility.

[1] Bernard-Louis, Marquis de Chauvelin (d. 1773), at Genoa 1751–53, then at Turin to 1765.

I was astonished I had no letter here from Madame Caze, and begun to perceive she had dropped me, as I had had letters before I left Lisbon telling me that the Imperial Ambassador, Monsieur de Kaunitz, paid his addresses to her and was very well received.[1]

The day after my arrival I landed all the merchants' money and went and dined at Monsieur de Chauvelin's. I lodged at my old friend's, the Consul, Mr. Birtles ; there was a most magnificent dinner indeed with about thirty-eight of the *premier noblesse*. I was seated by Madame de Bernis and paid all my attention there, tho' she was to go away in a day or two. The next day I had an audience of the Doge, Monsieur Grimaldi ; by his son I was introduced, Franco Grimaldi, a very sensible amiable young man. I supped at Monsieur de Chauvelin's again, where was a Monsieur de la Gari, Major-General of the forces in Corsica, and he undertook to introduce me to all the ladies of the first class, for at Genoa the *noblesse* is divided, the Old and New, and they little associate together, they are all very proud. I was introduced to Madame Doria, and her daughter Madame Grimaldi de la Pietra,[2] Madame Settiametti Grimaldi, pretty woman, Madame Pallavicino, Madame Carnavari who was very pretty, cicisbee to Felix Balbi, and several others. Monsieur and Madame de Bernis set out this morning for Venice ; she cried at our parting. The next day, 1st December, I was invited to a great dinner at Monsieur de Chauvelin's, who told me that it was for me, and he invited all the ladies again, but I soon found out he intended to place me as cicisbee to Madame Momina Grimaldi de la Pietra to give pleasure to Madame Doria, her mother, who was his lady—at least the old lady was in love with him. So I gave a little but not much in it, as I did not like her very much, but was set myself on Pellinetta Brignole, who I had seen the day before and who I liked much, very handsome and sensible for an Italian, but not very, very young—about twenty-seven, I believe.[3]

[1] " [Kaunitz] ne vie qu'avec nos financiers et financières, il fait l'amoureux de quelques beautés de finance, et, les voyant ainsi, il tire d'eux le véritable état des mauvaises finances du royaume." D'Argenson VIII, p. 79.

[2] She was Geronima (Momina), daughter of Marcantonio Doria and Lilla Grimaldi, his wife ; her husband was Giovanni Battista Grimaldi.

[3] She was Pellinetta Brignole-Sale, daughter of Giorgio Domenico Lomellini (not, as Hervey says, a Balbi) and Emelia Pallavicini his wife. Her husband, Rodolfo, was Doge of Genoa 1762–64. According to Soulavie's *Vie Privée du Maréchal de Richelieu* (the authenticity of which, to say the very least, is highly suspect) the Duc de Richelieu was her cicisbeo at Genoa in 1747–48—but he never managed to make the final conquest ! She is described as " une grande

I supped several nights at Monsieur de Chauvelin's and Madame Doria's *conversationis*, as they call them, being made for me. I found it was absolutely necessary to be that thing called a cicisbee here in order to be well received among the ladies. 'Tis an odd custom, and an odd part to play; 'tis expected you should attend the lady everywhere she goes, to accompany her chair on foot, in short to be a dangler for ever about her, and with her all hours, except dinner and bed-time. And every other liberty you may take that your merits and your assiduities can obtain from them, which is not put at too great a price or too far out of reach, any more than it is necessary to avoid the husband's immediate observance of too much familiarity, or not quite prudent ever to trust the servants. Indeed there is no occasion for it, as you may see them at all hours, at their toilettes, etc: etc: etc:

The 4th I went out to Sestri to dine with Madame de Marana that I knew at Leghorn, and whom I would not drop, tho' not a *dama di premiero ordine*. The evening I was at Madame Doria's as usual. . . .

The 7th I had a great deal of company to breakfast, and had a concert. The famous Galliotti[1] played on the violoncello; he is a Neapolitan residing here with the Durazzo's. The 8th I went to Madame Brignole's, and there was another Madame Brignole called Annetta who had been at Paris a good deal and who I had seen there[2] but indeed I found out the women to be most egregious fools, and the Italian men not one degree in a form better. . . .

[Hervey entertained Lady Townshend with his opinions of Italians of both sexes in a letter dated 27th November;[3] she knew him too well to take his account of his own state seriously. ". . . For my part, unless I could send you a month's sun or a basket of fruit, I know of nothing in this country that would give you a moment's pleasure or amusement. For unlike our Lady Carolines or our Lady this, our Lady that, our Miss this, our Miss that, the women are all so poor that their outsides are no better adorned than the insides of the men; they are as dirty and as frippery as their gallants are vain and ignorant, and the commerce of the one is as little desirable for want of a right

---

brune, bien faite et très–jolie; elle étoit gaie, aimoit le plaisire, et jamais conquête ne parut au duc plus facile a faire; il fut bien trompé dans ses calculs." (Paris edition, 1791, Vol. II, p. 101.)

[1] Perhaps Francesco Galeazzi (1738–1819), author of one of the earliest methodical instruction books for the violin.

[2] See p. 90.

[3] *Hist. MSS. Comm. Townshend*, p. 379.

pride, as that of the other is of a wrong one. There is nothing more common in Italy than to see a great princess, who will return a visit to nobody of an inferior title, strolling round the streets for amusement and in a continual conversation with her own footmen, who to facilitate this entertainment walk on each side of her coach holding by the doors. They play for half-pence with the utmost avidity; and he that will be cheated of three and sixpence never fails to go away with the reputation of being the most gallant man of the company. I was delighted with a thing said the other day by one of their own countrymen which put their understandings in a light equally true and ridiculous. The Italian women (says he) are such fools that if three of them are got together; 'tis possible that one may say that 2 and 2 makes 4, another that 2 and 2 makes 5, and whilst the dispute grows warm the third shall be embarrassed which to decide for. The men are not in a form one degree higher; they are too proud to seek or suffer the company of their inferiors; too jealous to be pleased with that of their equals; and too ignorant to be able to bear their own. However I have had the good fortune to meet with two or three here who both know 'tis possible to communicate one's ideas in other languages besides Italian and have a notion of their being inhabited countries beyond the Alps; two branches of knowledge that few gentlemen or ladies on this side of them arrive it. I pass a good deal of my time with them and with more pleasure than I have done any part of it since I left Lisbon. Indeed I have been ill with a pleurisie, and therefore bad health, or bad objects, I don't know which, or perhaps both, have quite cured me of flirting; 'tis so long (tell Lady Caroline) since I have seen so spruce a toilette as hers,[1] that I have hardly the idea of one; and if I venture ever again to accost a fine lady, I believe it will be blushing, stuttering, twisting my thumbs, and so much in the style of Sir Willfull Witwood,[2] that if the lady refused *to fetch a walk* I should be extremely puzzled for a second question to put to her, and in much greater confusion to ask her the last favour, than any woman in France or Italy ever felt in granting it. Your Ladyship won't credit this change perhaps, and I wish I did not feel it, but I am absolutely an old fellow. I rejoice in basking in the sun; every limb is a barometre and foretells rains, winds, snows etc. I begin to tell stories of what I was; pretend to despise pleasures I am past taking; rail at wine because I drink none (nor have not since I left England), condemn gaming because I have no spare money to play; and like the dog in the manger stare at every charitable gentlewoman that throws her oats to these animals who are glad to eat them; tho' perhaps like most other reformers my only quarrel to

[1] Lady Caroline Petersham was said to owe her charms to the fact that she "makes her old face every morning a new one".

[2] Sir Wilful Witwould is a middleaged country squire and bachelor in Congreve's *The Way of the World* (1700).

the banquet is not being bidden or not having an appetite. Now, dear Madam, after what I have acknowledged myself dwindled into, 'twill be impudence to expect your Ladyship will allow such a creature much of your time; but till I come to a pair of spectacles, a newspaper and a pipe, and confine my whole conversation to virtue and vice without having a view to either in my conduct, I flatter myself now and then you'll hear me relate extraordinary things over a cup of Mrs. Johnson's[1] good chocolate in a morning; and when Mrs. Frinch or Lord Waldegrave's ingaged, sometimes allow me to make a fourth in an evening at whist. . . ."]

This afternoon Monsieur de Chauvelin carried me to Madame Norrina Doria and to Madame Victorina Lascari's, who were sisters, and there I got acquainted with Nicollini Doria, a very pretty amiable young man, designed to command their little cruisers—for God knows little enough is their force become at sea, who were once so famous. I saw here a miniature family piece of fourteen figures done by Rubens in water colours in the year 1607, the finest picture I ever saw.

There was a silly thing happened which I will just mention to remind myself of the customs, as well as follies, of these Italian ladies. After coming from the nunnery this morning [21st December], Monsieur Durazzo and I drove out of town airing in his coach. We soon after met Lilla Mare Spinola in her coach. She turned about, drove after us, and would come into our coach with her cicesbee. As it had been said this lady had no aversion to me I was apprehensive of the *guaio* it would make with Madame de la Pietra, who would hear of this, and, tho' I did not love her enough to care about it on that account, yet I knew this would displease that family that I was now so intimate with. And so it proved, for at night this was the only subject talked of, and I was attacked how I could be so false to Madame de la Pietra, and all such stuff. However I cleared myself very well without sacrificing the other; and I believe I was the better received afterwards for it, for Madame de la Pietra was a very fantastical lady, required much attendance, and scarce knew what she would be at. Her husband was at Rome, and they say did not care much about her. Others said he was *impuissant*. At the Opera I went with Madame de la Pietra and, strange to say, I held her by the —— the whole time almost.

I endeavoured to get out now and go on to Naples, but could not, and I had the pleasure to find that the Brignoles and Spinolas

[1] Lady Townshend's maid.

were all endeavouring to get me into their coterie, for there is a great pleasure amongst these ladies when they can get a cicisbee from any lady that is remarkable for being at all, and I was silly enough too, tho' not in love, to be eternally sending presents, serenading with musick etc: The 26th I went to the Doge's palace to a great *conversationi* there where every one goes to give the Doge a merry fête. He and all the Senators are dressed in their ceremonious gowns, and the latest married ladies are always in their *habits de cour*. I stayed there very late and kept constant attendance on Madame de la Pietra, with whom I succeeded very well.

The 30th in the morning, having taken my leave of every one at Genoa, and being very sorry to leave a place I was so well received in, I received a very pretty letter from Madame de la Pietra Grimaldi, and sailed about noon. . . . I own I felt the regret of leaving Genoa.

Next day 1st January I was between Corsica and Capraia; the 2nd I was coasting along the Roman coast, having at my own expense hired a pilot at Genoa to teach me all the coast this first voyage, that I might be master of it for the future, and in my sea-journals there will be seen what pains I took and what descriptions I have left for any one to make their use of them as they please. The evening I made the island of Ponza, I saw the cupola of St. Peter's at Rome at a great distance, and all the shore of this coast and the different islands, tho' in this dreary season of the year, made a sweet appearance, Ponza, Ventotene, Palmarola. I went within, and stood close into Mount Circello and to a town called Terracina, which was what was called Antium by the ancients. These islands were then called Pontice, Palmeria and Pandataria. The descriptions of these and the manner of sailing amidst them I have explained in my journals of that voyage, but which would be of little amusement here, and of no use to me who have them there.

I anchored in the night the 4th January in the Bay of Naples, running up for my soundings and by the pilot's knowledge. The next day early I found there had long been orders to give me immediately pratiqua and all assistance I could want, so that I was presently in the mold and a very good one it is, and going in I was saluted by all the Dutch and English there. I found the Neapolitan fleet all there, which consisted of the four men-of-war, one of 64 guns, one of 40, and two of 30. These were laid up there, and miserable ships they were. However Don Michael Reggio, the General of the Marine, sent a Captain of the Port with compliments to me and sent a coach down to desire I would dine with him, but I excused myself, having the consul, Mr. Allen, and others to dine with me. After dinner I went to wait of the General, where numbers were that had dined and most of the foreign ministers. The Court were at a hunting-seat of the King's at Caserta, but expected Tuesday. Several English on their travels were here, who came to see me. At night I went to the Princess of Franca-Villa's, for whom I had letters, and was very well received there. This lady is sister to the Princess of Borghese's at Rome, and married to the Prince of Franca-Villa here, Great Chamberlain to the King, a nobleman of great hospitality and very magnificent.

The next day an unlucky accident happened to poor Mr. Allen's house (the Consul); it failed, and all his goods and things were going to be seized, but, as the King's arms was upon the door, this was prevented, and in three or four days I had letters from all the Factory to desire I would take them under my protection, as at this time they had several disputes with the Court about their privileges. I assured them I would do everything in my power to represent any grievances they had either to the ministers here or at home.

I went to the opera, which was very fine and the largest theatre in Europe. Caffarelli[1] was the first man, and Visconti the first woman. I went with the Marquis de Ruggi, the Marquis de Vasto, with the Prince Cimitino St. Severino, who was named Envoy to England, and others to the Princess of Franca-Villa's where a great number of ladies and gentlemen were; the Princess d'Aliano, beautiful, the Princess Rucelli, Duchess of Barrotta, and several others I was presented to, and the next day I received a very polite letter by the King's orders from the Marquis de Fogliani who was Prime Minister. And the Tuesday the King returned to town from Caserta; as he passed the strand by my ship I saluted him with twenty-one guns.[2]

In the evening I went to Monsieur de Fogliani and had a long conversation with his Excellency. I told him my arrival there was accident, but that as I was one of the ships in these seas to protect the trade of His Majesty's subjects and as I had been applied to by this Factory in respect to many grievances they lay immediately

[1] Gaetano Caffarelli (1703–83) the most famous of the evirati; Groves' *Dictionary of Music and Musicians* says he had "a career of marvellous success, always ridiculous, always odious, and always a contrast to the modest Farinelli."

[2] Don Carlos, who reigned at Naples from 1735 to 1759, when he became Carlos III of Spain.

under, I looked upon myself in their situation as obliged to give it them, and particularly in the affair of Mr. Vernon, an English gentleman on his travels who had been arrested and was then a-trying for his life for having been detected in what they called a rape, which was no more than his having dressed his washer woman's daughter in men's clothes to carry her to Sicily with him, with whom he had lain months before. The father and mother, wanting to make money of it, had the girl seized just going in this disguise in the boat, and made her swear against Mr. Vernon.[1] I represented this to Monsieur de Fogliani as too trifling an affair to make so serious a one of it, when he enquired into the characters of that family and the manner Mr. Vernon had lived with them so long. In short, the Marquis was not inclined to enter on this affair, which was become a party affair between the interests of two contending powers in the Court.

The next day I was at the King's dinner where he was with the Queen, and afterwards, as the custom is there, presented to him in a long gallery, where he stopped and spoke a good deal to me, as did the Queen.[2] I dined afterwards with Monsieur de Fogliani, where was a number of people, Lieutenant-General Mahony and his lady, both of Irish extraction, but he had long been in this service, very good people, and very civil to me. They carried me this evening to the Duchess of Minervino, Countess de Palena, and the Countess de Potenza. At night I went to the opera to Madame Franca-Villa's box, tho' I had two boxes put into one for all my officers or the English that chose to go. I perceived the Prime Minister was paying great court to Madame Franca-Villa, and therefore thought I had better not give in to her allurements, who was a very amusing Princess and delighted in the English. Soon after, she gave me a great ball.

The 13th I received a memorial from Mr. Vernon stating all his case to present to the King. 'Tis too long to insert, especially as I have touched on the heads of it before. I went to Monsieur de Fogliani to desire he would give it His Majesty. I told Monsieur de Fogliani that I had no orders from Court to take cognizance of this, because they could never suspect such treatment from Naples to a British subject, but I relied on his Excellency's good disposition towards us to represent this to His Majesty in the

[1] Vernon's Christian name was John, but I have been unable to identify him further. The official correspondence relating to this incident is in *P.R.O. State Papers (Foreign)* 93/32.

[2] Maria Amelia of Saxony, who had married Don Carlos in 1736.

most favourable light, and to have him released from such a persecution. He told me there were orders given to put him in the castle. I said that would then acquit him of his parole, and that I thought this a very ill-timed rigour towards the English, and got up, made him a bow and came away.

I dined at the Duke de Lassano's, the King's favourite, but who did not meddle in state affairs. The Neapolitans all complained of the treatment Mr. Vernon met with here, and so did all the English that were here; there was a Mr. Cross who travelled with Mr. Vernon. This night Vernon was to go to the Castello Nuova, which was in the centre of the town. I wrote next day letters to Lord Holderness, who was Secretary of State, and gave him accounts of everything that was passing here publick and private. The English would have all had Mr. Vernon not surrender himself but have been treated with violence. They would have wrote a strong memorial, all of them, to the King, and me to sign it, but I opposed both these measures and desired they would let a little time operate and be silent on it, only to go constantly and visit Mr. Vernon.

I was now in very close friendship with the Count de Solayo, the King of Sardinia's Ambassador, and who was much dissatisfied with this court, and gave me many anecdotes of the falseness of the Minister, some traits of which I had experienced in this affair. I found the French Ambassador was the only one who had influence here. The 16th I was at a great ball given by the Prince de Canoca; I danced with the Marquesa de Motta, who I think one of the prettiest women of Naples; Donna Terrassina de Strango, her sister-in-law, not inferior; the Princess de Palma Reggio was still handsome, and talked much of Lord March to me, whom she had been very much in love with.

This night, whilst I was at this ball, I had laid a whole plan with my officers and some others for Mr. Vernon's escape out of the castle, which he did dressed in an officer's coat in the coach that they all went in to the castle, and came away unobserved by the guards, by the assistance of Mr. Lee, a nephew of Sir William Bunbury's who was there.[1] They got on board all of my ship safe, and I had given orders that if ever he should come on board that I was not to be acquainted with it, but they should be kept below. The next day all their servants were seized that were suspected to

[1] This is the earliest recorded exploit of Charles Lee, a quarrelsome and impulsive adventurer, who became a major-general in the American Revolutionary Army; see the D.N.B.

be aiding, and nothing was talked of but this escape of Vernon's. The officer in the castle was put in arrest; the General sent an officer to acquaint me of it, and to say that he had surely escaped on board my ship, and therefore to demand him. I told the officer that was impossible, and that I concluded they had murdered Mr. Vernon, and I must expect him to be produced, for that it was customary in our ships if any strangers came on board for me to be acquainted. Hitherto I had not been told of Mr. Vernon's being on board nor did I therefore believe it, but that if he was ever to come I should certainly never give him up. A vessel was hired that night, and in three days they were sent away to Civita Vecchia. Naples dwelt on this a long time, and then it blew all over, and there was an end of a very silly affair of both sides, and which might have ended in a very serious one.

We had nothing but balls and entertainment this whole Carnival, and was prodigiously entertained. The ladies are all gallant to a degree, and live in these times most sumptuously, none of them go out without two magnificent coaches, one for themselves, the other for their pages. Madame Mahony took care to place me very closely about her friend the Contessa de Palena, one of the greatest and richest families, and she was very much attached to me.[1] Madame Mahony's was always the scene of our meetings, and she herself retired to her dressing-room regularly and left us for two or three hours generally together in which we lost no time, and this almost every other night. We met here to go the balls or the opera, so that we were now declared cicisbees, but yet I played some infidelities often, as I own I was rather taken by a kind of surprise here than from any inclination of my own. Madame Palena was not the youngest nor the handsomest, tho' she did not give up her pretension to either. However she was about twenty-six, and tolerable well in beauty, but very, very lascivious, and very jealous, which I too often put to a trial.

The 27th I went to Caserta to pay my court to the King and Queen, but I would not stay, and, tho' I went to Monsieur de Fogliani's house as the Minister, yet I would not dine there, but dined at the Princess of Franca-Villa's who I —— twice that afternoon and returned late to Naples.

The 29th I went to see the King's palace of Portici, which was

[1] She was Ippolita Pignatelli, who in 1737 had married Antonio d'Aquino, Conte di Palena, later Prince of Caramanico. Unless she was married at the age of ten or eleven, she seems to have concealed a few of her years from Hervey.

very well worth attention from being so very full of all the curious antiquities that had been for many years taken out of the ruins of the city of Pompeii and was daily finding in those new discovered ones of the Herculaneum of Heraclea. I went with the Abbate Camillo Pardorni who had the care of them all, and innumerable they were indeed of every kind, bronzes particularly, fine statues, several utensils of all kinds in gold and silver, rings, seals, in short everything that can be named; the most curious workmanship, and yet preserved, tho' so many hundred years they had lain under ground. There were several very fine equestrian statues, vast pillars of various different fine marbles, bronze figures eight feet high. I went down into the Herculaneum to see the nature of their working there, and to view the amphitheatre they had discovered, but which they could show but little of as they were obliged to fill up with the lava they dug out in order to support the foundations of the palace, which was in part built over all this famous city, destroyed 1,800 years ago. The paintings are all taken up and preserved, and some are still very fresh, and very fine mosaic work there is. The gallery round the amphitheatre and several of the seats are preserved. 'Tis prodigious the variety of things here. . . .

The 10th February we diverted ourselves a very large part of us to run different masquerades, wherever we heard there were any, and had very good sport in this work, and had I not been so engaged that I was well watched I could have had very good sport here, as I think the ladies of this country are scarce exceeded by those of Portugal in their inclinations for intrigue, but not being so much watched here as there, it makes it more convenient and and much more easy to obtain everything one can desire.

The 11th I made a party out to see the environs of Naples about Baye and other places. It was a most delightful day, and the Count de Gazzola had prepared boats and barks as well as chaises, so that now and then we went by water, and now and then by land. I could not help just taking a sketch of an old ruined Temple of Venus, just by the entrance of Baye. It stands on a rising ground, the sea near it, and, at a distance, ruins as if belonging to it. It has eight great windows in it and seventy-three steps remaining in it. We dined here on cold things brought us from Baye, and returned very late at night.

In the morning I had the Duke and Duchess de Calabritto on board to breakfast. They stayed and dined and went on the water, and we afterwards went on shore to the ladies' ball. Here had like to have been a scene, for the Princess d'Aliano, who was very handsome, and with whom I had made some intimate acquaintance with, coming up to me and whispering me at the ball about only a supper for next evening, Madame Palena grew very violent, quite rude to the d'Aliano, and told the Duchess of Minervino she was helping on an intrigue between Madame d'Aliano and me. I was confounded at all this. However it went off without any consequences but a coolness between the Palena and me the rest of the night.

I was now preparing to leave Naples, the carnival having almost wore me out, being one continued round of dining, supping, dancing and ——. The 21st I got my ship out of the mold, went to Court, took leave there, went and made visits everywhere of leave. I was very late with the Palena this evening at Madame Mahony's, and then went to the opera with them where I left them and came on board, sailing that very night out of the Bay. I was met with great civilities here from every one, altho' the Court was not very well pleased with my having got away Mr. Vernon, and yet 'twas as good a thing as could happen to them, as they would have been embarrassed had Mr. Vernon been condemned for so little an affair. The nobility here hate the Spaniards abominable, and love the Germans and the English. The lower people are ever ready to revolt, as they detest the French by whose councils they think this Court is governed, and indeed it appears but too plain that the French is the most favoured nation there. We have very little trade there ourselves for want of encouragement, or we might make it a very good magazine and a better one for the Turkey trade than Leghorn.

I soon cleared the Gulf of Naples the 22nd, and determined to push down to Gibraltar at once, if the wind continued easterly, as I knew Mr. Edgcumbe would want a ship below. The 6th March I got into Gibraltar where I found numbers of letters and old orders from Mr. Edgcumbe, the Commodore on this station, who was now arrived and at Mahon. I did not stay at this place longer than to get my provisions and stores, and then went to Cadiz, where I arrived the 9th, and was obliged to perform nine days quarantine, coming from Gibraltar, so that finding there was not a great likelihood of a freight I got under sail for Lisbon and arrived there the 19th, having met with contrary winds. Here tho' I had a letter from Paris with the disagreeable news of Madame de Mortyn's death at St. Cloud, yet I found my friend Governor Trelawny here in his way to England. I was admitted to pratiqua this morning, and went ashore to see Mr. Trelawny, who I found complaining much of his health, but looked very well. He was married since I saw him, and had his lady with him. Then I went to see Signor Don João who had been ill. I found the merchants of Lisbon wanted to bring me to lower the freight to half per cent, as Captain Howe[1] had been here and taken his on board so, but I would not on any account consent to it, and told them I did not think three or four of us upon this station were authorized to take such a step that might affect the whole corps. I amused myself as usual here among the Portuguese, and the nuns, operas at court, and chiefly with Don João, and very seldom with the Factory, and not often with our Envoy, Mr. Castres, who lived in a very niggardly manner here. The 5th April I had named for my sailing, and having got on board 63,533 moydores[2] for the different remittances, I sailed, and being down at Paça d'Arcos I refused to take on board 3,000 more belonging to Monsieur Grenier and Pury because they would not put it on board the day I had named.

I got to Cadiz the 8th and went on shore to Mr. Solier's, made visits as usual, and I went all over the *carrachas*[3] where they were building their ships. There were two line-of-battle ships of 74 each on the stock, two very fine snows purposely for cruising in the Bay of Campeachy, and five frigates. They were very exact in exercising all their Marine, their gunners particularly, and indeed everything was in great order here. We stayed in the country three or four days at Mr. Bahicks and Monsieur la Baller's. Just as I was going to sail, I met Lord Huntingdon coming into town with the Governor, who had gone out to meet him. I went to his inn to make him my compliment, came on board and sailed immediately, and scarce got any money here this time. I got to Gibraltar the 20th in the morning and landed the garrison's money. I found Captain Howe in the *Dolphin* here, and we did not at all agree about their having taken the money at half per cent, and I told him I should therefore have nothing to do with it, as I was convinced that it was not the way alone to get money, because I that had stood out had got so much at one. He said he should not alter his method till he knew what Mr. Edgcumbe would do. I

[1] Later Admiral of the Fleet Richard, 1st Earl Howe, victor of the Glorious First of June, 1794. He was nine months senior to Hervey as a captain, although two years younger.

[2] About £87,350.

[3] Presumably this means dockyard.

said that was as they pleased, for I should continue my way of acting, and therefore share with no one. I sailed again that evening.

I fell in off Cape de Gatte with two Spanish men-of-war that were cruisers upon the Algerines. They were going before the wind under tripple-reefed topsails tho' I had top-gallant royals out. They never attempted to chace me, tho' I was far in shore of them. I had but little winds, and only got off Mahon the 2nd May. I found Mr. Edgcumbe was gone a-wooding to Formentera, so I sent in the money and then sailed into the harbour when the sea-breeze came in, and found several of my very old friends and acquaintances there; Colonel Rufane, Mr. and Mrs. Mace, Colonel Lockhart and General Blakeney who I dined with.[1] Mr. Edgcumbe came in the 9th and we were very glad to renew old friendships. I went to the Freemason's Lodge held by Brother Boyd;[2] I was admitted member of it, and drank three times three to the Brethren of it. The Chapter and Psalm were read. We were very merry whilst I stayed at Mahon, making parties to Alayor and Cittadella, and shooting. I sailed for Marseilles the 14th, but was obliged to put back again the 16th with a hard gale of wind. Lord Colville arrived in the *Northumberland*, and Latham in the *Eagle* with Rich's Regiment to relieve some here. Edgcumbe, Lord Colville and myself were by the General made members of the Blue and Orange, which Rich's Regiment was the protector.

I sailed again the 25th with a contrary wind, and got to Marseilles the 30th. I found a Dutch man-of-war there who saluted me. As I could not get pratiqua, I delivered the money at the Pratiqua-House, so that I saw nothing of the town; the port seemed a very fine one indeed, the narrowest entrance I ever saw, and all the within quite a basin, the ships laying close to wharves, as at Bristol. The bay was very open, the citadel did not much command it. The country about it looked delightful and full of country houses.

I sailed Thursday the 31st for Genoa, was off Villa-Franca the 3rd June, and got into Genoa the 6th, but not being able to have pratiqua in eighteen days I determined to deliver the money and sail for Leghorn. I stayed only three days, many people coming off in boats to me and I went in my boat, and so with that farce

[1] Lieutenant-General William Blakeney (later Lord Blakeney), now aged 81, and Lieutenant-Governor of the island since 1747. He had served in all Marlborough's campaigns, and had successfully defended Stirling Castle in the '45. In 1756 to be one of the chief actors in Byng's tragedy.

[2] The civilian storekeeper, later General Sir Robert Boyd, K.B., who distinguished himself during the siege of 1756, and again at the great siege of Gibraltar 1779–83.

we kept conversing for hours together. I sailed however the 9th and got to Leghorn the 10th. I went to the Pratiqua-House. Mr. Goldsworthy was at Mount Topoli, but I had many gentlemen came down to me, Count Bellrusst, Jermy and Howe. The Governor sent me word not to go away ; he had sent to Florence an express purposely to let me be admitted to pratiqua, and did not doubt obtaining it. He sent me two bucks and five dozen of Monte-Pliciani Wine. Several ladies came to the *lazaretta* next day. I carried my musick there and we were very jolly, tho' we could not touch one another. In the morning at day-break I got pratiqua by special order from Florence, which my good friend the Marquis Ginori obtained for me. I waited of his Excellency immediately to thank him, and dined with him, and the evening went to the Signora Bonfiglio, who I found as handsome as ever, but she had been ill. I had letters here with the account of my poor friend Monsieur Caze failing at Paris, which I was very much hurt at on her account.[1] I received a letter here from Lord Bath to get him 400 yards of crimson damask. I had letters from Madame de la Pietra Grimaldi reproaching me with not waiting at Genoa to obtain pratiqua which I answered very well to show them the difference of attention they had for me at Leghorn to what they had at Genoa. I wrote to Francisco Grimaldi to the same purpose, in order that the Health Office might know it. . . .

The 17th I went to Pisa to see the illuminations for Saint Janierri, made every third year. . . . The next day Mr. Mann, Lord Tylney, Lord Pembroke, Lord North, and Lord Dartmouth came to see me, they all came with Mr. Mann from Florence.[2] The bridge was very finely illuminated indeed, and so was the old royal palace ; the whole was worth seeing in this way. I left Pisa at 2 in the morning, the town being so full, and returned to Leghorn. Lord Dartmouth and Lord North came on board my ship and dined.

The 22nd I had a very fine box of flowers finished that had been bespoke a year. They were put in a box of blue velvet embroidered with silver, and the Orleans arms over it, that was put in a white satin case, embroidered with gold, and the direction "To the Duchess of Chartres" in gold letters embroidered, and these I

[1] D'Argenson (VII, 376) says that M. de Caze went bankrupt owing two million livres. By 1755 they were reduced to the level of mere *bourgeoisie*, his original annual pension of 35,000 having been cut to 4,000 livres.

[2] Henry, 10th Earl of Pembroke was an intimate friend of Hervey's ; Lord North was the Prime Minister of the American War ; the others are John, 2nd Earl Tylney of Castlemaine, and William, 2nd Earl of Dartmouth.

sent by the French Consul for the Duchess of Chartres, and some weeks after had the pleasure to hear they were received and liked.

The 23rd I dined with the Spanish Consul, Marquis de Sylva, where was a Monsieur and Madame Scarlatti from Florence, who was beautiful. I now got acquainted here with a very pretty woman, the Testori, the commissary's wife, with whom I passed many very agreeable evenings at Leghorn. The 25th I remitted 375 pounds to Mr. Henshaw to pay Mr. Powell, on account of the agreement for the empty vessel I had taken at sea.[1] This day too I read in the English gazettes of my sisters having had the titles given them by the King, as if they had been Earl's daughters, that is, that their father had outlived my grandfather. I was very glad of it for their sakes, as it would please them, but thought my brother had better have got something more material.

The 29th I had a concert for all the ladies, and had the famous Nardini[2] to play the violin, who was really beyond any I had heard. There was one Millar, who is in the Custom-House here, who I saw play the harp, harpsichord, and flute all at the same time. I had also Champion who played and composes very well. . . . The 10th July I gave a very great entertainment on board to the Governor. The Count and Countess de Resta, Milanese and Grandees of Spain, and several ladies also dined with me, and in the evening we went all over the canals all night with musick. Madame de Resta is beautiful, but I got a pain in my side by it today. The next day, tho' not very well, I went and dined with the Governor with the same set, then to the comedy, and afterwards I gave them an illumination upon the canals and bridges, with musick and a cold collation; the great bridge was finely illuminated with Madame de Resta's arms. There were thousands of people along the streets, following up as we rowed along the canals thro' the town. In this manner I passed the time away at Leghorn, till the 20th that I sailed for Naples in order to take in 200,000 dollars[3] for Marseilles.

I had a very fine passage along the Roman shore, going close to it all the way. I went between the island of Portici and the main, and anchored at Naples early Sunday the 22nd. There could not

[1] On 17th May, 1748; see p. 68.

[2] Pietro Nardini (1722–93), the most eminent of Tartini's pupils. The poet-musician Schubart wrote: "his playing brings tears into the eyes of stony-hearted courtiers; nay, his own tears run down on his violin!"

[3] About £45,000.

be a more agreeable, pleasant and quick passage. I received pratiqua immediately, and went to wait of Monsieur Fogliani notwithstanding former disputes. I went in the evening to Madame Franca-Villa, then to the Marquesa de la Mota and with them to a fair, and bought a great deal of the chinay of the King's manufactory, because there were always the names of those that purchased carried to the King at night; 'tis bad chinay, but the painting and gilding is very fine. To this fair we went every evening till supper-time. The 25th I went to the Court to the King's dinner; both His Majesty and the Queen spoke to me. The Contessa de Palena being reconciled to her old cicisbee, I could not hear of her. . . . There was a charming woman here, Donna Andreanna Morota of Capua, with whom I grew very intimate and went constantly to the fair together. . . . I sailed the 31st July for Marseilles, having got a poor opinion in general of the Neapolitans, tho' they are very civil; but if they cannot get three and sixpence by you at play, the men, I mean, they lose their aim, for they are all great gamesters, and never play to lose.

I had a very good passage and got to Marseilles the 10th of August and went on shore. Mr. Whatley, our Agent there, a very pretty kind of man, came off with me to dinner. I went to the comedy in the evening which is a very good one. The next day I made acquaintance with several ladies; among the rest were Madame Seymondey; there were young ladies with whom we walked the Corso, like our Mall. This is a whole street with trees on each side, and goes thro' the whole town. I supped at Madame Gramfests where the Seymondeys were invited. The next day I got acquainted with a very fine French woman, Mademoiselle Sarrazin, who lived with an officer, a colonel of a regiment. The next day I determined to sail, and Mademoiselle Sarrazin insisted she would go away with me for a voyage or two; and she would go, so that I could not refuse carrying her. So that night she came on board with one of her maids, and I sailed. She was a delightful fine woman.

The 18th I got off Minorca and sent in the mails, got Mr. Edgcumbe's orders off, and sailed for Gibraltar where I arrived the 22nd, and I found General Braddock commanded here. He wrote me a letter complaining of the Moors at Tetuan and Tangier, but, however, as he was in treaty about them I sailed for Cadiz, where I met the *Dolphin*, Captain Howe. As I was in quarantine for four days I sent my orders to Captain Howe to peruse, but he did not much like I should go to Lisbon and he remain to watch the Sallymen.[1] On which he sent me orders at first to remain here. This I represented against, and at last in very strong terms, which made a breach entirely between us; but at last he sent me orders to pursue my former orders. I sailed the 5th September and got the 12th to Lisbon, and I went immediately on shore to my old lodgings at Guards.

[1] The Moorish pirates.

VIII

A MYSTERIOUS ABDUCTION

Lisbon, 1753

I FOUND Mrs. Pitt at Lisbon, sister to Mr. Pitt the Paymaster; she was a very extraordinary woman, I thought—clever, but mad.[1] Captain Buckle was here in the *Unicorn*. My old friend, little Jamineau, came in a packet from England in his way to Naples where he was appointed Consul. Monsieur de Baschi and Madame I found Ambassador here who I had known at Compiègne with Madame Caze, and very glad to see me they were and desired me to make their house as my own.[2]

Here I diverted myself as usual, only that now I got acquainted with the Princess de Holstein, who lived close to the French Ambassador's, so that we could with the greatest ease talk out of the windows. At Bairro Alta I took a quinta for Madame Sarrazin and was mostly out there with her. A French man-of-war, Monsieur de Chessac,[3] came in here. He was Captain of the company of Gardes-Marines at Brest and had therefore a number of them on board, and this little dirty frigate made more work than is to be conceived. There was a Count de Forlynge here that was I believe a gamester, but much at the French Ambassador's. The 15th October we had a very great dinner on board the French man-of-war, and to make it more pompous for the French Ambassador Monsieur de Chessac borrowed his plate and his cooks and indeed fitted his ship very prettily for the purpose. The next day I had the same set to dine with me and made them an entertainment

[1] This was Elizabeth, Chatham's youngest sister, who was then on her way from France to Italy; she had " the face of an angel and a heart of all the furies "; see *The House of Pitt*, by Sir Tresham Lever, Bt., pp. 93–99.

[2] According to D'Argenson, François de Baschi " est le plus grand nigaud de France ". His wife's relationship to Madame de Pompadour qualified him for several diplomatic posts.

[3] This is probably Bide de Chezac, who as a lieutenant had distinguished himself at the taking of the *Northumberland* in 1744; he was Marshal de Conflans' flag-captain in the *Soleil Royal* at the battle of Quiberon Bay in 1759.

quite in a different style as I possibly could, and they stayed till supper.

The next day I went with the French Ambassador to see the House of Braganza where the King kept all the royal wardrobe in a manner. Virgolino and his wife received Monsieur and Madame de Baschi, as they were the keepers of it, and gave us an elegant breakfast. The finest things there I thought were five pairs of very high candlesticks and a cross about seven foot high and very finely wrought indeed for a church. The gold toilette that was for the present Queen when she married (which she has never seen) is very finely finished, and the Brussels lace that covers it all and the bed is beyond whatever could be seen of that kind. There are several valuable pictures, and the present which the Emperor of Chinay sent the present King makes up a great part of the curiosities of these apartments. There are two rooms full of all kind of uniforms and furniture of different nations for troops, and a curious collection of all the regimentals that have been time out of mind belonging to the King of Portugal's troops. There are many odd kind of things that have cost great sums and are of no kind of use, but in a manner buried there. . . .

Saturday the 23rd in the evening as I was coming from Odivellas convent and over Campo Pequeno, my chaise was stopped by a man on horseback, who very civilly pulled off his hat and said he must speak to me. I asked him what he wanted and if he knew me. I was extremely surprised and thought it was some design of assassinating me. He said my name was Hervey and he had something to speak to myself. I never went without pocket-pistols, and therefore held one in my hand and told him to come and speak to me. He came up, and begged me not to be surprised, that on the other end of the *campo* in a by-lane, there was a chaise which waited for me and had orders to conduct me to a lady that would and must speak to me. I said I knew of none that I would risk such an adventure for, and that if he did not go off I would shoot him. He said that might be, but if I did, me and my family would repent it; that he was not surprised at my receiving him so, but that he would deposit himself in the hands of my servants and remain in my chaise till my return, providing I would give my word of honour not to be followed, nor suffer him at my return to be followed, and that he could assure me I should have a reason to thank him. Whilst he talked thus another came up, and told me I must go. So, in short, I found myself in a manner taken, and thought I might as well go by fair as foul means. I could make nothing of it, but began to find it was not to rob me however. I got out of my chaise and left orders for that to wait there till my return. I walked with these two across the *campo*, where I found a chaise called a pacquet-boat, that is an Italian chaise, four wheels and six mules in it. The servants had brown liveries. I got in and they immediately drove like the devil. I then indeed began to fear I was nicked and going to be sent to some d——'d place for some work or other of the convents that I was discovered in, and knew I could not help myself.

'Twas now about two hours in the night when I arrived at a little quinta, after having been turned and turned about I knew not where or how. We stopped at a wall, and I was conducted in at a small door at a garden, and conveyed in the dark to a house that seemed pretty large, up a small pair of stairs. I was quite struck with all this, as not a word passed, but one of the men led me by the hand without a syllable, and I knew all resistance would be vain, and if I was to be murdered there needed not this ceremony. At length I came into an apartment, small but very finely furnished, and with six large wax tapers in it. Here I began to take a little comfort. I was however left and told to wait here. I could not conceive what this was to end in, and a thousand ideas took possession of me by turns, and so quick that I had not possession of myself to form any conjectures. But soon after I was brought a pen, ink and paper and bid to write to my servants to wait for me till daylight in the same spot, or at least to be there at that time. This I complied with, and liked that very much. Soon after this a small hanging door opened, and I was called by a female voice into another room that was very finely hung, and a very rich bed in it, only one silver lamp on a table.

The lady was of a very fine stature, fine hair, fine teeth and eyes, much painted after the Portuguese manner. She caressed me very much, and told me if she had not seen me so, she should have been the most miserable wretch in the world, as she had been ever since the bull-feast last year that she saw me, and perceived I had taken notice of her. I could not recall any thing about it, nor was I recovered of my surprise, it appeared all a dream to me. She perceived the amazement I was in, and caressed me the more. However, feeling myself in the arms of a very fine and a very luxurious woman, those sensations soon began to get the better of all others, as they were ever ready enough to do with me. A maid-servant soon after brought some sweetmeats and water. I took only a dried apricot and ate it. She told me our time was short and we must go to bed, which I did not hesitate as she had fired me all over. I put my pocket-pistols under my head, and passed a most joyous night.

About 3 or 4 in the morning she told me I must dress and be gone. I asked her if I was not worthy the repetition of this feast, and if I was not to be trusted with whom I was indebted for it. She told me 'twas impossible for me to undertake anything, that I might be sure whenever she could she would see me, for she had long had no other happiness, and much to this effect that all this preparation had been long bringing about to have me here. She cried very much, and said she would rather die that moment than not hope to see me again soon. In short, she gave me every proof that she was very much in love with me, and I had reason to believe it. She told me she would send the same person to me that first came to my chaise, and who should now conduct me back, and that I must always do as he directed me and never attempt to alter the time or even an hour of her appointment, as hers did not solely depend on herself. She then slipped a very fine diamond ring on my finger and told me to keep it, but I refused it and gave it her again and asked her for a lock of hair, which she gave me, and a little bawbling ring she had on her finger. I told her I would keep that and no other. She kissed me and pressed me to take the other, but I would not, and threw it on the bed, and told her I should be very much affronted if she insisted any more. I took my leave of her, intreating I might soon see her again, for I was very much in love with her.

I was drove back by a chaise and pair only, and the man that drove me was he that first accosted me before. I offered him greatly to tell me only the place, but his only answer to me was that 'twas the securest always for me not to know the place or person. Away I came, and amazed, to my own quinta—and then I had a quarrel to make up with Mademoiselle Sarrazin for staying out all night! So I e'en told her I had been at play and lost my money. This she suspected and grew jealous of the convents, as she knew I was much with them. The next day I lay in bed most of the day, and could not recover my surprise, and was uneasy to find out who it was. . . .

I was at the opera at night the 26th at Court; Gioacchino Gizziello, *suparana*, and Giovanni Manzuoli, Antonio Raaff, tenor,[1]

[1] Gizziello (1714–61), Manzuoli (b. 1725) and Raaff (1714–97), were three of the finest singers of their age.

Domenico Luciani, first woman and Giuseppi Gallicini, second woman. The 4th November I was invited to an opera in the King's private apartments, which was very pretty, composed of the above performers and a reduced orchestra. Some few of the Portuguese ladies were there, none of the men, and this I have reason to believe was made for the young Marquesa de Tavora, who I could perceive was very well with the King. . . .[1]

The 7th Don João's mother was to go to the convent of St. Ann, and I was invited. The nuns were all very pretty, but there was one, Donna Maria Peregrinia da Conceicão, that was charming; Donna Maria Felice, Donna Isabela Caetano and Donna Brazzi Theresa were all very pretty. We stayed very late here.

As I was going to Bemposto I was stopped by a man who gave me a letter, which I soon found to be from the lady I had been with from Campo Pequeno. I read it, and only made answer I would comply. The next evening I went to Odivellas by way of cover to where I was appointed, for in the same spot I met a chaise and pair of horses, and was carried but a very little way off to a quinta, which was not the same and I believe only hired for the purpose. However I found the same lady, and with the same *empressement* and same tenderness as before, and was with her from 7 to 11 only, and was carried back with great promises of meeting me soon again, but constant charges never to endeavour to find out, as also, that if by chance I should chance ever to meet and recollect her, never to make as if I knew her.

The next evening the 13th I went to the English Ball there, which I opened with Mrs. Hoissard. In the morning I sent to Captain Howe my Lieutenant to know if he had any commands, that I proposed sailing the Sunday following. He sent me word that he should send me orders to proceed the 15th as I had said, but should not mind a day or two. Now Sunday was but the 18th, and I thought this very extraordinary. The next day I made visits of leave and went to Odivellas, where I saw Donna Louisa de Menezes, a beautiful woman, daughter of the Marquis d'Abrantes by Ellena Paghetti. The 17th Saturday I went down the river with my ship, Don João on board of me. The King and Queen went

[1] Here is evidence that the attempt on the King by the Tavora family in 1758 was not political in origin; see also p. 179. When that family was destroyed in Pombal's reign of terror, the life of Theresa, "the young Marquesa", was spared, and she was immured in a convent.

down the river with me with their yachts. The next day I sailed over the bar and was very sorry to leave Lisbon without discovering or even having a guess with whom my adventure was. I knew it must be someone of the first quality but I could not imagine who, but determined on my return to run all risks to find it out.

IX

MOORISH DIPLOMACY

1753

THE 23rd November I got into Gibraltar Bay in the night; having no money on board I only victualled and prepared for sea. The next morning General Braddock, the present Lieutenant-Governor there, acquainted me that the Moors of Barbary had been very insolent to the Consul at Tetuan, that they threatened to cut off all communication with the garrison, and, in short, wanted presents and had totally broke the Treaty. General Braddock wrote to me to desire I would go over there and endeavour to settle all things for them. As soon therefore as I was victualled, I determined to go myself over to the Bay of Tetuan and endeavour to settle all things. The 28th I sailed over for Tetuan Bay. This is a very fine bay with a westerly wind, but very dangerous with an easterly one. There is a small tower with three or four bad guns on the beach at the entrance of a small river that runs up almost to Tetuan which has a very bad bar on the entrance of it even for boats, and has no defence. The town is on a hill about four miles from hence. It is a very neat one for a Moorish town, unfortified, but a very fine palace for the Alcaide[1] who resides here. His name is now Mahomett Lucas, who was a page to the present Emperor, but being at such a distance from Morocco they are not very strict in their obedience to their Prince but when it is their interest to make use of his name, and Tetuan, as well as Tangier, has often been in rebellion to the Emperor, and he has been obliged to march down his army.

On my arrival in the bay I sent a letter up to our Consul, Mr. Petticrew, to acquaint the Alcaide with my arrival, and to let him know I was extremely sorry to hear the treatment he had given my Master's subjects, and that I would not leave the place till I had some redress. Petticrew wrote me that he had been that morning early ordered to leave the town, and that things were going to the greatest extremity. . . .

[1] Governor.

[Hervey wrote to Petticrew telling him to stand firm, for his leaving at this juncture would be taken as a sign of weakness. He thought the ministers at home did " not desire to be embroiled with a dirty State that we can no ways effect but in depriving some of their particular trading people of their present gain, when they, by their situation, have a possibility, if not a probability, of doing great detriment to our commerce." He was therefore resolved " to support the honour of our Royal Master in as lofty a strain as prudence will admit, at the same time to keep them ignorant how little is our interest to quarrel with them."

To the Alcaide Hervey wrote thanking him for a letter containing assurances of friendship, " and as I have no reason to doubt of the sincerity of them, I am certain Your Excellency will be pleased to give the same assurances publickly to His Majesty's Consul in the presence of any three of your chiefs, of which I do desire Mahomett Benbaleb may be one, and that afterwards he and they do come in Your Excellency's name to give me the same pleasing assurances, that I may send to my Royal Master those proofs of your desire to remain with the English nation in that harmony and friendship we have ever proved to have preferred to animosities and violences, which Your Excellency knows from your superior good sense and judgement that my Royal Master has it more in his power than any other Prince in Europe to do himself and his people justice and take whatever satisfaction it shall best please His Majesty."][1]

I had no letter from the Alcaide, nor Mr. Petticrew in answer to these, Mr. Petticrew saying he was afraid his letters would not come safe. This made me very angry, as an hour's loss at this season in this place was a great deal. I therefore wrote a very peremptory letter next morning to the Consul to come off and let me know what chiefs were to be depended upon, in case I consented to put the scheme of a general revolt in execution, which was what Mr. Petticrew had persuaded me the chiefs wanted and were prepared for, if I would not succour them.

Whilst I was treating in this manner a most fortunate event happened. A tartane[2] came in the bay from Alexandria and Tunis with several passengers for this place, among whom was one of the principal men of this town. He was their saint or high-priest, Sede Hedge Ahmet Barracha; he had been four years absent to visit their Prophet's tomb at Mecca. His four wives were on board and several servants, also several great men of the town. I sent orders to bring the vessel near me, and not to suffer any

[1] The full correspondence can be read in *P.R.O. Adm* 1/1888.

[2] A small single-masted vessel, lateen rigged, with a foresail.

one to land without my immediate orders. I soon after sent for Barracha on board, and ordered my barge to be well covered all over, knowing how strict they were about their women being seen, and I told Barracha all that had passed with the Alcaide and us, and what a confusion the town was in from his conduct. In short I explained the whole, and endeavoured to make a friend of him, as I now knew he was adored by all these and could do what he pleased. I then told him that I had determined to detain him till all was settled, but that in consideration of the long time his family had been at sea, I had fitted my own barge close for them, and he should himself go and land them all and his children and all his things, and then return to me. This he seemed delighted with, and expressed his happiness for my behaviour to him. He went, therefore, and landed his family and things. He kissed the ground the moment he landed, but he would not go from the water-side, sent his brother and children with his wives and servants, and came off. Thousands came down to the beach hearing of his return, and all Tetuan was in an uproar when they heard I had detained him on the Alcaide's account.

I told Barracha on his return that the chiefs of Tetuan and myself were as one; we were acting on the same principles, which was endeavouring to prevent the cruelties and rapacious conduct of Lucas from plunging them into a war with us, which would destroy all the trade of Tetuan and consequently impoverish and ruin all its inhabitants; besides, if we could once settle this point, that the chiefs should become security to me for the Alcaide's promises, that then it would make them more considerable in the place and lessen his weight, and give them pretensions ever after to be a check on his authority. Barracha seemed to like this doctrine. He was a thorough, honest, worthy man. He was about sixty and had a very venerable appearance, a very long white beard, but his heart was nobler and better than most Europeans I ever dealt with, as he proved throughout all this.

I sent to acquaint the Alcaide what I had done, and that I had determined I would not suffer any communication to be with the town till he had settled all things with me and ratified the Treaty between us. I explained to the Alcaide the many advantages the Moors of Barbary had by their peace with us; that in case of any disasters they had always Gibraltar and Minorca, good ports, open to them, when they knew they had not another in the whole Mediterranean, except on the African coast, if they were caught anywhere; and that, besides, our trade supplied the whole town of Tetuan with silver and gold, besides constant necessaries they could not do without. All this I wrote fully to him.

Allah Sallah came on board of me, who was one of the people I had let go on shore with Barracha's people. He told me the Alcaide had been in a great rage at my stopping Barracha, for that the town was all in an uproar, and attributed this restraint on one of their saints to the Alcaide's tyranny. The chiefs with whom I entered into correspondence desired me now to let Barracha go on shore as they wanted his assistance. Therefore I sent for him, and after letting him perceive that I relied wholly on him, and after giving me his parole to return to me whenever I pleased, I let him go on shore. All the great people of the town came down to receive him and kissed his robe. I went to the mouth of the river with him and saluted him, made him many presents, and in short he was delighted with my treatment of him. On the beach, as I landed him, Mahomett Cresse, who was a Governor of the port, had some discourse with me, and he pressed me much to go up to the Alcaide. As I went off, the castle saluted me. There came in a large Swede, to whom I sent and forbid having any communication with the place till I had finished, as I was determined the Moors should feel what we could do.

The next morning, 1st December, Mr. Petticrew wrote me word that all the civilities I had shown Barracha had had a very great effect on the minds of the people, that he returned most nobly and resolutely among the people, and that on the Alcaide's telling him he should come off no more, he declared he would sooner die than break his word with me and therefore would come off the next day.

I went the next morning early to examine the bar and the river. I found that in one part of the bar large boats could easily go over, flat-bottom boats anywhere, and then one might row up within two miles of the town without any apprehensions, for the country is so clear there is no danger of bush-fighting, and wherever you've an enemy you can see him.

I received a letter from the Consul saying he could obtain nothing from the Alcaide, who insisted to treat with me only. I therefore sent up word if Barracha came down I would go up, as I had determined to keep Barracha and two more chiefs on board as hostages for my security of return, for I was not pleased at all with the Consul's dilatoriness, and think the chiefs had either deceived him, or him me.

The next morning, 4th December, the wind came in all of a

sudden easterly. I saw Barracha on the shore with my glass, ready for my boat, but I was obliged myself to cut my cable and go off for Gibraltar, the wind blew so hard easterly. . . .

[He got back off Tetuan at 5 o'clock in the afternoon of the 5th.]

I found things still in the same situation. The chiefs were for driving things to the utmost, and yet had not courage to stand forth. I therefore determined to send for Barracha, and go myself and sign the peace with the Alcaide, and rely on his promises. In order, therefore, to save time, I went at 9 the next morning to a place in the river called Mortines, where I had appointed everything. There had been an old fort there and half-a-dozen houses, and here the Alcaide's row-boats and half-gallies lay. I found the Consul there waiting for me with Barracha, several of the chiefs, and twenty horses from the Alcaide to carry me and my companions up, and a guard of forty men on horseback to escort me up. I settled presently on the spot with the chiefs what was to be done, and telling them that we must endeavour to overthrow the Dutch weight and influence here, who I looked upon as having been at the bottom of all these disputes between the Moors and us. Barracha swore by his Prophet that he believed the Alcaide sincere in his intention to keep the peace and beseeched me to go up to treat with him, and that he would be my security.

Whilst this was going on and I ready to go, the wind came again easterly, and the ship made a signal and got under sail, which made me immediately return on board, so that we left things in that confused way again. I run over to Gibraltar and got there in the afternoon. 'Twas the 12th before I could run over again, and then found a letter from Mr. Petticrew to let me know that the Alcaide would expect me the next morning, and that all should be ready to attend me at Mortines again, where I went with six of my officers at 9 next day.

I made Barracha come up with me to show them I was not afraid of them and relied on his word. We had above a hundred horse to escort us. The fort saluted as I went off, and the whole way was lined with Moors, the women all covered to their eyes that one could see nothing of them. After riding about six miles over a fine corn plain, we arrived at the town, which is built on the side of a hill that had a very easy ascent, full of orange and lemon trees. The town being walled, we went thro' a gate, and thro' several covered ways, all arched, the streets very narrow, that our horses could hardly get along for the number of people that were about us. At length I alighted at Mr. Petticrew's house, where we drank lemonade whilst we acquainted the Alcaide by Mahomett Cresse of our arrival. He sent me a Bashaw and a present of all kinds of fruit to welcome me, and to say that he waited with impatience to bid me welcome.

About noon I went with Barracha, Cresse, the Consul and my officers and a conquest of people to the Alcaide's house, where he received me in a sort of open gallery. He was sitting on a cushion, and a carpet under him, about ten chiefs about him standing, a secretary kneeling, and a chair for me was placed close opposite to him. The Jew interpreter being come, I told him earnestly that he must relate every syllable as near as he could to the Alcaide, and in the same language. The Alcaide seeing me very earnest asked the interpreter what I said. On telling him, he laughed and said " Star-bon, star-bon Inglise ", and told Barracha I was very young.

I then told him I was very glad to come on such good terms, and to have the honour of an opportunity of being personally known to one who had the character of so brave and so sensible a man; that it was equally pleasing to me to be the means of strengthening that cordiality and friendship that had so long subsisted between the two nations; that the assurances his Excellency had wrote me were most welcome to me, as being the result of that judgement which convinced his Excellency we were the only safe and certain allies of Tetuan, and that he must on every occasion feel this both for himself and his people.

He bid the interpreter tell me he never complained of a true, legitimate Englishman; that 'twas the Genoese boats that were permitted under English passes and colours to come over and commit all irregularities; that he had reason to complain of our correspondence with that pretender and rebel (as he called him), Mully Mustadee, Prince of Arzula,[1] who had given such disturbance to the inhabitants of all this part of the country, and that we were enriching him with our trade and furnishing him with arms and the means of repeating these disturbances; that he entreated my good offices to break this all off with Arzula; and that we should ever remain good friends. He then held out his hand for me to touch, in token of the peace we were to sign.

I then told him to remember that the English were the only power in Europe that the Moors were at a peace with that could

[1] Arzila, 25 miles SSW of Tangier.

be of use to them, by being the only ports (Gibraltar and Minorca) that the Moors had refuge in; that even the Spaniards were so well convinced of this, it was their chief inducement for desiring to have Gibraltar restored to them; that, as to other nations purchasing their alliance, 'twas very proper, for that they had no other method of making their Mediterranean trade sure, whereas we were always safe by our ports, and a sufficient force to correct our enemies; that I appealed to every chief and every man of this town who heard me what the effects were to this town of their communication with Gibraltar, and of what consequence our friendship was to them; that I had yet another motive which assured me of his friendship, and that was his great renown for bravery, and that all brave people had a fellow-feeling of each other, and I believed none dispute the bravery of the English nation, and that his Excellency was, was out of all doubt.

He then held out his hand again and smiled, told me I must be his friend on the other side of the water, and remove the idle prejudices interested people had given against him. The rest passed in reciprocal compliments. He got up, and then said he hoped I would stay some time in the town, that he would give me a boar-hunt, and amuse me with shooting. I told him I was obliged to go away very soon now, but should return soon and make his Excellency a personal visit. It being past 1, it was their hour to go to the mosque, being their Sabbath (Friday), so I took my leave of him after signing the peace, which was only the old one renewed.

Barracha and the chiefs came to me at Petticrew's where I dined. I sent the Alcaide ten barrels of powder. We made a very indifferent dinner from the damn'd bad cooks. Then I walked about the town and the top of the houses, from which you have a communication over the whole town, the parapets of each being so short. Here of an evening all the women divert themselves, tho' veiled, of which we saw numbers. I gave fifty dollars to the servants of the Alcaide, which I could not help, and returned on board after 6.

The next day being quite calm, I went a-shooting, and had great plenty of game. Mr. Petticrew dined on board of me with a girl he calls his wife. The Alcaide of the port came on board to me and told me the Alcaide had expected I had sent him ten whole barrels of powder, instead of half ones, but I said it was ten casks such as the King allowed us to have on board. In short these were all craving thieves. It cost me above £100 in presents to different people, of which I never got a farthing again.[1] I was then to have a boar-hunt next day, but would not remain and sailed at daylight the 16th for Mahon, and arrived there the 24th December in the evening, where I found several letters from England and several orders the Commodore had left for me.

[1] Hervey had to wait until 1757 before their Lordships bestirred themselves to pay for the powder; the protracted correspondence will be found in the Captains' Letters series in the P.R.O. In the first letter, dated 12th December O.S. 1753, he wrote "I give . . . my word of honour [the powder] is by very far a less expense than what I myself have been obliged to be at with bribes, presents, rewards, fees, and messengers, which from the custom and disposition of these people is absolutely necessary to carry on any business—much more to succeed in any."

X

ENAMORADA NA ITALIA

January 1754 to July 1755

I WENT next day to wait of General Blakeney, the Governor of Minorca, Colonel Rich and his lady, and several of my old acquaintances, and prepared to careen the ship here. I found my ship's sheathing almost all off, so I pulled off the remainder, tho' there was no stuff here to sheath her with, and I would not let them saw up new stuff. I diverted myself very well here, having Mademoiselle Sarrazin always with me, but who wanted sadly to return to see her mother whom she heard was very ill at Aix. The 9th January was the first day I ever felt the attack of the gout, and that I did now in my left foot, and I could not use it for above ten days. Then I began to move about a little and ride. . . . The 20th I was pretty well recovered again and went about.

I was tired of Mahon by the time my ship was ready and therefore sailed in order to put Mademoiselle Sarrazin on shore, she was so uneasy about her mother, tho' I was very sorry to part with her. I sailed the 11th February, but meeting with a very hard gulpher off Cape Croisette obliged me to bear up for Hyères Bay, where I anchored, and it blew harder than ever I remembered it. The 13th I sailed again, and the 18th I anchored in La Ciotat Bay, a very pretty looking place, a small basin for small ships, and a very little dirty town, but fine country about it. I hired chaises here, and the next day went on shore with Mademoiselle Sarrazin, to whom I gave two hundred half-skinner pieces, about 360 pounds. I was extremely sorry to part with her, tho' she was ever sick at sea, too, poor thing; she was the best tempered creature that ever breathed, always in good humour, cheerful and ready to oblige; she made time pass away very agreeably.

I sailed again the 20th, and got to Gibraltar the 1st March; in one 24 hours we made 278 miles (or 92 leagues and 2 miles), a prodigious run. As soon as I had got provisions and stores I went to Cadiz to see what was going on there, but having no prospect of anything, I went the 7th to Lisbon, and arrived there the 11th. I found from my pilot that the day before the *Dragon* man-of-war (Spaniard) arrived from Vera Cruz with six millions on board. They were almost starved for want of provisions and water, having had a very long passage, so that I missed this again by very little, for he would have put on board all his unregistered money certainly. When I went to Don João I found his mother was retired to the convent of St. Ann's, not by her own good will tho'; the King had ordered her in, and Diego de Mexico[1] to his estates banished, as he was going to marry that lady. The King intended Don João to be High Admiral, and he was therefore to command the next Guarda-costa squadron. All the time here was spent in the usual dining about, and the evenings with the Portuguese.

The 20th I had a letter come on board from the lady I had been with when here before, and I determined, *coûte que coûte*, to endeavour this time to find her out. I was desired to go directly to Campo Grande, and by 9 I was there in my chaise, and there I found a close one which carried me to the same quinta I had seen before. I remained there till 3, but could not discover anything about her; she appeared to me much handsomer than before, and I found she was served with great respect by the servants that did appear. I was carried back again.

I diverted myself at Odivellas, St. Ann's, Cellas, and with the foreign ministers. I found it reported my brother Bristol was coming Envoy here, tho' I knew nothing of it from him.

The 29th again I was sent to, and found a close chaise at the Marquis d'Abrantes's apartments in the evening, and I went into the country to the same quinta, where I supped and stayed very late till very near daylight in the morning, with all the luxury possible, but she never would hear of my knowing who she was, or that I should ever see her in any other manner. I give the driver a thirty-six shilling piece, and came on board early in the morning and lay in bed most of the next day.

The 31st a packet came in and gave us an account of Mr. Pelham's death which made great confusion in the Ministry at home. In the morning of the 1st April the Brazil fleet began to move. Don João with the Conde de Aveiras, Don João de Sylva and others came on board me, breakfasted, and took mean his yacht to accompany the King over the bar, who would go out with these

[1] A mistake for Diogo de Mendonça, Secretary of State and Minister of Marine.

ships, and we stayed very late. I was obliged to go, tho' I had Captain Buckle and several gentlemen to dine on board of me.

The 4th I rode out to Odivellas, and returned early in the evening, and then went in my *capota* to make a visit to a young lady I had often made love to at her window. I met her at a third place now by appointment; she is called Donna Felliciana de Sylvera, a beautiful creature about fifteen, very tall and well made, and after two or three hours being together I at length prevailed with her to let me make the best use of our remaining time, and had as much joy with her as ever I remember to have reaped from the same delightful employment. I went home about 4 in the morning. This young lady and I met frequently afterwards, and was very often very happy together.

The 10th I went to Cellas to a grate there. The Condessa d'Atougia was there, and looked like an angel. There were many people there also. I stayed late and then returned home. Nothing happened very well worth relating all this time. I employed two bawds, Maria Josepha and Ellena, very famous, about a certain lady, but without success. I received several letters from Donna Maria Peregrinia da Conceic˜o at St. Ann's and went to see her often, and often she ———————————————— at the grate. I went to Cellas with the Infant Don Manuel[1] to hear Donna Marguerida sing. The 2nd May I received a letter from the Princess de Holstein to go and see her, which I did, and that very evening in a little closet we sat in I —— her. She was a very fine woman, but very fat. I went and supped at the French Ambassador's to recruit.

The 12th I received a letter from my Brother Bristol that at the Bury election Lord Petersham was chose, but the votes for Felton and me were equal, 15 to 15, so there must be another election for us.[2] The 19th being my birthday, Señor Don João came on board very early with many people to dine on board; we stayed late as the old Marquis das Minas drank very hard. His grandfather was the Maréchal de Villeroy that was governor to the present King of France.

The next day, the 20th, I received a letter again that a chaise was waiting for me at the corner of Rua Formosa to carry me to the old place. As it was long since I had been sent to this surprised me,

[1] A brother of King João V.

[2] In December the House of Commons declared Uncle Felton Hervey elected. A description of the election will be found in W. S. Childe-Pemberton's *The Earl-Bishop*, I, 42–46.

as I begun to think 'twas all over. I now therefore ordered one of my servants I had formerly prepared to follow this chaise with one of the mules of mine at a distance, and to observe well the house I might go to, whether on foot or in the chaise, and to inform himself carefully but secretly whose house it was, or whom hired by etc, and all about it. And that the man might not think it was any intrigue, I told him I wanted to hire it but did not care those in it should know of it, lest they should take it ill of me. At 4 I went to the Rua Formosa where I found the chaise and was drove a great way, and towards 7 I perceived the man drove so slow that he was ordered to waste the time till dusk. I took no notice, seeing my servant every now and then at a distance. We arrived however at the quinta about dusk, where I found the lady with a million of excuses for having been so long without sending for me. I stayed however till near 3 in the morning. I pressed her very hard this night to make a confidence to me who she was as I had no idea, but we might contrive to see each other oftener and keep our own councils in publick if we met, but she never would. When I got home my servant told me the quinta belonged to one Sylva, but was hired by a lady of the Court, who came there very seldom; that this lady lived next door to Lavres in town, so that I now thought it easy to find this out. The next day I went about in my *capota* and to Lavres' house. I found no one lived there but the Morgade d'Olivares. She was of the Bedchamber to the Queen, but I knew her and that it was not that person. So that after searching in vain, I went home again.

I dined at the Spanish Ambassador's with Signor Don João, and went in the afternoon to Belem. The King and Queen were riding in their *pickeria*.[1] He sent to Don João to go in and to carry me with him. They both came and spoke to me very graciously, and asked me how I liked the opera, and a great deal about other operas. We stayed there till near 7, till their Majesties went out of the riding house, and then we returned to town.

The next day I did all I could to find out about this quinta, but could not. The 24th I had another letter from the lady, and went there soon after dark, ordering my man to follow me as before, and to remain hid after I left it somewhere and watch any chaise or carriage that should go from it after me. When I arrived she was just ready to go to supper, which we did together and to bed till 3 in the morning when day began to break, and I left it, and her very uneasy fearing she should not be able to see me again

[1] Riding-school.

before I left Lisbon. As soon as I was up next morning my servant came to me and told me that he remained there till past 9 in the morning when a Pacquet-boat, as they call them, came out with six mules, and drove to town, and I found it was no less than the D——s of Ca——l! I own I was surprised when I found it was her, but she had so well avoided ever speaking French and telling me she did not understand a word. However I was well pleased with the discovery. She is sister to the Count de Brionne in France, now Monsieur le Grand, and a Princess of the House of Lorraine.[1] I determined to manage this prudently, tho' I longed very sillily to show her I had found her out. I could not certainly do a worse thing, because it could tend to no good and was only a piece of vanity to shew her my dexterity, but I never considered that by doing this I had discovered her to a third person. In short, the 27th I went to Odivellas and stayed late, and at night I went to the Duchess of Cadaval with a letter to desire to speak to her. I found her at home, and said 'twas a petition I had for her. When I went in she seemed surprised to see me. The pages being withdrawn (before whom I made, as she observed, as if I had a great favour to request), she told me the step I had taken was in that country a very dangerous one, but that she supposed by letting her see I had discovered her I trusted to her not being a Portuguese. She then asked me how I had done to discover her, but I took care not to tell her the truth. I said I saw her in her coach one morning go by, and that I knew her, and was determined to shew it her, that I could not avoid it. We sat together some time; she was very pensive, but company coming in, I went away.

I was introduced some days afterwards to another set of women, Donna Anna de Bivar, her sister Donna Louisa and her daughter Donna Felliciana, beautiful.

The next day Don João told me that Monsieur de Carvalho (the Minister)[2] had desired him to tell me all that passed between himself and Mr. Castres relative to the affair of Mr. Shirley,[3] who had been banished Lisbon by the Court for his insolence to Mr. Crowle the Consul, whose protection as a kind of minister Monsieur Carvalho had given, and now Mr. Castres had orders from Court to solicit the repeal of this banishment. Monsieur

[1] Henrietta-Julia-Gabriela, daughter of Louis, Prince of Lambesch, married in 1739 to Don Jamie de Mello, 3rd Duke of Cadaval; the duke had died in 1749.

[2] The patriotic reformer and tyrant, later Marquis de Pombal, King José's chief minister throughout his reign.

[3] William Shirley, a minor dramatist.

Carvalho told Castres that the King of Portugal did not interfere in it, that if the King of England desired such an insolent fellow as that was to be forgiven and recalled, the King of Portugal had no objection, but that henceforward they must never expect the Court will interfere in the Factory's affairs if they use the Minister or the Consul ever so ill, and that the King of Portugal was extremely sorry for Mr. Crowle's recall, for he had always shewn himself a very honest and good man, and that any misunderstanding between the two Courts he (Carvalho) looked upon them as owing to some very different representations and shicanneries, and in short gave Castres to understand that neither the King nor himself were so well satisfied with his conduct. I mentioned this to Mr. Castres that he might be on his guard with Carvalho.

The 9th June I received a message from the Duchess de Cadaval and went there, but did not stay long at her house as I knew it must be full of spies. The next evening I was at a quinta of Donna Anna de Bivar, and got in at a window, no one knowing I was there but herself. But her daughter, who grew jealous of her mother, had, I found, some suspicion. I owned it to her afterwards and told her I never should have consented but for her sake. We settled matters very well sometime after this. She was very handsome and not above nineteen, with very fine hair and sung mighty well. The 14th I went to see the procession of Corpus de Dios at Odivellas, which was very fine and shewed all the nuns to great advantage.

The 15th I was taken ill with a violent pain in my stomach, which went to my side, and now and then to my feet, but did not continue. I continued very unwell the whole time I was at Lisbon after, and was attended by Dr. Wade.

I sailed the 21st still very ill, and anchored at Cadiz the 23rd, where I found a small French squadron, a 60 gun ship and a 30, commanded by Monsieur de Rochfeuile[1] who sent immediately on board to me. The 26th I went on shore to Monsieur Solier's house, tho' very weak. The 30th Mr. Edgcumbe appeared off, and four French men-of-war anchored here, commanded by Monsieur de la Galissonnière.[2] Mr. Edgcumbe did not come on shore, nor

[1] Which of two brothers this was is not certain; probably it is the Comte de Roquefeuil (capitaine de vaisseau 1746, chef d'escadre 1761, Lieutenant-Général 1766, and Vice-Amiral 1781), not the younger Vicomte de Roquefeuil (capitaine de vaisseau 1754 and chef d'escadre 1771).

[2] Roland-Michel Barrin, Marquis de la Galissonnière, one of the most able of French admirals; he had played a leading part in the French expansion in America, and was to command against Byng at the Battle of Mahon. He died on his way to Paris very soon after that triumph.

could I go off to him. He wrote to me about them and seemed uneasy to know their destination. He sailed for Gibraltar soon, leaving orders about them. I continued growing better, and went on board Monsieur de la Galissonnière in the *Sage* of 64 guns, and I soon found they were only exercising their officers and people, and made a mystery of this equipment. The Chevalier de Rohan came often to see me. He was only a Lieutenant of one of these ships, but a very active and wild one, yet from his great quality he must soon rise in the service.[1] I was much fêted here, for tho' there was such number of French officers always on shore, yet they made such a work and came so dirty, so shamefully dirty always dressed, that the Spaniards would take no notice of them, and thought it was done to affront them. I took advantage of this, and ordered all my officers to be particularly attentive in their dress whenever they came ashore. I was frequently at the Governor's conversations in the evening. The 10th July the French men-of-war sailed to exercise their men. The next day I sailed for Gibraltar, and took Monsieur la Baller with me and a Mr. Brown, a young man that was with him. I got to Gibraltar the 13th, where I found Mr. Edgcumbe.

The 15th Mr. Aspinwall came in the *Raven* sloop with the King's presents for Algiers, and Mr. Edgcumbe desired I would carry them and the Consul, which I did, and sailed the 18th for Algiers, where by calms and contrary winds I did not arrive till the 30th. I found it a very open bay and a very dangerous one in the winter time, as very open to all the sea winds and a great swell setting always in. The town appears very large and strongly fortified, but the mold not at all so, and tho' the guns are numerous and large yet I think their fortifications very ill built. But the safety and strength of their place lays in the shoals about it and the great swell always in it, so that no shells can with any certainty be thrown, and cannonading would be rather at too great a distance. The Turks are numerous and brave here, and everything relative to their Marine seems very well planned. As soon as I anchored the fort saluted me with twenty-one guns, which I returned. The Captain of the Port then came on board of me with an interpreter, and the dreger-man of the nation, as the interpreter is called, and each nation has its dreger-man. Mr. White, the vice-consul, came off and brought me compliments from the Dey, and a present of fruit.

[1] Later Prince de Montbazon and Lieutenant-General of Marine. He was captain of the *Raisonable* when she was taken by the *Dorsetshire* in 1758; he perished in the Terror.

I asked an audience for the next day and obtained it, and accordingly landed with the Consul and several officers next morning, and was saluted with nine guns. I went to the fort where the Great Admiral sits every day to give audience and regulate all about the Marine. He had about thirty captains and officers round him, and was called Mahomett Reese Mustee Reese, (Reese means a Captain.) We dined at a Mr. Gibson's, merchant, and a very great dinner we had. At 2 we went to the Dey's palace. He was sitting in a kind of alcove that was in a long gallery, and his kitchen at the end of it. His head cook is the Prime Minister, which is by way of not being poisoned, and he was sitting a little way from the Dey, to whom I was presented, and soon after presented the Consul to him. The Consul and all the merchants immediately kissed his hand according to the custom. I shook hands only with him and saluted his cheek. Soon after, the King's letter was read and interpreted to him word for word. Then all the presents were brought and carried to another room by him, where all are deposited. He seemed to take scarce any notice of them, except one very fine fowling-piece. As it went by he stopped it and looked at the lock of it, and said, " Starbon ", but all the bales of cloth, the trinkets, watches, furniture etc. he scarce looked at as they went by. He was a little swarthy old man, and was affable and civil. (Poor man ! he was murdered not many months after by his guards as he was paying them, which the Dey does himself every month.)

When the audience was over with the Dey I went down to the Hazzah-Gee, or High Treasurer, and to Sede Hasse who is Hazzah-Dau ; he is chamberlain. We were received very well by all these. I went off in the evening and found the Dey had sent me a present of ten bullocks and a great quantity of fruit and greens which I gave my people. The next morning I got a Turkish dress made for me. The 31st I went on shore to the Marine and saw all their vessels and all the ware-houses for their stores etc. I dined at Mr. Logi's, the Swedish Consul, who had two very pretty daughters. I was very well entertained here. The next day I went with Mr. Logi to a country house of his called the Garden, a very pretty place, and there met the Fathers of the charitable hospital, which were Spanish friars. I gave twenty zechins[1] to them for the slaves. In riding thro' the town I saw several burial places, each family has one. They are little enclosures, and here the women go and weep over their father's and husband's graves, and often find

[1] About £9.

new ones, as 'tis the place where they can best see their lovers. At some little distance we saw many women, but the instant we appeared they veiled themselves, sometimes in such a manner as left us time to see them whenever they were handsome. The country appears very little cultivated. There are many country houses which have a little garden about them, but all for garden-stuff. 'Tis amazing the quantity of putrifications that are about here, and some found on the top of high hills, sea-shells, and fish etc.

The next day, the 2nd August, I went and took my leave of the Dey. He was very civil, and I took my leave of all the officers etc. who had been very civil to me. The Hazzah-Gee gave me two tigers which I intended for the Emperor, thro' my friend the Marquis de Ginori. Miss Douglas gave me an antelope, a beautiful creature. I was to have carried her mother Mrs. Stanyford and her off, but Mr. Aspinwall begged me not. I sailed the next day, and glad to get away, and got to Mahon the 6th, where the troops were in want of money which I had on board for them.

The 9th I sailed from Mahon for Marseilles, having left all the garrison in confusion with Colonel Rich's quarrels with the General, who at last confined him. I got to Marseilles the 14th, but could not get pratiqua under eighteen days, so that I could not get to go see Mademoiselle Sarrazin, and I would not let her come to this villainous pratiqua-house to me. I sailed the next day, and the 17th was off Villa-Franca, and kept the coast close on board to go to Genoa, where I arrived the 21st and was to lay ten days' quarantine. I did not care much, as most people were in the country. Madame de la Pietra Grimaldi was at the baths at Lucca, but I saw many of my friends at the pratiqua-house. I wrote to Monsieur Rivarola, Chief Magistrate of the Health, to desire pratiqua. He assembled a Magistracy and wrote me word they had ordered me pratiqua that day. I went to Madame Norrina Doria's that evening in the country, and was there very late.

The next evening I went with Franco Grimaldi to a great conversation at Madame Pellinetta Brignole's and here that intimacy began which lasted all the while I was in the Mediterranean, and which friendship can only finish with myself. She was of the Balbi family, and one of the finest and most accomplished ladies of Genoa. My time was now taken up with attending Madame Pellinetta Brignole, to whom I made great court. I found the Dorias did not like this, but I did, and that carried me on. The

1st September Lord Pembroke arrived here with the Arena,[1] who had followed him from Florence, and I went to see them the next morning in order to carry him about. The next day I dined at a very great dinner with Monsieur Rodolpho Brignole, husband to Madame Pellinetta. After dinner I went in the coach with Madame Brignole, which was a sort of declaration of my being her cicisbee, as the ladies go only with them out airing to St. Pier d'Arena and about. Monsieur Marcellino Durazzo had been Madame Brignole's cicisbee; that fine palace in Rue Balbi is his. We had a conversation at Madame Grillo's to which I carried Lord Pembroke, as I did every day somewhere, and introduced him to every one. The next day I gave a fête to Madame Pellinetta Brignole and thirty others on board my ship and danced on board almost all night. I dined sometimes with Madame Angelo[2] Spinola, sister to Madame Brignole. There was great parties in this affair of my being cicisbee to Madame Brignole; Madame Serra, Victorrina Lascari, and most of Madame Brignole's *parents*[3] were for me; the Dorias, Grimaldis and Pallavicinos against me, but I carried it *bon train* whilst I stayed. She was exceedingly kind to me, and made me many professions of love, esteem and friendship, but I could not obtain any stronger proofs of it than a constant attention to me, and her time. She was very handsome, about thirty, perfectly mistress of musick, but had long been given up to devotion, not perfectly happy with her husband who was a very sour, niggardly, ill-looking man, and had very little attention to anything but his money. This lasted till the 13th, and then I sailed for Leghorn, carrying Lord Pembroke and the Arena with me.

The 16th I got into Leghorn and went on shore with Lord Pembroke and her. They set out for Florence directly, and Captain Dallin[4] with him, who was with me. I gave the Governor my two tigers and a fine present of birds for the Emperor. Mr. Goldsworthy came off to me and many of my old acquaintances. I now kept off from any cicesbeing work with the Bonfiglio or the Testori, or any, as I had promised Madame Brignole I would, as ours was an affair so *déclaré*, and so talked of. In this time the Signora de la Pietra Grimaldi with her husband, brother and many

[1] The Arena, or "Countess" Rena, later came to England where she was for many years (off and on) the mistress of Lord March.

[2] This should be Argentina.

[3] i.e. relations.

[4] John Dallin, a captain in Rich's Regiment at Minorca.

others came from Lucca, and the Governor offered me his coaches and everything to entertain them. I had them on board ship with a great deal of company, and I peeked [*sic*] myself to show them all the honours I could, as she had heard of my attachment to the Brignole. The evening there was an opera for them that was dedicated to me. We dined with the Governor, and had a number of ladies there and a ball at night. The Governor next day made me a present of a set of chinay with my arms on it of his own manufactory.

I took my leave of all this company at the opera, and determined to send the ship to Genoa and proceed myself to Porto-Specia by land, there take a felucca and go to Genoa. This I did in order to show the Genoese the absurdity of their conduct at their Health-Office, as my ship coming from Leghorn must lay quarantine, and yet by land going from Leghorn I can enter their state without being liable to the same inconvenience. The 23rd at daylight Mr. Goldsworthy, Dallin, five servants and myself set out for Pisa, and the ship sailed. We passed Pisa, Torretta, Viareggio, Pietrasanta, Massa, Avenza, Sarzana, and Lerici. I thought Massa was a very neat charming town and very pretty women in it, even to the common labouring ones. I got to Lerici at sunset, where I found a felucca ready for me. I gave but five zechins and a half[1] for it, and it carried us to Genoa by light in the morning, where we landed without difficulty. My ship was there and in quarantine, which was made a great joke of by every one. I lodged at the St. Martha. Madame Brignole I found was gone to her country house at Torazzo, six miles off and a bad horse-road. However I often walked it there, and when in town lived mostly with her sisters, but as we were short of provisions in the ship, I sailed the 29th, tho' Madame Brignole had contrived to come to town to stay two or three days. Her brother Niccolini Lomellini accompanied me on board.

We had very little winds and calms during the voyage. I was off Minorca the 3rd October and landed Captain Dallin to his regiment, he having been only to make the tour with me. I went on to Gibraltar, but kept the coast of Barbary on board for the western currents, and had one day, by calms and currents, very near been on shore off Tanga, about eight leagues from Tetuan, but a breeze came off from the land and set us off, and got into Gibraltar the 9th.

I was again applied to to go to Tetuan to accomodate the affairs

[1] About £2 10*s*. 0*d*.

there again. I therefore dispatched a messenger to Malaga for the *Raven* to join me. Here I entertained the General and his lady, (Mr. and Mrs. Fowke),[1] and several officers. The 16th the *Raven* joined me. I met the *Dolphin* off the bay and ordered them to follow me. I sailed over for Tetuan, and the next day anchored at Tetuan, and wrote to the Alcaide that I was arrived and had My Master's orders to protect the trade of His Majesty's subjects to any part of Barbary they pleased to trade to, and that he was surprised at the Alcaide's being offended at our trading to Arzula. The Alcaide sent me a very short answer the next day, but importing that he did not care who traded to Arzula, but supposed the Emperor would soon send his orders on that subject. The reason of this jealousy of Arzula was because Mully Mustadee, the present Emperor's uncle, who had been in arms against the Emperor, was retired thither and was opening a trade with us which supported him very much, and, besides, it gave a jealousy to the Tetuaners lest we should open such a trade there as might lessen that with Tetuan, or at least make our dependence less there. But none but Moors could judge so ill, as Tetuan and Tangier were places very essential for Gibraltar. However the easterly wind setting in next morning obliged me to go to Tangier before this could be settled.

On my arrival at Tangier the weather was very bad, so that I only sent an officer on shore there to the Bashaw with my letters. He invited me on shore and desired to remain good friends. I run down with the *Dolphin* and *Raven* to Arzula, and was saluted as soon as I landed there. It is a miserable fortified town on the side of a hill, and Mully Mustadee was retired here, and had about 10,000 men with him. The streets were lined with armed men for me to his house. He was sitting on an English mahogany armed-chair, a very fine old man. He told me he wished very much to have a strict friendship with the English, that the people of Arzula desired to open a further trade with us, and that he was in hopes the Emperor and him should be soon reconciled, as he was determined to support his own right. Mully Mustadee then told me he knew the English esteemed their horses, and therefore he desired me to choose one out of his stables. He ordered his horses out and he gave me a most beautiful one, all caparisoned, which I embarked. I gave him a very fine gun, a pair of pistols, and 6 half-barrels of powder. I sailed that evening and got to Gibraltar the 23rd. . . .

[1] Lieutenant-General Thomas Fowke, broken by the King for his part in the military council of war at Gibraltar in 1756.

The 18th November I got off Lisbon; being bad weather and no pilots out I run the ship in myself, and went on shore to stay the next day. The King was at Palma, up the river, and Don João at St. Mora, a house of his, to be near the King. The 21st I went with the French Ambassador to see the new opera house the King was building. One Bibiena[1] was the architect, who built the theatre at Siena; the extent of this will exceed any in Europe, as well as the magnificence and taste of it, and will cost above 200,000 pounds Sterling. The evening I spent at the French Ambassadress's. I went the 23rd to see the Princess of Holstein with whom I renewed my acquaintance. The 25th the King arrived, and Don João came on board of me. We passed most of our time together as usual, convents and visiting.

The 5th December the Queen had a musick, and I was carried there, and very fine it was; the Princesses sung, only the Spanish Ambassador there and about eight of the nobility, no ladies but those in waiting.

The 9th I went with Don João to the palace at Belem. The King was just going into his *pickeria* to ride, and as he came out he stopped me and spoke a long time to me about the Genoese ships that were building at Genoa, and some of which were already arrived here for His Majesty. He was in a very good humour; he opened the garden door and called the Queen, who was in a riding-habit, and a little *capota* over it that made her look delightful, with a hat and feather. She brought a little Maltese dog in her arms with her, which I had had the honour to present her Majesty, and she said she was much obliged to me for it, but if I did not carry some females down for it the Princesses would be very angry with me. They asked me if I went away before their Majesties went to Salvaterra, and very civilly told me they were sorry I did not stay to go there. The King soon after run away, and the Queen went into her apartment. Then Don João and I went away. I dined at the French Ambassador's. The evening I had a swelling in my foot. I was extremely sorry I could not stay to go to Salvaterra with the Court, as it is a very jovial life the Court lives there during the thirty days it stays to hunt, and all at the King's expense, which is immense, very near a million of crusados[2] the expense of that journey to the King, so much is he cheated.

[1] The new opera house was opened on the 31st March 1755, and was destroyed in the earthquake of the same year. João Carlos Bibiena came from an Italian family of fashionable baroque architects; see p. 179.

[2] About £150,000.

I went to Odivellas the 17th to see all my friends there. I passed my time extremely well here, being always amused among the Portuguese nobility and the convents. The 21st Don João took me in his yacht, and we went to Cascaes with the Pernambuco ships. Afterwards we returned to town and went directly to the King's apartment, who asked me many questions about the ships that were anchored on the bar. I was the evening at the Princess of Holstein where I stayed alone with her many hours, he (Calhariz) being at his quinta. This was the time exactly that I got a very fine Salloa[1] on board who had been endeavouring for these two years to get out of the country. Her name was Joanña, and a very fine beautiful woman she was. I kept her all the time I was here on board.

When I had got the garrisons' money on board, which was only 6,400 moydores and about 6,000 more for Italy,[2] I sailed the 4th January and got to Gibraltar the 7th, where I found Mr. Edgcumbe. After being stored and victualled I sailed the 11th at night, having waited several hours for my steward, Cradock, who kept my boat, by which I lost two men and left my valet-de-chambre. In striking Cradock I hit my nuckle against his teeth and cut the tendon, so that my hand swelled very much and was very painful a long time. I got off Mahon the 17th and sent my boat in with the money, and then made sail for Genoa, had very bad weather and my hand continued very bad, we got to Genoa the 2nd February where I sent on shore for pratiqua. The Health Office made some demur, us coming from Gibraltar, but after persisting that I had been so long at sea and not a sick man in the ship, they told me I should have pratiqua the next morning. So I walked directly up to the Consul's house and told them they might pursue their forms if they pleased, for then I would go on shore.

I went that evening to Madame Brignole's, who had, in her child's late illness, made a vow not to go to the opera this carnival, such was the weak superstition of this beautiful and (otherwise) sensible lady. I found Monsieur de Kinsky, the French Envoy's nephew, did all he could to be received as cicesbee to Madame Brignole and I was told that they had all done their possible, but not succeeded, so that my vanity and my love for her made me determine he should receive some publick mortification to make him desist. I reproached her with her having given the least hopes or encouragement, which she absolutely denied, and very readily

[1] A woman from the immediate vicinity of Lisbon.

[2] A mere £17,050.

agreed to give him the negative I wished, so that in a day or two she gave a very great entertainment and dinner, invited a number of people and many of my officers, and left out Monsieur de Kinsky, which was taken as I wished, and he never more came near the house. In short I stayed all this carnival at Genoa, and was very well satisfied with Madame Brignole's attention to me, as that of all her family, and indeed there never were two people more together than we. Madame Lilla Mara Spinola, the Contessa de l'Arriano, Momina Grimaldi, and a very pretty *sposa*, Angelina Airola, all endeavoured to break my union with Madame Brignole. The last indeed gave some uneasiness to Madame Brignole as she was very pretty, very young, very lively, and very rich, and had made more than commonly up to me, but I cleared it up by an entire devotion of my time to Madame Brignole, but then I exacted in return that she should let me lay one whole night with her, *malgré* all the difficulties and risks that would attend it. But in short I was set upon it, and obtained consent, whenever I could manage it.

I short the 26th I undertook it, and I believe never man run a more hazardous and dangerous undertaking. She feigned an inflamation in her eye for a day or two before, and kept her room darkened. In the evening I was there as usual with company, and went out as if to go away, giving her the signal, on which she desired the company to go into the next room a moment, when I, by a turning, got round into her cabinet, and so into her bed-chamber again by her cabinet, and taking off my coat and shoes only, placed them under the bed, and got into bed myself to her, which was covered by one of their great thick sort of down quilts. However the bed was one of their very large ones, and high, with crimson velvet curtains richly embroidered with gold and lined with worked satin, which on account of her eyes were all drawn except on one side where there were no lights, and where the company sat some distance from the bed. As soon as I was so placed, she let them in again, and all this in a few minutes. Among the rest her husband came in. In this situation I lay for near an hour, when all went away. The husband came in after supper to take leave of her, and I was frightened at his d——'d *douceurs*, and especially when he offered to bring a light to the bed-side to show her some India handkerchiefs he had that morning brought for her, but which she put off, and away he went, leaving me in the arms of one of the loveliest women that ever was. I lay till near daylight and performed wonders. I contrived to get out of the house and home without ever being seen or suspected by any one.

This very successful night encouraged us both rather too much, for some nights after I repeated the same by getting under the bed, and staying there two hours before I could get into bed, which we did, and I got away next morning after being horridly frightened by finding all the doors locked, which never used to be, so that I was obliged to be hid behind a great *portière*,[1] till Madame Brignole was dressed and going to Mass with all her servants in the chapel of her apartment, when I got out unsuspected. But this so frightened her that we attempted this no more. But indeed it was mere wantoness, as I was with her every morning before she was out of bed, and every evening after the conversation. We were very happy together the whole time. . . .

About this time we heard of the preparations making in England and France for war.

The 10th March she took the Cross she wore about her neck and swore to me she would never make any intimacy with anyone else as long as she lived, nor admit any one to make addresses to her. But I had already experienced that the use of confessions and absolutions with these ladies made all that very easy when the passions cooled, or new ones succeeded. I sailed the next day, having stayed several at her particular request. I gave her a green enamelled box set with diamonds that cost me £300 at Paris. Birtles the Consul went to the lanthorn with me, and I got off Cape della Melle by the evening. I made Minorca the 15th and went into the harbour, and found I was very much in love with Pellinetta by my being displeased with everything about me.

I dined with General Blakeney the next day, and found all the conversation was on the thoughts of war. Here I hove down the ship and found our false keel all eat away. We took off the sheathing. I passed my time here with the officers and were very much together. I wrote constantly by way of Marseilles to Genoa. The 13th April, having refitted, I sailed. . . . [to Lisbon where he arrived the 23rd.].

The 26th I went in the evening to the Secretary of State's, and then to the Spanish Ambassador's, as I never went near old Castres, our Envoy. I wrote my letters to Genoa by a ship I found bound immediately thither. I went to the palace at Belem to a concert with Don João. The King came and spoke to me, and as he went away he said joking, " Vosse e micoi triste que vai, e

[1] A curtain hung over a doorway.

e enamorado a Italia" [*sic*].[1] His Majesty never waited my answer but the Princess of Brazil[2] joked me afterwards about it. The next day I received a letter from the Secretary of State enclosing me a ticket for the King's opera, which is the most magnificent theatre I ever saw, and everything in it truly royal; *Alaxandre nell'Indie*, Caffarelli did Porus. I was at St. Ann's convent to music there, and the next day went to Paço d'Arcos to Don João's quinta. The 19th I went to Odivellas with all the Gratias family, and saw all my old friends at the grate. The 22nd all that family dined on board of my ship, with musick the whole evening on the river and a ball and supper for them on board, and I was very well with Donna Felliciana. The 31st I was at Mr. Burns' quinta and went to Chillies. I dined with the Spanish Ambassador and went with him and the Nuncio to Odivellas, where all the nuns came to the grate, the bells ringing, and all the friars walking before the Nuncio; we had several grates for the Nuncio to see the whole. The 6th being the King of Portugal's birthday I dressed my ship, and fired. I dined with Don João and was at the opera at Court at night; it was *La Clemenza di Tito*. Here I perceived the Marquesa de Tavora was very well with the King; they did nothing but eye each other as much as they dared in the Queen's presence. The scenery of this opera surpasses anything I had ever seen of the kind. I gave a dinner the 8th July to Signor Don João, the Marquis de Tancos, Marquis das Minas, Conde de Aveiras and his son, Marquis de Nisa, Conde de Villa Mayor, Don João de Sylva, and Abbate Xavier. In the evening we all went to the Italian comedy, where was the Marquesa de Tavora with whom I flirted, tho' I was on my guard, knowing I should ill pay my court by any assiduity there.[3]

The 10th I went with the Conde de Villa Mayor to the Patriarch's quinta at Marvilla to dine with the French Ambassador, Monsieur de Baschi, who was to make his publick entry and was to be entertained three days there at the King's expence. There were thirty-six people at dinner, a table of three services of forty-eight dishes, a dessert of above a hundred, numbers of gentlemen waited, and the service of plate was magnificent, and everything well dressed and delicately served, the King's music playing the whole time,

[1] Hervey's Portuguese is corrupt; what the King probably said was "Vocé está muito triste que vai, e está enamorada na Italia", meaning "You are very sad at leaving—and all the time you are in love in Italy."

[2] King José's eldest daughter, who, as Maria I, succeeded him in 1777 and died insane in 1816.

[3] See p. 153 and note.

and numbers of people going thro' the apartments to see them. The bed for the Ambassador was very magnificent, and is the one King John the 5th had made for his wedding. We returned to town very late and went to Madame de Baschi and played there. The 11th I went to the Spanish Ambassador's to see the French Ambassador's entry conducted by the Marquis de Valencia. It was very fine for that kind of show of coaches and liveries. The next day I went to Don João, being his birthday and then twenty-nine years old.[1]

The 18th I had a great many of the Portuguese to dine on board, and fell down the river with my ship, intending to sail the 20th. I had intelligence early that there were nine sail of French men-of-war at anchor at Cascaes, and whose boats I saw go by.[2] I went immediately to the Envoy, and found the poor old man as yet ignorant these ships had been anchored near sixteen hours. I wanted to know the most expeditious way to acquaint the government of these ships. From this I went to Bemposto, and with Don João to the palace. The King, I thought, seemed much displeased with the arrival of these ships, and said angrily that but six of them should come in, according to treaty. In the afternoon Signor Don João and I went down among them in the yacht. These was the *Formidable* of 80 guns, *L'Inflexible* of 70, *L'Heros* 74, *Le Palmier* 76, *La Veille* 64, *L'Aigle* 54, *La Fleur-de-Lis* 36, *L'Amethyste* 30, *L'Heroine* 30. The Chef d'Escadre was Monsieur le comte de Guay. We returned to the palace about 8, and gave the King a minute account of them. I wrote to the Admiralty an account of them. The next morning the six largest came up the river and anchored before the palace. I dined at the Spanish Ambassador's and found by him the King was much displeased at these ships being sent here.

The 23rd I went down with the ship to Paço d'Arcos; Don João's barge run mine down and I was obliged to leave her behind. The next day I sailed, and the 26th I got into Gibraltar, and having received all my letters by express from Cadiz and victualled here, I sailed for Mahon, and arrived at Mahon the 13th, where I found the Commodore out, but he had left no particular news from England, nor nothing to prevent the continuance of my route; so I sailed on the 17th for Genoa, and met the Commodore the 20th, who told me Mr. Byng was sailed from England the 10th for the

[1] Some reference books say he was born in 1719.

[2] They were from Brest, whither they returned, by way of Cadiz, at the end of August, narrowly missing an encounter with the Western Squadron under Admiral Hawke.

Mediterranean.[1] I left Mr. Edgcumbe in the evening, and went to the Villa Franca, where I arrived the 21st, and sent a packet to my brother at Turin.[2] I remained four days in quarantine, and the 25th I had pratiqua. The commandant of the gallies, Monsieur Gibair, came on board with me with the other officers of the gallies. I went with the Chevalier de Bellona to Nice to see General Paterson who was ill. The next day I sailed, and arrived at Genoa the 27th and had immediate pratiqua. I went on shore to Madame Brignole's.

[1] He was told wrong; Byng commanded the Western Squadron in the autumn of 1755, but was not ordered to fit out for the Mediterranean until the 11th March following.

[2] On 15th June, George, 2nd Earl of Bristol, had arrived to assume his appointment as minister to the King of Sardinia; in return for this favour the Duke of Newcastle held his proxy vote in the Lords.

XI

PREPARATIONS FOR WAR

August 1755 to May 1756

The war which was about to break out had long been smouldering in America. Under the leadership of Galissionnière and Du Quesne the French had been pushing a line of forts from their colony of Canada down the Ohio and Mississippi rivers to New Orleans on the Gulf of Mexico. They hoped in vain that this tenuous strand would confine the virile English colonists East of the Alleghanies, and thus preserve the vast wilds to the westward for French exploitation.

Early in 1755 both sides began to pass reinforcements across the Atlantic; in the British force under General Braddock which sailed in January went Hervey's youngest brother William as a volunteer in the 44th Regiment. These movements and the protection of homecoming trade brought several French squadrons to sea, and the ministers at home, realising that war was bound to come, gave orders to our Admirals to strike before a formal declaration should a prize of sufficient worth present itself. De Guay's squadron which Hervey had seen at Lisbon would have been such an object. But the danger was that this scheme might go off at half-cock; some officer might misjudge the value of a target and at once do too much for diplomacy to excuse and too little to have any effect on the course of the war. This very thing happened when Boscawen took the *Alcide* and *Lys* on their way to Louisbourg; he put England morally in the wrong without any compensating military advantage.

The war was not formally begun until 17th May 1756, but during the preparatory stages the French cleverly misled Newcastle's government into thinking that an invasion of England was their first objective; in fact this was no more than an elaborate cover-plan for their expedition to Minorca, and its success was complete. Hervey tells of the intelligence, preparations and events in the Mediterranean leading up to Admiral Byng's disgrace which was the result of the fundamental error made by the cabinet in thinking that England, and not Minorca, was in the greater danger. A few of the ships which were standing guard off Brest or which, in answer to the entreaties of the City, were spread out to guard our commerce against the depredations of French privateers, would have given Byng a decisive superiority in numbers; even in that admiral's too cautious hands such a fleet would certainly have won the day off Mahon.

THE 30th we had news of Mr. Boscawen's having taken two French men-of-war in America, no war being declared; and this made a great noise everywhere, as a war was inevitable. This Republic dreaded the consequences, as foreseeing it must become general and that they would be obliged to take some part or other.

The 2nd August I had the three sisters Pellinetta, Argentina and Angelina on board to musick etc, and in the evening at Signora Victorina's. The 5th Madame Brignole carried me to a villa of Monsieur Durazzo's to dinner about six miles from Genoa on the road of the Ponte Severa, a great deal of company there, and a magnificent entertainment we had. In the evening we returned.

The 6th the Consul told me an odd event; it seems the King's arms over the door was found in the morning with a t——d stuck upon it with a paper, and wrote on it some very scurrilous words on the King. This was looked upon as by the French, and made a great noise. I advised Birtles not to take notice of it, but he complained and Franco Grimaldi wrote to me to desire to see me upon it. But I treated it as a low blackguard thing not worthy notice. It went off so.

The next day I went with Madame Brignole to her brother-in-law, the late Doge, to Albaro, a very fine palace he had there, and talked with him a long time on the present situation of things. He talked of a neutrality, and how much he wished the Court of England should know that was the sentiments of the Genoese, but as I knew this great man was entirely Frenchified I gave very little credit to anything he said, but however took care he should not see my opinion of him, that did not suit neither with my situation in his family. We returned to Genoa in the evening and supped at Madame Lascari's. . . .

The 14th I received an express, in which was a letter from Sir Thomas Robinson, Secretary of State, to read to all the trade to warn them of an approaching war with France. I made the signal for all masters of merchant ships, and this was read to them.

This whole time passed in love, mirth and voluptuousness.

* * * * *

Monsieur Rodolpho Brignole, her husband, and I had a very long discourse on the present situation of affairs, and of the steps the Republic would take to endeavour to secure, if possible, a neutrality for itself. I told him I thought it the best thing they could do would be to send some person of weight immediately to England as minister, and he asssured me this was now under consideration. A French officer arrived here from Toulon to inspect into the ships that were building on the coast here, in order to purchase them if they were found fit for their purpose, as also to engage so many sailors.

The 2nd September I prepared for going away. It was very bad weather and a merchant ship was lost in the port here. In the afternoon a bomb-ketch, the *Speedwell*, Captain Webb, arrived with an express from England in thirty days. He had packets for all the Consuls and commanders of men-of-war. There had been a sad mistake in the packet, one paragraph omitted that should have been sealed up and put in it, so that we learnt nothing of her whatsoever but that a war was unavoidable, and the next day I advised Captain Webb to sail, as he ought not to have landed here without laying quarantine from Gibraltar. The next morning the bomb-ketch sailed. The next day I pressed several of the senators about sending a proper person to England, and I found the Abbé Celesia[1] was to be fixed on to go as Minister with appointments of about 16,000 livres, that is about £650 a year. The next day Abbé Celesia came to me and talked over several things. The next day I got out of the port, but very little wind and a great swell prevented my getting clear away till the 7th, when I was very sorry to leave.

* * * * *

Off Villa Franca the 9th I sent my boat in, and by newspapers found our troops had been defeated in America, and General Braddock killed.[2] I got into Mahon the 12th, and gave my ship a very large heel alongside the wharf, having all the reason in the world to expect a declaration of war immediately. My ship being ready by the 30th, and several Turkey ships being here bound downwards, I took them under my convoy and sailed the 2nd October. The 12th, as we were off Adera Point, I fell in with the *Bedford*, Captain

[1] Piero Paulo Celesia; when minister in England he married the widow of David Mallet, who pamphleteered for the Administration against Byng.

[2] Before Fort Duquesne on the 9th June.

Douglas, and *Portland*, Captain Baird, from England with the outward bound Turkey trade and a storeship for Minorca. By these ships I received orders from the Admiralty dated the 27th August to seize all French ships and send them to some British port. (This was a bold but very wrong, injudicious and impudent step of Lord Holland's, and will one day or other be a precedent for a stroke that will cost us very dear.) Captain Douglas and I exchanged the convoys, he was to proceed down again with mine, and I went up with those he had brought, and therefore took Captain Baird of the *Portland* under my orders. I was to go up as high as Candia with the Turkey ships. We parted in the evening in very bad weather, and the two convoys each went their respective ways. The next day I saw a sail and make the *Portland's* signal to chace her, who soon brought her to me, being a very large French ship from Marseilles bound to Martinico. We put people on board him and sent him in to Mahon the 16th, and went in myself. We sealed up the prize's hatchways, and the *Portland* sailed for Italy the 19th with the trade, and the 22nd the Commodore appeared off, who confirmed my orders by Mr. Douglas, and I sailed the next day.

The 29th I took a French pollacre in my way up from Alexandria to Malta. I took her with me. The 2nd November I was off Cape St. Angelo, and the 4th my boats took another French pollacre from Smyrna. The next day I parted with the Turkey convoy, there being no ships of force in these seas and I determined to continue cruising a few days. The 5th I fell in with and took a French ship from Smyrna to Marseilles being the *La Mariane d'Esperance*, a very rich one she was. The 8th the wind being very hard westerly I bore away for the island of Argentiera[1] which is a better road than Milo, as you can get out at all weathers and there are three passages, whereas Milo is a very fine bay but you cannot get out with any wind. I arrived at 2 in the afternoon of the 8th. I found a Dutch man-of-war there with a convoy, and between the main of the island, where the town of Argentiera is, which is a walled one on the summit of it, and a little low island on the larboard side, there were several sail of French ships whom I soon fired at and sent my boats to take possession of, there being no fort here nor any kind of government. Only in the village I saw a French flag flying, which proved to be in the French Consul's house. There were only Greeks in the town. Our Vice-Consul, whose name is Leonardo, is a Greek, he came off to me and brought

[1] Now called Kimolos, one of the Cyclades, three miles N.E. of Milo.

some Turks who solicited their properties that was in the ships. In short this day I put men on board the prizes, and as I could not obey my orders by carrying these all down with me, I determined to ransom some of them, and to do everything I could to satisfy the Turks.

The next morning the Greeks sent two of their chiefs and five of their *papas* or chief priests to me in the name of the town to present the keys of the town to me and to ask my protection against the cruisers of Malta, who annoy them greatly. The French Consul came on board of me and wrote me a demand of these ships, being found, he said, under the Turks' protection, and no declaration of war, but I cleared up all that to him, not seeing any right the Turks had to give protection where the inhabitants was obliged to seek it from those who came there. The day after being the King's birthday, I dressed my ship and entertained all the chief Greeks on board. In the afternoon the Dutch captain and officers came to see me and I returned his visit next day. I sent away an express to our Ambassador at Constantinople by way of Smyrna with all that had passed, lest the French should misrepresent it and put us ill with the Turks. My letter, I found afterwards, had the desired effect with Mr. Porter our Ambassador,[1] tho' not with the Turks, whom my old friend Monsieur de Vergennes had worked up against this proceeding, and in short the Porte demanded the restitution of these vessels, which some months afterwards I was by an order from the Admiralty obliged to comply with, and, as most of these were afterwards (as will be seen) left at Minorca by Commodore Edgcumbe when that place was taken by the French, I was much out of pocket by this event, as I was obliged to pay for those I had ransomed here for goods, as I lost those goods at Mahon.

The 13th a Tripoline cruiser came in here, whose captain was a French renegado. His name was Sicar, a famous man. He came on board and wanted several stores and things. There was a drunken dispute happened on shore between the Dutch and Tripolines; both parties came next morning to me as mediator, several having been wounded on both sides, and I obliged the Tripoline to ask the Dutchman pardon publickly by saluting and punishing his people, and so ended that affair. He was very troublesome, too, in the town, but we got him away.

I was very tired of staying, and sailed the 16th with a scanty wind and all the prizes, as did the Dutch. The next day a very

[1] Sir James Porter, Ambassador to the Porte 1746–62.

hard gale of wind obliged me to bear away again for Argentiera; where the Dutch went I know not. As soon as I returned the Greek chiefs came on board and told me they had sacrificed for me when the bad weather came on, and prayed God for us in return to all the charities I had given at the island. The 20th the wind was northerly and fine weather, I sailed again, and charming it was to go among all these islands that once was the seat of empire and the envy of the world. But the weather soon grew bad again and obliged me to return a third time to Argentiera. Whilst I remained here I went all over the island. I went to Milo, to Zifanti, and about. The Dutch I found was put into Milo.

The 25th we had fine weather and a northerly wind and I sailed again, and soon got out of the Archipelago. I took two prizes more in my way down to Malta, but was so reduced now that I could pursue no more. I was obliged to watch with my master watch and watch till I arrived at Malta the 3rd, for which place I was obliged to bear away for, being quite wore out having been up in bad weather three nights running, and lost company with one of the prizes. I got into Malta in the afternoon, and the Consul, Mr. Dodsworth, came to the pratiqua-house to me as I could not be out of quarantine.

Malta is a very fine and very strong port; the Maltese are all governed by French consuls, and are in fact a French arsenal in time of war, neither more or less. I had strange accounts from the Consul of them, tho' the Grand Master is a Portuguese and ought naturally to be inclined to us, but he cannot control. His name is Don Manuel de Pinto. His Eminence sent the Conde de Ponte, who was Commissary of the Health Office, to me the next day with compliments and excuses for not being able to let me on shore. Here I learnt of Mr. Fox being Secretary of State in the room of Sir Thomas Robinson and other changes in consequence. The 5th several chevaliers of the Order came off in boats and accompanied me in mine all round the harbour to show me as much as they could in this way of it, and they were personally very civil to me. I saw all the gallies and their ships. They have creeks called Port l'Anglois, Port Francois, and so on.

The Consul told me that it was given out industriously by the French that the Grand Master had detained me here on account of the French ships I had taken without any declaration of war, so I determined to go out for a few days to prove the falseness of this and that it might not be spread. I therefore told the Conde de Ponte that I was going to sea to look for one of my prizes that had separated, and accordingly sailed to the astonishment of everyone, as I found people really believed I was detained. I was no sooner out than I saw a sail, which soon after I took, being a Frenchman who was come from Smyrna going to Marseilles I took her about twelve leagues from the island. The next day the weather continued so bad that I bore away for Malta with the prize. In the afternoon I went to the Health Office to meet the Consul; by him I found the French party was highly offended at this proceeding and was doing all they could to make me restore this vessel. I told several of the *commandeurs* that if they had seen this vessel they should have sent to me when I was going out that a French vessel was off and desired me not to touch her, or else to detain me till she came in, but this vessel was at such a distance and I saw her so long after I was out, there could be no excuse for their claim. . . .

In the evening I received at the Health Office the Conde de Ponte and the Chevalier d'Argent, the two commissaries of the Health Office, sent by the Grand Master to me with this message: "Monsieur, son éminence nous a ordonné de vous faire part que Monsieur le chevalier de Bocage, Ministre de France, a rèclamé la prise que vous avoit fait hier, et puis de scavoir votre rèponse là dessus; mais que son éminence ne faisoit là dedans que vous donner part de ce que c'est passé avec Monsieur de Bocage, et que votre rèponse suffisoit et que son éminence n'entre pas plus là dedans."

My answer was: "Messieurs, je suis très obligé de l'attention de son éminence; je serai très fâché de donner aucune juste occasion aux religions de Malte de regretter la reception que le vaisseau du roy mon maître trouvoit ici; mais je suis très supris de la rèclame qui a fait le ministre de France. Je suit bien aise que ce n'est pas de la part du Grand Maître. Je regarde le prise légallement fait, un bâtiment si eloigné de votre port. Ainsi, Messieurs, le Ministre de France peut ètre assuré que je ne la rendrai pas."

The Conde de Ponte afterwards assured me the Grand Master had nothing to do in it, that I was entirely master to keep her or not as I thought proper, he only let me know what the French Minister had done, with other hints to that purpose. Afterwards the chevalier de Breteuil, brother to Madame de Breteuil who I had known in France, came down to the Health Office, and in discoursing I explained to him the affairs of this vessel, and they all agreed that in a port so open to all passers-by as this was, a man-of-war might be kept in for ever if detained for every vessel seen off. In short nothing more was said of it.

I found myself obliged to ransom some of these vessels as I could not carry them to Minorca. I put the prisoners on shore to the *lazaretta*. As I could not go on shore I was amused with making signs to a very pretty young woman who was daughter to a great merchant, and lived at a corner house directly opposite my ship.

The next day, the 9th, we had the sad news of the fatal earthquake that happened at Lisbon, with many of the particulars of that misfortune, and that it had been felt in many places of Europe, and even across the ocean to Barbary. Machinesse[1] in Barbary suffered greatly at the same time. These are frightful events, and ought to inspire reflections that should mend the lives of individuals in order not to deserve such chastisements from Providence.[2]

I had several slaves deserted and swam off to me; all those that had not stole anything or done any crime I protected; those [who had], I gave up. I ransomed three vessels, and then begun a correspondence with this young lady, whose name was Margherita Carcas. We continued this correspondence tho' I could never get on shore.

The 17th I got out of Malta with my prizes, having been obliged to put in once before, and got well down to the westward. I got into Cagliari on the island of Sardinia the 21st, and there I found my two prizes that had separated (Mr. Foulks and Mr. Purdy)[3] were sailed the 4th for Mahon. The 22nd I saluted the King of Sardinia's fort with seventeen guns on assurance from the Viceroy of the same number being returned, which was done, and I went on shore and found the Viceroy's coach ready for me. I went to wait of his Excellency, the Conte de Trinita, who had about forty officers with him. I dined there, and he pressed me much to lay at the palace, where he had an apartment ready for me. He told me all the news there was and confirmed to me that terrible

[1] Meknes.

[2] This terrible earthquake, which destroyed more than two-thirds of Lisbon, occurred on 1st November, when the churches were thronged for the festivals of All Saints' Day. The destruction of the Royal Palace, the Patriarch's Palace, and twenty convents, must have been a cruel shock to Hervey.

[3] Peter Foulks, First Lieutenant, and Andrew Purdy, master's mate.

account of Lisbon, which made me very uneasy for my friends there. I sailed the 24th with my prizes and had very bad weather the whole passage. However I got into Mahon harbour on New Year's Day, having been obliged to lay one night in the road, and here I found the Commodore, but no declaration of war yet.

I had many rich and valuable prizes now in here; we sealed up all their papers and hatchways etc, and laid them in safety. The 4th January, the Commodore sailed with the *Louisa* and *Portland*, and left me to refit, and then to follow him according to my rendezvous. I diverted myself very well at Mahon with my friends of Cornwallis's Regiment, and was lucky enough to get in with a very pretty girl, daughter of Smallridge that kept the tavern. She and I agreed very well, and I kept her all the while, and a sweet pretty creature she was, so that she engrossed my whole time here, and as I lay at the house we had no interruption. I hove down the ship here and prepared for sea as soon as I could, expecting a war every minute.

We received now intelligence from all parts that the French were meditating the taking of Minorca, and were assembling a great fleet and army at Toulon for this expedition. This was so confirmed on all sides, and the island in so little condition to receive such an enemy, that the General, Blakeney, thought it was proper to call a grand council of war, and for that purpose sent to me, as commanding officer then in the port, to meet at it, which I agreed to, after settling that I should sit next to the General, with precedence of the colonels whose commissions were junior to mine as Captain of a man-of-war, and to have the honours of the guards etc. We met the 5th February:

General Blakeney, *Lieutenant-Governor of the Island.*

Hon. Captain Hervey	Lieutenant-Colonel Jefferies
Lieutenant-Colonel Rufane	Lieutenant-Colonel Thorne
Major Pool	Bastide, *Chief Engineer*
Flight, *Captain of Artillery*	Major Innes, *secretary*

Here I refer to the original minutes of this famous Council taken on the spot.[1]

This Council met the 5th about 11, and continued so to the 22nd, almost every morning and evening. I was also employed in fitting my ship, getting all the King's stores on board one of my

[1] Appendix B.

prizes for security and to be ready to be sent away if the French came, and all the prizes in readiness to go to Gibraltar. The council of war sitting and making resolutions on resolutions, but none ever put in execution from the great indolence of the General and his ill-judged tenderness to the inhabitants, who were all this time betraying us to the French, inviting them over, and making ready to assist them when they came. We had good accounts of the French forces and their designs, and yet nothing was done here. The island was in a very bad condition for want of stores, of officers, of men, of provisions, and in short had been much neglected, and tho' continual expresses were sent home, yet such was the neglect at home no assistance came till too late. I will answer for it had the ministry even sent one regiment out, and the officers to those that were here,[1] the French would not have dared to have attacked it. In short I was so wearied with constantly proposing things to this council which was ever agreed to and never executed, that as soon as my ship was ready I determined to sail for intelligence. However I determined to speak my sentiments plainly to this council, whom I thought very remiss, and therefore after having, as the original papers show, met day after day, I told the council I would go over to Villa-Franca myself to get what intelligence I could, and accordingly sailed the 25th, and got to Villa-Franca the 29th and found Captain Noel had been sailed a few days for Mahon, and the packet for Leghorn to join Mr. Edgcumbe who was still loitering away there, and had left me an order to join Mr. Edgcumbe at Leghorn; but I continued my pursuit as knowing it most for His Majesty's service.

The 2nd March I went to Nice, and received from General Paterson a very circumstantial account of the French armament and intentions. I wrote every particular home to the Secretary of State and to the Admiralty, and then sailed the 3rd. I arrived at Mahon the 10th, and a council was called. Captain Noel was there. I gave my report to the General and the board with ample intelligence of the preparations making at Toulon, and all which are said to be against this island. I was very circumstantial in all the intelligence as to ships, regiments, transports, general officers, etc, etc. I told them I could not but rely upon the intelligence; that I thought it was against this island, and wished to know

[1] Absent were: Lord Tyrawly, the Governor; the Colonels of the four regiments of the garrison, of whom three had seats in the Commons; nine other officers and nineteen newly-commissioned ensigns.

whether our former resolutions were put in execution, and desired some method would be found out of obliging the inhabitants to put their part in execution. This Colonel Rufane seconded strongly, and I received the thanks of the council for my diligence, which they came to a unanimous resolution for.[1]

The 12th another council was called. Captain Noel and myself had been employed to get a boom ready to lay across the harbour, and had prepared everything for sending away all the stores, careening gear and prizes. But I found the same remissness as ever in the General to make his preparations, so that I was resolved they should know my sentiments fully, especially as Colonel Jefferies and Colonel Rufane was of my sentiments but would not speak out. So when there had been some proofs brought to the council of the inhabitants not having complied with the orders given out I begged the council would let me give them my reasons for a motion I must make, and said:—

"The time draws near to guard against which we have been so often summoned by the Lieutenant-Governor, and now, gentlemen, I think our loyalty to His Majesty, our obedience to you, Sir, the Lieutenant-Governor and Commander-in-chief here, and our own justification calls very earnestly for our most serious and deliberate reflections in this situation, an open and sincere opinion on the result of those reflections, and a most speedy and punctual execution of all the orders that is thought necessary to be given in consequence of these consultations. We have had very often the honour of being summoned here on this occasion, and I have observed with great pleasure and admiration the General's attention to whatever any one of us has thought proper to propose, or give his reason for objecting to; and with equal satisfaction I have found the General ready for giving out his necessary orders, and I will therefore leave you gentlemen to judge with what concern it is that I have seen and continue to know the little vigilance that has been used in the execution of those orders by every degree of people among the inhabitants. Sir, I look upon every man here responsible for his conduct and liable to be called to an account if any accident happens to this island, which has cost so much obtaining and such infinite sums to maintain to the Crown. And therefore I shall never confine my opinion to my profession when I think it can be of any service to give a hint here towards the promoting anything out of it. I therefore declare, Sir,

[1] At home on 11th March, Byng, now Admiral of the Blue, was commissioned to fit out ten ships of the line for the Mediterranean.

that I know it to be a just, as well as universal observation, that the natives of this island have not complied with their duty as subjects in any degree. Your great tenderness, Sir, as Lieutenant-Governor, ever shewed them and your pressing speech on the beginning of this alarm to them, (now six weeks past), has had no effect on them. I leave you, Sir, to judge if your own expectations and desires of them, much less those of the council, have in any degree been answered. Have the Magistrates shewn their activity in putting your orders in execution? Have the people of any degree shewn a desire of being employed in defence of the island? Have the clergy been known to preach up and propagate to the people a spirit of heartily joining His Majesty's troops, and giving all assistance cheerfully? Have they not done the reverse? Have the principal inhabitants and those who have received mark of your indulgence set any example of the just sense of their happiness under His Majesty's protection and your mild government?

"Indeed, Sir, I know not, nor have not heard, of any one step taken by any one inhabitant that seems to comply with your request to them or to shew their duty as subjects to their Royal Master. Sure, gentlemen, if this be allowed, how much more essential is it, how much more justifiable are we, and how much more necessary will it be thought to take such measures as shall without any regard to the natives best answer the sole view and end of our meeting here, which is the defence of the island and easing as much as possible His Majesty's troops in the execution of their part of it and providing in every degree for their welfare and plenty, on which alone any dependance is to be had. Sir, let us speak out. Let us cast off this ill-timed and ill-bestowed tenderness towards these inconsiderate and, I fear, these treacherous people. Therefore I do desire that orders should be immediately sent to the commanding officers of all the out-detachments to summon before them the Chief Magistrates of the *terminos*[1] they are in, and to tell them that you do expect, Sir, that such a number of beasts are to be kept continually in the spot they reside, to be ready at a moment's warning for any service the commanding officer shall have for them for the service, and that for the present execution of removing the baggage or any other labour for the beasts of burthen, additional ones may be employed, that the number I propose to be in the town with the troops be ever ready to accompany them.

[1] Administrative districts.

"Next, Sir, and principally, as we are now very short of money, and what is expected may be delayed or intercepted, and the very necessary remittances are already out for the daily support of the troops, what may be the consequence of a want of a military chest when blocked up? Intelligence may be wanted and must be paid for; services may be required that must be encouraged and ought to be rewarded; the native labour must be paid in coin or they will not attend; many other exigencies will be found requisite and may be lost for want of money, and I believe no one ever heard of an army without a military chest. But, Sir, as yet no money is thought of, and the time elapsed that we might expect the enemy to land, from our intelligence, I therefore move the council Sir, that a military chest be instantly levied, and if the principal inhabitants will not by way of loan to the Crown furnish a sufficient sum on this occasion at the island interest of 8 per cent., that then some tax be immediately levied to obtain a military chest."

Colonel Rufane and Colonel Jefferies seconded this, then 'twas debated which way to raise it. It was resolved at last that the principal inhabitants attend the council of war Monday 14th to lend a sum of 30,000 dollars[1] on the island interest of 8 per cent., and every man putting his own seal upon his money bag, but if not made use of to be returned in the same specie with the interest from the day paid in.

The 14th I kept urging the council to put the island under martial law, yet nothing was done that could in the least help the defence of the island. I spoke to the different members of the council about this strange remissness. They most of them agreed to it, except just the poor old General's tools, and I found there were two or three who were afraid that the estates and houses about St. Philip's would suffer if this took place, and therefore they rather run a risk of the whole.

The inhabitants appeared; I delivered in an account of every principal inhabitant of the island, and what they were each reckoned worth at a moderate computation of land, stock and money.[2] They were called in, and I was desired by the General and the council to explain to them what was required, but they shuffled and prevaricated so much that 'twas easy to see they meant to do nothing at all, and I plainly told them so, and urged the General to raise money on them.

[1] £6,750.

[2] His detailed account is not published; he reckoned the "Minorcines" could afford to lend 77,600 dollars, and the Jews 12,000.

The 17th, Mr. Edgcumbe being arrived from Leghorn the 15th, he was present, and I was desired to continue of the council. The inhabitants came in again, and the whole amount of their subscription was Cittadella, 2,493 dollars; Alayor, 283 dollars; Mahon, 4,451 dollars; the Jews, 4,000 dollars. I represented this as indecent trifling with the Crown and the present critical situation of the island, and that methods should be used to oblige them to comply, and at the same time to learn the motives of this conduct. Then I desired the clergy to be sent for to talk with them, but to as little effect.

The 18th the harbour's defence was considered by the council; two fireships were proposed, and a boom. By this means Lieutenant Paul Ourry got a command, and Lieutenant Phillips.[1] I moved that all the prizes might be sent down to Gibraltar, and all the King's careening stores embarked ready to send away.

The 22nd the clergy brought in a return of their loan—400 dollars. I then moved for the clergy to be sent off the island, excepting just as many as would serve each parish. In short I was tired of seeing the shameful inactivity of those who ought to have put the island in a better state of defence by breaking up the roads, demolishing the town of St. Philip's, and driving in all the beasts of burthen, and retard the enemy all in our power. This evening I was ordered off the island for seven days to give notice of the enemy's approach, tho' it had been proved useless at the council. The fact was the General wanted to get rid of me out of the council now. I therefore sailed the next morning, and kept off the island all these days with very bad weather. Nothing appearing, I bore away the 28th and got in about noon, and they had had no news since I left them, nor was anything done of any kind towards putting in execution all the orders of the council. I received orders to go to Villa-Franca or Leghorn for intelligence. I should have sailed next day but the wind right in prevented me, so that I could not go out till the 5th April, and opened my orders off Fornelles.

The 10th I made Leghorn, and got to anchor in the evening. I sent in, but had no news. The next day I went on shore to the

[1] Paul Henry Ourry (a Captain in Feb. 1757 and later Commissioner at Plymouth) and Henry John Phillips (Captain in January 1757) were respectively First and Second Lieutenants of Commodore Edgcumbe's ship the *Deptford*; their first commands were the *Proserpine* and *Blast*, both subsequently lost in the harbour.

lazaretto. I delivered to Mr. Howe bills for 6,000 livres[1] to pay Mr. Porter or his order for the ransom of those vessels I stopped at Argenteira, by order of the Admiralty. By letters here I found Mr. Byng was coming in the Mediterranean with Mr. West and ten ships, but I feared he would be too late to hinder the descent, and too weak to conquer their fleet.[2] The next day we had news the French were sailed the 10th from Toulon. I sailed that afternoon. Off the island of Hyères I found French letters on board a tartane which I opened and found the French sailed the 13th, with a whole detail of their fleet for Mahon. I got into Villa-Franca the evening and had it confirmed—twelve sail of the line, four frigates, 180 transports with 12,000 men, all under the Duke de Richelieu and their Admiral, Monsieur de la Galissonnière. It was amazing to all Italy that as long as this armament had been fitting and declared for Minorca that England was so long without sending ships out, after all the intelligence that had been sent them, both by the General and myself, two months ago. Had the fleet sailed from England a month sooner, the French would never, I may venture to say, have landed at Minorca. This is a fatal and dishonourable stroke to England, for which the leading ministers deserve to lose their heads.

I went to Nice next day to consult with General Paterson. There I saw Lady Primrose and Miss Pultney. I wrote to the Admiralty, to Mr. Fox and my Brother Bristol full accounts of all this.[3] I sailed the next day with Captain Ourry in the settee[4] he had been sent out in to get intelligence. I was ill with the rheumatism and took James' powders, and sailed on for Mahon. The 19th I was in such pain in the night that I was blooded in the night and lost twelve ounces, and remained ill in bed all the 20th. I

[1] About £250; he wrote to the Secretary of the Admiralty "my being obliged to make good the sum with £97 out of my own pocket as they overvalued the effects they paid their ransoms in, is what is the least concern to me"; for the happy outcome, see p. 226.

[2] Byng had sailed from St. Helen's on 6th April.

[3] Hervey's recollection is at fault here—perhaps purposely. In his letter of 17th April, which reached London on 7th May, he gave the French fleet as only ten of the line (one 80, two 74s, six 64s and a 50) and five small frigates; in fact, as he says above, there were twelve of the line (one 84, four 74s, five 64s and two 50s) and one of the five frigates was of 46 guns. Henry Fox, seeking solace in this inaccurate intelligence, wrote to Newcastle "There is bad as well as good in [Hervey's letter]. But if its contents are true as to ships of war, Bing is undoubtedly superior to La Galissonnière." *Add. MSS.* 32,864.

[4] A small, decked vessel with a long sharp prow, two or three masts, lateen rigged, and very fast.

remained so the 21st, 22nd and 23rd. The 24th I prepared my letters to be sent in by Captain Ourry in any creek of the land, and was uneasy at not making the land this day, but it was very thick. I continued all night under an easy sail.

Sunday 25th, at 4 in the morning I tacked in for to make the land, and immediately made the island about five leagues off, and saw several sail of large ships all round us. They chaced me as soon as the day broke, and I stood away from them. I saw the French Admiral's ship plain making signals. Three ships continued chacing me. I cast off the settee and Captain Ourry went away from me. I told him to stand a different way from me. I told him my scheme of going to Majorca, and he told me he would endeavour to get into the island. By the time these ships had chaced me several hours they perceived they gained little or nothing on me, and the next morning I was clear of all of them, therefore I stood away to the northward determining to go to windward of the island, and so to Majorca and try if I could get a boat over from thence to the Commodore, if he was not got out. The French were all off Fornelles, so that I judged they had landed there. The next day I felt a violent pain in my left great toe, which I found was the gout got down there. In the morning we perceived a large ship in chace of us. I got on deck and, tho' foggy, I saw the ship was of two decks. I made ready to engage. It blew very fresh in squalls, and as I found he came up with me he began to reef his topsails, I took that opportunity and threw out my top-gallant sails, and by the great time he was reefing I got such a start of him that he never after got near me, till night he gave over chace. The next day I made Majorca, and took a French tartane loaded for the French fleet with twenty bullocks which we detained, and lived well on. I got into the great bay of Palma on Majorca the 29th at 5 in the afternoon, and saluted the fort, lay about half a mile from the town, and was returned gun for gun.

I sent on shore an officer to the Marquis del Cayro, Viceroy, and found on my officer's return our Consul, Mr. Scot, was a poor old man not able to move from age, and the Vice-consul a fellow of the island in the French interest. I here found the Duke de Richelieu had landed the 19th at Cittadella, and under concert with several of the principal inhabitants of that place, that they were preparing for the seige of St. Philip's, having met with no opposition in conquering the rest of the island. I found the people here almost all glad of this attack, altho' they hate the French, and yet astonished at our supineness in England, for which I could make no defence but wish the ministers brought to a scaffold.

I found myself rather better the 30th, but could not go on shore. Various was the reports here daily.

The next day, 1st May, there was a report brought me of two French men-of-war being off cruising for me that came from the other side of the island. The 2nd, Monsieur la Rivière, a Protestant from Mahon, came off to me and told me that a fisherman told him that in the night a French man-of-war's boat boarded them and asked several questions about my ship, and whether I lay moored or single. I also learnt here that the Duke de Richelieu had imprisoned several inhabitants in our interest, Doctor Creux, Doctor Colveran, Doctor Gumillier, Doctor Bennet, and that John Saura and all that family was every day with the Duke de Richelieu. I this day sent Mr. Spicer[1] away to Barcelona with my letters in a settee I manned for that purpose. This day I heard that Mr. Edgcumbe had got away from Mahon with the men-of-war, and had left Captain Scrope of the *Dolphin* there with several men, that all the prizes and all the stores were left in the harbour. The 3rd I went on shore to wait of the Viceroy, who sent his coaches for me and received me in great form and state, was very civil to me, and made me offers of all the refreshment there was, and said he was determined to maintain a very strict neutrality between the two nations. (How well he kept up to this will be soon seen). I told his Excellency I was very well satisfied of the entire neutrality now of the Court of Spain, but that I could not but comment I had seen great proofs of the reverse here, for that every partiality was shewed to the French that was possible; that everything was sent to Minorca they could want, such as horses and other necessaries; that the Spanish xebeques, I observed, was employed continually for the French; that a great partiality had been shewn here with regard to quarantine, the French vessels from Minorca having now immediate pratiqua when all my Master's subjects coming from that island were made to lay a months; that the rigour shewn to English masters of vessels in not letting them come in their boats to speak to me at a distance was unheard of, for, suppose I had directions to order them all away to another place, how could they obey without they had liberty to come within hail to receive their orders? He only answered in very polite terms that the Health Office had

[1] William Spicer, a master's mate in the *Phoenix*; he became a Lieutenant in 1758.

its forms which they must comply with and he could not interfere with, and repeated several times that he would observe a strict neutrality; that what the French wanted he could supply them with, as he would us. I told him that was very easy to say, as our people could obtain nothing, being besieged and blockaded. I then asked his Excellency if the Majorca xebeques employed as pilots and carrying over horses and mules for the French, going with their despatches, carrying provisions and everything required of them, was a proof of their neutrality. The General asked me to dinner, but I refused, and left him soon after.

This town seems pretty clean for a Spanish town, and the people very civil. I offered 400 dollars for a boat to go over to Mahon with a letter. The 4th I went off in the evening early, being still weak and tired. I fitted out the tartane I had taken, and sent Mr. Spicer to Barcelona with my letters to the Admiralty. Don John Troyols came off to me in the afternoon; they told me there were five sail of French men-of-war in Alcudia Bay yesterday, no news from Minorca but common reports; every vessel that came in was examined at the pratiqua-house with centuries to keep people off, that we might not learn what was going on at Mahon.

The next morning the 5th at daybreak, two French men-of-war, *L'Hippopotame* of 64 guns, Monsieur Marquezan, and *La Gracieuse* of 30,[1] appeared cruising in the bay close to me, and in an hour the *Gracieuse* anchored close to me. In the evening the *Gracieuse* got under sail again, and both kept plying off and on about the bay, and sending their boats on shore frequently. I kept now going on shore every day to walk of a morning and evening to recover my strength. The 7th several of the French officers rowed round my ship. The next day I went to see the Viceroy and told him I was sorry to be so troublesome, but that I now thought it my duty to represent to his Excellency that as the two French men-of-war had now remained four days in the situation he saw, that I could not help desiring to know from his Excellency on what footing the French looked on themselves with regard to this port; that one being anchored close to me, the other cruising within my buoys, that I was quite blocked up by them in this neutral port; that before the arrival of these ships I could have lain further out and stopped several French vessels, but would

[1] Usually rated 50 and 26 respectively; M. de Rochemore commanded the former, and M. de Marquizan the latter.

not offend the neutrality of the port on any account; that I desired to know, if I wanted to sail, what measures I was to take with the one under sail in the bay. The General told me he did not approve of their conduct, that he had sent to them to let them know he should look on me as a Spanish man-of-war there, and give me every protection, but he begged of me not to think of moving, as he could not in that case answer for their conduct. He was much on the reserve, and as I knew there had been many mules shipped off again last night for Minorca, I determined he should see I knew it. However I would not exasperate him too much in the present situation of things, as I thought it not for my Master's service, and as he asked me to dine with him to-morrow I accepted. Don John Troyols attended me everywhere with his own coach.

The 9th I found that Duke de Richelieu had issued a proclamation recalling all the Minorcines on pain of forfeiture of their lands and cattle, and this was read at the pratiqua-house here, which I complained of. I found the French kept all their transports and store vessels at Fornelles and the squadron off Mahon harbour to prevent succours getting in. I went on shore and dined with the Viceroy and his lady, who was very ugly, about fifty, had been maid of honour to the Queen Dowager of Spain. We were only eight people, and I thought but an indifferent dinner, and few attendants.

The next day an English snow[1] came in from Barcelona, and luckily escaped the French men-of-war. By him I had news of Captain Ourry's getting safe into Barcelona, but no news of my own tartane. I was surprised that in the present critical situation of things the Consul of Barcelona sent no letter of news or any kind of intelligence to the Consul here, but I found that they were allowed nothing for their letters, and the Admiralty refused paying the postage of any packets sent. By all reports we heard on the 11th that Admiral Byng was certainly in his way out hither with a fleet, and therefore I determined to push out the first strong easterly wind to endeavour to meet with him.[2] This day I sent a memorial

[1] A small vessel, rather similar to a brig, with fore-, main- and try-sail masts.

[2] Byng had arrived at Gibraltar the 2nd May, had written home a despondent despatch full of forebodings and complaints about the dockyard, and had sailed for Minorca on the 8th. He should have taken on board a battalion of the Gibraltar garrison which was ordered from home to be thrown into St. Philip's, but a pessimistic council of war of land-officers had refused to part with it, as they were advised a landing on the island would be impossible. Byng therefore had on board only Lord Robert Bertie's Regiment, which was serving

to the Viceroy (a copy of which is in my letter-book) to represent the manner of the French men-of-war blockading this port. Soon after I had sent it, the *Hippopotame* stood in and anchored a mile from Porto-Pin Point, which is about two leagues within the North-West point of this bay. I was ill, and could not wait of the Viceroy, but sent him a memorial on this point by my Lieutenant, which he only answered by saying as the French were out of reach of his cannon he could only represent their conduct to his Court, to whom he would send my memorial. In the morning of the 12th an English snow coming round Point-Pin and in the Bay was attacked by one of the French men-of-war till she struck her colours, and the Frenchman sent his boats on board and took her and hoisted French colours over the English. On this I went (ill as I was) to the Viceroy, and delivered in another memorial, complaining of this fact committed in the bay not a cannon-shot from me. The Viceroy told me if the French brought in the vessel he would seize her. I argued with him much on the conduct of the French, and he repeated his promise to to seize the vessel if she came in, but tho' the French man-of-war brought in the vessel that evening, yet the General only wrote to me a letter, telling me he could not comply with his promise yesterday, but had put two Spaniards on board till further orders from his Court.

In the night the *Gracieuse* had sailed, and the 14th the *Hippopotame* was off Cape Dragonera making signals all day. I concluded they must have had some intelligence of the approach of our fleet. The next I went to the General and gave him letters to send over to Sir Benjamin Keene with duplicates of them I sent to Barcelona. The 16th my tartane came and Captain Ourry in her with letters from Barcelona, by whom I learned our fleet was at Gibraltar. I went directly to the Viceroy and told him as I had observed a strict neutrality since I was in his port, that I now intended to sail, that I would go out in the morning, and if the *Gracieuse* came near me I was determined to engage her, which I hoped to do in sight of his town to-morrow. He replied that ship would be too strong for me, 36 guns and 300 men. I replied we would try. I complained to his Excellency of the partiality of the Captain of the Port. Don Juan Troyols dined with me and saw my ship all prepared for

---

as part of the complement of his ships in place of the proper Marines left behind at Portsmouth. He also carried small drafts for the regiments already on the island.

action, but before we had dined we observed the *Gracieuse* sailing with all she could crowd and making many signals. Soon after this from our masthead we saw two sail standing in, and at 5 we saw seventeen sail. I rowed out and met the *Experiment*, who gave me the account of Mr. Byng being those ships in sight and that he came here for intelligence.

XII

THE BATTLE OF MAHON

May 1756

THE next morning, the 17th May, having but very little winds, I went off with my boat to the Admiral and my ship went between Majorca and Cabrera. The Admiral expressed great satisfaction at my being with him, and told me a ship was coming out of England for me. Rear-Admiral West and most of the Captains were on board, and my friend Gardiner was the Admiral's Captain. I gave the Admiral all the intelligence I could of the situation of the enemy off Minorca, and what progress they had made on the island. Lord Effingham, Lord Robert Bertie, General Stuart and Colonel Cornwallis, with several officers, were in the fleet to be thrown into St. Philip's. I told the Admiral at last that I was extremely sorry to see him so thinly attended, that I thought two or three more ships would have done the thing completely, and that it was an object that deserved this preference. He told me 'twas worse than I saw, for his ships being almost all the worst of the fleet, that even they were not manned, that the troops of Lord Robert Bertie's regiment, which were to be landed at Mahon, made up the compliment now of the fleet; such was the situation of this fleet, and that his instructions were to secure Gibraltar as well as relieve Minorca. In short, Lord Anson, the First Lord of the Admiralty, only sent the very worst of the fleet whilst he kept the rest cruising at home, no hospital-ship, no fireship, no storeship, nor any tender, and if the Mediterranean squadron had been cut off and kept into Mahon, as it might have been, where then could he have shewn himself? What a reflection on Government!

But here are now the squadrons as they are off Minorca:[1]

[1] For convenience the names of the British captains have been added to Hervey's table; he was junior to all save Baird, Everitt, Lloyd, and Gilchrist. The ships of Edgcumbe's original Mediterranean squadron are indicated by

BRITISH				FRENCH		
	Guns	*Men*			*Guns*	*Men*
Ramillies	90	780	Admiral Byng Arthur Gardiner	*Foudroyant* (M. de la Galissonnière)	84	950
Culloden	74	600	Henry Ward			
Buckingham	68	535	Rear-Adm. West Michael Everitt	*La Couronne* *Le Guerrier*	74 74	800 800
Lancaster	66	520	George Edgcumbe	*Le Téméraire*	74	800
Trident	64	500	Philip Durell	*Le Redoubtable*	74	800
Intrepid	64	480	James Young	*L'Hippopotame*	64	600
Captain	64	480	Charles Catford	*Le Fier*	64	600
Revenge	64	480	Frederick Cornwall	*Le Triton* *Le Lion*	64 64	600 600
Kingston	60	400	William Parry	*Le Constant*	64	600
Defiance	60	400	Thomas Andrews	*Le Sage*	64	600
**Princess Louisa*	56	400	Thomas Noel	*L'Orphée*	64	600
**Portland*	48	300	Patrick Baird			
Frigates						
**Deptford*	48	280	John Amherst	*La Juno*	46	300
**Chesterfield*	40	250	William Lloyd	*La Rose*	36	250
**Phoenix*	20	160	Augustus Hervey	*La Gracieuse*	30	250
**Dolphin*	20	160	Lieutenant Benjamin Marlow, *acting*	*La Topaze* *La Nymphe*	24 24	250 200
**Experiment*	20	160	James Gilchrist			
	926	6,885			982	9,600

The morning early the 18th I went on board of Admiral Byng and did lament his not having more force, when he told me that Lord Anson sent all the best ships cruising with his favourites, and, all he could do, he could not obtain two or three more, tho' he might with ease have brought them. He ordered the next day the *Chesterfield* and *Dolphin* under my orders, and I was to endeavour to get a letter into St. Philip's if possible at daylight. Therefore I was within pistol-shot of the Lare of Mahon,[1] when it fell calm, and I got my boats to tow. The English colours were

asterisks. *L'Hippopotame* and *Le Fier* were in fact 50s; *Le Constant* should be *Le Content*; there are several other minor inaccuracies.

[1] Isla del Aire, off the S.E. end of Minorca.

still flying on the castle of St. Philip's, which the enemy were firing upon from all parts, and French colours on Cape Mola, and many other parts of the island. But soon after, the signal being made for the enemy's fleet, my signal was made on board the Admiral to return, which I obeyed, and found the fleet preparing for action. I then went and offered my service to the Admiral as a fireship, as my ship was old and that he had ne'er a one, and I had material on board with which I could make her one. He consented, and I prepared her accordingly. I put several men on board the *Revenge*, and several on board the *Deptford*. I fixed graplings everywhere, made a great quantity of shavings, picked oakum, dipped them in rosin, pitch, brimstone and gunpowder mixed, and twisted rope with these combustables all about my rigging and decks, which were scuttled. It came on foggy in the afternoon and scarce any wind, that we lost sight of the French, but in the night took some tartanes that were carrying out some piquets of soldiers to the French fleet.

The 20th we saw the French fleet about 7 in the morning, and a signal was made for all cruisers. About 10 a signal was made for the fleet to tack, which was to gain the wind of the enemy, and soon after a signal for the line of battle ahead. I then went on board the Admiral to wish him good success, receive my orders, and fix on the signal to be made from him for scuttling my decks and priming, and sent all my things and useless people on board a tender prepared for me. About 11 our fleet was all formed and standing towards the enemy, which were then sixteen sail, twelve appeared large and of the line, which then formed, and as they saw we had gained the wind they waited for us. Their evolutions were pretty and regular. Our fleet stretched out to the westward till the van was the length of their rear, then the Admiral made the signal for the fleet to tack together, which was performed at once by every ship except the *Portland*, who missed stays.[1] Our line was then much to windward of the enemy, about four miles I believe. The Admiral then made the signal for the ships that led the van to bear away, intending all should go down close to the French line slanting and regular, but the *Portland* and *Defiance* that led did not go down as the signal directed, tho' I repeated it three different times. The Admiral, perceiving this, found as he himself edged away that he had nothing for it but making the general signal to engage, as they were then about $2\frac{3}{4}$ miles from the French, and that everyone then would bear down on the ships of the

[1] i.e. failed to go about.

enemy's that fell to him. A few minutes after 2 this signal was made.[1] The Rear-Admiral and his second, Mr. Edgcumbe in the *Lancaster*, bore down upon their ships and engaged, tho' I thought at too great a distance. The ships in the van bore down but slowly to close the enemy. The Admiral in the centre was then going down and made the *Deptford's* signal to quit the line and lay by for a reserve, as we had twelve and twelve without her, but the *Kingston* (Parry) instead of closing the line left this vacancy and lay sometime with his main topsail to the mast. The *Culloden* also appeared to me a great way from the Admiral, and that the *Ramillies* was exposed to much fire when they began.

A little time after the Admiral began to engage I saw the *Intrepid* had lost her foretopmast, and very unfortunately was driving down upon the other ships astern, as they had no command of her head sails. But this accident making the *Revenge* and others back to avoid the *Intrepid*, this divided the Rear-Admiral's division and the Admiral for some minutes.[2] The ships ahead of the Admiral laid all aback, which obliged the Admiral to do the same for fear of being on board of them. The *Trident* also threw all into confusion by not bearing down with the Admiral at first, tho' often called to. This unlucky accident I look upon as the cause of this day's disgrace, if one may call it so, for the French, tho' superior, certainly avoided a close action. The Admiral made the signal for closing the line, and threw out all the sail he could as soon as the *Intrepid* was clear of him, and ordered the *Deptford* to supply the *Intrepid's* place, and the *Chesterfield* to lay by the *Intrepid*, but 'twas now easily perceived that the French ships wronged ours much in sailing, and kept edging away the whole time. I saw the French Admiral fire several shot at one of his own men-of-war which Mr. Byng had drove out of the line, and boats sent after her. By the time our van and rear were closed, the French had got a great way to leeward and ahead withall, and then the French put before the wind.[3] Our two leaders, the *Portland* and *Lancaster*, stood on with all their sail and was greatly separated

[1] See Plan I; these plans have been traced from original drawings by Hervey preserved among Henry Fox's papers at Melbury. He drew them about 26th June (see Appendix C, p. 322). No other plans made so soon after the action have come to light; they almost certainly show the *Ramillies* closer to the enemy than she ever was. For a contemporary anti-Byng plan see *Papers relating to the loss of Minorca*, edited by Admiral Richmond for the Navy Records Society.

[2] See Plan II.

[3] See Plan III.

from Mr. West, so much so that I was going to send to acquaint the Admiral with it, lest in the smoke he should not see it. The French body kept bearing away to join their ships to leeward and endeavour to rally them, for I think they had flown. But our ships in the van soon were disabled in their rigging and masts, tho' they kept a constant fire on the enemy. The Admiral kept all his sail out going after the enemy, but they outsailed him much, and he was then obliged to make the signal for his van to tack, that they might close him, or he would run a risk of losing them as night drew on. The Admiral saw that the French might soon tack and gain the wind of him, made the signal to tack himself, which closed the action, the French being then so far ahead. The disabled ships were by this manoeuvre covered from the enemy, and by this may be said to have kept the field of battle and gained the victory, for the French might have continued and fought on if they pleased. The Admiral immediately brought to about 8 o'clock in the evening.

I went to the Admiral immediately and found he was very sensible of the many errors of some of his captains. He sent on board to Mr. West to know how he did, and Mr. West came on board him late as it was. Then it was these two admirals saw the effect of having been sent with the worst ships in England. However an account was to be had immediately of our situation, and the fleet got ready as well as they could for action next morning, for this I know was Mr. Byng's determination when I left him with the Rear-Admiral, for he then told me Lord Anson had sold him, but by God he would fight till every ship sunk before he would give this up, if the council of war did not think his instructions bound him otherwise. I saw the consequence of this early battle in a different light. I told the Admiral the day before I thought the best thing would have been to have landed all the officers and troops for the garrison if possible before any action, as that was the material object now the French were landed, and then, if he thought proper, come to an engagement and try them, because if we were beat, (having thrown in what succours we could) it was of no great consequence, there must soon come up other ships; whereas if the enemy by their superiority obliged us to retire without throwing in any succours, then the consequence would be fatal to the island; but now the event proved what I said to be true, for the fleet had been disabled and lost so many men and had so many sick, and ne'er an hospital-ship for them, nor no storeship, and no port nearer than Gibraltar, that it was giving up all to think of retiring thither. In short I left the two Admirals together to consider what was to be done in this very critical affair.

The next morning it was very thick weather, the *Intrepid* and *Chesterfield* not in sight, and we were all laying-to. The *Dolphin* and *Phoenix* were sent to look for the *Intrepid* and *Chesterfield* whilst the rest of the fleet were refitting and many of them appeared like racks. The next morning, the 22nd, the Admiral sent for me and told me as Captain Andrews of the *Defiance* of 60 guns was killed he would give me that ship, which I accepted of, altho' a perfect rack and the worst manned ship in the service now, and I was obliged to borrow men to fit her, but had her in order that evening, when the *Intrepid* and *Chesterfield* joined us. The next day we lay to refitting the ships. The Rear-Admiral found great fault with Captain Ward and Captain Parry for not closing the Admiral in the action, as also with Captain Cornwall of the *Revenge*, and was for bringing them to a court-martial, which would have been better if the Admiral had listened to.

A council of war was called the 24th of all the land and sea officers. To this council the Admiral shewed his instructions first, which were to endeavour to relieve the island of Minorca, but to take care to secure Gibraltar, and in case the French fleet should be passed the Straits (in that case) to send a number of ships after them. The Admiral made no comment on these absurd instructions, tho' others did. The present state of the shattered fleet was taken into consideration next, and which proved how unfit they were to engage again if they were to protect Gibraltar, as they found they could not relieve Mahon, already so closely besieged. The Admiral told them his instructions were peremptory with regard to Gibraltar, and desired the opinion of the council of war relative to the situation. They all agreed, first, that the fleet was in no condition to attack the enemy's again, which was so superior, without risking every part of the instructions, as the French might then go down to Gibraltar and attack that place also. I was of this opinion with the rest. Mr. West particularly said we ought on no account to risk another engagement, on which the Admiral said if there was any officer that thought we ought he would attack them to-morrow. The next question was whether we ought not immediately to proceed to Gibraltar to cover that place. This was agreed to by all but myself. I said I thought we should send an express there, but keep off here till joined by some other ships, and endeavour at some opportunity

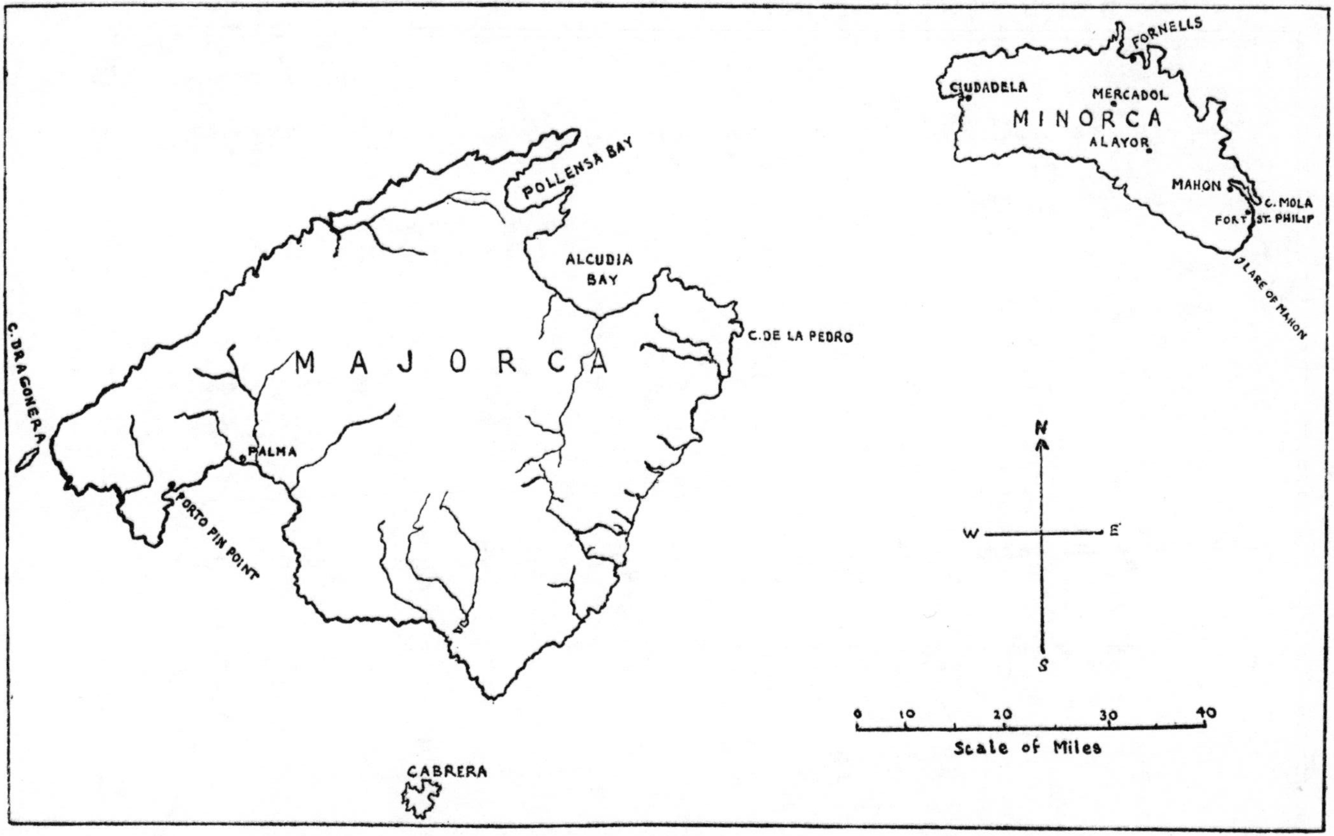

Majorca and Minorca.

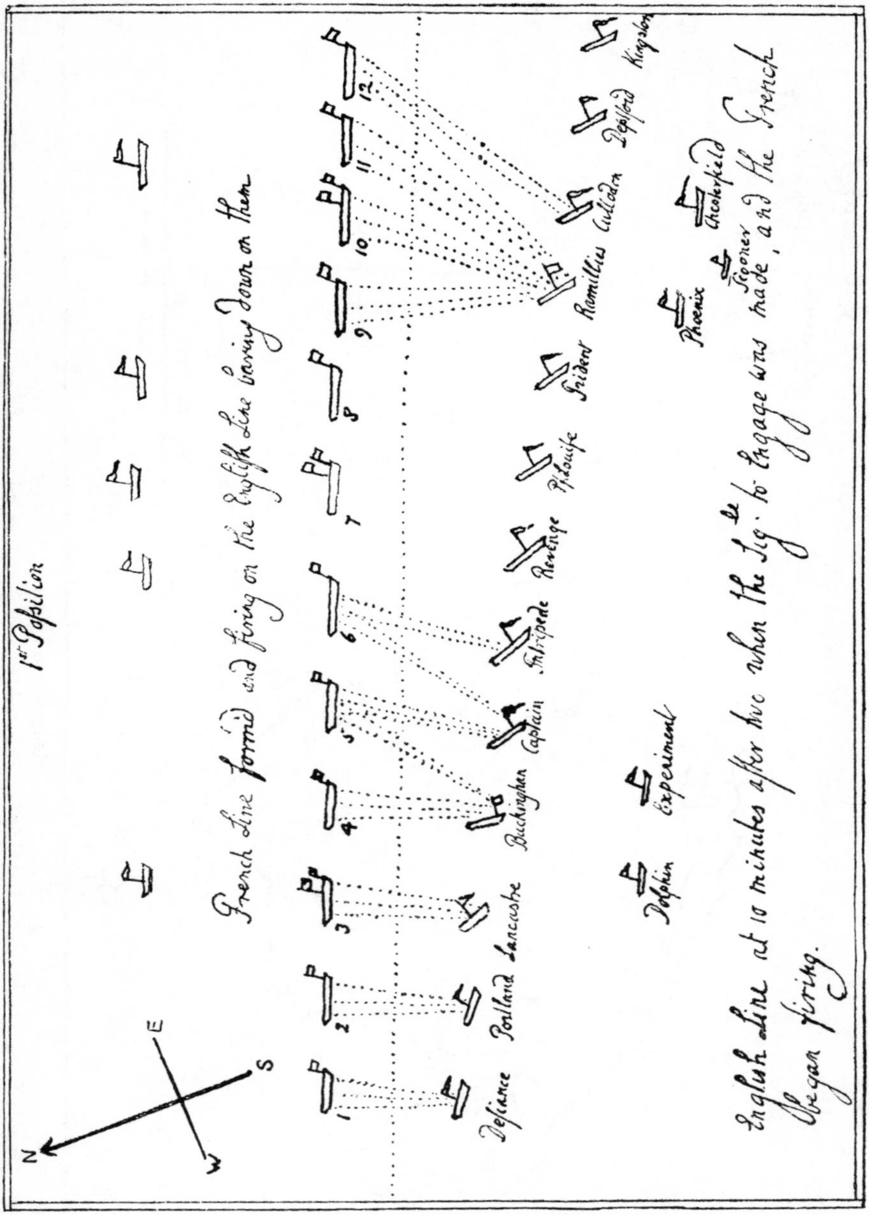

The *Foudroyant*, wearing M. de la Galissonnière's flag, is No. 7 in the French line. Hervey is wrong to show M. de la Clue's flag on ship No. 10 (*Lion*); in fact, he flew it in No. 11 (*Couronne*).

PLAN I: A little after 2 p.m.: Wind SW by W.

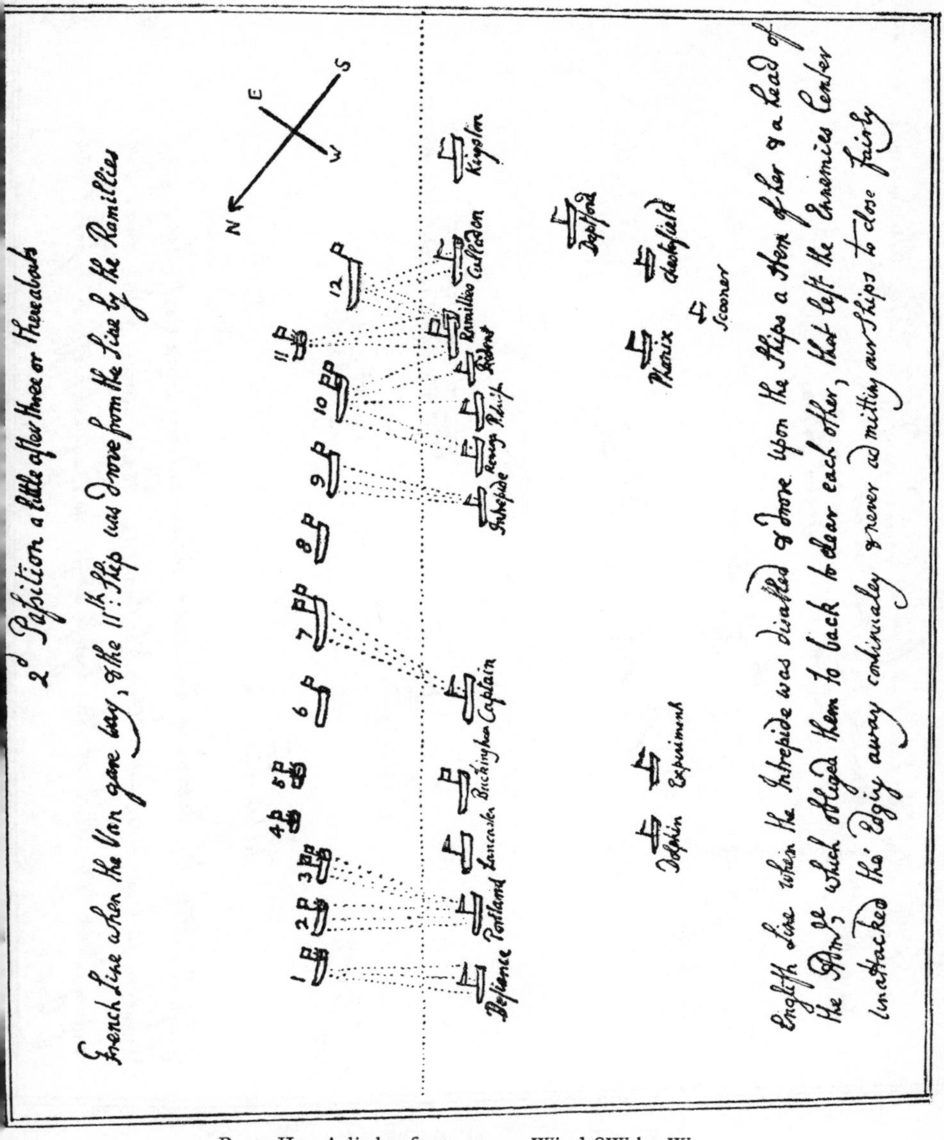

Plan II: A little after 3 p.m.: Wind SW by W.

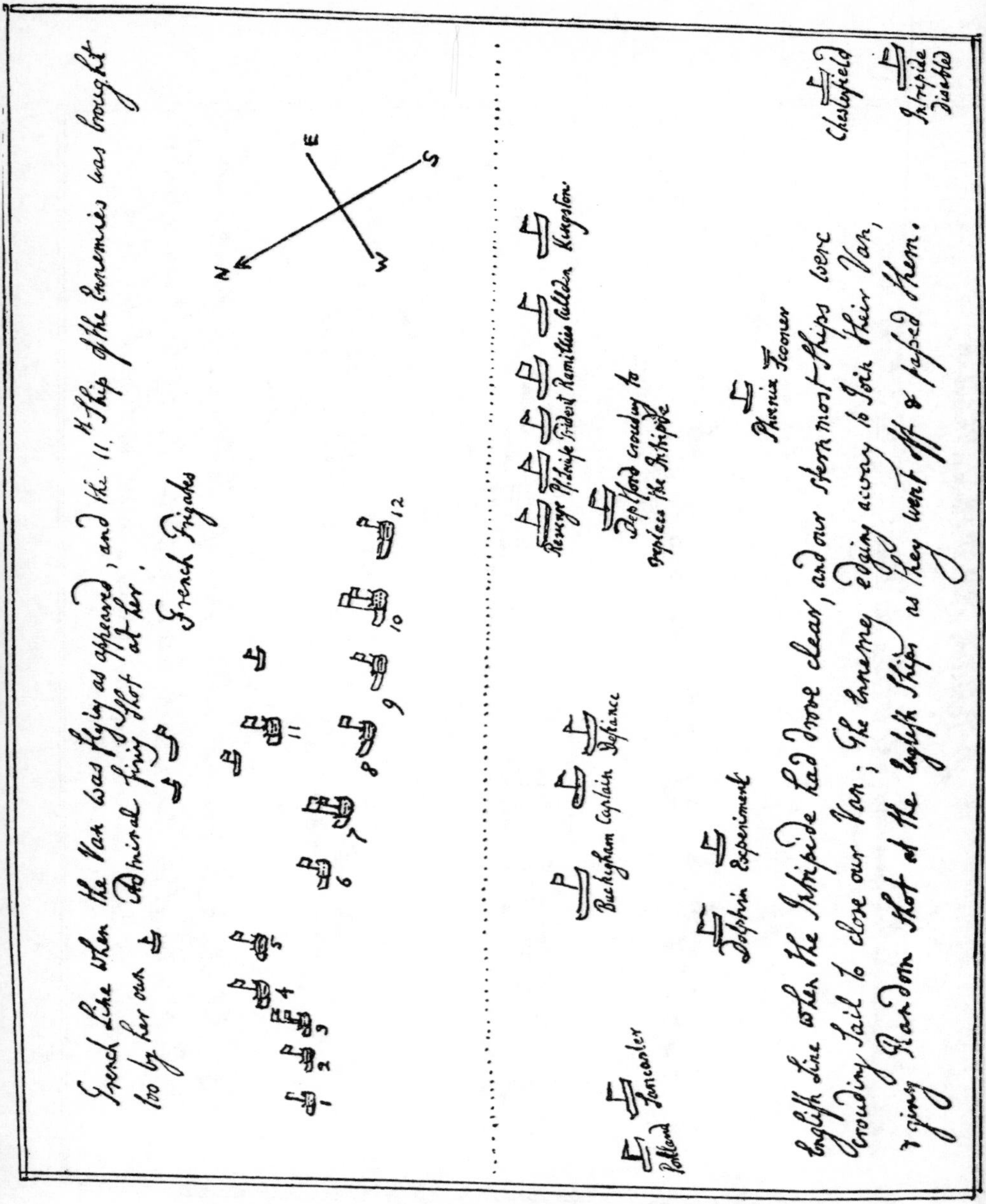

PLAN III: About 5 p.m.; the action ends: Wind SW by W.

to throw in succours to Minorca, and be ready to re-attack the enemy as soon as re-inforcements arrived, which would keep up the spirits of those in the castle, and be doing, I thought, the best service to publick. Mr. West particularly exclaimed against this, and said it would be risking both places, and acting directly contrary to the Admiral's instruction. I answered that I did not pretend to contend or debate it, but I had done my duty as one called there and given my sincere opinion. Then Mr. West and Lord Robert Bertie were for inserting resolutions and reasons for those resolutions, which were only reflections on government for sending such a force. This was opposed.

Mr. West at first refused sitting at this council with Captain Ward and Captain Parry, and said their behaviour in action, as well as Captain Cornwall's, was such that he could not submit to sit with them. The Admiral, who had no inclination to bring a slur on the action, replied to that, that if he, Mr. West, would accuse them, he would confine and try them. But Mr. West could not do that, and there it ended, with only bad blood among them. The council broke up after a resolution to proceed to Gibraltar, cover that place, and land our sick and wounded.

The 25th early in the morning I went on board the Admiral and helped to write his dispatches on this lame affair, one to the Admiralty, one to Lord Anson, and one to Sir Benjamin Keene. I wrote to Mr. Fox also (vide my letter-book) a whole account of this affair, but I believe my letter was not shown to any one, as it condemned the conduct of the ministry very freely.[1] These dispatches went away to Barcelona, and we were in the interim putting the ships in order as much as we could. Had the French come down upon us any time these three or four days, we must have been undone, so shattered were we, with our masts and yards all down repairing, but I must say I never saw so little activity among any set of officers. These were indeed in general the very scum of the fleet. My ship was very ill manned indeed, and very sickly and many wounded, and all I could muster when I went on board fit for service were 226 men out of 400, her complement. Such was the situation of those ships chosen by Lord Anson to go with Mr. Byng on the most important service just then that could be, but that Lord ever sacrificed the interest and service of the country to the interest and favour of a few individual favourites of his own.

We were all these days making our way down to Gibraltar,

[1] See Appendix C.

and kept the coast of Barbary on board so near that one day I went to beg the Admiral to keep off this coast as a most dangerous one, and that very afternoon, the 28th, we had near been on shore most of us in a calm and a great swell. We had a long passage down, and I was mostly on board the Admiral every day, and sometimes with Mr. West and others. I found great dissatisfaction on every quarter, as natural on such an affair in which some were to blame and all were disappointed. The 7th June Captain Noel of *Princess Louisa* died of his wound, who was to be regretted as a good officer and sensible man. I advised my friend Amherst to ask for her, but he did not care to leave the *Deptford* which was well manned. The next day I found Captain Gilchrist and Captain Lloyd on board the Admiral; both had asked for the command of the *Princess Louisa*, and if Lloyd got the *Louisa*, Gilchrist wanted the 40-gun ship. The Admiral told me all this, and at the same time did not care to give that dirty fellow Gilchrist the ship. I therefore advised the Admiral to tell Gilchrist that it was but fair Captain Scrope of the *Dolphin*, who was now in the castle of St. Philip's, should have the 40-gun ship, if he chose her, when he came out, and therefore that ship should only be commanded by order for the present, and the two 20-gun ships filled up entire at present. Lloyd therefore had the *Princess Louisa*, Amherst not caring for her. The Admiral then conversed with me on the action, and shewed me Mr. West's minutes of the action. I told the Admiral I thought that the too precipitate bearing down of the van, and the backing of Captain Cornwall's ship and the *Intrepid*, I looked upon to have been a misfortune, and to have given the enemy a very great advantage. In short this was fought over and over again, but alas, to no purpose. In these days as we had little winds we went on board each other's ships, and there had various dissertations on the engagement, but I never heard a word hinted against the Admiral's conduct till we came to Gibraltar.

The 12th I was ordered to make the best of my way to Gibraltar and get the hospital ready, and stores etc: to fit the fleet with all dispatch. I spoke to a Dutch man-or-war from Cadiz who told me the French had sent expresses everywhere that we were beat and they had gained a complete victory, and the Admiral killed. I arrived the 16th at Gibraltar where I found Commodore Broderick and five sail of the line[1] arrived yesterday from England with a regiment on board. Alas, had these been sent out with Mr. Byng Minorca had been saved, the French fleet destroyed and the Duke

[1] *Prince George* 80; *Hampton Court*, *Ipswich* and *Nassau* 64s; *Isis* 50.

de Richelieu's army obliged to lay down their arms. Such was the inexcusable error of our wicked Ministers, that detested wretch Lord Holland, and that poor contemptible one Lord Anson. Among these five sail the *Hampton Court* of 64 guns was sent out for me, commanded by Captain Knight who was to have the *Phoenix*. I went on shore and dined with the General, gave a faithful account of the engagement, and told them the French were too strong and too good sailors, our fleet in too shattered a condition to re-engage, and the instruction too peremptory to leave Gibraltar exposed, as they could not hope to relieve Minorca. We had a council of war next day on board the Commodore, when a ship was proposed to be sent out to look for the Admiral, and I proposed the whole squadron going out to join him, but it was carried against me.

The 20th the fleet came in in a very sickly and shattered condition. I pressed the Admiral much to sail the next day with all and take some troops on board and press every seaman in the bay, but tho' he determined to go as soon as he said he could, yet I was very uneasy. I attended poor Captain Noel's funeral.

The next day I found Captain Cornwall of the *Revenge* had asked for a court-martial on himself about the battle, which the Admiral was too averse to, I thought, but his reasons were that it would delay us. However Cornwall insisted so much that one was ordered. Admiral West was President; Captain Amherst, Captain Lloyd and myself declined sitting, as by our situation we must be evidences as to the *Revenge's* conduct. This made a bustle. On my getting up and protesting to my sitting they were for sending for more Captains. In short here was a confusion, and they adjourned the court to Monday. After this was over Admiral West desired every one to be attentive to him, and then threw out that he had been told that it was reported he was the promoter of these enquiries, which he absolutely denied; that he knew court-martials were always a disgrace to a fleet, tho' sometimes necessary; that all he had said was that five of our van beat five of the enemy's, and that our van was not supported—he did not know the cause; that he accused no one, nor ever had; that it was true he had refused to sit at a council of war with some Captains but he had accused none. In short he dwelt a long time on all this, with very artful insinuations that I thought reflected on Admiral Byng. On which I got up and said that I knew the Commander-in-chief was very averse to court-martials for the same reason Mr. West was, and wished to have postponed this, but not to have suppressed it. But that I did not see what Admiral West meant by not accusing when he says five of our van beat five of the enemy's and that the van was not supported; that, indirect as this is, I insisted it carried an accusation on the rear of the fleet, and therefore ought to be cleared up; that, had I have been of that line of battle, I should have thought myself engaged in honour to have asked Admiral West when he objected to sit with some Captains at a council of war whether I was one, and I therefore should think it the duty of every officer there to know who and why he objected to them, but as I was not, let those sit still who may, for my part I rise only to justify the Commander-in-chief, to whose conduct I was so situated as to be a judge of that day, and I could with truth and honour, and would, justify to the last, but that I knew Mr. West had said Captain Cornwall might have passed the *Intrepid* as well as the *Buckingham* passed another ship, (the *Defiance*). Mr. West then took this up, and acknowledged it, and said he thought so still. However this occasioned two or three sharp replies between Mr. West and me; but I cared not, I saw what he was at. In the evening General Fowke sent to me and wished me to endeavour to reconcile the two Admirals, but I begged to be excused interfering with anything more than pressing the Admirals to sail.

I was all day the 26th employed with the Admiral to assist in writing his letters. The 28th a signal for a court-martial was made on board the Rear-Admiral. Captain Cornwall appeared, and there being no accuser, the Judge-Advocate making proclamation three times for it, it was agreed that Captain Cornwall's letter desiring a court-martial, being founded on reports heard, were not grounds sufficient (as no one appeared to those reports) to proceed on, and so adjourned the court.

The 31st the Admiral and Mr. West went on shore together, which pleased me very much, as I was in hopes they would be well together. I kept pressing their sailing immediately to endeavour to find the enemy, and wish my advice had been followed for the next day Admiral West had a letter overland that himself and Mr. Byng were recalled. And sure enough the 2nd July at 10 in the morning the *Antelope* of 50 guns in thirteen days from England arrived with Sir Edward Hawke and Rear-Admiral Saunders[1] to relieve Mr. Byng and West, Lord Tyrawly to relieve

[1] Sir Charles Saunders, K.B. was one of Anson's favoured pupils of *Centurion* days. He was joint captor of Quebec with Wolfe in 1759 and is known as Pitt's favourite admiral. The picture Hervey gives of him as an indolent second-in-command is a new one.

General Fowke, Lord Panmure to relieve General Stuart, Captain Batten and several other officers;[1] the gentlemen relieved were all to proceed to England immediately, Mr. Byng as a prisoner. Mr. Broderick was made a flag and to go home also. The land officers were superceded for their council of war at Gibraltar before they went up, and not complying with the King's orders, and here the whole garrison were astonished to find a set of gentlemen stigmatised only on the accounts of the French admiral, which were the only ones received when these sailed. They did not give time for the arrival of Admiral Byng's express, such was their determination to sacrifice that officer to screen their own wicked heads. Even Sir Edward Hawke, whom I went to see, condemned the hasty manner in which it was done, and much more so the unprecedented infamous reports Lord Holland, Lord Anson and the Duke of Newcastle encouraged everywhere against Mr. Byng's character in order to raise the mob against him and turn all the resentment and just indignation of the people from themselves to Admiral Byng.

The next day I was wholly taken up writing with Mr. Byng, who I found worked up with the greatest indignation against the Government, and no wonder. He came on board my ship that evening as he would not stay in the *Ramillies*, Sir Edward being very pressing to be on board and be gone up off Minorca, tho' it was evident they would be too late for any business. Every one seemed really hurt at the conduct towards these two Admirals, as nothing could have appeared in England to have deserved such treatment. The next day the Admiral went on shore, and I attended him. Sir Edward Hawke wrote him word he thought himself obliged to superced all the Lieutenants of the *Ramillies* in the action, which he did and filled up the vacancies. The next day I felt the stroke of this attention to Mr. Byng, for they took eighty of my best seamen away from the *Hampton Court* to put in other ships. This was a poor, mean, dirty spite, and could scarce have first entered into the head of anything but a dirty secretary, whom Sir Edward was ever cursed with.[2] The 8th poor Mr. Byng went on board the *Antelope* with Admiral West, their Captains,

[1] Called by the wits the " Little cargo of courage ".

[2] This was one John Hay, whose unofficial minutes of a joint naval and military council of war caused trouble after the Rochefort expedition in 1757. Horace Walpole (*George II*, Vol. III, 50 and 77) who is never fair to the Admiral, says Hawke was " childishly abandoned to the guidance of a Scotch Secretary ", a gibe to which Hervey affords some support, *infra* Chapter XIII, *passim*.

Lieutenants, and General Fowke and his lady, and Admiral Broderick. I think they were between thirty and forty in that 50-gun ship. Such was the reward of forty years services for Admiral Byng, the son of Lord Torrington, to whom this country owed so much! The 9th the *Antelope* sailed, and here I own I was hurt to see this officer go away in such a manner. Sir Edward in the evening sent for me and talked a great deal of the late affair, told me he hoped I would look upon him as a friend too, and that he honoured my gratitude and attachment to Mr. Byng.

XIII

HAWKE IN COMMAND

July to November 1756

THE 10th July we all sailed about noon and had a regiment from Gibraltar. We were sixteen sail of the line and five frigates. I was in Rear-Admiral Saunders' division and one of his seconds. We kept making up for Minorca with little winds contrary, and exercising the fleet in lines of battle. The 15th we fell in with all the French transports having on board General Blakeney and his garrison of St. Philip's, who surrendered to the Duke de Richelieu the 27th of last month. I went on board to see the officers of the garrison, and found many dissatisfied at the giving it up. General Jefferies was taken. The assault cost the French 1,200 men. We certainly lost the most useful island to the English in a war that could be, thanks to Mr. Fox, the Duke of Newcastle and Lord Anson, and there I lost all the prizes I had made by Mr. Edgcumbe's leaving them in that harbour.

The 16th we had a strong gale westerly, but I do not find we made the most use of it, having never set a steeringsail the whole time. The 19th we were all off Minorca, and saw French colours on St. Philip's and a number of men at work on the fortifications. They fired a shot at one of the men-of-war as she was wearing off. We found the French fleet were gone, and I was anxious to know what would become of all our blustering, and what this mighty fleet was to perform, which, had it been sent earlier, would have given the finishing stroke to France. We heard there were about 5,000 troops left on the Island. I thought we might easily have forced the harbour had we had troops. In short we satisfied ourselves with cruising off and on this harbour to no purpose in the world, to our eternal shame and the reproach of those who gave the orders, till all our men fell sick with despair and scurvy, and when we were sure that nothing could be obtained by it. I was frequently on board Admiral Saunders, who I found very uneasy at our situation and not at all approving of our manoeuvres.

We had several chaces at tartanes and small vessels along the coast of Mahon, but as our water now grew scarce the Admiral was thinking where we could get it most convenient for the fleet, as they would believe the French fleet was to come out again, which was a farce. They had done their business and had no business to come out purely to fight an exasperated enemy. The 28th we missed of a number of French victuallers by our being to leeward of the island. To be sure, there never was such poor work in the world as this, signals three times a day for all Lieutenants about the most nonsensical things possible. I was indeed quite tired of this inactive, dispiriting work, and found Mr. Saunders more and more so every day, especially as our men fell down sick every day in the fleet, and that we all knew Sir Edward Hawke was totally governed by a damned interested Scotch secretary, a fellow without a grain of understanding who had been bred up to business in a shop and had the impudence to show his ascendancy over the Admiral to the whole Fleet.

The 1st August there stood into the fleet, as we were putting water-casks on board small vessels which were intended to go and fetch water for the ships, a vessel who belonged to the Jews at Mahon. I had the curiosity to go on board of her, and found that the French used the Minorcines very ill, which I was very glad of, as the treacherous dogs deserved it for their behaviour to us. This day the *Chesterfield* sailed with four vessels to fetch water for the fleet, and which could not bring us above four days water. Therefore it was obvious it was not worth while all the trouble we had of putting our casks on board, sending men in with them, and spoiling our water-casks by being tossed out of one vessel into another in such a manner. 'Twas impossible this method could keep the fleet out longer, and, if it could, to what end off this place?

The 2nd was an idle day. The 3rd at daylight there was a signal for Flag officers, and soon after for all Captains, when the Admiral told us that he had intelligence by a Dane that the French fleet lay with their topsail sheets hauled home at Toulon and were determined to come out and fight us. Then he made us a fine speech that he was determined to run close up to them, and that the honour of our country required we should do our very utmost to destroy these ships and he did not doubt that we should, with a great deal of all this sort of stuff. For my part I told Mr. Saunders that I was certain this was all artifice of the French in sending us this sort of intelligence to keep us useless here, where we were effectually destroying ourselves, that the French could have no view or interest in coming out to fight us merely for blows, that they were not apt to risk all without any point to gain, and that here they had none whatsoever, and that therefore, tho' I wished them to give us this opportunity of signalizing ourselves, yet I despaired of it. He was of my opinion, but yet thought it right not to speak it openly and discourage people.

The 4th there was a continual firing in at Minorca. I suppose the French were blowing up some of the works. For my part I wonder they do not effectually destroy the harbour, which is so very narrow and therefore might easily be done, and can be of no use to them, and they may be almost sure we shall insist on the restitution of it at the peace, and that at any rate 'tis worth their while to make it useless as they cannot expect to keep it.[1] I had ninety-six men sick at this time in my ship, at which I should have been still much more uneasy, if possible, could I have thought we should have had a battle, as I was determined to distinguish myself by some exploit that should have given my ship's crew everlasting credit. We were employed in cutting up the French tartanes continually for firewood, and also to get rid of them. We had calms with great seas and nothing to occupy us. The Rear-Admiral sent to me to go dine with him the 9th, which I did and found he had been on board Sir Edward Hawke this morning to persuade him to send something of our own to look into Toulon and get intelligence, but all to no purpose. Mr. Saunders seemed very uneasy at our situation; he told me he looked on Sir Edward as a very honest man, but thought he was lost from this expedition wherein we made so silly and useless a figure. The *Experiment* was sent the 11th down to Gibraltar with prizes, yet this ship could not be spared a few days ago to go for intelligence. The 12th the fleet had many of them near been on shore, for we had stood so close in with the land that, the wind dying away and having a great swell on, our boats could scarce keep our heads off the shore. The *Intrepid* made a signal of distress, being so near the shore that she was in great danger. This was a pretty situation. If a breeze had not sprung up four or five large ships must

[1] Although Hervey puts this passage in the future tense, he is writing *after* the Peace has been concluded and Minorca restored. For he has already referred to Henry Fox as Lord Holland, which peerage was not conferred on him until April 1763, two months after the treaty was signed; the Preliminaries containing the main terms had been agreed in the preceding November. Probably Hervey has copied the passage verbatim from his Journal to show how right were his thoughts at the time.

have been thrown on shore which would have completed the expedition.

The next day a signal was made and a circular letter sent to us of his intentions to water at some of the Majorca bays. The 13th early I went on board Mr. Saunders, who I found very uneasy that the Admiral had determined to run into some of the bays of Majorca and water the ships, and particularly Poyance Bay[1] for which no one had pilots, and that it was uncertain whether we could get water, and besides never to have sent a compliment to the Viceroy of the island, or ask leave. However the Admiral made the signal for the line of battle about 9, and before we were formed he hauled it down and crowded away for Poyance Bay. We got off there by night, and there he run the whole fleet in following each other, without one of us being acquainted, anchored all about midnight confusedly, and the next morning the Admiral found himself with the whole fleet of great ships anchored in a very deep bay where there was scarce a hut to give us the least refreshment and not one drop of fresh water to be found. I went on board to breakfast with Mr. Saunders, but found him gone to the Admiral, and soon after my signal was thrown out. I went to Sir Edward and found him much shocked at the precipitate step he had taken. Well he might be so, for it would be an unpardonable step in a young officer to have carried two or three frigates into such a place, in such a manner and at such a time—much more so such a fleet without ever consulting with any one, or sending a vessel in to know if the fleet could lay there, or could get water when there. Sir Edward asked me about it. I told him had I known of his intentions time enough, I could have told him he would not be supplied here. He then asked me what I thought of Alcudia Bay. I said I never was there, but heard there was water, but that at Palma Bay the fleet could soon be watered, tho' we lay a great way off, and that on any occasion the fleet could turn it out of the bay, and get out at any time. I recommended Barcelona to him, as he might also hear in a few days of the French's motions at Toulon, and command the passage between the main and the islands if they wanted to go down the Straits, and I could not conceive they had any further business in the Mediterranean, but that if he proposed carrying the fleet there, it would certainly be necessary to send some vessel before to the Marquis de las Minas, Viceroy of Catalonia, as by treaty we could not carry in but six ships at a time without leave. Mr. Saunders who was then

[1] Pollensa Bay.

present with the Commodore and Captains Young, Taylor, Sir William Burnaby, and Lloyd seemed all to like this advice. The Admiral then said " Well, gentlemen, Barcelona is the word, we'll go." I then reminded the Admiral that I had a Minorcine on board who could be landed here and carry a letter over to Captain Gilchrist who was at Palma Bay (the other side of the island) with the vessels to water us, and that he should be ordered out immediately to join us at Barcelona. The Admiral liked this too very much, and told me I should have his letter in half an hour and thanked me much for this assistance. We all went on board, and just as I was sending the man to him, he sent me the letter, so I was obliged to send it back again to desire he would write some directions for the Consul to dispatch this man in the packet to Barcelona should the 40-gun ship be already sailed from Palma. Then I went to dine with the Rear-Admiral, and there I received another letter from Sir Edward that he had just recollected he must go for a few days to Minorca again, and therefore would not send the man, and so returned him to me. In this time we were warping out and endeavouring to get the ships out of this deep bay, which we were fortunate enough in doing in the evening late by a land wind setting right out of it. At daylight the Admiral sent for my Minorcine on board him again to go in a tender to Palma Bay, as he first proposed. About 8, as I was at breakfast, he sent this man back to me again, with his compliments by the officer and he would not send him now. At 10 the Admiral sent the tender to me with Mr. Strawn,[1] his Lieutenant, and desired the Minorcine again who I sent, but was astonished at all this irresolute work, and to find that in trifles as well as essentials 'twas all alike, nothing fixed, nothing could be determined. I had no sooner sent the man, and the tender made sail with him, than the signal was thrown out to call the tender in again. When we had all bore up above three hours and had already passed Alcudia Bay, the Admiral fired several guns to make the tender perceive the signal. For my part I was not surprised the officer could not understand it, as he could never suspect such contradictory work, as this was the fifth time the Admiral had changed this since yesterday noon. I mention these things only to show the disposition of the Admiral.

In the evening we were all close off Cittadella, but we were all lamenting that this was so much time lost with regard to

[1] Later Sir John Strachan, 7th Bart.; he was appointed Captain of the *Experiment* in September, and was an uncle of the Strachan of the Walcheren expedition of 1808.

watering the ships and refreshing the sick. The next day the 16th the *Jersey* brought in a tartane with another report of the French being put to sea as yesterday with eighteen sail of the line and 200 transports. How we could be so often the dupe of these reports was astonishing, and not find out that they did it merely for the sake of keeping our fleet useless off this place and destroying our people, whereas, as I have said before, the sending only an officer with twenty men into one of these tartanes to Villa-Franca would bring us certain accounts of the enemy. The 17th the *Chesterfield* joined us from Palma Bay with the vessels and water, which was not three days watering for us, and no news. Mr. Saunders told me to-day that Sir Edward was now determined to go for Barcelona to water. The 19th there was a signal made to tell the Captains that we were now steering for Barcelona, that we were to go in in a line of battle by seniority. In the afternoon the Admiral sent to speak to Mr. Saunders, and changed his mind again, and now determined to go and water at Altea Bay. This was a strange alteration, as it carried us above eighty leagues to the westward, and that we might this time of year be very long going thither, and that when we are there we shall hear no more of the French than if we were out of the Straits, and then afterwards have all this way to return back, when by that time we shall have no more provisions left, having now but thirty-eight days bread on board, and that at Barcelona he might constantly have heard from England. I reflected what chance did for some people when a fleet could be so commanded and yet get on.

We steered away to the westward the next day, and the 24th we all of us anchored in Altea Bay, after having mistaken two others for it, which was amazing that the Admiral could not inform himself if there was no one in the fleet that was acquainted with the coast, as it was evident no one that was in his ship knew anything of it. The day we got in we chaced a Dutch convoy of ten sail, taking them for the French fleet, but they did not lead us far. Altea is a very good bay, a dirty village, but easy watering here, having a river that supplied very plentifully, greens and fruits also sufficient, and the country people brought down all kind of provisions to us. The people were very civil, and the country about very fertile.

Whilst we lay here a very extraordinary thing happened to us considering an Admiral of the Blue commanded. A French ship was chaced in by the *Isis*. She had an English jack flying. As she approached the *Lancaster*, who was an outward ship, she put out French colours, on which the *Lancaster* fired at her, and the

Admiral fired two shot at her, and several other ships. On which she dropped her anchors and her colours. She was immediately boarded by an officer of the *Lancaster*, an English colour hoisted on board her. Admiral Saunders and myself were walking on shore and saw these strange proceedings in a Spanish bay, under a Spanish fort, and where we were suppliants for refreshments. We went on board to Sir Edward and represented the consequences of this. She was a ship from Marseilles bound for Martinico, and before night French colours were hoisted on board her again, and the ship restored to the Captain. They soon after complained of having been plundered, some amends was made the Captain, and the thing silenced.

Whilst we lay here several ladies and gentlemen of quality came from Valencia to see the fleet. I had them two or three times on board to dinner, gave them a ball, and carried them on board the two Admirals' ships. They were Signora Donna Anna Sisterres, wife to Don Mauro Antonio Osser y Bono, Rexidor perpetua a la Cuida de Valencia and sister to Donna Francisca Sisterres de Casteleon de la Plana, her brother Don Manuel Sisterres and others. She was very handsome. They went to Valencia and returned here to us again and were very agreeable and amiable.

We remained in this bay till the 1st September when we sailed at 5 in the morning, having the old story played upon us of the French being off Minorca. I was surprised Sir Edward and his ignorant secretary could attempt to play this upon the fleet so often. In short we went all to short allowance of all species. The 7th I was at breakfast on board Admiral Saunders, and we saw the *Buckingham* and *Intrepid* go on board each other. The former lost her bowsprit and all her head, the *Intrepid* little or no damage. I could not learn who was in fault, but it appeared a sad affair at this time that we were supposed to be at the eve of an action. We all brought to and sent boats, carpenters, etc: to assist. The 8th in the morning I had a note from Captain Hood (the Rear-Admiral's Captain)[1] that Gilchrist, who had just joined the Fleet, had brought word that at the island of Formentera they had reported on our going to Altea Bay that the French had again drove the English fleet from Minorca. We were waiting these two days for the *Buckingham* of 68 guns, and losing this fair wind. I could not help saying one day (perhaps imprudently) on the Admiral's quarter-deck that I perceived notwithstanding I had heard it said we were ships enough to blow the French out of the water yet we were willing

[1] Later Admiral of the Fleet Alexander, Viscount Bridport.

not to leave one of our force behind, tho' Mr. Byng was tore to pieces for not renewing his engagement the next day when he had four ships out of ten disabled and one out of sight, and yet we can now run the risk of not seeing the enemy by waiting for one of 68 guns, when all the rest of the ships were in so much better a condition and so much superior.

We lost Captain Catford of the *Captain*. He was buried the 9th and Captain Amherst was removed out of the *Deptford* into the *Captain*, and Gilchrist into the *Deptford*.

The 11th we got off Mahon, but no French, nor any intelligence of them. The 13th we were joined by the *Colchester*, Captain O'Brien, who brought orders from England for myself and nine other Captains with several officers to go home in the *Colchester* to attend at Admiral Byng's trial, and it was a very extraordinary thing that all the captains of that fleet should be ordered home but one, and that one Captain Durell, who was the Admiral's immediate second in that action, and was the occasion of the Admiral not being able to get into action the second time. By this ship we heard very much of the most infamous and shameful unheard-of treatment Admiral Byng had met with in England, all occasioned by a hired mob to insult him, and by papers being sent about everywhere to poison the minds of the people and prejudice them against him, in order to screen those wretches Newcastle, Anson and Fox.

The 17th we still remained useless off Mahon, just where the French could wish us, without the least appearance or, indeed, possibility of our being able to be of any annoyance to the enemy, and out of the way of being of any use to the very little remaining trade we had in the Mediterranean. This day a small boat that came from Leghorn with letters for the fleet had the good fortune to get on board the Admiral's ship just before a very hard gale of wind came on that must inevitably have sunk the boat. By this boat, too, I received several letters. Among the rest was one from Mr. Porter, our Ambassador at Constantinople, telling me that the sum of 6,000 livres I was ordered to refund to the Turks for the ransom of some French ships was not claimed; that he, the Ambassador, had supported the right of what I had done, tho' the Admiralty had been so ready to condemn me, and so hasty in ordering me to refund. I had a letter from Genoa of Madame Brignole being brought to bed of a girl the 13th April this year.[1] This afternoon the Admiral at last made some distribution of his ships.

[1] Unidentified.

'Twas a long time before he could be persuaded to it, and put me in mind of a child with his playthings. The *Jersey* and *Isis* went to Leghorn for the trade, and the *Dolphin* to Gibraltar to prepare them for our exhausted and sickly condition. The 18th the *Prince* of 90 guns joined us from England. This ship was sent in order for Mr. Saunders to hoist his flag on board her. I own this made me reflect at the conduct of our chiefs. At a time when they ought to know that nothing more could be done or could be feared in these seas, they were constantly sending out ships to re-inforce, and when they knew the French were superior to us and had a design on Minorca, then they would not send only a few of the refuse of their ships at home, whereas had this 90, the three 64's, and one 50 been sent with Mr. Byng that has since been sent out, he would have totally demolished the French fleet, relieved Minorca, obliged the French army to throw down their arms, secured all our trade, turned the politics of Europe in our favour, and made us esteemed as the true maritime power of Europe, but with all the present force we were only beating the seas off Minorca and destroying all our people, without a possibility of being the least advantage.

We were now on our passage downwards, and one morning I fell on this paragraph in the 2nd volume of Campbell's *Naval History*, in King Charles II's reign, 1673. Speaking of Prince Rupert's conduct in the battle fought between him and the Dutch the 4th June he says both sides claimed the victory, and that " some Dutch writers pretend Prince Rupert did not distinguish himself as he used to do, for which they suggested reasons void of all foundation. The truth is the Prince was for fighting the enemy again, but it was carried in a council of war to sail for the English coast in order to obtain supplies, as well as ammunition as provision, for want of which a great many captains complained loudly, besides the fleet being so poorly manned that if it had not been for the land forces on board, they could not have fought at all, and these being new-raised men, we need not wonder they did not behave so well as our old sailors were wont to do."[1] Now even in these Dutch wars where so many valiant commanders' praises are sung down to us, they could retire from the enemy, even tho' on equal terms, with the opinion of a council of war, and yet neither the commanders-in-chief nor the council of war

[1] Hervey would have had the first or second edition of John Campbell's *Lives of the Admirals*. The passage occurs at p. 308 in the first, and at p. 314 in the second.

met with the treatment which this ungrateful age is pleased to bestow on the present commander-in-chief and the council he called, tho' they had such stronger motives that authorized their determinations.

The 29th I was much surprised to find the Admiral shorten sail tho' we had very little wind, and considering the condition we were all in for want of bread and wine and the *Buckingham* so disabled, I thought no time was to be lost. The next day the wind came hard to the westward, and I then wondered we did not put away for Malaga, which was under our lee, instead of risking the being drove up again, for from Malaga an express would have gone to Gibraltar in ten hours, by which the Admiral could have given all his orders and have had everything ready against our arrival, whereas, if we miss Malaga, and the wind continues we do not know to what we may be drove to. The next day we had less wind, and the 2nd October it shifted and we all got into Gibraltar.

Whilst I was here I could gather from the officers of the Minorca garrison that it had been given up too soon, and in short great complaints made. On the other hand great parties were raised even here to censure Admiral Byng's conduct. Whilst we lay here I was preparing to go to England, and leaving all my things at Mr. Crutchett's. Mr. Saunders and several officers were continually with me. Lord Tyrawly who commanded the garrison here refused my request of letting poor Smallridge set up a publick-house here; he had kept one at Minorca a long time, and had formerly been in the Navy, was ruined by the French taking Minorca, but all solicitation was in vain with Lord Tyrawly, who was as insensible to others' distress as incapable of gratitude for others' favours to him. For I had had some claim to such a trifle from the long care I had taken of his worthless son whilst on board my ship.[1]

Sir Edward Hawke shewed me a favour in telling me he would give me his packets for England, that when I arrived I might immediately go to Town with them, wherein he said he had desired I might be sent out to him again as he wished to have me with him, and that he had done this to show he distinguished me from the rest. The 27th it was before we could be dispatched, when I embarked on board the *Colchester*, Captain O'Brien, with Lord and Lady Effingham, Captains Cornwall, Amherst, and Marlow,

[1] Peter O'Hara; he became a Lieutenant in 1758, and disappears from the Sea-Officers List in 1760.

several land and sea-officers, about thirty-two in all, and with the *Deptford*, Captain Taylor, and several transports and the trade. We left in the bay sixteen sail of the line of battle, and some frigates. We had a tolerable passage on the whole, were very sociable on board, and Captain O'Brien endeavoured to make it agreeable to every one. The 9th November we struck soundings, and the 15th we got to Spithead, and I landed immediately and went to Town.

XIV

JUSTICE IN DISGRACE

November 1756 to May 1757

The campaign of vilification against Byng had not succeeded in deflecting the whole of the public's rage from the ministers. When Hervey arrived in November the Government was falling ; Newcastle, Hardwicke, Fox and Anson were for a brief six months deprived of office. But so firm was Newcastle's grip on the votes of the House of Commons that his support proved indispensable to the administration, and in June 1757 there came into being the Pitt-Newcastle coalition which was to sweep the French from the seas, destroy their American empire, and draw off important bodies of troops from their armies campaigning against Frederick the Great in Germany. Hervey is writing about the period before this famous ministry was formed, when the Duke of Devonshire was Prime Minister and Pitt his chief lieutenant.

THE 17th November I went to Lord Anson with the packets. He asked me several questions about the fleet and who was come home. He told me that no Captain was sent to my ship, and only to have her commanded by order. I went to Lord Temple, just made First Lord of the Admiralty. Mr. West came in whilst I was there, and they appeared to me to be much against all the proceedings that were carrying on against Mr. Byng. I dined at my mother's where I met with many of my acquaintances, and all of them at me about the Mediterranean affair, which was now the great subject of conversation. The next day Lord Rochford, as Lord of the Bedchamber in waiting, was so good as to call of me and carry me to Court, when I was presented, but His Majesty did not deign to speak to me, nor even enquire the least about his fleet, tho' I was the only officer come from it that he was likely to see. Such was His Majesty's attention. The Chancellor (Lord Hardwicke) resigned the Seals this morning.

Mr. Fox sent me a note at Court and desired to see me. He called of me, and stayed an hour with me, but I was well on my guard with him, tho' he insinuated to me that he had nothing to do with all the proceedings against Mr. Byng and disapproved Lord Anson's conduct on the whole. All this minister's discourse with me was full of arts, and endeavours to see what he could get of me, by way of weakening any part of Mr. Byng's defence. In the evening I found my mother talked to me much of the great imprudence there would be in me to appear too warm at this time in Mr. Byng's defence, that I might be sure of making myself great enemies at St. James's, but all that I little regarded. The next day I went to Lord Temple's, who desired me to assure Mr. Byng that he should have all the justice possible in his trial, and that his Lords thought the late Admiralty's proceeding with regard to Mr. Byng quite shameful. Yet I did not find that there was any mitigation with regard to the severity in which he was confined. I went the next day, the 20th, down to Admiral Byng to Greenwich, who I found with his usual good spirits, and speaking with a manly contempt of all the ill-treatment he received.

I returned to Town and dined with my mother where was the Abbé Celesia, Minister from Genoa. As he knew I had been very much there, he began to talk with me about the Republick's affairs, that he might find out what kind of impression I had brought away from thence, as he imagined I might be much questioned here with regard to the conduct of the Republick in admitting the French troops to Corsica, building ships for Toulon, and sending numbers of Corsican seamen to France. I told him fairly I always should consider Genoa as an arsenal for France, but, alas, he was mistaken in thinking I should be questioned here about it, our ministers never take the pains of enquiring from any of their officers concerning any places they come from.

Two or three days after this at Leicester House, where I was to be presented to the Prince of Wales[1] who received me very graciously, Mr. Boscawen[2] told me a commission was gone out for Sir William Burnaby to command the *Hampton Court*. I immediately went to Lord Temple and had this affair set right and my ship not given away.

I was continually employed in Mr. Byng's affairs and assisting him. I wrote several pamphlets on this occasion in Mr. Byng's

[1] The future George III.

[2] Edward Boscawen, then a Vice-Admiral, later captor of Louisburg and victor of Lagos. He was the sole member of Anson's board to remain in office when they resigned on 19th November.

behalf, and circulated several papers. . . .[1] At this time Lord Harrington died, by which Bury St. Edmunds became vacant, as Lord Petersham was now Lord Harrington, but I did not stir in it as my brother was abroad. The 18th or 19th December I published some drawings of the different positions of Mr. Byng's and the French fleet at the time of the action, to shew the publick the falseness of the assertions in regard to Admiral Byng's distance.[2] In all this time there was nothing very remarkable but the constant ribaldry published to prejudice people against Admiral Byng, whose trial was drawing near. I got to Gosport the 26th, and chose to lodge with Captain Gardiner there at one Mrs. Wilson. I went the next day to Admiral Byng, who was in great spirits, and looked over all his defence, and remained with him most of the time.

The Monday morning of the 27th at 8 in the morning a signal was made on board the *St. George* by Admiral Smith, Vice-Admiral of the Red, for all Captains, tho' they did not settle upon sitting to-day and deferred being sworn till the next morning. There were several people came from London to attend this trial, especially Lord Morton and Lord Willoughby of Parham, both creatures of Lord Hardwicke and who were thought, as far as they were able, to do all they could to prejudice every one against the Admiral, who was brought on board the *St. George* on the 28th in the morning with all the solemnity and attention of guards etc. as if he had been inclined to make an escape. There were boats full of soldiers to attend that in which he was in. The Court —this most INFAMOUS Court—assembled, and were selected to be there at Portsmouth by Lord Anson for this purpose:[3]

Thomas Smith, Vice-Admiral of the Red . . . *President*

Francis Holbourn, *Rear of the White*	Henry Norris, *Rear of the White*
Thomas Broderick, *Rear of the Blue*	Charles Holmes
Francis Geary	John Simcoe

[1] Appendix A.

[2] A set of these prints, beautifully executed in great detail, is preserved in the British Museum (*Crach.* 2. *Tab* 6. *v.* 6) and another set at Greenwich. The ships are shewn in the same positions as those in the plans reproduced in this volume, and the whole presentation is favourable to Byng. They were republished in the next year as a supplement to a two-volume edition of the trial.

[3] Walpole reports Boscawen as having said at dinner, " Well, say what you will, *we* shall have a majority, and he will be condemned " ; *George II*, Vol. II, p. 287.

John Moore — William Boyce
James Douglas — John Bently
Augustus Keppel — Peter Denis

Mr. Fearne, *Judge-Advocate*

These chosen gentlemen were all swore, and proceeded to trial. When the charge (such as it was) was read, every person present showed their surprise that the charge was not confined to the day of the action, but had a retrospection to the hour in which the Admiral sailed from St. Helens, so that the resentment of the nation which was raised against the Admiral for his supposed cowardice and all their attention which was carried on to that period was now dwindled to an enquiry into all parts of his conduct from the time he unfortunately accepted the command of that pitiful squadron. This struck every one present with indignation. I shall not here repeat all the particulars of the trial and the evidence given, as the pamphlets printed and the papers published at that time are all to be seen, many of which I wrote myself, as will be seen in my papers of manuscripts. The Court adjourned at 2 o'clock, on Mr. Byng's having applied for Lieutenant Clark being allowed to attend his papers, as he had been summoned by him. He said he would wave his evidence, as it was immaterial, Lieutenant Clark having been quartered in the action on the middle gundeck, but Mr. Byng was told by the President after a debate, that could not be, as there was no destination of evidence, but the whole were called to support the charge and to inform the Court what they knew of the action of that day, and that there would be no distinction of evidence either for the Crown or the prisoner. In this case it appeared a very great hardship on Mr. Byng, as this gentleman had been employed in the setting to rights all his papers and preparing them for this great event.

The next day Admiral West's evidence was given, and appeared greatly in favour of Mr. Byng. In the course of his examination the President asked Admiral West to give the Court his opinion with regard to the action of the 20th May. Mr. West, greatly astonished at such a question being put to him, very warmly told the Court he was surprised to find such a question put to him, which he thought himself not at all obliged to answer, nor would not, as they could rest no opinion or evidence upon it; that he was there to answer facts and not to his own opinion; that if he could have had one moment's opinion of the rear of the fleet not closing the van in that action, he might have had very good reasons since to know how impossible it was, but that, on the whole, he thought that a very illegal question. The President offered to wave it, but Captain Moore said as the Court had heard that question, they must clear it, to debate whether it should stand or not. The Court soon after adjourned, and the next day met again, and waved that former question of the President's. Mr. West run on a great deal which was to shew his own conduct, but never once threw any blame on Mr. Byng.

Old General Blakeney was called, who made a very poor figure, read a paper which he confessed was collection from the observations of others, and shewed he was put on to every thing he said, as the whole of his evidence tended to throw what blame he could upon Admiral Byng, tho' it was manifest the old General could be no judge whatever of what passed in that day's action. The next day the 31st the Court sat, Mr. Boyd of St. Philip's and Captain Everitt were examined, but their evidence was of little consequence to the charge.[1]

The 3rd January I was summoned to the Court-martial, and was called in after Captain Gilchrist, who I was told had given his evidence as unfavourable as it was possible in such a cause, and I was not surprised at it, as I had ever found him the most fawning sycophant that ever cringed to power. The President asked me where I was stationed the time of the action the 20th May. I told him abreast of the Admiral commanding-in-chief to repeat his signals. He desired I would relate to the Court all that I observed, from the time of the signal of battle till the end of the engagement, which I did in a very long narrative, and which took up the whole day. I was then ordered to attend the next morning. I dined with Admiral Byng who seemed very well satisfied with the manner I had related the truths of that day. The next morning I was called in early to Court and cross-examined with no small acrimony by several, but I had the satisfaction to find I had not made an improper answer, and had given several of them very severe ones. Nor did I ever fail to throw in everything in my power that I could to prove I thought that the failure of that day's success should have ALL laid at the doors of those infamous ministers who sent such a weak squadron out, after all the repeated intelligences they had had.[2]

[1] For Boyd see p. 144; Everitt was West's flag-captain in the *Buckingham*.

[2] Mrs. Montagu, the Queen of the Blues, wrote to Mrs. Boscawen on the 12th January, "I admire Captain H——y's method of watching the battle. I have known people boil an egg with a watch in their hand, counting the

The next day Captain Amherst of the *Deptford* was examined, and very soon confounded by the Court, so that his evidence proved of little consequence to the Court. The evidences were all gone thro' that the Crown called, wherein it was observed thro'out that no one question had been asked by the Court that could give an opening to favour the prisoner, and yet not one reply given that could tend to accuse him of any one crime. This was glaringly declared by the numerous spectators about the Court.

The 16th *The further address to the publick* that I wrote was published and sent down here to us.

The 18th the Admiral called his evidences. Captain Gardiner (his own captain) proved the courage of the Admiral, his coolness in all his orders, and his readiness and wishes to bring the enemy to a closer engagement. The next day the Admiral had agreed to call me in, but when I was attending I found the Admiral called his own secretary only, and closed his evidence. This sudden change surprised me, and the very abrupt manner in which he closed the whole of his defence. It must have been some peck between himself and Mr. Clark that morning. I had no conception of it, it hurt me much, and therefore I determined to go to Town the next day, as I could only be of use to him there now. He was so certain of being acquitted that he desired me to write a letter for him to be ready to send to Lord Temple, that he might hoist his flag for a few days, which I did, and set out the next day, and was very busy in Town giving the most favourable accounts of Mr. Byng's trial.

But it was easily perceived there was a sullen determination in the King, the Duke of Cumberland, Lord Anson, and the Duke of Newcastle (which was artfully conducted by that determined, implacable villain, Mr. Fox) to sacrifice Admiral Byng in order to screen themselves from the just resentment of the people for the loss of Minorca and other infamous misconducts. And indeed, the 27th at 3 in the morning convinced everyone of this, as Mr. Lawrence (secretary to Admiral Byng) came up express to me to

minutes, but I never heard we were to do so when we basted the French. If I had been in court, considering the delicacy and effeminacy of the family, I should have asked if he had not his tweezer-case on his left side. By this noble gentleman's evidence I conceive Mr. Byng's to have been the most bloody engagement that ever happened. The Blakes, Van Tromps and de Ruyters, though men of some courage, must strike the flag to Admiral Byng. I do not believe we shall lose this brave commander by any untimely death. He has abused the late Ministry, which I take to be an antidote against ugly incidents." For a different view, see Appendix C, p. 325.

acquaint me that the Admiral was condemned to die by the Court-martial; that the sentence had been pronounced at 4 o'clock that afternoon, and which at once acquitted him of cowardice or disaffection, and in the strongest terms declaring they found him guilty contrary to their consciences, only in obedience to one severe Article of War which left them no alternative. I shall not here dwell on this most astonishing sentence,[1] given by the most infamous set of judges. It has been so fully wrote upon, and so severely handled, that every one may see the whole at length. When the news came to Whites', where Mr. Fox happened to be at supper with many others, the conscious and concealed persecutor was not satisfied with the wording of the sentence, and declared in these very words, he would rather be Mr. Byng than one of his judges, for they deserved all to be hanged. In short he feared, by the strong recommendations to mercy expressed in the sentence, that the Admiral would escape, and then himself and others be called upon to answer for their neglect of Minorca, which the battle of the 20th May had no more to do with than the Battle of Malaga, 60 years ago.[2]

In the morning I went to Lord Temple, to Lord Egmont, Mr. Dodington, in short to everyone I could to stir up all the assistance I could to shew a face against such an infamous violation of justice. This affair made a great noise, the King referred the sentence to the Judges, everyone cried out against the Court-martial for condemning a man against their consciences, having acquitted him of every crime that could have condemned him. The iniquity of this proceeding was seen thro', and people everywhere was open against it. The 3rd February I was re-commissioned for the *Hampton Court*, and to go out to the Mediterranean again passenger to her, as Admiral Osborn[3] was to go commander-in-chief there,

[1] The 12th Article was: "Every person in the fleet who through cowardice, negligence, or disaffection, shall in time of action withdraw or keep back, or not come into the fight or engagement, or shall not do his utmost to take or destroy every ship, which it shall be his duty to engage, and to assist and relieve all and every of His Majesty's ships or those of his allies which it shall be his duty to assist and relieve; every such person so offending and being convicted thereof by the sentence of a court martial shall suffer death."

The sentence recited that Byng had neglected to do his utmost to relieve St. Philip's and defeat Galissonnière, but in a letter accompanying the sentence the Court gave to understand that they thought him guilty of an error of judgment only.

[2] In 1704.

[3] Henry Osborn, Vice-Admiral of the Red; his brother had married Byng's sister Sarah.

it was reported. In the meantime I was entirely taken up printing things for Mr. Byng's case, and stirring up his friends. Lord Bath told me he thought it was impossible they could execute such a sentence. Sir Edward Hawke, who was come home, told me the morning I was with him (the 5th) that he would go live in a cottage rather than serve to meet such treatment, and said that Mr. West had been very false in all this, and rose on Mr. Byng's ruin. This indeed was but too true, but Sir Edward was as double in all his boastings, and was ever so about it. I got *Some queries* printed the 8th in the papers.[1]

The 9th I met Mr. Keppel at Lord Temple's levée. He asked me about the third of a freight I carried up from Lisbon some years since. He named Admiral Norris and Captain Moore, and I Admiral Forbes, to leave it to their decision, who gave it unanimously in my favour some days afterwards.[2]

The Judges were to meet to consider of the legality of the sentence on Admiral Byng, and on the 17th declared the sentence to be legal, which made everyone despair of justice being done the Admiral. In short the King was such a hardened brute that he was determined Mr. Byng should not escape, and this very night I heard that orders were sent to Portsmouth for the execution of Admiral Byng. Admiral Forbes, one of the Lords of the Admiralty, having his doubts with regard to the sentence, refused his signing the order for the execution, which made a great noise. Lord Temple, Mr. Elliot and Doctor Hay were the only three that signed it.

I dined with the Patriot Club the next day, and Sir Francis Dashwood (since Lord Despenser) determined to move to have the sentence with the letter of the Court laid before the House of Commons. Mr. Fox opposed it, but the motion was not dropped. I went to Mr. Pratt[3] and got his reasons for repealing the 12th Article of War, and blended it with Mr. Byng's case. About this time Admiral West, commanding a squadron at St. Helens and going to sea, and one of the Lords of the Admiralty, wrote to resign his command, for that he would not serve under such an article as the 12th Article of War (see his letter and reasons printed at large in a pamphlet),[4] but his near relation Lord Temple being First Lord prevented that timely resignation.

[1] They were by Horace Walpole, and are printed as Appendix D.
[2] See p. 124.
[3] Charles Pratt, later 1st Earl Camden and Lord Chancellor.
[4] Unidentified; the two letters are printed by Charnock, Vol. IV, p. 421.

There was now a petition to the Parliament now set on foot to be signed by the members of the Court-martial, desiring the sentence not to be executed. I went so far as to speak to Denis, Norris and Mr. Smith, who all said they would sign it. I carried Lord Egmont at Richmond Mr. Pratt's arguments and reasons for explaining and amending the 12th Article of War. The 21st I went to Lord Temple and told him the scheme there was to get the Duke of Bedford and himself to join in the petition to the King for a pardon. Lord Temple told me plainly that he thought he should hurt it, for that the King would rather be against any measure that he could recommend. I told him if we could get it moved in the House of Commons that he might influence many people, which he promised. In short the great work was to get the members to sign the petition to the King for a pardon. I sent Rodney[1] about to several, whilst I went to others, but we could get nothing determined, so that I went the 22nd to Sir Francis Dashwood, where Sir John Cust came to meet me, and we consulted what motion was best to make in the House of Commons, where I was so unfortunate not then to have a seat. However Sir Francis Dashwood kindly and generously came to a resolution to move in the House an explanation of the 12th Article of War, to blend it with Mr. Byng's case, and to shew the great hardship that officer and all others lay under from the severity of that absurd Article. Sir John Cust undertook to second it, and Mr. Dodington (since Lord Melcombe) to take it up and speak to people's passions and to move the House. Sir Francis accordingly opened the debate and spoke very strong with regard to his opinion of the treatment given Mr. Byng, the whole conduct of it, and how little he deserved the fate he meets with. He was seconded by Sir John Cust. Mr. Fox opposed the motion and said that Mr. Pitt (then Secretary of State), nor the Admiralty, have not said one word in favour of Mr. Byng to the King, but had left all the odium on His Majesty. He concluded with saying the Minister might represent truly to the King that not one man in the House had spoken against mercy. Mr. Pitt then took it up, and declared openly he wished for mercy, and that he thought it was not for the honour of national justice that this should go into execution. Sir Francis Dashwood and Lord Egmont said that Mr. Byng's blood would lie at the door of

[1] George Brydges Rodney, later captor of Martinique, victor of Finisterre and The Saints, was then a captain. He was five years older and senior to Hervey. He was a Tory, whose glorious days were to come in the reign of George III.

those who do not explain what they meant, that if any one was to read the resolutions of the court without knowing the sentence, they must conclude they all tended to acquit him; one of the resolutions says that the witnesses saw no backwardness in him, then, for God's sake, of what did they condemn him? Mr. Dodington said he should be glad to know of what he was not condemned, and it was the acquital of cowardice and dissafection after such severe enquiries that supported him under all the cruel treatment he had met with. He had been, even by SUCH JUDGES, condemned of nothing that stained the soldier or the subject; that the world must know the sentence to be extremely cruel, and was even thought so by those who gave it. It would therefore be more mercy to his judges than to him to pardon him, for they plead the distress of their consciences, and their expressions clear it from clashing with the King's promise.[1] They shew that they think their own sentence unjust. Lord Strange said that the motion for repeal of the 12th Article of War would be more absurd than anything but the sentence that was given up for an infamous one on all hands. Mr. Pitt said again more good might come from mercy than rigour under such a sentence. Lord Barrington, that wasp of power and snake of ministerial dirt, opposed the motion, and said that discipline was relaxed, and that they found the good effects of some punishments which he cited.

I got Mrs. Osborn[2] to go to the Duke of Bedford to present a petition to the King, but in vain. Some of the members of the Court-martial intreated Lord Temple to enforce their letter to the King for mercy. In short there was now more cry against the Court-martial than against the unfortunate injured prisoner. . . .

I was with Sir Francis Dashwood and Mr. Walpole[3] to-day the 24th, but found the Court party in the House of Commons was adverse. At night at White's, that infernal black demon, Mr. Fox, told me he was surprised the Court-martial could shew their faces, that he would much rather be Mr. Byng than one of the thirteen members of the Court-martial. I made him no answer, but went away.

The next morning, as I was at Mr. Walpole's, General Conway[4]

[1] That he would save no delinquent from justice; made in reply to a petition from the City.

[2] Byng's sister Sarah, mother of Sir Danvers Osborn, 3rd Baronet.

[3] Horace Walpole, who has left a detailed account of these days in the second volume of his *Memoirs of the Reign of George II*.

[4] Walpole's cousin, Henry Seymour Conway, a gallant soldier and later Field-Marshal.

came in, who told us there was nothing to be done unless I could get some of the members to have themselves moved in the House to have their reasons accepted for being for mercy, for that the King had absolutely refused Mr. Pitt and Lord Temple, who were both with the King yesterday. Sir Francis Dashwood and Lord Talbot called on me as I was dressing, and they told me nothing could be done in the House of Commons unless we could get some of the Court-martial to say they desired to be released from their oath of secrecy. I called on Mr. Rodney, and got him to go and speak to some of the members, whilst I would go and speak to Mr. Keppel. In my way I met Moore, and talked with him upon it, and as we were both going to see Keppel, we met Admiral Norris, who agreed and acquiesced with me. We did not find Keppel, so I proposed going to the Admiralty that we might know whether the power of the respite did not lay in them. Mr. Forbes was the only one there. He asked Mr. Cleveland,[1] who was of opinion it was not in that Board, and must be an Act of Parliament to dissolve the members of the court-martial of their oaths. I then went to Mr. Keppel's house and talked with him much on it. He seemed rather irresolute about speaking on it in the House, but I rather thought him inclined to it, and therefore went down myself to the House, and told Sir Francis Dashwood and Walpole, who got hold of him, and Sir Francis took an opportunity of introducing it into the House, and Mr. Pitt called on some of the members of the Court, as he saw some there, to speak out. Mr. Keppel then got up, and stammered out something of his desires to be released from his oath of secrecy in order to divulge the reasons which had induced him to so strongly recommend Admiral Byng to mercy and saying they had condemned him against their consciences. The House thereon gave the members of the court time till tomorrow to determine whether they would divulge their opinions without an act, and, if not, to make an act for it, and in the meantime to address the King for a respite of the sentence till these reasons were given. All this was done in a very short time, and some of the old ministry could not help showing and expressing their dislike of this tendency to justice, and consequently to mercy.

The next day Mr. Pitt (as Secretary of State) acquainted the House that His Majesty had thought fit to order a respite of a fortnight of the execution of Admiral Byng, as he had heard that a member of the Court-martial had got up in his place and spoke

[1] John Cleveland, Secretary of the Admiralty 1751–63. Walpole speaks of him as a creature and tool of Anson.

for a bill to be brought in to Parliament to absolve the members of the Court-martial of their oath in order to communicate something that had passed and their reasons for being so much for mercy. The House debated the motion for a bill, but 'twas carried, a bill ordered and read twice, and ordered to be committed and read the third time. Very strong debates and great abuse between Mr. Pitt and Mr. Fox. At night I was at supper at White's, where Mr. Fox openly called all the Court-martial a pack of fools and knaves. He said were he now to advise the King, he should not employ one of them.

I was the two days following very busy, as I heard most of members had recanted, and would not speak out if absolved of their oath, which astonished every one. However the 1st March the bill came into the House of Lords for absolving the members of the court-martial of their oath, in which debate Lord Hardwicke and Lord Mansfield seemed like two attorneys at assize pleading for the blood of a man, and using all the dirty little quirks and tours of the law. Lord Halifax and Lord Ravensworth spoke very well for the bill. The members of the Court was ordered to attend next day, and the bill put off for their attendance. The next day the members were all called in to the bar, one by one, and asked two questions by Lord Mansfield and two by Lord Halifax. They all declared, except Moore, Norris, and Keppel, they did not want the bill, and even those three almost denied what Mr. Keppel had himself declared in the House of Commons. The bill was therefore rejected, by which Mr. Byng's death was sealed. Nothing could equal the shameful figure every member of the Court-martial made. The amazement which was expressed on everyone's countenance was sufficient to shew their dissatisfaction and indignation at the Lords rejecting this bill, which would certainly have brought to light some infamous work that lay concealed under all these proceedings. But what amazed me was Lord Temple, at the end of the debate, congratulating the House that the sentence was proved to be a legal one, and which made most people imagine there was some compromise between the late and present administration to screen those most infamous delinquents, Lord Anson, Mr. Fox, and Duke of Newcastle.

I was very uneasy and unhappy at seeing my friend and benefactor so betrayed, so treated and so sacrificed, but determined to set out for Portsmouth to take my leave of Mr. Byng, and to see if there was not a possibility to help him to escape out of the hands of these blood-thirsters. I set out the 5th and lay at

Ripley, where I left a set of horses. The next day I dined at Petersfield, and ordered four horses to be ready for me any time night or day that I might return, agreeing to pay three pounds a day for them, and determining if possible to convey Mr. Byng to London as the surest place to get him off from, and wrote to my servant William Cradock to have horses constantly ready saddled for me, as I should want, I said, to go out of Town, and made him hire a Dutch fishing-boat to send a servant to France. But all this proved in vain, as I got to Portsmouth Sunday the 6th, and found Mr. Byng was a prisoner very narrowly watched on board the *Monarch* (Captain Montagu), even centuries in his gallery and in boats moored head and stern of the ship, an officer in his cabin night and day, and people every four hours to look in his bed to see if he was there. All this was very cruel and very shocking.

The next day Mr. Byng wrote to me to go off to him. I found him very composed, cheerful, and seemed quite rejoiced to see me. He told me 'twas hard he should pay for the crimes of others with his blood that had never before been stained, that his only happiness was that the Court-martial could not with all their endeavours charge him with cowardice and dissafection, and was acquitted of both. He often repeated the very harsh manner he had been treated with, which he freely forgave. He was persuaded to petition the King to turn his sentence into perpetual banishment, but it had no effect. Mr. Pratt drew it up. I offered my services to him, and shewed him two or three schemes for his escape, but he told me that he thanked me, but would never think of it, he would rather die than fly from death that way. I left him in the evening and had determined to go off no more, as it really hurt me too much to see a man so treated, who I knew had deserved so much better a fate. But the Admiral wrote to me a note the next morning to press me to go off to him, which I could not refuse. I there penned down the heads of what he was to leave behind him in case he suffered, which he proposed giving Mr. Bruff the Marshal, a copy of it to send Mrs. Osborn. Whilst Mr. Bramston[1] and he went into the bed-place, I stole away and begged of them to tell him I could not bear the taking leave of him, and only prayed earnestly I might see him again, which I own I never expected, knowing the hard heart of the King, who was merciless, and his old ministry ever revengeful. I set off therefore that evening for London.

At Ripley I stopped a day with Mrs. Onslow who was there,

[1] Edmond Bramston was the Admiral's first cousin and legal adviser.

and the 11th I got to Town and found all in great confusion about Mr. Byng's case. Yet he was to suffer. I determined to return now to my ship, the *Hampton Court*, at Gibraltar the very first opportunity, and as I was setting off for Portsmouth my servant William Cradock told me he was married and could not go with me, which was a very great inconvenience and obliged me to stay a day or two longer.[1] But I got to Portsmouth the 16th, where I met Mr. Bramston who gave me the melancholy account of poor dear Admiral Byng's death the 14th, who was shot on the *Monarch's* quarter-deck after the most heroick and modest behaviour which was admired by all his friends, and envied and dreaded by all his enemies. I was sorry to find he had changed the paper I had drawn up for a more moderate one.[2] I went to Petersfield, not caring to lay at Portsmouth till poor Mr. Byng's corpse was removed from Hutchin's where I generally lay, who was boatswain of the dock. Captain Gardiner in the *Monmouth* was to have carried me, but he was ordered to wait a convoy from Portsmouth. The 21st I wrote a paper of *Queries to Captain Cornwall* and sent them up and had them printed, which put that fellow's conduct in it's true light, altho' he got a pension of £200 a year for the loss of his arm, but I believe it was for the evidence which the fellow gave at Mr. Byng's court-martial.[3] Jack Byng wrote me word the Admiral had left me in his will a clock, which clock I have, and will keep as long as I live.[4]

The 23rd I went to Town to wait for the ship being ready that was to carry me to the Mediterranean. I found Admiral Osborn was appointed Commander-in-chief to the Mediterranean, and he offered to carry me, which was very agreeable to me in every light, as a worthy good man, and a great friend and some connection with my late friend Mr. Byng. I went to Portsmouth to wait for my passage the 3rd April, and diverted myself about with

[1] He had married none other than the maid Ann, who was to be the last surviving witness of Hervey's marriage to Miss Chudleigh.

[2] Appendix A.

[3] Frederick Cornwall had lost his arm at the Battle of Toulon in 1744, where he had greatly distinguished himself in the *Marlborough*.

[4] The will says " to my worthy and sincere friend . . . my French clock ornamented with Dresden flowers which I desire he will accept as a small token of our friendship ". Lord Stanley of Alderley saw it in Hervey's house at Norwood many years later, when he was told it was " the clock . . . that Admiral Byng had sent Lord Bristol a few days before he was shot, with the words May time serve you better than he has served me ". See *The Early Married Life of Josepha Maria Holroyd*, by J. H. Adeane.

different parties to Havant, and about the 5th there was another change of administration, Lord Winchelsea at the head of the Admiralty. Mr. Osborn chose the *Prince* for his ship, and I remained mostly with him, settling his signals for him, and different orders. I wrote for the *Invincible*, but could not get her, so that I was much dissatisfied, as well as at my long stay here, and which promised to be still longer, as I knew nothing going on and could not amuse myself.

The 30th Mr. Osborn arrived from Town, Lord Robert Bertie, Lieutenant-Colonel Smith and others came down to go out to Gibraltar with us, which I was glad of. The 6th Admiral Osborn embarked on board the *Prince* of 90 guns. The squadron was the *Prince*, *St. George*, *Monmouth*, *Revenge*, *Monarch*, the *Ludlow Castle* with the American fleet, the *Greyhound* and *Deal Castle* frigates with the Lisbon trade, all of them too weak for the service. The 8th we sailed from St. Helen's, and next day off the Start we had intelligence that all the Brest fleet were at sea, and concluded they were either gone after Admiral Holbourn, who with ten sail of the line sailed a few days before with all the transports for America on which the fate of America depends, or that they were to cruise for us who would be an easy morsel, having only five sail of the line with a hundred sail of merchant ships. What absurdity in the Admiralty proceedings were here! No sooner was Holbourn gone with his ten sail than they order away the *Invincible*, *Nassau* and *Defiance* to sail immediately after him, which were only three or four days before us and much too late to overtake him, so that they risked those three ships falling into the enemy's hands, and would not detain them three days to sail with us, which would have been an additional strength to this great convoy, and we might have always gone on as far as Cape Finisterre in our way together, and then each pursued at least risk his different instructions. And at Spithead lay ready for sea the *Royal George*, *Ramillies*, *Royal Sovereign* and *Neptune*, these four prime manned ships. In the harbour was the *Magnanime* with 750 men on board, the best seamen in England, cleaned but two months before, and only waiting in the harbour that Admiral Mostyn may have all his officers and men ready for the *Royal William* that was not yet ready to launch, nor could not be ready in two months more. The *Torbay* with 680 fine men had lain six weeks in the harbour and not to be docked that Mr. Keppel might not be obliged to leave Town whilst the different enquiries went on. The *Devonshire* docked two months before, now ordered into the harbour to dock again. Why were not these ships employed to strengthen Mr. Osborn's squadron as far as the Cape ?

The 12th we had accounts confirmed of the French fleet being sailed for America ; they were met at sea the 7th. The 14th it blew so hard we were obliged to put into Plymouth, where we heard Captain Moore was ordered to the Windward Islands with a board pendant ; that was for his behaviour on the court-martial. The 17th I was surprised, with a northerly wind and ebb-tide, that we did not sail, and went down and spoke to the Admiral (as Clark Gayton was his Captain, a poor creature, tho' good boatswain he would have made) who immediately ordered them to make the signal and to weigh, and down Channel we went, and off the Land's End next day I could not help observing how little discipline there was in this ship, and how unfit a man for such a command was his Captain.[1]

[1] Clark Gayton commanded the Jamaica station 1776–8. Charnock (Vol. V, p. 390) says that a " rough pleasantry " was natural to him, and cites as an example his refusing to trust to bankers and their bits of paper ; instead he insisted on taking home his considerable fortune in prize-money in specie on board an " old and crazy frigate " !

XV

THE CHIEF OF STAFF

May to November 1757

The three chapters which follow describe the next eighteen months' operations in the Mediterranean. Hervey discusses the strategic problems which arise, and reveals the manner in which the business of the fleet was conducted. The loss of Minorca was a severe handicap, as there was now no advanced base within the Straits.

THE 24th we parted with the Lisbon trade, and Colonel de Cosne went in the *Greyhound* in his way to Madrid, where he was going secretary to the Embassy. I wrote in to Senor Don João. We parted with the Cadiz trade the next day, and we spoke with the *Lyme*, Captain Vernon, who gave us an account that Rear-Admiral Saunders had assembled all the ships on that station at Gibraltar in order to cut off the passage of the French ships that were supposed to be sailed from Toulon in order to join the rest of their fleet sailed for America. The next day we got into Gibraltar Bay, where was Admiral Saunders with the fleet. Mr. Saunders acquainted the Admiral that he had the night before received accounts from Genoa that the Toulon fleet was fitting out with great expedition, and that eight sail was destined for America, that the French had eighteen sail of the line at Toulon. The Admiral was determined to go and cruise in the Straits and wait to intercept these ships, and to go up the first westerly wind off Toulon, and so return with an easterly wind.

I was busy in taking possession of my ship the *Hampton Court* from Captain Swanton and found her ready for the sea. I never liked her, but kept her on account of my people. But I was very glad to be here with Admiral Osborn, as he had great confidence in me, and flattered me that I was of great use to him and assisting to make the different dispositions of his fleet, and writing all his letters, orders, etc. I persuaded Admiral Saunders to change his flag to the *St. George*, which he did with all his officers and men.

I sailed the 2nd June with the *Revenge* (Captain Storr) under my command to cruise in the Gut. The whole fleet joined us in two days, and we continued cruising. The days I was always on board the Admirals. I found by Saunders that at Gibraltar the clerks of the offices there made a practise of purchasing all the King's condemned stores and selling them again to merchant ships etc, by which practice the King had often very serviceable stores condemned. A very glaring instance of this was a Mr. Barber (the Commissioner's clerk) and a Mr. —— (Naval Officer's clerk) joined in and bought a very large parcel of the King's stores that were condemned and sold at public auction, but so managed that one Finsey, a Jew and a fiddler, purchased them in his name, the bargain was struck off, tho' one named —— would have paid half as much more, and these people got about two hundred per cent by them, and sent them to Leghorn. The same Barber offered my purser to purchase all my seamen's tickets that were discharged, and said he would give cheaper than anyone. On being asked by the purser, he offered ten Peistrines or ten penny pieces for a pound sterling, if above £10 the tickets, then twelve Peistrines for a pound sterling. This I only mention by way of proofs what infamy is going on in every office, and which ought to be known to be enquired into and prevented.

We were now all at sea, except some cruisers gone up, and our fleet were the following ships :[1]

Prince	90 guns	Admiral Osborn Captain Gayton
St. George	90	Rear-Admiral Saunders Alec Hood
Culloden	74	Smith Callis
Berwick	70	Robert Hughes
Hampton Court	70	Hon. A. Hervey
Revenge	64	John Storr
Swiftsure	70	Thomas Stanhope
Monarch	70	John Montagu
Monmouth	64	A. W. Gardiner
Princess Louisa	60	William Lloyd
St. Albans	60	James Webb
Portland	50	Jervis Maplesden
Ambuscade	40	Richard Gwyn

[1] All the captains of the ships of the line were senior to Hervey, except for Hood, Lloyd and Maplesden ; Gwyn of the *Ambuscade* was also senior to him. It is rare to find a 40-gun ship put in the line at this date.

Frigates

Lyme	32	Edward Vernon
Experiment	20	John Strachan
Fortune sloop		William Hotham

The 14th the *Swiftsure* (Stanhope) joined us, which made us twelve sail of the line the whole fleet, which was very insufficient for the different great objects in the Mediterranean. The Admiral exercised the fleet in lines and firing every day. The great view was to prevent the French fleet getting thro' the Straits, that they might not send any more ships to America, where everything was now pushing, but where our Ministry had sent a commander-in-chief for the Navy whom no-one would have scarce trusted a line of battle ship with—Admiral Holbourn, and the success of his fleet proved my observation.

There was nothing happened worth notice till the 17th, when the Admiral gave me orders to take the *Revenge* under my command and go off Toulon, and endeavour to make myself master of the French force there, and to get what intelligence I could afterwards at Villa-Franca. We afterwards settled a kind of plan for the fleet's proceedings in case I should not find the French in any readiness to come out. I went on board Rear-Admiral Saunders in the evening, and afterwards separated from the fleet.

The 20th I chaced a ship in the evening off Majorca, which, with little wind, I could not get up to, but made her a French frigate of 32 guns. The *Revenge* could not get up at all, it was so little wind. The French ship rowed and towed, endeavouring to get into Alcudia Bay, but could not get round the point, a little breeze of northerly wind took her, and she run into a little creek just to the southward of Cape de la Pedro. It was now almost night, I was very near in, and therefore kept all my own boats and the *Revenge's* to keep my head off shore, determining to destroy her in the morning if I found there was no fort or town to protect her. At daylight, therefore, I ordered the *Revenge* to stand off and on in the offing, and towed my own ship in. As I approached her and sent in my boat with a flag of truce to command them to surrender her, I saw their people all running on shore, as the French ship lay close to the rocks, and they carried a French flag on shore. My officer hailed the French man-of-war and told him, as there was no inhabitants here about, there could be no protection for him, that therefore I command him to strike and give up. One of the officers on board hailed and told mine to keep off and row away, on which I fired at him, and he immediately set fire to his ship, and as his guns were all pointed into me, and I feared his blowing up so near me, I immediately fired a broadside into him, and she sank on one side immediately. I stood to sea, and tho' I could not learn her name then, afterwards I found it was the *Rose*[1] of 36 guns and 220 men, for which I afterwards received the head-money.

I got off Mahon at 8 that night to look into that harbour. At day-light next morning I found myself becalmed off Cape Mola, and had the mortification to see a French frigate towed into the harbour without being able to get at her, tho' I afterwards took a small ship from Toulon that was under her convoy. In the harbour I could only see the Intendant's flag flying on board a ship in the harbour. The *Revenge* took in the offing a small ship from Genoa under French colours bound into Mahon, loaded with different merchandises. There were two women passengers on board who desired earnestly to go on shore, and I gave them the boat of the ship and two men to sail them in with all their baggage, and went off. I saw there was no alteration made at St. Philip's. Next morning I re-took the *Eagle* sloop that had been taken eight days before by a privateer of 24 guns. I continued my route towards Toulon and the 26th took a French snow, four days from Toulon with ship-timber for Mahon. He told me that he left in the road of Toulon four ships of the line that would be ready in ten days for sea, and five more preparing but wanted men. Next morning I got close in with Cape Sicie. I hoisted a Dutch flag at the fore-top masthead of my own ship and both our ships had Dutch colours flying. I went on board the *Revenge* as a lighter ship to look close in, and also that Captain Storr might see whatever observations there was to be made of the enemy. In Toulon road I saw four sail of the line, one had a *cornette*[2] at the mizzen topmasthead ; five or six more in the basin, and the rest were small ships. I was within four miles of the shore and could not wish for a better view, nor a clearer day for it. We had but little wind or should have taken several ships standing into Toulon, as also a privateer who brought a snow in tow in from the sea. However I re-took the snow with my own ship, but the privateer got off. The *Monmouth* and *Princess Louisa* chaced in, who told me the fleet were about twelve leagues off. I dispatched away the *Revenge* with my

[1] In fact she was the *Nymphe*.

[2] A broad pendant.

letters to join the Admiral, and sent the vessels with her, and stood away myself for Ville-Franche.

Next morning the 28th I sent my boats and took a little tartane that came from Tunis bound to Toulon. The next day, as I did not care to be troubled with this vessel, I (with the consent of my officers and people) sold the vessel to the master of her for 180 sequins,[1] and sent her away and got into Ville-Franche at 4 in the afternoon. I got pratiqua next day, and went to Nice to General Paterson, who was Governor of the province and Lieutenant-General of the King of Sardinia's forces. He told me that as to our whole fleet going into Ville-Franche, he had no orders about it, but would write to the Chevalier Ossorio by an express; that it were to be wished we did not come in all together, that they avoid at this time any essential jealousy to the Court of France; that as to five sail, there would be nothing in it, and he hoped soon to have an answer from Court; as to cattle we might have what we wanted. I dined here, and his Excellency shewed me an English newspaper that told me I was returned Member for Bury. We had an opera at Nice and I returned on board very late, and wrote several letters to my brother at Turin, and others to England and Genoa. Next day 1st July, I dined at Monsieur de Gibair, commandant of the gallies, sold my prize for 36,000 Genoa livres, and distributed it directly, about £1,600 sterling. I was very anxious to get out, but the wind was from the sea the whole day. I could not get out next day, so I went to Nice, and was at the opera with Madame la Barrone Tonda. Next day I got out of Ville-Franche with the assistance of the gallies' boats, who were sent me, and whom I paid out of my pocket, as indeed I often did on these occasions, no allowance being made for those extra (even necessary) expences. I got off Antibes this evening, and next day off Cape Sicie, but could see nothing of our fleet on the rendezvous.

The 8th I chaced three pollacres which a Catalan vessel had told me were French. It being calm I sent my boats to chace them with Mr. Shenery and Mr. Holmes (2nd and 3rd Lieutenants),[2] and by night they were within pistol-shot of them, but finding they were all lashed together and one of them appearing a vessel of force, they thought it most prudent to return, and got on board

[1] About £80.

[2] St. John Chinnery became a Commander in 1761 and a captain in 1773. Lancelot Holmes was an elderly officer who had been in the merchant service; he became a captain in 1762 and died in 1785, aged 97.

about midnight. I was very surprised they had not made sure at least of what they were, and expressed my dissatisfaction at not leaving a boat to follow them with false fires, that the ship might go after them if there came wind, and, if not, that I could send more force after them. The next morning however, at dawning of the day, we saw the three vessels, and being scarce any wind, we only saw the white of their ensigns, on which everyone on board declared them French. It inclining to calm, and a whole day before us, and these vessels not above three leagues from us, and having found fault with the officers the night before for not seeing at least what they were, I determined to go myself to set them an example of their duty, and in consequence set off with the boats at 7 o'clock, and by 2 in the afternoon was within musket-shot of the three pollacres, all lashed together, as they had done before, designing to defend themselves with all their people, taking us for Algerines. I ordered the barge and yawl to row on the larboard bow, whilst I attacked the starboard quarter with the pinnace and longboat, having swivel guns and thirty men in her. But I went in the pinnace to head the boarding, and fired several swivel guns at them. They called out, and at last got poles to spread their colours which till then hung down only white. Just as we were rowing under their quarter, we perceived arms in their colours, and they called out they were Neapolitans, but were all hid at close quarters for our reception. This damped us all at once, having taken them for French to that moment. I went on board, and as there sprung up a breeze of wind, I made one of them tow us down to the ship, whilst I refreshed all the people on board them, paying the master for the wine and onions he gave us. He got us on board by 5 in the afternoon, and I set them at liberty, being Neapolitans bound to Leghorn and Naples.

I stood away for Ville-Franche, and sent my boat in for news the next morning to enquire after the Admiral and fleet, but with strict orders to the Lieutenant not to say that we had not seen the fleet, but on the contrary came in with letters from it. At 4 in the morning Mr. Baker[1] returned in the boat, no account of the Admiral. I received several letters from Genoa and other parts, and was much hurt at finding my Brother Bristol was then so ill. I made sail to the westward, and took a French sloop coming from Marseilles bound to Palermo, and sent her into Ville-Franche. Soon

[1] James Baker, commander of the *Fortune* sloop later in the year and a captain in 1758; at present he was First Lieutenant of the *Hampton Court*.

after, I took another Livornois vessel, whose Captain, on examination, confessed his cargo to be all French, and shewed me the real bills of lading, telling me if I had him his freight he did not care about the rest. I made sail to the westward and kept him. At midnight the *Fortune* sloop joined me, going to Nice with letters from the Admiral and to look for me. I stopped him to return with me to the Admiral, who was near me, and whom I joined the next morning the 12th at 9 o'clock.

I found the squadron very sickly and the Admiral surprised at my dispatch having been twice on his station to look for him. He told me his plan, that being very sickly and no account of any French ships coming out, he determined to go to Leghorn and refresh. I took the liberty to tell him that as the French were now in the utmost consternation for having divided their force at Toulon, the great object must be to keep them so, and for the ships that were in the Levant to fall in his hands, that therefore he must secure the passage between Cape Taular[1] on the island of Sardinia and the Barbary shore, and also that between Corsica and Leghorn; that he might very well do this, and water his ships also, by sending Admiral Saunders with a detachment to water at Cagliari by two at a time, whilst the others cruised off Cape Taular, and so on till joined by the Admiral; that the Admiral with the rest should go to the northward, and water either at Leghorn or at Ville-Franche, and then go down to join Rear-Admiral Saunders and pursue the rest of the plan that shall be found best for preventing the enemy getting their ships from Malta. This opinion I gave to both the Admirals together, who, after considering the whole, approved, and that evening Admiral Osborn desired me to draw all the necessary orders, which I did, and next day Admiral Saunders went away with the *St. George*, *Swiftsure*, *Revenge*, *Monarch* and *St. Albans*. We kept sailing for the N: E: land to range the coast for Leghorn. The Admiral gave me orders to increase my compliment of men to 520, by bearing 40 supernumaries for victuals and wages. The morning of the 13th I received on board Mr. Perceval from Admiral Saunders, a son of Lord Egmont's, but with a very indifferent character from Saunders of him.[2]

These days we were sailing along the coast and I was examining the papers etc: of the Livornois vessel, when the Admiral on Saturday the 16th threw my signal out, and gave me orders to

[1] Cape Teulada.

[2] Hon. Philip Tufton Perceval, a captain in 1761.

go into Genoa and enquire of the Republick into the truth of the report of their building ships for the French, and to examine into everything that was going on in that port, and know about their shipping cannon for Toulon. I left the Admiral that day and, having little wind, it was the 18th in the morning before I got to Genoa. Mr. Holford the acting Consul came to me, who I appointed as agent for the Livornois vessel. He told me he was afraid it would be four days before I should get pratiqua, and I told him I would not wait for it. He gave me an account of the Ministry in England, and wherein I found Lord Anson again as First Lord of the Admiralty, which I very sincerely lamented, for my own sake as he has ever been very adverse to me, for my country's sake as a most ignorant man, and for the sake of the service as a prejudiced weak head that was only led by three or four interested people nearly as ignorant as himself, and this to be at the head of what I think the most important Board for England that is, especially in a war.

This afternoon, notwithstanding what the Consul told me, the Health-Officer boat came off and told me I had pratiqua and was at liberty to go on shore, which I did directly, and went to the comedy with Madame Brignole, where I caught cold, and in the night had the gout in my left foot, so that next morning I could not bear it scarce to the ground. I therefore went on board to write my letters to the Admiral and dispatched a boat to him in Leghorn to let him know the situation of things here, which I very well collected last night from the Count de Lavariano, the Sardinian Envoy, an old acquaintance of mine. I was confined by the gout today the 20th on board, and had many people on board to dinner with me, the Grimaldis and Niccollini Doria, Constantino Nigroni, Giacomo Durrazo, and others. A Monsieur Lilla came to me next morning, who was one of those flattering sycophants that introduces himself in all companies, and is ever well with the ladies. After much round-about work, he told me he would make me a confidence which he begged I would never tell, and after much work told me Madame Brignole, for whom he knew I interested myself much and was much attached to, had during my absence lost about 4,000 livres at play, and was afraid her husband should know it, and did not know what to do to pay it, as she had a delicacy about it to speak to me of it, and would never forgive him if she knew it. I made him no answer but said I was very sorry, and turned off the conversation, knowing him to be a rascal who perhaps had won it, but more likely employed (after the Italian fashion) to tell it me from the lady, in order to get it—and I was fool enough next day to give her 200 pistoles in a box when she came with many ladies to see me!

I received this afternoon a letter from Admiral Osborn from Leghorn telling me of his arrival there, and which fretted me very much, as he told me he had saluted the town first, which I knew had never been done to the Grand Duke's territories, and which the Emperor (as Grand Duke) wanted much to bring about, and therefore threw a bait out to all our people to tell them that unless they saluted the forts first and would receive gun for gun (which crowned heads do) that they would be taken no notice of on shore by the guards or centinels. This was so trifling a ceremony that, had I been at Leghorn, I should have entreated the Admiral to have waved all those considerations, and if the Governor took no notice of him, not to take any of the Governor and only do the business of the fleet with the Consul, and return on board, as his stay would be so short, only to victual and water the fleet, and I knew the Livornois would soon make the Regency of Florence sensible that the town of Leghorn would lose much by giving any offence to the British squadron, as much money was always left there by our ships. This day however I received a counterbalance to this letter by one from my Brother Bristol at Turin, telling me he was recovered and that I was chose Member for Bury the 26th May 1757, by a majority of one vote. I had 11, Sir Robert Davers 10.[1] The next day the 23rd I went on shore (being pretty well) to the Doge, and after supping at Madame Lascari's with Madame Brignole, I had the gates opened for me, and went off at 2 in the morning to sail, which I did about 4, but was obliged to anchor in the road with a calm, where I stayed all day. Niccollini Doria and others dined with me, and we went on shore in the evening to Madame Angelina Spinola to meet

[1] Brother Bristol assured Newcastle he had a new supporter in Parliament; "I have acquainted my brother Augustus with his being chosen for Bury, and I have reminded him at the same time of the many professions he has made of adhering steadily to me and my friends, of which list I have placed your Grace at the head; I hope I may congratulate you upon your having an additional friend in the House of Commons. . . ." *Add. MSS* 32,871.

In October he renewed the assurances: "My brother Augustus has not long since confirmed to me his former assurance of having no other connections than mine, and has particularly mentioned his resolution to serve your Grace. I hope the zeal of our part of the family for you will in some measure compensate our want of abilities. I am one that will adhere to you till you drop me. I really value your character, and neglect alone can alter me. . . ." *Add. MSS* 32,875.

Madame Brignole. The evening brought the wind off the land, with which I sailed and got into Leghorn late the Wednesday 27th.

The Admiral had a number of people to dinner with him on board from Florence and other parts. I went to him, where there many pretty Italian women that come to see the fleet. The next day the Admiral called on board my ship. Mr. Howe the merchant was with me who was my agent there. We went on shore together to dine at Mr. Dick's, the Consul, who I found a good agreeable sensible coxcomb. Count Bellrusst, my old acquaintance, came to see me. The 29th and 30th I dined with different people, lay at Mr. Howe's, the Admiral lay at Mr. Dick's, and the 31st Sunday, having finished all the Admiral's letters to England that went by express, and laid the plan of all our transactions and made several proposals home with regard to the fleet here, I went out with Mr. Howe to a house of Mr. Jermy's at Monte Nero to dine there, where was a Mr. and Mrs. Lefroy, and Mr. Sherron, and after dinner we went to the Testori's house (the Commissary's wife) where was the *sposa* St. Pierre, the Ricci, my former cicesbee and whom I made up to again, and several others. The Ricci was jealous of the St. Pierre who was very pretty, and who, she had been told, I should certainly make up to. So early in the evening the Ricci would come to town, tho' there was a ball that evening at the Testori's, and she insisted on my going with her, which I did in her chariot, and held her by the —— the whole way. I spent the evening at her house, where was a great *conversationi*. . . . The evening the 3rd August I went to the Ricci's, who gave me some hair, and a little garnett ring, which she bid me keep, she cried much as I was to sail next day. Sir Horace Mann came in, who was come from Florence to see the Admiral. The wind coming in very strong from sea we could not sail. I therefore dined with the Comte de Bellrusst where was the Ricci, and the Marquis and Marquesa de Corsi come from Florence to see the fleet. In the afternoon I carried them all on board the Admiral with the *sposa* Damiera, and then to my own ship, where we supped and afterwards all went on shore. The next morning we all went out at 5 o'clock. I wrote a letter to the Ricci, which I sent enclosed to Mr. Howe.

I was on board the Admiral most of the days laying out the plans. The *Berwick* and *Louisa* the Admiral determined to send off Marseilles for a few days, and myself to take the *Revenge* and me off Malta to look for the French cruisers said to be there. The 9th the Admiral, Captains Hughes, Gardiner, Callis, and Gayton came and dined on board my ship, as it was calm. We were going down the coast of Italy, and got off Ville-Franche the next day, and sent the *Louisa* off for letters and intelligence. We cruised off Toulon till the 19th and then went away to join the ships off Cagliari, having formed and delivered a plan for the fleet to the Admiral. The 21st in the morning we were off the island of St. Pierre, South-West end of Sardinia, and at noon were joined by Admiral Saunders and the ships cruising with him, and three prizes they had taken, one of which was worth £30,000 taken by the *St. Albans*. They gave us intelligence that the French were at sea from Malta, two between Malta and Sicily, three between Malta and Tripoli, and two off Cape Matapan. I was for going up immediately with four sail, but Mr. Saunders was not, so it was postponed to be considered of tomorrow.

The next day at daylight my signal was thrown out on board the Admiral, who desired I would freely give my opinion to him as to the distributing the ships or keeping them together. In consequence I told him that I thought Mr. Saunders' scheme of keeping them together till the 15th September was making the fleet of twelve sail of the line to be only acting against three ships and four frigates of the enemy, and leaving all the other services unattended to; that as we knew those ships of the enemy's were at sea, we should endeavour to get at some of them, or prevent their return home; that if three or four ships were to go round Malta, and two others off Marseilles, with strict orders to be off Cagliari by the 15th September, whilst Mr. Saunders with five sail kept between Sardinia and Galita to guard that passage, the French could not well escape us. In the interim the Admiral might go in with the *Prince* and *Revenge*, both sickly, that in this manner we could all be of service, and be together the 15th September to wait the return of the express from England. This proposition the Admiral considered over, and approved after I had put it all on paper. He therefore desired I would write the orders out for those ships he picked out for these different services, whilst he sent for Rear-Admiral Saunders, who dined on board and liked the distribution very much. In short, these gentlemen would never give themselves the trouble to weigh and consider the intelligence they received and the different objects which such a fleet as ours were able to fulfil, but if ever they trusted their instructions and intelligence to others, I never found but in general they were glad to have all that work done for them. I was dispatched away that evening with the *Monmouth* and *Princess Louisa* to go round Malta after the men-of-war, the *Swiftsure* and *St. Albans* to go off Marseilles, the *Berwick* to be ready to go home with the convoy the beginning of September. Captain Storr being sickly was obliged to go in with the Admiral and being disappointed of going with me, I let him share that cruise with me till we rejoined. That evening we chaced Algerines, Captain Gardiner of the *Monmouth* was the Commodore.

'Twas the 26th before we got off Malta being little winds, and chaced several neutral vessels. We determined to go over to Cape Passaro first, and then cross over, and round Malta. The 30th we took a French ship called the *St. Thérèse*, Captain Cain, a ship of 18 guns, 36 men, from Marseilles to Alexandria. Gardiner determined to go away to Cagliari as his orders were out, and leave me with the *Princess Louisa* to continue some days longer. I took Captain Lloyd under my command and kept cruising off Malta and off Pantellaria till the 11th September without any material intelligence but of their being four sail of French at Malta, and three gone up the Levant. The 10th I took a French pollacre with my boats, called the *St. Antonio*, Captain Claud Guigon, who was wounded by a musket from the boats, and one of his men killed in the boarding. He came from Marseilles bound to Smyrna, but not rich. He had 400 quintals of coffee in him, which surprised me to find they sent West-India coffee to Turkey. I found by all the letters we had had but bad success in Germany.[1]

The 13th I made the land of Sardinia, and the 14th joined the Admiral off the Bay of Cagliari, where I received sixty-three letters from England, but was sorry to find the Admirals had changed their plan for the fleet, altho' by the Admiralty's answer to the express all was left to them, only desired to weigh well whether they could be supplied in any of the Italian ports with stores and provisions, and to send another express to the Admiralty when they had determined finally. This I told them was leaving all to them as they could wish. Notwithstanding, Mr. Osborn told me they had not wine or provisions and therefore would go down, leaving the *Monmouth* and *Revenge* to cruise off Cagliari, and afterwards to go to Naples and bring down any trade there that might

[1] The Duke of Cumberland had been defeated at Hastenbeck in July; in consequence he had to surrender all Hanover to the French, and the Duc de Richelieu entered the city on 11th August. On the 8th September Cumberland signed the convention of Klosterzeven which brought about his recall and disgrace. Frederick the Great was being pressed on all sides by the French, Austrians, Swedes and Russians.

be bound homewards. For my own part I could not help disapproving this arrangement, and when they both asked me about it, I said I would consider it all over, and tell them in the morning. I went on board my own ship, read my letters in which I had nothing material, and then threw before me the whole situation of our fleet and the enemy's situation. But before I delivered my sentiments to the Admiral I determined to go on board Rear-Admiral Saunders and see what his real opinion was. I found on conversing with the Rear-Admiral that he could not justify our going down so early with the whole fleet, and I found he expected orders to go to England and therefore wanted to be down soon to be ready to sail. I very freely told him what I thought, and found that as long as I did not hint at his remaining up it was very well. I soon after went to the Admiral, who I found impatient to know what I had planned out, as the good old man never could be brought to digest his own thoughts, however sound his judgement was and however good his intentions for the service alone.

I told him that, first of all, the retiring with the whole fleet in the month of September to carry down eight sail of the trade will be rendering the fleet of no use, and leaving the Mediterranean exposed to the few French ships that are about and to those, as it is reported, they are fitting out at Toulon. He acknowledged this, but as he had already answered the Admiralty's letter before I joined him (which I found Saunders had induced him to do) and told the Admiralty he would go down with the fleet, he thought he must now comply with it, or that he would appear to be unsettled. I replied to this that he might in one sense answer both purposes, only by making the distribution for the fleet's going down different, and not let all Europe imagine we were leaving the French masters of the Mediterranean, and also not be all flocking in together to Gibraltar. "However, as to myself, I am totally against the fleet going down till October, but on the contrary would advice our all going immediately off Toulon, but if that can't be, at least take down the great ships, *Prince*, *St. George*, *Cullodon*, *Monarch* and *Berwick*, let the *Monmouth*, myself, *Revenge*, *Swiftsure*, *St. Albans*, *Princess Louisa* and *Ambuscade* go off Toulon, remain four or five days to show them we are desirous of meeting them, if none of them come out or appear in readiness for sailing, let the *Monmouth* and *Revenge* go to their destined station, the *Swiftsure* and *St. Albans* go down the coast of Spain and collect all the trade homeward bound and carry them to Gibraltar, myself with the *Louisa* go off Mahon, see what they are about and alarm them of the fleet's approach, then go to Gibraltar, and the *Ambuscade* go from off Toulon directly to let you know what is going on there. This squadron will be answering all the purposes, and, at the same time, ease you at Gibraltar of having all the ships in together to refit, so that by the time some of these are down, you will have two or three ready to go to sea on any occasion, and, in my opinion, have a very different appearance from that of going all down together."

The Admiral made me lay this all out on paper, whilst he sent for Admiral Saunders, who, as usual, approved all without giving himself much trouble to consider. The orders were immediately wrote out, and signals were made to distribute them. I remained late on board the Admiral and drew out the heads of his letters to the Admiralty etc that was to be sent on his arrival at Gibraltar. As soon as I went on board my own ship, we all joined the *Monmouth*, Captain Gardiner, and the next morning separated from the fleet, tho' little wind.

The 18th we dispatched the *Ambuscade* to look for the *St. Albans* who was thought to have stood into Cagliari with some prizes. The next day the *Ambuscade* joined us, and told us the *St. Albans* would be with us next day. The 20th the *St. Albans* joined us, and having strong North-West winds we made no way of it. The 23rd Captain Gwyn and myself drew up an agreement to go shares whilst he commanded the *Ambuscade* and I the *Hampton Court* in the Mediterranean. The time advancing I represented to Captain Gardiner that I believed he would think of our separating soon, as these winds had retarded the Admiral's schemes very much. The 25th as the winds continued, Captain Gardiner made a signal for all Captains, and told us that he thought this gale would continue, and therefore was desirous to have us all together before we separated, which he said we should do tomorrow if the wind did not shift, as ten days had elapsed since the Admiral left us and we were not ten leagues advanced, by the winds and currents being so much against us. The next day the 26th we had chaced a French pollacre from Ciotat bound to Tripoli, empty and rotten. We sunk her. Two days after Captain Gardiner made our signal to separate, at the same time for the *Revenge* to chace. However I saw a sail, and being within twenty leagues of Cagliari, I determined to chace these vessels and go water at Cagliari which would lose no time. At 2 I found myself alongside a French pollacre called the *Vierge de Montcarmel* from Tunis bound to Marseilles. I just dropped my boat on board, and pursued another in sight which I soon made to be a tartane, and the *Revenge* coming up with her I left off chace, joined the *Louisa*, and run into smooth water under the islands of St. Pierre before night.

The next day I got into Cagliari, and found the *Monmouth* and *Revenge* standing in also. I got pratiqua next morning. We found water very scarce here, not being able to get above twenty tons a day, so that the *Revenge* and *Monmouth* sailed this evening, having got ten tons each only. Next day I went to the Viceroy (Count de Trinita) and made him a visit, ordered Captain Lloyd to go and water under Cape Poule,[1] as he could get water with greater ease there, whilst I completed here. I dined with the Viceroy, who gave me a most splendid entertainment, but gave me a sad account of the people of the island, and the afternoon shewed me the King's stables with very fine horses in it, which was all I saw worth notice. This Bay is a fine one, water is scarce, wood and provisions plentiful. In the morning came on board me a Captain Bartholomeo Carcas, a native of Malta and brother to Marguerita Carcas whom I had had signals from at Malta. He told me he had a vessel here, and was loading for Ville-Franche but confessed to me he was loading for Marseilles a cargo of corn worth 50,000 livres, that his contract was made with a Monsieur Audibert, a French merchant here, to go to Marseilles, that if I would give him the notis [*sic*] and 10 per cent upon the goods, he would meet me on Tuesday or Wednesday next off the islands of St. Pierre, and I should seize him, and that on searching in his yellow letter-case I should find the French contract, which case should be in a blue coat-pocket. In short all this plan he settled, and the 4th I prepared to sail, having sold my prize to the Maltese captain for 9,000 livres, received the money, and sailed the 7th at 3 in the morning, and in the evening was off Cape Poule. It blowing very hard, the 9th the carpenter reported the brickwork of the coppers almost all down and was in danger of fire getting there. I therefore bore away for Cagliari and got in that night, and as it continued blowing very hard whilst there and water coming on board very slow, I determined to go lay under Cape Poule to water faster, as well as to know that place in case of emergency. So I went away Tuesday, and went on shore in the evening, finding it a very convenient place. I let the people all go on shore in different parties to refresh themselves and play about, and Thursday being complete, I weighed and went to sea.

Nothing remarkable till the 16th, that I chaced and took with

[1] Cape Pula.

my boats a French pollacre from Bona bound to Marseilles with wool, hides, wax and 6 guns and 24 men. We had hard gales till the 19th, when the wind came easterly. I therefore determined to go to Gibraltar and join the Admiral at once, having this prize that would otherwise retard me. The 22nd the wind changing to the westward and blowing very hard, I gave Captain Lloyd orders to remain with the prize, whilst I pushed away for Gibraltar, least the Admiral should want my ship, and both of us staying with that vessel was useless. In the afternoon it blowing harder, I saw Captain Lloyd bear up for Table Round Bay under Cape de Gatt, and I kept plying to the westward. It was the 27th before I made Gibraltar Hill, and got in that day, and received many letters from England of little importance.

I went on board the Admiral, and that night Captain Lloyd and my prize came in. The Admiral told me he had sent the *Rainbow* to Naples to fetch the trade down and to dispatch the *Monmonth* and *Revenge* without any, as he expected the French ships down soon. We dined with Lord Robert Bertie that day and Lord Home[1] and others. I went off in the evening and dedicated the next day to the Admiral's business, and therefore went to him early, when he desired me to read over the Admiralty letters and then sketch out the orders for the ships, which I did. The *Jersey* and *Louisa* to cruise between Cape St. Mary's and Cape Spartel, one of them to look into Cadiz every fourteen days for orders; the *Louisa* to go on this service when the convoy sails, and not to part from them till joined by the *Portland* from Cadiz; the *Fortune* sloop and pollacre to proceed to-morrow out of the Straits, and carry orders to the *Jersey* to cruise off St. Lucar; the *Fortune* to proceed to Cadiz for the garrison's remittances, and the pollacre to her station in the Straits. The *Ambuscade*, as soon as fitted, to proceed along the coast of Spain up to Ville-Franche, and bring down any intelligence of consequence to the Admiral, and if there is none, to write down by the post only that he is arrived off there and proceeding on with his orders (which the Admiral will understand), and then for him to go off the island of St. Pierre and up above Malta to Cerigo at the entrance of the Arches, and cruise for six weeks up above according to the best intelligence for the destrution of the enemy, then to proceed to Leghorn for further orders. The *Berwick* to heave down after the *Ambuscade*; the *Swiftsure* and *St. Albans*, when arrived, to refit, and the latter to relieve the *Louisa*, and the *Monarch* to relieve the *Jersey*; the *Swiftsure* to

[1] William, 8th Earl of Hume, Lieutenant-Governor of Gibraltar 1757–61.

attend the coast of Spain, as also the *Monmouth* with the *Revenge*, on any cruise that was wanted, as the two best sailers and best cruisers. The Admiral to remain in the bay with the *Prince*, *St. George*, and *Culloden*, with always five ships in out of those that are cruising about here. The *Hampton Court*, with any frigate, to go and scour the coast of Spain and Provence, and to get intelligence wherever she could, and if none material, to cause her to return to the fleet, then to proceed up to Malta, cruise there, and then to Leghorn, victual, and bring down the trade with the *Rainbow*, *Guernsey* and *Lyme*. This was the distribution I made for the ships, and which the Admiral approved and gave directions for the orders to be prepared.

We continued fitting the ships at Gibraltar without anything material, till the 5th November that the *Tartar's Prize* (Captain Ballie) came in express from England in twelve days, but only with orders for the Admiral to enquire into Captain Stanhope's conduct of the *Swiftsure*, having drove a French vessel on shore on the coast of Sardinia, and very improperly landed after the people. The Admiralty's orders were very peremptory and strong on this occasion, that if Captain Stanhope had acted in that manner, he was to be superceeded and sent immediately home, with the officers also so offending. By this time we heard of the miscarriage of the expedition against Rochefort under Sir Edward Hawke, which I thought was likely, as I had had much experience of that officer's not having a head to conduct an expedition, however he might and certainly had a heart to gain an engagement.[1] The 6th I sent a bill of £200 to Mr. Henshaw to pay off Mrs. Voll's bill, my former tailor, in full. We were all this time fitting, and no resolution could I bring the Admirals to of sending away the ships, tho' they approved the disposition for them. Only the 9th we got the *Ambuscade* to sail on her destination. The 11th the *Swiftsure* came in, and brought in a Swede and a French pollacre. The Admiral shewed Captain Stanhope the orders he had received with regard to himself, which Stanhope was struck with, but acknowledged the fact was so, that he had chaced a pollacre on shore on the island of Rossa[2] at Sardinia and his people had landed

[1] This attempted raid in the Basque Roads was the first of several by which—and by the threat of which—the elder Pitt successfully diverted French strength and attention from the main battlefields in Germany. Though Hawke had contributed to its failure by his uncooperative behaviour towards the military, the greater blame must be laid on the General, Sir John Mordaunt, for his halting conduct, which exasperated the Admiral.

[2] Five miles N.E. of Cape Teulada.

after them. Stanhope came to me in the stern-gallery and desired I would take this in hand for him, make an answer for him to the charge, and prevail with the Admiral not to suspend him, but give it a favourable turn home, so at least as to gain time. But tho' I did not much like Mr. Stanhope or his conduct here, yet I thought it but good natured to assist him now he seemed so much distressed, tho' it was not an easy thing to evade a fact so openly committed. However I undertook it, providing Mr. Saunders would go hand in hand with me upon it, for he commanded the ships of that detachment from which Stanhope chaced. So we turned it about, and Mr. Saunders wrote also to Lord Anson, and we heard no more of it.

I was much tired of this place and nothing to do. The 14th we were diverted with a private anecdote of a Captain Leviston,[1] great friend of Lord Home, who run away with the Genoese Consul's daughter (Mademoiselle Denina) a good handsome girl.

[1] Perhaps Adam Livingston, a Major in Lord Robert Bertie's regiment (21st Foot), then stationed at Gibraltar.

XVI

THE MOONLIGHT BATTLE

November 1757 to March 1758

This chapter describes the thwarting of the French plan to send part of the Toulon squadron out of the Mediterranean to America; that attempt culminated in one of the most famous single-ship actions in the history of the Royal Navy—the Moonlight Battle fought by H.M.S. *Monmouth* against the *Foudroyant*.

THE 19th November I was so tired of this silly idle life I desired the Admiral to let me go out with the *Louisa* for a few days to the westward and cruise for the sake of my people, which he gave me orders to do, but a strong westerly wind coming in prevented us and the convoy, and the 22nd we had letters from Carthagena and from Captain Gwyn that nine sail of French men-of-war were off that port the 14th determined to go out of the Straits the first easterly wind. This hurried us all to go out immediately to cruise in the Straits for them, tho' I looked upon it as an artifice of the French to keep us all together. However the wind continuing westerly, we worked to get the *Swiftsure* and *Berwick* out of the mold. We sent an express to Cadiz to call in the *Portland*. I drew out a new line of battle for the fleet, and the wind continuing westerly. The 26th we got the *Berwick* and *Swiftsure* out.

In this interim the Admiral shewed me letters from Messieurs Lee and White from Smyrna of the 26th August, setting forth the situation of our own and the French trade to and from the Levant, and wishing some men-of-war could be spared that way. They made it evident that in 1750 there was exported from Marseilles to Smyrna only to the amount of 1,562,029 dollars, and shipped at Smyrna for Marseilles above 1,764,713 dollars, so that to judge from this of their Levant trade to all the ports, and especially to Aleppo and Constantinople which is more, we may judge what it would be to destroy this, that twenty to thirty ships go annually from Marseilles to Salonica, which with the trade to Egypt and the coast of Syria and the other scales[1] of the Levant makes (they believe) above ten million of dollars annually, that in the year 1756 it was near double the usual amount, from the loss of Minorca and our credit then with the Turks. In short the conclusion of this letter was an application for ships to attend this important branch of the French trade, as well as to protect our own from the enemy's privateers. Indeed I always thought the Levant too much neglected by our instructions from England, from an apprehension we had of offending the Turks, which is of no manner of consequence to us at present, the French having total possession of them, and from what I have ever seen of all the different Mahometan states, nothing is ever to be gained by them but from the consequence you make yourselves of to them and the fear they have of the harm you can do them. They do nothing from any other motive, since for interest the French must ever carry it, as they under-sell you everywhere and at every market.

The wind coming easterly the 27th, the Admiral made the signal to unmoor, but the wind returning to the South-West, we all moored again. Next day I went on shore to a wedding, Captain Carrey, only son of Lord Falkland, was married to Miss Leith, a daughter of a very honest Captain in the Artillary, and a very fine young woman she was, tho' her mother had been a kitchen-maid.[2]

The next day brought us in the *Monarch* and *Jersey*, which latter the Admiral was inclined to send up with the trade, who had petitioned for a convoy, but I strongly represented against parting with any ship at present, because if the French came down I imagined they would endeavour to push thro' the Straits what they could, and then the more ships we had the better chance to prevent them. When Saunders came on board, without opening my lips, he was fully of my opinion, but he was not quite so as to my wishing to be at sea, lest the French should slip by us on the first spirt of an easterly wind before we got out of the Bay. However we lay still with a westerly wind.

The westerly wind continuing, the 3rd December the Admiral desired I would go up to St. Roque to settle some affairs there with General Buccarelli, the Spanish commander-in-chief of all

[1] Trading ports.

[2] Lucius Ferdinand Cary, a captain in the 14th Regiment, died before his father the 7th Viscount Falkland; his bride was Anne, daughter of Colonel Alexander Leith.

the troops about the lines, and I rode out thro' the Spanish lines with Colonel Renton, Captain Edhoes and Mr. Crutchett, a merchant, and went to St. Roque, where I was received by the General very politely, and settled all our points about the French privateers lurking under the islands of Tarifa for our trade, our sailors running tobacco, and many little things of this sort that had bred ill blood between us. In short, I dined with him, and came away in the evening very well satisfied with my visit. Next day we had the news of the King of Prussia having defeated the Austrian Army.[1]

The wind continued westerly, and no accounts of the enemy, till the *Lyme* appeared off the 7th and sent in a boat to tell the Admiral the French were off Cape de Gatt. I was immediately sent for to the two Admirals, whom I found together. It was determined to wait for an easterly wind and secure this pass, least they should slip by. I was sent to Lord Home to let him know the result of the Admirals' consultation. The *Syren* came in and brought us a list of the French ships that were out. Winds continued strong westerly, and we all waiting with impatience for a change of wind to bring the enemy down, or go to them. The *Tartar's Prize* (Captain Ballie) came in Tuesday from Ville-Franche, but he had seen or heard nothing of the French. I had a touch of the gout in my left foot, which was troublesome. In the afternoon the wind came up easterly, we all weighed, and the convoy for England did so also, but in the night the wind came to the westward, and we found ourselves, convoy and all, at the back of Gibraltar Hill. The wind increasing, we were drove up as high as Malaga by the 18th, when the wind returned to the eastward, and we stood for the Straits, and the convoy made the best of their way. But the wind returning to the westward, and we cruising till the 22nd, and having intelligence by land that the French were in Carthagena ever since the 6th with six sail of the line and two frigates, we run into Gibraltar Bay.

I advised to send the *Lyme* and *Tartar's Prize* off Carthagena to watch the enemy, one of them to return with the most perfect account of them and the other to watch their motions and find whether they persisted in coming to the westward. I was not well all this while with the gout, so the Admirals came and dined with me, and, the wind coming again to the eastward, we weighed, but the wind returning westerly anchored again, and had the news of

[1] Meaning the brilliant victory over the French and Austrians under Soubise at Rossbach on 5th November.

Sir Benjamin Keene's death, our Ambassador at Madrid, and which at this time was of great prejudice to our affairs, as I believe we were endeavouring to prevent the junction of the French and Spaniards at this time, and France using all her power to get the Spaniards to enter into the war with them.

The 26th early in the morning the Admiral wrote me a letter, and enclosed me one he received from Consul Banks of Carthagena with a very particular account of the French squadron under Monsieur de la Clue in that port, who had the 10th instant received an express from the French Ambassador at Madrid acquainting Monsieur de la Clue (as was said) of the number of our ships here, and therefore telling him he ought to remain at Carthagena till further orders from Paris, or till re-inforced from Toulon; that a council of war had been held on board the *Océan*, and it was reported to be unanimously resolved to wait the return of an express from Paris; that they were fitting out two fireships and expected five sail more from Toulon with Monsieur du Quesne, a *chef d'escadre*. I wrote back word to the Admiral that I would see him next day, but to recollect that the very steps had been taken by the French which I foretold. The next day, being better, I went early on board of Admiral Osborn, and he sent for Admiral Saunders, and we found that Captain Rowles in a privateer had last Monday stood close in to the French squadron, and came down with a fresh easterly wind as far as Malaga, that this intelligence was good, and we were certain by appearances that they would not stir from Carthagena. I was for going up to the Bay of Escombrera[1] and anchoring there, where we should keep them ever from stirring without fighting us, and nothing could go into them but must equally pass us, that the Spaniards could not object to this from having permitted the French to lay so long in Carthagena with eight sail of ships. Mr. Saunders said he knew not this road, and that the Straits seemed the best place to put a stop to their going out. The Admiral's master was called to know if he had any knowledge of the Bay of Escombrera. He said he had never anchored in it, but to all appearance it was a better place to lay in at any time than this Bay, and certainly commanded the harbour of Carthagena. Notwithstanding this, here we remained, going out every little spirt of a Levanter, and anchoring again in Gibraltar Bay every return of a westerly wind, which made this work the most laborious for our men and officers this time of year, and for the ships also, as it was one continual scene of hurry and attention.

[1] Five miles S.E. of the harbour mouth of Carthagena.

We had no more intelligence of the French till the 9th January Captain Baker came on board of me and told me he had spoke to a Dutch ship from Carthagena who had left the French men-of-war the 30th December in that harbour, moored head and stern waiting a reinforcement before they would come out. I went to the Admirals immediately and urged to them the necessity of running up there with this westerly wind, that we might have an opportunity of intercepting their reinforcement at least, as we were sure with that wind they would not stir. Whilst we were in this way, the *Monmouth* (Captain Gardiner) joined us with a privateer he had taken, and hearing that the *Montagu* (Captain Rowley) was at Cadiz, I proposed sending for her, which was done overland, whilst the *Fortune* was sent by sea for her. The Admiral also took notice how unaccountable it was that by this ship he had no letters from England, nor had he had any one answer to any of his letters, excepting that by express from Leghorn, for these several months. The *Montagu* joined us from Cadiz the 26th, which made us now thirteen sail of the line, with which we sailed from Gibraltar again this day, being the seventh time in these few weeks. I was for making two squadrons, one to go off Carthagena, the other remain here. The Levanter came on so very hard the 29th that we were forced out of the Straits, and we lay to under a ballanced mizen, which was the finest opportunity for the French to escape had they been out, as it was so hazy we could see but a little way, and could not have engaged for the sea. It grew moderate the 1st February, and I went on board the Admiral the 2nd, who shewed me two letters he had by the *Fowey* from Carthagena, by which we found the French were there the 12th of last month, waiting for a reinforcement from Toulon. We plied into the Straits by the 5th, where we imagined the French might have come out with this Levanter, and, if a westerly wind came up, put into Malaga. I therefore pressed the Admirals that if that should be the case, as was generally imagined, that they would atttack them in that open bay if they were joined, as it would then be an object to destroy ten or twelve sail of the line, and that the Spaniards would not in that case dare to resent it. However the Admiral seemed rather cautious about this step.

In short whilst we were cruising in this eager and very slavish manner, it gave time now and then for very serious reflections on the conduct of those who had the charge of our naval affairs at home, which here I will examine a little, as the critical situation we have long been in here with regard to preventing the passing of this French squadron is wholly owing to the neglect of the Admiralty, and to them alone, if the French get thro'. For tho' he [Osborn] had been many months intent on preventing the return of the seven French men-of-war to Toulon that had been at Malta to collect their Levant trade, and had blocked them up several months, till he wanted stores and provisions to bring him even down to Gibraltar, yet he no sooner heard of the equipment of a squadron at Toulon to pass the Straits, than he immediately collected all his force (looking upon this as the chief object) and put to sea with every Levanter, cruising in the narrowest of the Straits as the surest place to intercept the enemy, by which judicious conduct he obliged Monsieur de la Clue with eight ships to shelter himself above two months in a neutral port, to the great disgrace of the French flag. But had the Admiral had a sufficient number of ships to have composed two squadrons, and whilst he guarded the Straits in this manner with one, have been able with another to have kept off Carthagena to intercept their re-inforcement, or even their return to Toulon, (which they were otherwise always at liberty to do) they would have been effectually secured, and rendered ignominiously useless. Why then were there not ships sent out of England for this service, when the Admiralty knew in July last that the enemy in these seas had ships fitted that were superior to ours? They also knew that ever since July Monsieur de la Clue's squadron was fitting with great expedition, and if they knew not for what design, at least it proves their want of intelligence. They also knew, ever since October last, of Admiral Osborn's return to Gibraltar with part of the squadron, and those (as they were told) all foul after so long a cruise, and their men harrassed. They knew many of the ships were attending the different services which this extensive station required for the protection of our trade, and they must know that the cleaning and refitting these ships is a work of considerable time from the situation of the place. These watchful guardians and directors of our navy also knew that the French did not sail from Toulon till the 8th November, that they put into Carthagena the 1st December, were reinforced the 22nd January, and continued still there waiting for four more ships of the line. Let me then ask if there was not time to send out of England five or six clean ships, that would have effectually secured this great object by enabling Admiral Osborn to have guarded the Straits at the same time that he either blocked the French in Carthagena or intercepted their re-inforcements from Toulon. But the same fatality attended the navy of England at this immediate era as it did at the taking of Minorca. I mean the same ignorant and obstinate First Lord of the Admiralty, Lord Anson, who only considered a few interested people that had sailed with him in his South-Sea voyage, and who were incapable of giving him better advice. Thus again this dictator in our naval department left exposed this great object, and which indeed was as well attended to by Admiral Osborn with the force he had as could be expected from the most experienced, most alert, vigilant and zealous officer that ever commanded, and for the truth of this I will appeal not only to the Rear-Admiral himself, who was Lord Anson's *élève*, but to every officer in the fleet, and, as far as land officers can judge of naval operations, to every officer of the garrison of Gibraltar. Thus was this service neglected for six months by those at home, and so much so that the Admiral never in this time had the satisfaction of having any one of his many letters acknowledged to have been received. These reflections I could perceive to work hard on the Admiral's mind, and he felt for the cause of the public as well as himself. A disagreeable situation in a country, and at a time when most people were but too apt to judge of people by the success of their actions.

All these reflections made me ever take all opportunities to induce the Admiral at all events to give the French some stroke, let them be where they will, and as we now, the 8th, heard by Captain Veron of the *Lyme* that the French were reinforced by the *Sovereign* and *Lyon*, two ships of the line, and expected four sail more from Toulon every day, which would make them twelve sail of the line and six frigates with which they were to force their way thro' the Straits, I pushed the Admiral to steer off Carthagena with a westerly wind, especially as the Agent-Victualler had reported to the Admiral that we had but twenty-six days bread in store for the whole fleet, and with which we could only be completed all to three months—such a neglect run thro' the whole at home. We put to sea every spirt of easterly wind, and this day Sir Charles Saunders hoisted his flag on board my ship, the *St. George's* head being loose and in danger of not being able to come out, so I requested the Admiral to come on board, which he did, but the next night the *St. George* was got out again, and Sir Charles returned to his ship.

We kept in this way till the 26th, when the wind was strong westerly, and I persuaded the Admirals to at least spread and stand along shore, as it was impossible with the wind at West-

South-West the French would go by us if they were out (as was reported). We stood all of us up to the eastward, spreading a great deal of sea to look out, and the 27th, by 4 in the afternoon, we were off Almeria Bay which we looked into, but saw it quite clear. We still stood to the eastward towards Carthagena, and the wind in the night died away. But just before dawn of day, I being near the Admiral's ship as his second, perceived two sail of large ships ahead of the Admiral, which he fired at, but which we could not then tell whether it was not [the signal] to chace. I gave orders immediately to chace and clear the ship, and as day broke we saw four French men-of-war spread ahead of us. The wind was then little and westerly. I gained much on the one I chaced, which I perceived with my glass to be of 64 guns. The general signal had been made to chace long before day by the Admiral. The *Monmouth* and *Swiftsure* chaced the largest ship in the offing. The *Berwick* and *Revenge* followed the one I was after, but the wind being westerly and dying away, they out-sailed me, tho' I had every sail set and were getting up fast with my chace. So that perceiving the *Monmouth* after the largest, I bore away after her to assist her, as I saw the *Swiftsure* a great way from the *Monmouth*. Soon after this it fell calm, and in an hour after the *Revenge* and *Berwick* engaged the chace which in three-quarters of an hour struck, and proved the *Orphée* of 64 guns. Another of our ships was in chace of another man-of-war, and the others of a fourth. I kept pursuing this chace, which I then was certain was Monsieur du Quesne[1] in the *Foudroyant*, and tho' Admiral Osborn made my signal to return yet I pursued, as I thought he could not distinguish, as I could, the force of the ship and the superiority of it to the *Monmouth*, for I then thought the *Swiftsure* had no chance. But it was so little wind, and she to the westward of us, that she brought up the airs, by which means she gained upon us all, and as night came on the wind freshened. About 7 we perceived the *Monmouth* engaged with her chace, and both before the wind with every thing out, and continued so till about 11, when I got near enough to see by the light of the moon that the *Monmouth* lay disabled, and her chace dismasted, and both their heads contrary way, but all firing ceased, and I saw the chace's French colours lying over her taffrail. I run under her stern, and gave orders not to fire, as they were calling to us for quarters, whilst the *Swiftsure* run ahead of

[1] Ange, Marquis du Quesne-Menneville was a descendant of the seaman of Louis XIV's reign. He had been governor of Canada, and the famous fort on the site of the present Pittsburg was named after him.

him, and Captain Stanhope too hastily threw in a broadside to the French ship and partly into me, when I called to him and told him my boat was gone on board, for that she had struck to the *Monmouth*, who was disabled and could not get her boat out. I went on board the *Foudroyant* myself, of 84 guns, with all her masts laying on her decks, 820 men on board, and Monsieur du Quesne, a *chef d'escadre*, going to reinforce Monsieur de la Clue at Carthagena with these four sail. Stanhope's officer soon after came on board, and desired that Monsieur du Quesne might be sent on board the *Swiftsure* as the senior officer. I thought that was right, tho' without a doubt neither the *Swiftsure* or myself had had the least claim to any of the honour which the *Monmouth* acquired by taking such a ship. The truth was the *Foudroyant* never could give a sheer to throw his whole broadside into the *Monmouth*, because that manoeuvre would give the *Swiftsure* and myself an advantage over him, and then he was infallibly gone, whereas he was in hopes to dismast the *Monmouth* and then get away from us two, which he certainly would have done, as neither of us sailed equal with his ship. Therefore I cannot see the poor Frenchman was so much to be censured as he was.[1]

I returned on board, and the *Monmouth* hailed me to say poor Captain Gardiner was killed, which was a very great loss to the service, being a very brave officer and a worthy good man. The next day I went on board Captain Stanhope to visit Monsieur du Quesne, and Monsieur de Lisle Callian his 1st Captain (who I found had commanded the frigate I had burnt at Majorca). A Monsieur de Fabre (a brother to an old acquaintance of mine mentioned in the beginning of these journals) was Captain of the ship. After breakfast I went on board the *Foudroyant* to speak to her people, as she lay there like a rack, and none would work. She buried about 134 men and had about 142 wounded, and by what I could find, the officers were obliged to kill several people to oblige them to go to their quarters. After having spoke to the people and given strict orders that none of Monsieur du

[1] Nevertheless the ship commanded by Byng's late flag-captain had performed a fine feat of arms in taking Galissonnière's former flagship. For the *Foudroyant* was armed with 42, 24, and 12 pounder guns against the 24's, 12's, and 6's of the *Monmouth*, and the French broadside weighed 1,222 lbs. to the English 504 lbs. The French naval historian Troude says that the crew of the *Foudroyant's* "second battery" deserted their guns early in the engagement and hid themselves in the hold. A seaman who saw the two ships lying near each other in Gibraltar Bay was heard to exclaim that "it was like the Monument overlooking a nine-pin".

Quesne's things whatever should be touched of any kind or sort, either as to stock or wines or anything, I returned on board, sent eighty men on board the *Monmouth* to help refit her, and then took her in tow, she was in so shattered a condition. Thus, the *Swiftsure* towing the *Foudroyant* and myself the *Monmouth*, made sail to rejoin the Admiral.

I took several officers out of the *Foudroyant*, Monsieur la Grange and Monsieur de Vialis, Lieutenants, Monsieur de Montfort and Monsieur de Montalet,[1] Ensigns. These ships were intended to join Monsieur de la Clue at Carthagena, who had eight sail of the line and one frigate, and which ships were short of provisions and only waiting for these to push thro' the Straits. Monsieur du Quesne, it seems, had attempted to get in eight days ago, but was prevented, and was standing in this very day to join them had we not intercepted them. 'Tis amazing Monsieur de la Clue did not come out to him, and not risk his being off there with only four ships, for I found Monsieur du Quesne was only to have accompanied de la Clue thro' the Straits and then returned with his division.[2] They left only four ships of the line at Toulon, and those could not be got ready for sea in any time, so that this was a great blow to them.

All these days we made little way to the westward. I spoke this morning to the *Royal George* privateer who told us he spoke to Admiral Osborn yesterday off Cape Palos, and gave me an account of their having taken the *Orphée* of 64 guns and run on shore the *Oriflamme* of 50, by which means I found there was an end to their expedition.[3] I made sail up and told Captain Stanhope the news. At the same time I said it was my opinion as the Admiral was so near that one of us ought to go and let him know our situation, especially as he might want reinforcement of our ships lest the enemy should attempt to slip out. However Captain Stanhope did not like parting, and desired me only to run ahead, which I did and soon after saw several sail that I made a signal

[1] This should probably be Montalais, who was killed when the *Superbe* was sunk at the Battle of Quiberon, 1759; his father was her captain and went down with her.

[2] Du Quesne was "prevented" by an absurd argument with La Clue. The latter, as the senior of the two, thought Du Quesne ought to come into Carthagena to meet him before making for the Straits, while Du Quesne wanted to dispense with that formality. This petty behaviour lost them three days. (Corbett, *Seven Years' War*.)

[3] The fourth ship was the *Pleiade* 26, which out-sailed her pursuers and got away.

for, when Stanhope called me in, desired I would take the *Foudroyant* in tow, and that he would go and join the Admiral. So away he went, and nothing extraordinary passed till Saturday morning the 12th the *Fortune* sloop, Captain Baker, joined me from the Admiral, who I joined the next morning and went on board him, meeting there the Rear-Admiral, Sir Charles Saunders. I very strongly recommended to the Admiral the giving the command of the *Foudroyant* to Mr. Carkett, the first Lieutenant of the *Monmouth*, as a reward for his behaviour and encouragement to other officers. I knew nothing of this gentleman, but from his conduct in this action I thought he deserved it, and the Admiral very kindly appointed him to the command of the *Foudroyant*.[1] We bore up this day for the Straits, as we were sure the French would now never attempt to stir after this blow. I asked the Admiral to give me the command of the *Monmouth*, if she could be soon repaired, which was agreed to, as she sailed so very well, and the *Hampton Court* so very ill. I wrote all the Admiral's letters on this occasion, which was enclosed to Colonel du Cosne at Madrid by the *Fowey* which we sent to Malaga. The *Orphée* was in company and an old ship of 64 guns, the *Oriflamme* of 54 was run on shore by the *Montagu*, Captain Rowley, under the guns of the Point Aiglos, and was left on shore there quite destroyed.[2] This was a stroke Monsieur de la Clue could have prevented had he sailed from Carthagena and waited Monsieur du Quesne's arrival off that port. Then they would have been together at least, and might have fought us and run into port together. 'Twas very bad management.

The 13th the wind returned to the westward so that we kept plying off Almeria Bay, having sent the *Swiftsure* and *Monmouth* on to Gibraltar with the *Foudroyant* and *Orphée*. I prepared everything for the distribution of the prisoners, which were very numerous, and then the Admiral desired me to make out a disposal of the fleet for his approbation, which I did, and wrote out orders for the *Preston* to go refit at Gibraltar, take the trade out and up to Genoa and Leghorn, and then go to Smyrna for the trade, and proceed according to the Admiralty orders to Scanderoon[3] and

[1] Robert Carkett, a lieutenant since 1745, was a doughty fighter, but no tactician. He was the officer who Rodney blamed for the failure of his action against De Guichen off Martinique on 17th April 1780. He was at that time captain of the *Stirling Castle*, and was drowned when she was wrecked in a hurricane in October of the same year.

[2] In fact she later got into Carthagena to join La Clue. " Aiglos " is the same as Aguilas.

[3] Alexandretta.

bring down all the trade from the Levant. I wrote a letter to Lord Winchelsea for the Admiral, giving a private account of the situation of affairs here, wrote to the Intendant of Toulon proposing the exchange of 500 prisoners, which were to be sent to us or to any place they would name, and the Admiral would send for them. Clerk[1] was made commander of the *Orphée* to take her home. I was to have the *Monmouth*, Captain Vernon my *Hampton Court*, Baker (who had been my first Lieutenant) the *Lyme*, and Mr. Cocks, the Admiral's 2nd Lieutenant, the *Fortune* sloop, and other promotions in consequence laid out. Orders were wrote to Commissioner Colby at Gibraltar to fit the ships as fast as possible, with a preference to the *Monmouth*, which was necessary to get ready for sea. I proposed to the Admiral that Monsieur Roy de la Grange and Monsieur de Vialis should be the officers to go with the letter to the Intendant in the flag of truce that they might transact the exchange. I took them also to Mr. Saunders to pay their respects to him, to whom I related all that was done, and intended to be done and who approved to all.

The next morning the 16th the Admiral sent me some letters which came in the *Gibraltar*, and desired I would go on board him, which I did, and met Mr. Saunders. We laid the plan for the general letter to be sent home with regard to the situation of the fleet, that of the enemy's, and everything relating to public affairs in this part of the world. I soon drew it up, and it was approved of. The *Orphée* was to be sent home to carry Monsieur du Quesne, the two Captains of his ship, and those of the *Orphée*. The Admiral wished me to get McCleverty to go home in the *Orphée*, which he at first liked, but on conversing with Mr. Saunders he changed his opinion. I dined with Mr. Saunders and sat late this evening talking of affairs, and I had some satisfaction in finding the Rear-Admiral had as much confidence in me as Mr. Osborn. The next day I wrote to my brother (as Ambassador to Madrid) for the Admiral, wrote also the Sir Horace Mann, wrote the orders for the *Gibraltar* to go home and carry Monsieur du Quesne instead of the *Orphée*. I wrote a paper to publish which I sent to Lacy (vide copy in the MSS).[2] We got the length of Malaga, when the wind changed about constantly. The next day the two French officers Monsieur Roy de la Grange and Monsieur de Vialis went away in

[1] The same Edward Clerk who had been 4th Lieutenant of the *Ramillies* at the battle of Mahon and who had prepared Byng's papers for the trial. He shot himself in 1764.

[2] Missing and unidentified.

the *Thetis* for Malaga, as there was no likelihood of our getting to Gibraltar very soon. They carried letters to the Intendant Commissary, Monsieur Mitchell, at Toulon for an exchange of 500 men. We were lucky in sending these gentlemen in today as the three successive days the weather was so very bad that no boat could pass, and we were mostly laying to under our mainsails. The 21st the weather broke up, and I went on board the Admiral. The next day it blew very fresh again, and we anchored under Roquetta Point, which is very safe riding with the wind to the northward of the West. . . . In the afternoon the Rear-Admiral came on board the Admiral, and I wrote a paper to be sent to the Consul at Malaga to put into the Spanish papers relating to our taking these French ships. I wrote several letters to the different Consuls. The worst was our men fell sickly and we could get but very bad sheep for them here. The wind continuing westerly we could not get down, but in the night it suddenly changed to the North-East. We weighed, but with difficulty weathered Adera Point.

XVII

CRUISING AGAIN

March to September 1758

"Poor dear boy, he is very unlucky; one admiral who was his particular friend was cruelly and scandalously murdered, and another who is also a great friend is unfortunately struck with a palsy, to blast his laurels and damp the happiness of his friends and family in the midst of his glory."

Lady Hervey to the Rev. Mr. Morris, 21st November 1758.

ABOUT noon the 25th March the Admiral sent for me, and I was extremely shocked to find that in the night, as he was looking out of his gallery windows, he was seized with a paralitick stroke. His speech I found very faulty, his mouth on one side, he seemed sensible of his misfortune, which he had brought on himself by his constant anxiety and watching the French and the different duties of the fleet, which he carried to too great an excess and minuteness for his time of life, being seventy-two then. I remained the whole day with him as he desired, and had a consultation of the surgeons of the ships and wrote to the Rear-Admiral, whom I acquainted with it. The surgeons were of opinion it might be attended with very bad consequence. We had a fine easterly wind the 26th, and was off Fougerole[1] in the afternoon when the Admiral's Captain came under my stern and desired I would go to Admiral, which I did and found him rather worse, but in tolerable spirits for his situation. He sent to the Rear-Admiral to remain out with the ships, whilst he went in to Gibraltar to get on shore and endeavour to recover. He ordered the Rear-Admiral to send me in as soon as the *Swiftsure* or *Jersey* joined. The Admiral bore away for Gibraltar, and I went on board to Mr. Saunders who told me he should be glad I would go into Gibraltar as soon as possible for that I might be near the

[1] Fuengirola, twenty miles S.W. of Malaga.

Admiral, and that he should correspond with me, for that I knew the whole designs of the fleet, and I knew it would not be right to leave the ships etc to Captain Gayton.

The next morning the *Jersey* joined us. It blew so very hard that it forced us thro' the Straits. The *Fowey* came out of Gibraltar and joined us off Cape Spartel, where we lay to, and Mr. Saunders sent for me and shewed me the letter he received from the Admiral by which it appeared he was much better, surprisingly so. The shock of the disorder was gone off, and he only wanted rest to recover him. Mr. Saunders desired I would go immediately in, take Mr. Osborn's flag on board my ship, and hurry all the ships out as fast as I could to him, as he would stay out and watch the Straits. He pressed me much to take the *Monmouth*, and by no means to leave the Admiral to the people now about him, lest he would grow weaker. I took my leave and got into Gibraltar next day, and found the Admiral much better, but not on shore as the weather had prevented their landing him. The Admiral seemed quite happy to have me with him and to get his flag on board my ship. I found the *Swiftsure* and *Louisa* still here. The *Guernsey* and *Syren* arrived with the trade from Italy. I was this day swore in for the *Monmouth*, Captain Baker for the *St. Albans*, and Webb was to have the *Hampton Court*. The 30th in the morning I went on shore with the Admiral to the Commissioner's house, and in the evening I hoisted the Admiral's flag on board my ship, blue at the maintopmasthead, and wrote the different orders in the morning at daylight for the ships. The *Prince* was to sail as soon as could be ready. I wrote to Admiral Saunders by Captain Lloyd in the *Louisa*, who I sent to sea directly with directions for the *Swiftsure* to go out this afternoon. Lord Robert Bertie and Monsieur d'Herville[1] embarked on board the *Gibraltar*, who went express to England to acquaint them of the Admiral's situation, who was desirous of going home for the recovery of his health. I wrote to Mrs. Osborn and my mother, and dispatched all the orders for the different ships before noon. . . . The 3rd April I received a letter from Mr. Saunders who very obligingly expressed the greatest satisfaction at my alertness and all that was done.

I was now employed in getting the convoy away for England, but met with many delays from Captain Milbanke of the *Guernsey* who I was obliged at last to threaten with a court-martial. He was drunk and like a madman, abused the Commissioner very much before me, but next morning was very penitent and sensible how

[1] Monsieur d'Herville had been Captain of the *Orphée*.

wrong he had been. The 5th in the morning early Rear-Admiral Saunders came in with the fleet, the wind being westerly. I went off to him, and we went together to the Admiral, who he found better than he expected. The Admiral desired the Rear-Admiral to refit as soon as possible, and at night the Admiral's flag was hoisted again on board the *Prince*. I gave Mr. Saunders a dinner with all the French officers, for whom I kept open table constantly here. I continued writing all the orders for the fleet, as also the Admiral's letters to the different Consuls about the trade etc. The 8th the Captains had a meeting on board the *Culloden* to choose their agents for the *Foudroyant* and *Orphée*, but I would not go as I thought only the three ships that were at the taking had the right of naming agents. However Mr. Brett, Mr. Stephens, Mr. Bately and Rudjard was named, the whole was very irregular. . . .

The Admiral grew better every day. The 18th he shewed me a letter from Malaga, where we found the French was so disheartened at their late loss and had missed their opportunity of getting out, that they had received orders to return to Toulon from Carthagena. Mr. Saunders appearing off, we sent him out the intelligence with orders to go off Carthagena with a westerly wind, and return should the wind come easterly. In the night my Lieutenant returned from the Rear-Admiral, acquainting us that the *Hampton Court* was at Malaga, being separated. This evening I had a great ball and supper for the Consul Loggie's family, Mr. and Mrs. Cary and all the women of the garrison, with Lord Home and others, the Admiral having been out airing today in a chaise into Spain.

The little wind there was the 19th was easterly, but soon came to the southward, the fleet not in sight, but the wind coming to the eastward the 21st, the trade sailed, and we got clear of them, I hoped. I went therefore and dined with General Bucarrelli at St. Roque, and in the evening Mr. Crutchett, a merchant whom I have already mentioned, carried me to see a most beautiful Spanish woman called Rosa. I offered her a good deal of money, and to her mother, but she would only let me toy and kiss her, and all that before her old mother. The 23rd the weather came in very bad to the South-West, and the trade all returned again. The *Fortune* sloop came in this day and brought an account that the French fleet sailed from Carthagena the 19th, and that he had left them twelve leagues to the westward of that port, steering to the westward, which account he gave to Admiral Saunders yesterday at the back of the Hill, and that, as the winds had been, he imagined the two squadrons must be near each other. The Admiral gave me direction to immediately hurry out the *Guernsey*, *Fowey*, and everything that could sail. I wanted to have gone on board the *Orphée* with all my people, but she could not be ready in two days, and Captain Cocks said it must be over before that, one way or another. Indeed I imagined the French intended returning to Toulon myself, but on these occasions it unfortunately happens that one must not proceed as one's own judgement directs, but as vulgar and popular notions will influence.

The 24th I hove the *Monmouth* down on one side, and found her bottom very sound. This morning the *Ipswich* hulk arrived, who sailed from England the 9th with a great convoy and Rear-Admiral Broderick in the *Prince George* of 90 guns, whom they reported to have been burnt in the Bay of Biscay, losing several of her people. The next morning Rear-Admiral Broderick arrived with 248 of his people in the *Glasgow* of 20 guns with his flag flying (Rear of the White) and ten sail of merchantmen. He gave a most melancholy account of the burning of the *Prince George*, and of the infamous behaviour of the merchant ships with him in not coming to their assistance, being afraid of the cannon. The Admiral swam naked above an hour to save himself; he lost everything in her, letters etc. Mr. Saunders appeared off the Bay in the afternoon, when I went on board him. The ships I had sent out to join him all missed of him, but no French fleet ever appeared. The same orders were continued to Rear-Admiral Saunders as before. The next day as the wind came easterly, the convoy was ordered away under the *Syren* and the *Fowey*, both frigates, and the *Crown* storeship, and the next morning the cartel ship[1] arrived with only 161 men, 21 having left her. Mr. Broderick, the Commissioner, Lord Home and several of the principal officers dined with me; they all sat very late and got very drunk. Admiral Broderick was very much so, and very full of his professions to me. I knew he was to be left in the command, but I knew very little of him; what I did made me determine to go home as soon as I could.[2]

Admiral Saunders sent the morning of the 28th to know if he might not come in as the wind was westerly, which Mr. Osborn consented to, and the fleet came in in the afternoon, and in the

[1] Bringing back exchanged prisoners of war from France.

[2] Thomas Broderick had been third-in-command of Hawke's Squadron at Rochefort. Hervey's distrust of him doubtless had something to do with his having been a member of Byng's court-martial.

evening there was a sort of consultation at Admiral Osborn's house to which I was invited. Rear-Admiral Saunders, whose leave to return home was arrived, would not go till he knew what was become of the French, and this I perceived would make a difficulty of providing for Mr. Broderick's Captain and officers, who he wanted with him, for Sir Charles Saunders going home would carry his people with him and leave his ship for Mr. Broderick, as he would have no doubt of getting them provided for with him in England whilst Lord Anson presided, an indulgence Mr. Osborn perhaps could not have obtained. But here it is necessary for me to take notice of the great remissness of the Admiralty at home in sending out the *Ipswich* of 18,000 tons [*sic*], out as a hulk for the government, and yet to send her quite empty, not a store or provision of any kind on board of her, when the fleet here was in such want of everything, and which Government must pay so much freight for when it comes in storeships. But this is all job work, and want of proper inspection and attention at home. The 29th I was obliged to write in Admiral Osborn's name to Colonel de Cosne, the *chargé des affairs* in Spain, for orders from Madrid to the different ports of Spain to permit the extraction of provisions for the use of the fleet, there not being one ounce of bread in store at Gibraltar for this whole fleet, altho' such a convoy was just arrived. Lord Home dined with me today and the Admirals. We came to a resolution not to make any distribution of the men that arrived in the cartel more than employing them till we had done with the French fleet. . . .

The 1st May it was as hard a rainy day as I had seen, the wind came easterly, and Mr. Broderick went on board the *Prince* and sailed with the fleet. The *Guernsey* and *Tartar's Prize* came in, but brought no intelligence with them more than the last of these vessels having spoke to a French ship who said he met the French fleet steering to the eastward off Cape Palos. . . . The *Swift* came in the 3rd, and brought us news that he met the French fleet off Alicant steering North-East with the wind at West-North-West, and by all accounts they were certainly ordered to return to Toulon. I had also this day accounts of my Brother Bristol being named Ambassador to the court of Madrid. The wind coming to the westward the 14th our fleet returned into the Bay, and the next day I got my ship out of the mold. When the wind returned to the eastward Mr. Broderick was not for sailing again, but Mr. Saunders was entirely of a different opinion and thought they should sail immediately to complete the work, and not wait till the *Glasgow* came down and confirmed the intelligence we received by the *Swift*. In short Mr. Saunders came and talked it over with me, and Mr. Broderick went to Mr. Osborn that he might endeavour to gain him to his opinion, but in vain. However this whole day and the night was lost for want of determining. The next day it blew a very hard Levanter, and in the night the wind came to the southward, and the next day to the westward so the fleet did not move. But had the French come down and given the slip, Mr. Broderick would have been very justly highly to be blamed. In short the weather continued very bad till the 11th, and we had various reports of the French fleet being arrived at Toulon.

I sailed with the *Monmouth* into the Bay, but could not paint for the rain. We had a court-martial on Captain Peyton for the loss of the *Prince George*, but he was acquitted. Admiral Saunders was taken ill of a fever, and it was determined he should go for England in the *Montagu* and the prizes go home under convoy of the *Revenge*. I wrote all the Admiral's letters for England, and having made out the disposition of the fleet I wrote out my own orders to go off Toulon, and afterwards a cruise. The 13th Mr. Saunders shifted his flag on board the *Montagu*, Mr. Broderick his on board the *St. George*, and I shifted Mr. Osborn's from my ship into his own. This night the *Greyhound* and *Ferret* anchored from England in twelve days from Plymouth, and without bringing a single order or letter, but one private one from Lord Anson to Admiral Osborn with congratulations on his taking the *Foudroyant* and *Orphée*. The Monday following, the 15th, the *Glasgow* came in without any particular news of the French, except a letter from Mr. Banks, Consul at Carthagena, which in my opinion only confirmed the intelligence brought by the *Swift*, as it said that a tartane arrived there nine days ago who reported that he met the French fleet off Iviza becalmed. Yet there was now a bustle to be made of the French coming down, and the fleet was to go out in a great hurry in order to retrieve their past conduct. So the 17th, as the wind coming easterly, out we all went to sea without the least prospect in my opinion of the French coming, and by this method we lost the refitting of all the squadron, and sending home the prizes. In short we cruised till the 21st, when Mr. Saunders wrote me word that a ship arrived who told them that several French officers had been arrived some time ago and a letter from the fleet disarmed at Toulon. I went on board Mr. Broderick, and, as the wind came westerly, we all went in that evening to

Gibraltar. I found Mr. Osborn very much recovered. This morning an express arrived from Malaga that a Swedish ship had put in there, who had a Swede officer on board passenger that had been a volunteer in the French squadron of Monsieur de la Clue's, that he left them all disarmed at Toulon. Two days after, notwithstanding all these repeated accounts, Mr. Broderick prevailed with the Admiral to let him sail again with the fleet as the wind came easterly, tho' every one saw the folly of it, and I saw the great loss to the public by not refitting the ships, sending home the convoys, and distributing the cruisers. I displayed all this to Mr. Osborn, but however Mr. Broderick prevailed, and away we went, till the next day the wind came westerly, and back we went to Gibraltar. All this dispirited our people now, as they found all their labour in vain.

The next day, the 17th, I prevailed with the Admiral to let me go out, and he gave me orders to go off Toulon, and then a-cruising according to my intelligence for two months, to take the *Ambuscade*, *Rainbow*, *Lyme*, and *Glasgow* under my command, and to do the best I could to distress the enemy. The 29th I gave Admiral Saunders a farewell dinner on board my ship, and had the Spanish General Buccarrelli to meet him, with the Commissioner and many others. In the evening Mr. Saunders sailed in the *Montagu* for England, and the *Revenge*, *Foudroyant* and *Orphée* with him. I also sailed this night to the eastward, and took on board Mr. Penton with me, who was a gentleman of fortune going on his travels and had come out with the *Prince George*. The next day I saw Mr. Saunders and his fleet at the back of the Hill. I steered away from Cape de Gatt, was off Cape Palos the 31st, and Saturday the 3rd June stood close in for Mahon harbour, where I took a French tartane from Toulon bound in. The captain told me that the 29th past the *Sovereign* of 74 guns and *Gracieuse* of 36 had sailed from Toulon as was said for Mahon, that the *Triton* of 64 guns with the *Rose* of 36 had sailed for the Levant and to touch at Malta with men to man a privateer fitting up there, and that the *Lyon* of 64 guns and two frigates were now in the road fit for sea, the rest all disarmed. With this intelligence I steered away for Marseilles, determining to range down all along the coast, look into Toulon, and try if I could get any intelligence at Villa-Franca. For this purpose I put some men into the tartane for a decoy, as I found she sailed very well.

The 6th I was off Toulon, the winds not letting me fetch Marseilles. The tartane took me four others, one loaded with timber for the King's yard. I was very near taking a large merchant ship, but it fell calm and boats came out and towed her in. I kept cruising two or three days without any more success, the coast being alarmed, and therefore I steered for Villa-Franca, where I arrived with my five little prizes the 10th, and went to Nice to General Paterson, Governor of the province and General of the whole. I dispatched away a foot-messenger to my brother at Turin. The Governor of the fort at Villa-Franca, Baron Tonda, Chevalier Maccarana, and other officers of the gallies came on board me. The next day I dined with General Paterson. There was a great deal of company, and among the rest a Madame de Gressy St. Sebastian who was waiting to go to her husband, a Colonel in Cagliari, and to whom she was lately married by contract. The Patersons pressed me much to take this lady and put her on shore as I passed Sardinia. Paterson assured me it would be taken very well at Turin, where my brother was Minister, and that she was a very agreeable lady, and daughter to the Marquis de Gressy, so that I consented to take her and servants on board, and we sailed the 15th. Being assured there was nothing stirring at Toulon, I determined to call at Leghorn for news, and to pick up the frigates with me that were thereabouts. The morning before I sailed I sold my prizes, and shared the money before I went out.

I had no sooner got clear of the land of Villa-Franca than I perceived two large ships in the offing making all sail towards me. We soon perceived them to be two French men-of-war of two decks, and with little wind I made from them and kept my own course, and, weighing what these ships could be, I concluded them ships bound up the Levant as a convoy for their homeward-bound trade. I lost sight of them by night, and made the best of my way to Leghorn where I anchored the 17th and receive pratiqua. I found the *Lyme*, Captain Vernon, here in quarantine. The *Ambuscade* was at Genoa, the *Rainbow* sailed for Gibraltar, and the *Preston* gone up. The intelligence which I had from Mr. Dick, Consul here, was that the *Triton* of 64 guns and three frigates were sailed up the eastward of Malta and so to the Levant to intercept our Turkey trade. This determined me to collect all the force I could and go after them. I therefore dispatched a felucca away to the *Ambuscade* to Genoa to join me, and as I found there was at Porto-Specia a cartel ship from Toulon, on board which there were 98 men who had forced the master of her into that port, I resolved to go there and get those men and discharge the vessel. Having settled all the proper orders from the intelligence I received,

I went on shore, made several visits, and saw the Ricci who I found with child. The next day it was too bad weather to sail, so I made up accounts with Mr. Howe my agent here, and remitted £524. 6. 8. sterling to Messieurs Gosling etc. The Governor Marquis del Monte asked me to dinner, but I excused myself on account of Madame St. Sebastian on board of me. The next day I sailed with the *Lyme* and got to Porto-Specia that evening, the next morning took on board 98 men out of the cartel ship, and sailed in the morning of the 22nd at daylight, and joined the *Ambuscade*, Captain Gwyn. With these two ships I made the best of my way off Sardinia, but had very little winds. I let the Captains into my plan of attacking the *Triton* and the three frigates, and that I was resolved wherever I met them to destroy them, because of the consequence it would be to the Turkey trade. In this time Madame St. Sebastian was very well, very good company and very agreeable, and I believe was very well satisfied with her situation. The 27th in the afternoon I fell in with two of the King of Sardinia's gallies close in with the land of Sardinia. I found it would save me a great deal of time if Madame St. Sebastian could get on board the gallies and go in to Sardinia with them. Therefore I recommended her to write to the General of them to desire him to receive her and carry her in, tho' I was very sorry to part with her; she was such excellent company, so sensible and so amiable without being handsome. She took my advice, seeing the necessity and propriety of it, and that evening embarked on board the General's galley, who sent the Chevalier de Balbiana to receive and conduct her. I saluted her as she left me, and immediately crowded all the sail I could for the island of Marittimo, in hopes of meeting the French, said to be between that and Pantellaria. I spoke to several vessels in my passage, but had no intelligence of the French, and made Pantellaria the 29th. The 30th at daylight in the morning we gave chace to three ships which we took for the French cruisers, when after a long chace and totally cleared for action, we found them to be three Dutch Smyrna ships bound to Amsterdam, but unluckily we found the *Lyme's* mainmast sprung and that it could not be repaired without being two days at anchor. I was very much vexed at this, but determined we should go into Malta for two days, as I intended sending my boat in there for intelligence to our Consul, and wait off there till the *Lyme* came out.

The 1st July in the evening we saw a sail off the West end of Malta that appeared a frigate. We chased her with little wind all night, and at daylight we saw her about four miles off and scarce a breath of wind. However I was to the eastward of her, and off the port of Malta the frigates were much dispersed by the currents and little wind. I made the signal for chasing, and sent orders to the Captains to destroy the frigate if possible at all events, as I had my reasons for paying very little regard to the neutrality of the island of Malta, as they regarded it so little towards the subjects of His Majesty whenever they could show a partiality to the French, and as I looked upon the port of Malta as little less than an arsenal for the French ships of war. For I knew at this time they were suffering the French to fit out a large privateer of 26 guns there in order to join the *Triton* up the Arches, who had brought men from Toulon to man her with. About 8 in the morning the French frigate was rowing and towing with a very light air of wind close in with the shore, endeavouring to fetch into Malta. The *Ambuscade* and *Lyme* were astern of her at three or four gunshot distance. I was to the eastward and standing close in, so that I was certain of cutting her off the port even with the very light air I had. She fired at me, and luckily gave me that handle to begin, which I did, when I found her struggle in in the break of the shore to weather a point just off the Lazaretto of the harbour. The instant I fired at her the batteries on shore, which were crowded with people, began to fire at me, being then about a musket shot from the shore. The French frigate, finding my fire very quick upon her, began to steer wild and run on shore, when I brought to and, firing on her still, made a signal for boats manned and armed and sent my Lieutenant with orders to destroy her under our fire, as we saw their people deserting her fast. But before this could be executed she took fire, and was instantly in a blaze, and about 10 blew up. I then brought to, finding it was the *Rose* of 36 guns, one of the *Triton's* squadron. The loss of this frigate gave me an opportunity of sending away the *Ambuscade* to reinforce the *Preston* now at Smyrna to bring down the trade.

I stood close along the town of Malta that was full of people, and wrote to the Consul in such a manner as that if the Maltese stopped it, they were very welcome to all they read. About two hours after this a boat come off with Maltese colours and a deputation from the Grand Master to know why I had in this manner broke the neutrality of the port by destroying a French man-of-war under their very walls. As they spoke this with some kind of menace, and that the Consul (Mr. Dodsworth), who accompanied this deputation, told me they had at first determined to fire upon me, I told them in French, " Qu'ayant eu l'honneur de voir son éminence le Grand Maître sur son balcon, je ne pouvoit faire autrement que lui donner un feu de joie ", and that was all the answer this deputation could obtain from me. At the same time I told them I would try in the morning whether or not the French party so prevailed at Malta as to induce them to attempt firing on the King of England's ships, on which, if one single shot was fired, I would immediately go and destroy their gallies, which I knew then lay at Sicily for corn. They went away. I continued all the rest of the day off Malta, and the next morning, having a very fair opportunity of wind and weather, I stood along the town of Malta within musket shot, my colours up, with all my lower guns out, and the two frigates following in a line with me. But nothing passed.

I continued cruising till the 3rd, and having then a fine westerly wind I determined to push for Cape Matapan to endeavour, if the French were thereabouts, to destroy them. In short if the wind continued I could be up in two days ; if it returned to the eastward I should be obliged to give it up, as my water and wine could not hold out to go such a distance with a contrary wind. But in the morning the wind veered about to a strong North-East, and by continuing fixed for fourteen hours I found myself obliged to give up my plan and return to the westward. I therefore gave Captain Gwyn orders to go and join the *Preston* at Scanderoon and her convoy and see them safe off Sardinia, and then go to Leghorn for my further orders. By him I wrote a letter to the Consul at Scanderoon and bid him go away that evening, which he did. I got off Cape Passaro the 6th, and the next day off Malta, when the Consul came off to me and told me that the *Triton* of 64 and *Minerva* of 36 was up the Arches waiting to be joined by the *Rose* and *Tyger*, the first of which I had destroyed of 36 guns and 300 men and the second was then fitting out at Malta. I desired the Consul in my name to acquaint the Grand Master that England would no longer shut her eyes on the notorious partiality of the Maltese in suffering their port to be only as an arsenal for the French. The Consul also told me the natives were all for us and against the French party there, who prevailed however over the Government. I found there was nothing more to be done hereabouts, tho' I had once some thoughts of attempting to burn the *Tyger* where she lay in their harbour, but thought it would be censured at home. However, as the *Tyger* was then lying fit for sailing, I sent him in word that if he would come out the next day and promise to engage the *Lyme* only of 28 guns, I would leave her off the port and charged the Captain of the port of Malta to tell the French Captain so. I was as good as my word, for I left Captain Vernon the next day alone off the port with directions to stand close in with his colours flying, which he did, and in the evening Captain Vernon joined me and told me that he had continued off the port with his mainsail furled till past two in the afternoon, when the Consul came alongside of him, but brought no answer from the French Captain, nor did the ship make any attempt to come out. This evening I therefore made the best of my way to Leghorn to victual and water, and determined to get the *Glasgow* and return again upwards if nothing interfered, but meeting with little winds and contrary, it was the 21st in the morning before I got to Leghorn, and meeting nothing remarkably in my passage.

I immediately waited on the Governor, Marquis del Monte, and received several letters from England. I resolved, if I could get away in any time, to proceed up to the Archipelago with the *Lyme* and *Glasgow*, in order to cut off the *Triton* and *Minerva*, and wrote to my brother at Turin that I intended doing so. I received a letter next day from a Mr. Russell, wrote to Mr. Howe my agent, demanding about £50 in full of all charges for the expences of the prizes I had taken in the Levant before the declaration of war. It was very bad weather all day, so that I could [not] have intercourse on float. I had a great dinner at the Governor's with many ladies and a *conversationi* at Mrs. Dick's in the evening. The next day Mr. Howe and myself with some officers went to Pisa, examined those immense fine brazen gates of the church, the burying ground, the place of baptism etc, and then went to the convent of St. Bernardo to see the nuns, of whom there was some acquaintances, Donna Francisca, Donna Crucifice, and Donna Clarica de Battachi. This last is pretty. We stayed there sometime, and returned to Leghorn in the evening, where I found the *Tartar's Prize*, Captain Ballie, just arrived with a small prize, by whom I received a letter from Genoa from my Brother Bristol which obliged me to lay aside my scheme of going up the Levant, as there was a letter inclosed in his from the Admiralty directed to any Captain of a man-of-war that might be at Leghorn to proceed immediately to Genoa and take the King's Ambassador to the King of Spain on board and land his Excellency where he chose. My brother was therefore very desirous, if consistent with the service, that I should carry him. I was as desirous of seeing him, and as I must have sent some ship, it would equally have prevented my pursuing my plan up the Levant, as making me too weak to pursue the French. Therefore I preferred going to attend my brother and distribute the other ships. I dispatched away a messenger to my brother at Turin, giving him rendezvous at Genoa. . . . I sailed in the morning of the 30th with all the trade, and tho' little wind off the land, I got without the Mallora[1] before evening. The next morning, being the length of Corsica, I parted with the *Lyme* and convoy, and bore up for Genoa. In my way I met with a Livornois vessel bound from Leghorn to Marseilles, who I stopped, having information of her. I seized all his papers and found the whole cargo was French. I therefore carried him into Genoa where I arrived in the evening late, having immediate pratiqua.

* * * * *

that evening at a *conversationi* at Madame Momina Grimaldi, where the whole town was assembled, but I left it early to go to the French Theatre, where

* * * *

and accompanied her home as usual. I sent away the *Glasgow* 2nd August with a convoy to Leghorn, and then to go a cruise off Cagliari. In the evening to Madame Victorina Lascari's, where Madame Annetta Brignole came. The 4th Monsieur Constantine Nigroni came to me in the name of the Government to compliment me on my arrival, and to express the satisfaction the Senate had whenever I was here. My whole time was passed here in festivals and conversationi's at different noblemen's houses, who live most splendidly on these occasions. The French Theatre was the only one open this season. A Dutch man-of-war came in the 9th and I got out twelve English seamen of him. . . .

* * * * *

out to Campo Morano to meet my Brother Bristol, who arrived there at 2, and with great joy we met each other and dined there, then came away to Genoa, where immediately came Monsieur Renieri Grimaldi, Pietro Francisco and Francis Grimaldi and Constantine Nigroni to wait upon my brother on his arrival. With these we went to the theatre, and to Madame Pellinetta's box as my cicesbee. The 17th my brother received and made several visits incognito. There dined on board with me to meet him fourteen of the *noblesse* with whom we went to the theatre in the evening. The next day we went about to see all the palaces, and

[1] The Secce di Meloria, a shoal immediately west of Leghorn Harbour.

had a great conversation at Madame Violante Balbi's. In the morning everything of my brother's was embarked, and his equipages and servants in a great Dutch ship he had hired for that purpose. I dined on board with my brother, and would have sailed had the wind let me. I found Genoa had been a very great expence to me this voyage, above £450. The next morning the 20th early, having taken leave of everyone here, we sailed, my brother taking on board only four servants out of livery and two in livery and a messenger, and on board his ship with the baggage was fifteen more servants.

I made sail over to Corsica and had very fine weather during the passage, and was surprised my brother was so little sick. We dined upon the deck every day almost. Just after I had made Minorca we saw two large ships, one of which appeared so French that we prepared for action as she stood end on to us with all sail. I would have persuaded my brother to go on board his baggage ship and part with us, as we expected to come to action and I thought the King's Ambassador with all his instructions etc: to Spain had no business in such a scene, besides being a delicate situation for me to carry him into, and it was the first time, I confess, that I was happy to find the ship did not prove an enemy, but a large Venetian man-of-war, bound down the Straits. We parted again, and the 30th we anchored in Alicant Road, where Mr. Coxswain the Consul came off with my old acquaintance Mr. Reevely. The Governor also sent off an officer to compliment my brother, but he would not go on shore till he set off for Madrid, which would be Sunday morning. First I went to wait of the Governor, the Marquis D'Olos, who was very polite and asked if he should not have the honour of seeing the Ambassador. I said I believed he intended setting out for Madrid the instant he landed. That evening my brother and I landed in the country and walked a good deal, then went off in the evening. Next day I wrote several letters by the messenger my brother sent to Madrid. A Dutch man-of-war came in, who saluted and cheered me. I went on board to see him, and he saluted me again. The Captain of the *Veer* (as she was called) complained of two of our Captains, Captain Barker and Lloyd,[1] having met him in his passage and sent an officer on board him to see his commission and to search his ship, which he refused, telling them he never heard of the States General's ships being searched, and that it was a very extraordinary demand, and that he believed the Captains exceeded their orders,

[1] Of the *Jersey* and *Princess Louisa* respectively.

that after twice sending on board him they went away. The Captain of the Dutch man-of-war told me that he had wrote to complain to the States of it, and that he had said these gentlemen must either have exceeded their orders or not complied with them, in either case they were culpable. I thought it a very just and severe stroke on them. The Dutch Captain came on board again, and told me this was to wait of the Ambassador, so that my brother went and returned the visit the next hour, and was received with the ship all under arms, and saluted with 21 guns at going on board and leaving the ship. At daylight in the morning the Consul came on board and acquainted my brother that his coach and chaises were all ready on the mold. As my brother did not intend to stop in the town we breakfasted and landed about 6. I cheered and saluted him with 19 guns, hoisted three flags, and the standard in his boat. The town saluted him with 15 guns on his landing and 15 guns on his going out of the town. He found a tape and seal of the custom house put on his trunk, on which he took out his sisars and cut before their faces before he stepped into the coach.[1] The guards were turned out as he passed, and to the officers he gave silver-gilt boxes, money to the guard, and money to the adjutants, which was the etiquette. My brother was rather surprised the Governor had not come off to see him, tho' it seems he had been on board the General of the Maltese gallies when in this place. The Governor came to me to the Consul's as soon as he heard I was landed. I went to the Treasurer of the Marine, and dined at Mr. Reevely, and went off in the evening and sailed at daylight the 5th.

I got off Barcelona the 6th, and went in the next. I sent on shore a compliment to the Marquis das Minas, Viceroy of the Province, but he was gone a-shooting. Here I had the good news of Cape Breton being taken, with five sail of French men-of-war being taken and destroyed there. I thought the Spaniards seemed to rejoice at the ill-success of the French, and yet not pleased with our triumphs. I here found a letter from Admiral Broderick to proceed to Gibraltar. I therefore weighed the next day and sailed with a fine easterly wind, till Tuesday the 12th that I made the Hill, and got into Gibraltar about noon and found my orders to proceed for England, which I was very glad of, but I had many ships to take under convoy and I was ordered to Plymouth. The wind being westerly and bad weather, I had little amusements

[1] An action which fully confirms Horace Walpole's description of him as "a very Spaniard in formality and pride".

here waiting to sail every day. There was an Italian troop of opera people came here whom I assisted much. The impressario was one Nicola, a good *buffo*;[1] he had Agatta Massi for first woman, whom I knew at Genoa at the theatre. I sailed with a Levanter the 24th, with about thirty sail of ships under convoy. . . .

[1] A comic singer.

CHAPTER XVIII

HOME AND CHANNEL

November 1758 to May 1759

(After a tedious passage Hervey had arrived at Spithead on the 29th October.)

I passed my time at Portsmouth with Admiral Holmes and women, and Barrington, Pigot etc, till the 11th November that the expedition sailed for Martinico, and I was very much surprised to find no notice taken of my ship from the Admiralty since my arrival. Lady Burnaby was here, and a Miss Ottley, who was very pretty and aimable and made my time pass away very agreeable here. Admiral Holbourn came down the 20th and relieved Rear-Admiral Holmes. I had asked for the *Resolution* and my people, but Mr. Forbes wrote me that he had spoke to Lord Anson who told him the *Resolution* was engaged. In short it was the 25th before I got any orders, and then it was to proceed to Chatham to dismantle and refit the ship there. I wrote to the Admiralty that I had the gout, and desired the ship might go round with a Lieutenant, but had not answer at all to it.[1] The wind coming westerly the 7th December, I prepared for sailing, but grew then distressed at leaving Lady Burnaby, with whom I had mostly lived these two months and who had been kind enough to shew great partiality for my attentions to her, and who, indeed, I had taken great pains to please and to insinuate myself into her favour, and had all the reason in the world to flatter myself I had succeeded, tho' I never saw the least inclinations to exceed the strict bounds of virtue. Yet I had every reason to be satisfied with the preference

[1] This is not truthful. In fact Hervey got an answer which said that a captain would be appointed to take the *Monmouth* round, to which he replied indignantly " that as their lordships think it improper the ship I command should go from hence to Chatham without a captain, I have only to say that I can bear a great deal before I consent to any other gentleman being sent to do my duty". *P.R.O. Adm.* 1/1893.

she always gave me, and which made us very seldom assunder; she was so unaffectedly charming in her manner and person 'twas impossible not to love her.[1]

I paid all my bills the 9th, and then sailed with eighty sail under my convoy. The 10th I got into the Downs with all the ships and took a pilot on board, but it was the 12th before I could sail and got that evening to the Gunfleet. The next day I got up to Blackstakes and got my guns out, but 'twas the 17th before I got up to Chatham, where I spoke to Mr. Cooper the Commissioner about my ship, and then went off for London, where I got about 5, and sat with my mother all the evening. I just went to my sisters and heard no particular news. At least I was then so hurried and so little taken up with domestic affairs that I cared very little about anything but my pleasures in these days, till I got to sea, and then my profession was all my pleasure.

The next day I was presented at St. James's to His Majesty, who did me the honour to rump me without saying a word or even looking civil. I met Mr. Fox at Court who took me down to the House of Commons with him to take my seat, but when I came there I found I had not the certificate of the Crown Office with me and therefore could not be introduced till next day. Mr. Fox was now Pay-Master General and first favorite to the Duke of Cumberland. I dined at my mother's where was company. I remained there the evening and the next day took my seat in the House as member for St. Edmund's Bury, being introduced by Lord Egmont and Sir William Rowley. In the evening I was at Lady Rochford's. I dined with Lord Egmont next day, and did not go to the House as it was to be adjourned till the 16th January. The next morning I was presented at Savile House to the Prince of Wales, who was very civil and spoke to me a great deal; afterwards to the Princess of Wales at Leicester House.[2] I was obliged to go to Sir Samuel Prime's, one of the oldest of the Bury Corporation, as I intended soon to go down to my constituents and entertain them. I went down to Rochester to speak to the *Monmouth's* people, and pacify them on 150 being lent to the *Temple*;

[1] She was Grace, daughter of Drewry Ottley, of Bedford Row, and had married, as his second wife, Sir William Burnaby, 1st Baronet (a Captain in 1742), a decidedly pretty officer whom Admiral Edward Vernon, in a moment of buffoonery, had affected to mistake for a dancing-master! Charnock, Vol. V, p. 131.

[2] George III's mother, Princess Augusta, to whom "Miss" Chudleigh was still Maid of Honour.

returned that evening, and dined at Lord Coventry's next day with Lord and Lady Pembroke and Miss Pelham, and passed the evening at my mother's, who was not very well. In short this was my sort of life till the 27th Wednesday that I got to Ickworth, where I lay, and Brother Frederick came to meet me there, who gave me a detail of the state of the Corporation at Bury whom I was to go and make my visit to the next day.

I therefore went very early this morning, the bells of Horringer, Chevington and Bury ringing all the way as I passed, and three or four thousand people met me about one mile out of Bury with flags, morrice dancers, music, and loud acclamations of joy. They in a manner carried my chaise into town, where I alighted at the Mayor's (Mr. Wright), and, in short, made twenty-three visits to the Corporation as they then stood. I found Mr. Jackson, who was at the head, as I may say, of my brother's party, was for filling up if they could make sure of filling up and get two Wigg's majorities on those to be elected. But as this was doubtful I would by no means give my advice for it. I invited them all to dinner the next day, but in the morning I went to Mr. Ottley and his family, whom I made great court to for the sake of Lady Burnaby. He had several daughters and nieces, very pretty merry young ladies, and himself a very hospitable *bon vivant*. I made several visits in the county, and then went to dinner and dined with the Corporation, Justices, and several neighbouring gentlemen. About sixty sat down to table; we sat till 1 in the morning, most of us very drunk and all very merry and very well pleased. I gave six hogsheads of beer to the populace on the Angel Hill, and there were great bonfires and rejoicings at night. I made several visits about and had many returned to me. I dined at Mr. Ottley's where were his daughters Miss Ottley and Miss Eddye, his nieces Miss Precy and Miss Eddye and about twelve other people. We supped there and stayed till 3 in the morning. I invited them all to my ball for next day, as I had done the whole county. The 1st January I went to Bury to the Town Hall where I was met by the Corporation, and was swore in member and to protect the freedom and privileges of the Corporation, and to renounce the wages formerly given to members. I dined at the Angel with a great deal of company, and at night gave a ball to the Corporation and gentlemen and ladies of the county. There were about 360 people, they danced 54 couple and sat down 330 people to supper. The Corporation had a supper by themselves in another room. There was nothing but mirth and joy appeared and satisfaction thro' the whole town, and everyone allowed they never had seen such a ball in the town at no time. I did not return home till 6 in the morning. The next morning early Lord and General Cornwallis came to see me at Ickworth, but I excused my not dining with his lordship as I was to go to town next day. I paid all my bills today and found this pretty jaunt had cost me £358, besides £40 I gave to the two parishes. That evening Mr. Alderman Wright took me in for £100 which I lent him on his bond, and the next day Sir Robert Smyth set out with me for Newmarket. We lay at Hockerill, and got to town next day.

I found my mother very well again. I passed my time visiting and feasting about, and nothing worth relating passed till the 11th, when I wrote to Lord Anson for the *Fame* of 74 guns that was just launched, as it would be May before my ship could be ready, and I thought it too long to lay by. Lord Anson sent me word he should be glad to see me, and Mr. Saunders told me at night at White's that Lord Anson was inclined to give the *Fame* to me, but on meeting I found him shuffle about it, and so I did not press him, not caring to be obliged to him, as I own it always went against me when my situation and his obliged me to ask anything of him.

I amused myself as well as I could whilst my ship was fitting, and Saturday the 17th, as I was at the Opera, the Duchess of Hamilton, half laughing and half earnest, gave me to understand she was much in love with Colonel Campbell, who will be Duke of Argyll. I took care to let him know it the next morning when he came to me, but he did not seem to be very fond of making a match then. However I saw he liked her very much, and this was the beginning of that union of those two great contending families of Scotland, the Hamiltons and Campbells, which ended in that marriage that made her mother to those two great Dukes of Hamilton and Argyll.[1]

About this time I was much taken up with a Dowager Countess who professed a great attachment to me, and who I could not understand what she meant to be at, as she was sensible of my situation, and yet she would not let me satisfy her passions or gratify my own, and at last I got in with Kitty Fisher which put an end to that silly loitering which only robbed Lady

[1] John Campbell married Elizabeth Gunning on 3rd March. In 1766 he was created Lord Sundridge, and succeeded to the Dukedom in 1770.

C——— of that good name which she really did not deserve to lose.[1]

The 25th I dined with our Club at the Star and Garter, Lord Egmont, Sir Thomas Cust, Sir John Gordon, Sir Edmund Thomas, two Colebrooks, Mr. Oakington, Mr. Oswald and Lord Strange. . . . I took a small house in Scotland Yard of Mr. Ripley for £35 a year, and furnished it in order to keep my things in whilst at sea. I was too much dissipated to mind much of what was going on in public business. The 2nd February we voted the Supplies £6,600,000 ; and was charged for the Navy £4,000,500 ; Army £2,700,000 and odd money ; foreign troops £1,978,177 ; Subsidies, £600,000 ; and many other expences brought in, amounting to ————,[2] and about which no one said one syllable, except Mr. Legge who was Chancellor of the Exchequer, and Alderman Beckford.[3] Mr. Hume brought a bill into the house against pressing, and the City of London was heard by counsel at the bar of the House against some clauses of it. Towards the close of the debate, in which I took a very warm part against the whole, Mr. Hume desired it might be admitted to go into a committee. Mr. Charles Townshend and Mr. Nugent gave it up to be so. I opposed that, but it was carried on a division to be heard in the committee. I was at the opera that night and much flattered on my conduct in Parliament. I was at a ball of Lord Sandwich's which was a tour that many took every week. I danced with Lady Stafford, Lady Caroline Seymour,[4] and Miss Courtney, and the next day dined with Lord and Lady Pembroke. On Friday 16th I dined with Admiral Boscawen to meet a Monsieur des Gouttes that commanded the French ships at Louisbourg, spent the evening with Lady Mulgrave, where was Lady C——, Lady B——y and Lady Caroline Seymour, to all which three I was laying in pretensions. On Sunday I went to Hammersmith to Mr. Dodington's

[1] There can be no doubt that the Dowager Countess beginning with C was Isabella, second wife of the 4th Earl of Carlisle, who had died on 3rd September 1758 ; on the 10th December 1759 she married Sir William Musgrave, Bt., of Hayton Castle.

Kitty Fisher was a notorious courtesan, then the very height of fashion, who sat frequently for Sir Joshua Reynolds.

[2] The total Supply voted to sustain the operations of the "Year of Victories" was £12,750,000. By the end of the war the unprecedented figure of £18,000,000 per annum had been reached.

[3] William Beckford of Fonthill, M.P. for the City 1754–70, twice Lord Mayor, and vastly wealthy.

[4] Elder daughter of the 2nd Earl Cowper, married in 1753 to Harry Seymour, nephew of the 8th Duke of Somerset.

with my mother to dinner. Lord and Lady Ilchester and Lady Susan Fox with many others were there.[1] The 19th the Northumberland House assembly was opened, and I believe there were 400 people in it, and a most magnificent apartment it is. Next day Mr. Hume brought in the third reading of his bill, which I again opposed, and it was thrown out. The next day the 21st to my great surprise and joy I met Mrs. Ord as I was coming out of Reynolds' the painters. I went home and dined with them in Bedford Row, not knowing they were arrived. I went on Friday to the Duke of Newcastle's levée and spoke to him about my Brother Frederick, as he had made me many promises before about him, which he only repeated now with the same false grinning countenance, and which I wrote my Brother word of, and telling him at the same time how little I relied on anything his Grace said. I drove away all this nonsense by going to Ricerrelli's Benefit with Mrs. Dent, and a very pretty woman, Mrs. Burrard, whose husband is Member for Lymington. The next day I went to my ship and found her in great forwardness and had had a very great repair. Prince Edward went down with me, or rather carried me in his chaise, and brought me back next day. We lay at Rochester, and each his nymph came down, and returned to town next day. . . .[2] I spent the evening of the 9th March with Lord Egmont who was very heavy on Mr. Pitt's conduct, and the heavy taxes he laid on to support this destructive war. We laid a tax on all dry goods, sugar, tobacco, tea, India goods and papers. The 10th I appointed Mr. George Marsh my agent, and to pass all my accounts for the future. . . .

The 24th I had a letter of the *Monmouth* coming this day out of the dock at Chatham. I was in the evening at Covent-garden playhouse and sat by accident by Miss D——ks, whom I held by the —— most of the time of the farce, and as it was a rainy

[1] Stephen, Lord Ilchester, Henry Fox's brother, had been Lord Hervey's dearest friend; his eldest daughter Susan married in 1764 William O'Brien of Stinsford, Co. Dorset.

[2] Edward, Duke of York was a younger brother of George III, and was the subject of many amorous anecdotes—several of them concerning Kitty Fisher. He was wild and irresponsible. He served in the Navy from 1758 until the peace; in 1761 his exalted station procured him the rank of Rear-Admiral when aged twenty-two. In 1763 Hervey, as Commander-in-Chief Mediterranean, was selected to conduct the prince round his command in the *Centurion*—first call at Lisbon! But this experienced and knowledgeable guide was prevented from performing that congenial task, for George Grenville's administration required his presence in the Commons at home. The prince died in the South of France in 1767.

evening I kept her in the house till all the people were gone, no chairs to be had, and took her into one of the open houses under the Piazza, and there passed our time till we could get a coach to carry her home to Pall Mall. The 28th I went to a ball at Mr. Mayne's, and danced with Miss Pitt, sister to Mrs. Dent. The next day I supped at Lady C—— and spent the evening there very late *tête-à-tête*, and had orders the next day to fit my ship with three months provisions for Channel service. I endeavoured to get to go to Guinea or to Jamaica, but found I had little chance for either, tho' my friend Admiral Forbes was at the Board.[1] I went down to Rochester and carried Kitty Fisher with me, and a friend of her's Mrs. Squib. We dined on board the *Monmouth*, and endeavoured to go down to Blackstakes but could not for the wind, so I returned next day to Town leaving orders for

* * * * *

The next day the 7th I was to carry Kitty Fisher out of town as she was to go down to Lord Poulett's in Somersetshire, who wrote to her that he would absolutely marry her if she would go to him. I carried her to Egham at 1 in the morning, having first cleared her of some debts for which she was arrested. We lay at Egham, and she set out for Hinton St. George in Somersetshire and I for London, desiring her at any rate to get a settlement made her. I found my ship was gone to the Nore, and therefore I prepared for going to her, settled all my things, and took leave of every one; wrote to Kitty Fisher that if Lord Poulett failed her, my little house was at her service upon a pinch.[2] I set out at 6 in the morning for Chatham, saw the *Sandwich* of 90 guns launched, and went down next day to Sheerness and found orders there not to wait for my men, but go round to Spithead. But it was such

[1] Hervey conceals the fact that he conformed to the practice usual for those soliciting such favours; he wrote to the despised Newcastle (*Add. MSS.* 32,889): " . . . I have little reason to hope for obtaining anything but from your Grace's goodness to me, nor shall I seek it thro' any other channel, as that is the most acceptable to my Brother Bristol and will always be the preferable one to myself. I have now been twelve years a Captain and have seen many favoured with commands that have given opportunities to distinguish themselves, who were much junior officers to me, tho' from my being kept so long a Lieutenant, have some little seniority to me as captains. . . . Your Grace's time is of too much importance for me to intrude on any longer, I will only beg leave to assure your Grace that I shall never be forgetful of, or ungrateful for any favour your Grace may please to confer on, my lord, your Grace's most faithful and most obedient, humble servant, A. Hervey."

[2] John, 2nd Earl Poulett did fail her; she died Mrs. Norris in 1767.

bad weather I could not have my ship paid till Tuesday 17th, when Commissioner Brett came on board and paid us up to June 1758.

The 18th I got under sail and went down the Swinn, and next day got to the Downs where I found the *Nottingham*, *Jason* and *Penzance* and several cutters. Being senior officer, I sent away one after the *Escort* who had 150 of my men.

* * * * *

a good kitchen garden. There is an unfinished tower they tell you cost £8,000, and which is only for a prospect. We dined at an inn just by the park gate, and returned in the afternoon to Deal, where I found the *Escort* and my people, whom I took on board and quartered etc. The next day the 21st I sailed and got to Spithead the Monday following where I found Admiral Holbourn's flag on board the *Royal Ann*, with the *Royal George*, *Union*, *Ramillies*, *Resolution*, *Revenge* and several frigates. I supped that evening with Sir William and Lady Burnaby, where was many of the Ottleys. Having no orders I made parties here with Lady Burnaby and others, sometimes to Stanstead, sometimes to Havant, and so about to pass the time. But Thursday Kitty Fisher came down post to me, and stayed till Friday, that I had orders to sail immediately for Plymouth, which I did, taking leave of Kitty who I had great difficulty to prevent going to Plymouth in my ship.

I arrived at Plymouth the 29th, where I found Sir Charles Hardy's[1] flag on board the *Hero*, with the *Dorsetshire*, *Windsor*, *Dunkirk*, *Chatham*, *Essex*, *Isis* and two frigates. Mr. and Mrs. Dent were here, as he was an Extra Commissioner; no orders for me, and all the ships above named cleaned and fit for sea. Two frigates were sent to look into Brest the 4th May, and two others to Rochefort, a gross error in the Admiralty to keep all these clean ships till the return of the frigates, because they will be foul by the time they are employed. The day after the frigates sailed for their destination, orders arrived for the *Chatham* to go with those off Brest, and the *Isis* with those off Rochefort, but the Admiralty had forgot the *Isis* had sailed for Portsmouth with £20,000 to pay that yard. The morning the 5th Captain Barrington in the *Achilles* arrived with a prize, the *St. Florentine*, pierced for

[1] Sir Charles Hardy (1716–80) was the younger son of a Vice-Admiral of the same name (1680–1744). He was second-in-command to Hawke and Boscawen in the Western Squadron 1759–62, and he succeeded Keppel as Commander-in-Chief of the Channel Fleet during the invasion scare of 1779.

60 guns, a great deal of indigo and sugar on board, and was a very good prize.

I dined the 9th with Sir Charles Hardy who talked to me of the Quebec expedition, and said he had been always made to believe by Lord Anson that he was to have gone and been prevented going to Bath for that purpose, and that he was astonished when he found Mr. Saunders sent for to command that expedition on Mr. Boscawen's refusing it, that this was the more extraordinary and false in Lord Anson as Sir Charles, who had long been Governor of New York and well acquainted with all America, had shewn Lord Anson several papers and charts etc, and that Saunders when named to the command wrote to Sir Charles Hardy for his advice and lights, declaring he knew nothing of the country, never having been thereabouts. Sir Charles said he found there were those about Lord Anson who were jealous of Sir Charles's rank and getting too much credit by any command. This only confirmed me in my opinion of Lord Anson's principles and abilities being of the very lowest class.

The 12th I gave Lord Edgcumbe a picture sealed up of Lady C—— to give my Sister Mary in town, which was to be returned.

The 14th May I received orders to put myself under Sir Edward Hawke's command, as did Sir Charles Hardy and all the ships here, and we were to sail immediately to Torbay, there to make up the fleet, which we did the next day with the *Hero*, *Dorsetshire*, *Essex*, *Revenge*, *Montagu*. We got in the next day to Torbay, and there lay till next day Sir Edward Hawke, Admiral of the Blue, on board the *Ramillies* joined with the *Royal George*, *Union*, *Resolution*, *Torbay*, *Temple*, *Chichester*, *Magnanime*, *Kingston*, *Fame*, *Dunkirk*, *Bienfaisant*, and *Pallas*. We lay here fitting; Sir Edward Hawke, Sir Charles Hardy, Edgcumbe, Denis, Geary and Storr dined on board of me, and Denis threw out as if Lord Anson would come and command, but the 20th cleared all that up by Sir Edward Hawke making the signal to unmoor, and soon after to weigh. But none got out that morning but the *Dorsetshire*, *Resolution*, *Revenge*, and myself. The evening tide the ships were obliged to anchor, and the next morning the whole fleet was under sail of twenty-five sail of the line, sixteen frigates and two fireships. We knew then our destination was off Brest, as the Marshal de Conflans had there a great fleet and a great army said to be intended to invade Ireland.

The 22nd the whole fleet being joined, we made sail to the westward with little wind, and made Ushant the next day, and the 24th the Admiral sent for a French pilot I had, and lent him to the *Nottingham*, who with the *Minerva* frigate was sent to look into Brest water. The next day the Admiral having intelligence that four sail of the line were coming from Rochefort to Brest to join Conflans' fleet thought necessary to send four ships to cruise off the Penmarks, and therefore gave direction to Captain Keppel in the *Torbay* to take the *Magnanime*, Lord Howe, the *Fame*, Captain Byron,[1] and myself in the *Monmouth* and go upon that service, and the *Southampton* frigate. 'Twas with great pleasure that I found we wronged all these ships very much,[2] that if we met the enemy I should at least have had the satisfaction of leading these noble companions into action. About 6 o'clock in the morning we brought to all of us in the Bay of Hodierne,[3] between Penmark Point and that of the Bec de Raz, which appeared a very fine country with many villages dispersed about it, but I thought this as good a bay for the fleet of Brest to come out to and join any force from Rochefort as where they lay. We cruised here about till June 3rd, when a frigate (the *Actaeon*) joined us from the Admiral with orders to rejoin the fleet. By this ship we had an account of Geary, Callis, and Rodney being made Rear-Admirals of the Blue, and we joined the fleet off Ushant at 4 in the afternoon, which was twenty-four sail of the line, and twelve frigates. I went on board the Admiral, and had many letters by which I found the French fleet were every day expected to sail with a great force which was collecting, and we were therefore enjoined to keep close in with the land as close as we could. Soon after we got on board from the Admiral it began to blow very hard from South-West with an appearance of very bad weather, and the 5th in the afternoon the Admiral made a signal for the whole fleet to bear away, and Wednesday the 6th we all anchored in Torbay.

The next day whilst we were watering, Captains Austin,[4] Storr, Porter and myself walked on shore. Sir Charles Hardy and several of the Captains dined with me next day, and that evening we unmoored and sailed the next morning, tho' a West-South-West wind and not promising a very good day. This weather continued very bad till the 11th without accident, till the morning of the

[1] The Hon. John Byron, second son of 4th Lord Byron. He went on a voyage of discovery in the South Seas 1764–5 and commanded squadrons off America and the West Indies 1778–9. Lady Carlisle was his sister.

[2] i.e. the *Monmouth* sailed better than the others.

[3] Audierne Bay.

[4] Joseph Austin, captain of Marines in the *Monmouth*.

12th we had more moderate weather, when we saw the *Hero*, Captain Edgcumbe, without her masts. The *Nottingham* was sent to take her in tow; the *Bienfaisant*, Captain Balfour, had broke two tillers, and the lower gudgin of her rudder gone; the *Temple* lost her bowsprit and had her foremast sprung; the *Torbay* split all her sails; and it was fortunate this very bad weather did not last. Rear-Admiral Geary hoisted a white flag at the mizen top masthead on board the *Resolution*. As the weather inclined to be bad again the Admiral made a signal to bear away, and into Torbay we all went again and anchored in the evening, the 14th.

I went Saturday morning the 16th to breakfast with Sir Edward, who expressed great concern at being drove in, and told me that he had destined me for a very honourable employment, for I should command his vangard in at Brest water to watch the fleet's motions, and that on my diligence and skill much must depend, but he was pleased to say he did not doubt of success in my hands. I went on shore with Storr and Mr. Lee[1] today, and we walked to Tor Abbey, an old mansion house of the Cary family, which is a pleasant situation but now much out of repair, yet some of the family we saw were there. Penton,[2] which is a village close to it, we dined at and many very pretty girls we saw there, particularly the Miss Fowlers, where we drank tea, and went to see Mr. Carter afterwards, parson of the parish, who had a remarkable pretty garden. I supped on board with many Captains. Nothing remarkable happened, everyone was employed in putting their ships in the best order possible and in the afternoon amusing ourselves with walking on shore. I generally went to the Miss Fowlers at Penton, till the morning of the 19th the wind was moderate to the North-West and we all sailed again to return off Brest. Sir Edward Hawke had lent me a book called *The Prince of Abissinia*, which I read at leisure hours, but could only find it was a very good moral simple tale.[3]

We got off Ushant the 21st, and the 22nd the *Magnanime*, Lord Howe, joined us from looking into Brest with an account of there being twenty sail of the line lying in the road and most of them their sails bent. The next morning we received a new line of battle and I found myself in the Admiral's division, therefore shifted my colours. We kept forming different lines of battle

[1] Thomas Lee, a lieutenant in the *Ramillies*; a captain in 1763.
[2] Paignton.
[3] Otherwise *Rasselas*, by Samuel Johnson.

every day when the weather admitted, and nothing extraordinary till the 28th when the *Belliqueux* and *Windsor* joined us from England, and the 2nd July some victuallers joined us with bread and beer which was taken out of them by the different ships close to Ushant. I had a very large quantity sent to me, as the Admiral sent for me next morning and gave me orders to take the *Pallas*, Captain Clements, and two cutters, and to go cruise close in with Brest and to look in on the fleet as frequently as I could, to annoy and distress the enemy every way I could, and to send the Admiral frequent accounts of their situation, and he would soon re-inforce me properly to keep that service on which, he repeated, much depended on my activity and judgement. I made sail away, and at 4 in the afternoon. . . .

Here, in the middle of a sentence, in the centre of a page, Hervey's memoirs come to an abrupt end. It is most unfortunate that he should have left off writing at this moment, for he has arrived at the opening of that chapter in his professional career which has earned him the highest praise from commander and historian alike. Between the 19th June and 5th November the *Monmouth* never once entered a friendly harbour. Throughout those twenty-one weeks, even when westerly gales forced Hawke's main squadron to take shelter in Plymouth Sound or Torbay, Hervey kept the *Monmouth* at sea, maintaining constant watch and ward upon the motions of the French fleet in Brest Road. This arduous work wore out both the *Monmouth* and her captain; two weeks before the victory among the rocks and shoals of Quiberon Bay Hawke had to part with the commander of his vanguard. The Admiral wrote that Hervey had " suffered much in his constitution by the fatigues of the critical station he has been on since the 1st July. Through the whole he has given such proofs of diligence, activity, intrepidity and judgement that it would be doing injustice to his merit as an officer not to acknowledge that I part with him with the greatest regret".

This is not the place to give a detailed account of Hervey's valuable work off Brest which led Hawke's biographer Montagu Burrows to write that " Hervey and Keppel were the eyes and hands of the fleet." But at Ickworth are two unpublished letters from Lady Hervey to her favourite son which illustrate how the fortunes of war had changed from the dark days of 1756, and how universal was the recognition of Captain Hervey's valour.

The first letter[1] came from Chevening, where Lady Hervey was staying with the Stanhopes.

[1] Dated 1st August, endorsed by Hervey " Recd. off Brest 13 Aug.; Ans. 17 Aug."

Indeed, my dear Augustus, if you go on at this rate you will quite blind me. I have been forced to read and write so many answers to letters of congratulation on your behaviour and success that I can hardly see; and this moment I have received your letter of the 22nd July with the pleasing account of farther and greater intrepidity, and, thank God, with safety still on your part. Four seventy-four-gun ships to be made retire by only two of sixty-four is indeed nobly done and must gain you immortal honour, though the account in the newspapers mentions it as slightly as possible "that part of the Brest fleet was under sail Monday sen'night to come out of the harbour, that the headmost ship had enchanged a few shot with the *Monmouth* and *Montagu*, but that on Sir Edward Hawke appearing and forming a line of battle they all returned and went to anchor again."[1] Lady Stanhope and Miss Hamilton, to whom I had told the contents of your letter, were so angry that they called the newspaper writers and admiralty (whose business they thought it was to have had the whole given with due commendations of you to the public) many harsh names, and they were very pressing with me to draw up an article in a proper manner, which they would have sent away immediately to be inserted in the first newspapers, but as your letter was so short, so little explicit, and by some omissions of words from hurry, so unclear, I could not do it; otherwise indeed I believe I should. Your first action[2] was very well and properly related in the *Evening Post*, perhaps the next newspapers may bring a better and fuller account, at least I hope so, when they may perhaps have a more particular information. I have this day received a very pretty letter from Ld. Chesterfield on this occasion, and last post brought me one from Mrs. Osborn with congratulations both in her own and the Admiral's name. Also one from Mr. Bateman very obliging. I had also one from Lord Lyttelton, who never wrote to me before, to congratulate me on *the glory you have gained by your brave and spirited action at Brest*. Mr. Walpole, who is always the first and most obliging on all such occasions, said they were all in joy and full of your praises at Holland House. This good family who, no more than myself, have not wore a smile for many weeks before, expressed the greatest pleasure and

[1] *London Chronicle* 28–31 July: Hervey's determination "not to be drove off the station" frustrated this attempted sortie by the *Dauphin Royal* 70, *Glorieux* 74, *Dragon* and *Inflexible* 64's.

[2] On the 14th July; supported by the *Pallas* he cut out some Swedish supply ships from under the guns of the forts of Conquet.

joy on this occasion, and Ld. Stanhope, who returned this day from London where he has been for some days, drank your health and wished this country produced many such gallant men as Mr. Hervey. He is just come into my room with Lady Stanhope and all of them with the newspapers of this morning which he has just got, in which there is a full and most delightful account of the action and of *Commodore* Hervey and at the end of it some verses of which these are the last two lines.

> " Britons exult ! all Gallia trembling stands,
> While *Hervey* executes and *Hawke* commands."[1]

They all beg I would make their compliments to you and assure you how great a share they take in your glory and in my joy. Ld. Stanhope came back after he had gone four steps to say very kindly and very prettily " Pray give my congratulations to Mr. Hervey as your friend, as his humble servant, and as an Englishman." God bless you, my dear Augustus, and keep you safe; now you have had an opportunity of showing yourself would to God we had a peace and my dear boy was safe at home. I will write to your brother, and make him as happy as I am with all this good news.

Lord Stanhope tells me Mr. Elliot of the Admiralty cried you and this brave action up to the skies; and that Mr. Pitt said your conduct had been equal to your courage, which was as great as possible. Thank God for all this good news. Oh that that dear good friend I have lost could have lived to have shared and increased my joy, which she would have done.[2]

[1] It was the message in the lines, rather than any poetic merit, which appealed to Lady Hervey. They were written to commemorate the events of the 14th July; *London Evening Post*, 31 July.

> . . . Full in their Sight two British ships engage
> Their Tow'ring Ramparts with resistless Rage.
> The *Pallas* frown'd, France shuddered at her look:
> The *Monmouth* thunder'd and the Mountains shook.
> Thy forts, Conquet ! no longer Succours lend,
> Too weak to save, too tim'rous to defend.
> The Ships auxiliar from thy Wings are tore,
> And Conflans, sorrowing does their Fate deplore;
> Unable to resist the Show'rs of Fire,
> Thy Guns lie speechless and thy Troops retire.
> Britons exult ! all Gallia trembling stands,
> While *Hervey* executes and *Hawke* commands.

[2] Lady Murray, who had died in June. Forty years before John Gay had praised her as " sweet-tongued Murray " in the same verse in which he had described Lady Hervey as " youth's youngest daughter, sweet Lepell".

Hervey received the second letter[1] when the shattered and leaking *Monmouth* dropped anchor in Plymouth Sound on the 5th November.

'Tis an age since I heard from my dear Augustus and ten days since I wrote to him. I have been extremely hurried since I came to town and, for some hours, again alarmed by those vile newspapers, they have put in an article to say the *Monmouth* was by a storm drove on the coast of Brittany. I immediately wrote both to Mr. Forbes and to Mr. Stanley lest one should not be to be found, but as it happened, it being Saturday, neither were in town; in the anxiety I was under I wrote a note to Mr. Cleveland at ten o'clock at night; he was not at home, but in half an hour returned and immediately wrote me a very obliging note to dissipate my fears, by assuring me there was no news of any kind come from those parts to the Admiralty, and 'twas very sure that a ship and a commander of that importance could not have had a misfortune of that kind without the Admiralty being first informed of it, there being so many ships in company; therefore he did not doubt that Captain Hervey was safe and would continue to render further service to his country. On Monday I received a letter to the same purpose from Mr. Forbes, and a visit from Mr. Stanley to confirm it. I called at Lady Mary Forbes' door on Monday and left my compliments with thanks to the Admiral for his letter, on which he very politely made me a visit on Tuesday and staid here alone an hour. He said he had taken the liberty to chide you about the affair of the boats and really said all the same things I had wrote to you about it; He said it was not an occasion worth risking an officer of such consequence as you was of, that your character wanted nothing extraordinary to be done; but when it was for some distinguished service, then, and then only, extraordinary risks were to be run. He spoke kindly of you; he seems to be a serious sensible reserved man. On Wednesday night between ten and eleven Mr. Cleveland sent me a letter to say he had that moment received an express from Sir Ed. Hawke with an account that you was well on your station on the 20th, which he hoped would make me quite easy on your account, that he thought himself happy to be so soon able to remove all my fears. In short, my dear, he has been most extremely civil and indeed obliging to me on this occasion, and I know that both he and Lord A—— have spoke very handsomely about you to different people. Why

[1] Dated "London, 27th October".

therefore perpetuate enmity and be perpetually blowing those embers that are near extinguished?

Mr. Fox, who was here yesterday morning, made me many compliments on your bravery and spoke very kindly of you, and Lord Huntingdon who was here last night said you was the constant toast of the City and the first favourite there, but what say you, my dear, to all our successes in the East and West Indies? Upon my word we now make a great figure, and my poor friends—how are the Mighty fallen! Neither ministers to plan nor officers to execute. The K— told Mr. Pitt publicly at his levee, the day the news came of taking Quebec, " All your plans have succeeded." Quebec is certainly a great acquisition, but 'tis gold bought too dear. Woolfe is an irreparable loss, such an head, such an heart, such a temper and such an arm are not easily to be found again. He was an excellent scholar, knew all the advantages of the Roman Phalanx and Grecian Discipline, had a memory that made all the past present to him and he could therefore profit by all the battles fought and seiges laid either by ancients or moderns: with all these public virtues he had also all private ones, was the most tender, most dutiful son in the world and the most humane benevolent master: he has left a young lady to whom he was to have been married at his return inconsolable—'tis a sister of Sir James Lowther's. His poor mother does not feel his loss, she has been insensible since she heard the certain news of his death—but what must that first feeling have been to have worked such an effect so immediately, poor, poor, miserable woman. I pity her from my soul. . . .

Since I begun this I have been at Lady Brown's where I saw a gentleman, I have forgot his name, but he lives in the City, is a man of substance and business; he says he drinks your health regularly every day, and that no man who lives in that part of the world dares to do otherways. Mr. Dodington came yesterday from Dorsetshire to Hammersmith where he proposes staying some time. I hope I should see him soon but this is such a day as " has made a great gulph between us so that he cannot pass from thence here nor we from hence there." It has rained pouringly incessantly ever since seven o'clock this morning. Lou's son Captain Smyth[1] was wounded in the head at Quebec, but so

[1] Hervey Smyth was the son of Sir Robert and Lady Louisa Smyth (see p. 84). He was one of Wolfe's A.D.C.s, and in Benjamin West's picture he is portrayed holding the dying general's right arm. He was an accomplished artist with the pencil; his profile sketch of Wolfe, now in the Library of the R.U.S.I., Whitehall, was said to be a faithful likeness.

slightly that he was walking about the camp the day after. The ball grazed on the top of his head, took off the hair and the upper skin without in the least touching his skull ; 'tis well he was not half a quarter of an inch taller. Poor William, thank God, was out of the fray with Amherst. I have asked you twice if the Darling's son[1] takes most after the father or mother ; as you have never made me any answer I conclude he patrisares—to be sure that is the best, should not a man be like a man ? Mr. Walpole is in the country, not at Strawberry Hill. I heard from him the day I came to town but shall not see him these ten days. He enquired after the " Black Prince ". . . .[2]

Adieu, dear Augustus, I hope I shall hear from you soon.

While the *Monmouth* lay in port repairing and her captain rested, the news came of Hawke's decisive victory on the 20th November. Hervey's disappointment at missing the battle must have been aggravated when he learnt that it was those very ships which the *Monmouth* had outsailed in June which went a-head during the chase and got into action first. Had the *Monmouth* been in the van perhaps Conflans' *Soleil Royal* would have struck her flag to the conqueror of the *Foudroyant*. That indeed would have been the answer to Hervey's prayer to distinguish himself by some exploit that should give his ship's crew everlasting credit.

Monmouth at Plymouth[3]
November 28th 1759.

Sir,

You'll please to acquaint their Lordships that notwithstanding my earnest Inclinations of proceeding to sea with His Mts : Ship under my Command yet I find myself under the Necessity of desiring their Leave to remain onshore 'till the recovery of my Health.

[1] In 1758 Constantine John Phipps (after 1775 Lord Mulgrave), eldest son of Hervey's sister Lepell, had been entered on the books of his uncle's ship as " captain's servant ". He was now aged 15, and at the beginning of a distinguished career in the Service and in politics. He became a captain in 1765, and in 1773 commanded the *Racehorse* and *Carcass* in an expedition to Northern waters, in which Nelson served as a midshipman. From 1777 to 1782 he was a member of the Board, and was a frequent speaker in Parliament in support of Lord North's Administration. Hervey's natural son " Little " Augustus was killed alongside him on board the *Courageux* at the relief of Gibraltar in 1782. He was said to have the finest naval library in England, and it was to him that Hervey left all his naval papers. Mulgrave died unmarried in 1792.

[2] Presumably Walpole thought Hervey's depredations on the French warranted this comparison !

[3] *P.R.O. Adm.* 1/1894.

Their Lordships will give me leave to have the Honor of Congratulating them on the Success of His Majt's: Fleet, tho' I shall ever Condole with myself for the Misfortune of not having had it in my power to contribute towards it.

I am Sir,
Your most Obed. Sert.
A: Hervey

John Cleveland esq.
Secretary of the Admlty.

APPENDIX A.

Pamphlets by Augustus Hervey

1746–57

1. *A letter from a friend at Jamaica to a friend in London, giving an impartial account of the violent proceeding of the faction in that island.* Published September 1746.

   This attack on Admiral Davers provoked a reply by The Planter in the *Daily Gazetteer* of the 7th October. Hervey thought this was by one Gray, formerly Agent-Victualler at Jamaica; they exchanged insults in the *Daily Gazetteer* of the 15th and 20th October and in the *Daily Advertiser* on the 6th November.

2. *THE NAVY BILL*, February to March 1749.

   Lady Hervey wrote the names of the authors on her copies of the pamphlets; the MSS. of Hervey's are at Ickworth. They were published in the following order:

   (1) Hervey wrote *A letter from a friend in the Country to a friend at Will's Coffee-House; in relation to three Additional Articles of War.*
   (2) Lord Barrington wrote *Considerations on the Bill for the better government of the Navy; by a sea-officer.*
   (3) Hervey wrote *A detection of the Considerations on the Navy Bill; by a Seaman.*
   (4) Temple West wrote *An Examination and Refutation . . . of . . . Considerations on the Navy Bill; by a real sea officer.* This is the best argued of them all.
   (5) Hervey wrote *Objections to the 34th Article of the Navy Bill.*
   (6) Hervey also wrote two broadsides: *Some short queries on the new Articles of War* and *Reasonable Queries.*

3. *BYNG'S TRIAL* 1756–57.

   This event provoked one of the most extensive pamphlet wars the country had ever seen. Hervey joined in immediately he got home in November. It is not possible to identify all he wrote on this occasion but the following is a list of the MSS. preserved at Ickworth.

   (1) *A further Address to the Public . . . Mens conscia recti*; British Museum.
   (2) *If Justice be done, may it continue!*; broadside; British Museum.

(3) *The Unfortunate case of Two Swedish Generals*; broadside ; also in the *Public Advertiser*, 5th Feb. 1757.

(4) *Some queries addressed to Captain Cornwall late of the* Revenge; broadside ; British Museum.

(5) An attack on Keppel for his conduct in the Lords on 2nd March 1757, when the bill to release the Court-martial from their oaths of secrecy was thrown out. MS. marked " Printed March 3rd 1757 —sent to the K—— in a letter." No printed copy to be found.

(6) *The Speech of the Honble Admiral Byng Intended to have been spoken on board the Monarque at the time of his execution . . . but his sorrow not suffering him he delivered it to a friend to be published.* MS. not at Ickworth. A printed copy is in the B.M., Crach 2. Tab. 6, v. 6, folio 20 ; Byng's authentic speech is in the same volume, folio 22.

Probably by Hervey are (among others):

(7) *Admiral Byng's defence as presented by him . . . containing a very particular account of the action . . . and the proceedings . . . during the six days* [*the Fleet*] *was off Minorca.*

(8) *A letter to a gentleman in the country from his friend in London* [giving an account of Byng's behaviour and death] . . . *Mens conscia recti.*

(9) Hervey was suspected by Richard Rigby, the Duke of Bedford's man of business, of arranging the publication of a garbled version of the oath taken by the members of the Court-martial.

" The House of Lords did not sit today, so your printers and publishers are not yet disposed of ; but I heard it so strongly suspected as almost to amount to a proof that Augustus Hervey sent to the newspapers the paragraph complained of. I shall not be sorry to have that proved upon him."[1]

The offending passage appeared in the *Whitehall Evening Post* for the 26th Feb. and in the *Public Advertiser* of 2nd March ; the printers of both papers were forced to beg their pardon on their knees in the House, and were discharged on payment of their fees. Responsibility for the passage was never traced to Hervey.

[1] Rigby to Bedford, 3rd March 1757, *Bedford Papers* II, 238.

APPENDIX B.

Some Minutes of a Council of War called by Lieutenant-General Blakeney at Minorca the 5th February 1756 and continued as follows. [For the members, see p. 190.]

[These minutes deal only with the days on which Hervey attended; they are not full, and are not an impartial record. Hervey sent a copy of them to Henry Fox. I print them for the light they throw on the state of the island, the indifference, if not hostility, of the inhabitants, and what Hervey thought was the indolent conduct of the General whose patience the Captain finally exhausted.]

Feb 5th The General's letters and Captain Hervey's read from Marseilles and from Barcelona, which confirmed the intelligence already received of an embarkation being intended against this Island from Toulon.

'Twas unanimously agreed that the intelligence was very minute and fully sufficient to authorize the most speedy and effectual means being taken to secure the island against any attempts on it.

The General then proposed Captain Hervey's sealed orders and rendezvous from Mr. Edgcumbe being opened and the execution of them deferred if they interfered with the present necessary service of the Island; *agreed.*

Captain Hervey moved that the General only might see the rendezvous; *agreed.*

Moved and agreed that Captain Hervey remains here to attend the service of the island; *agreed.*

Captain Hervey moved for the packet's being immediately dispatched to Leghorn, and endeavour to find the Commander-in-chief of H.M. Ships; *agreed.*

Proposed that the chief inhabitants and others be assembled, and that the General shall let them know that the island is threatened with an invasion, and that their aid and assistance to the troops is required. *Resolved*; that as the garrison is in want of provisions, that the cargoes of fish now in the port, brought in as captures, shall be secured.

Several other Resolutions come to this day with regard to the detail of the defence of the island; adjourned till next day.

6th Met at 4 in the afternoon.

Friday Several resolutions with regard to the fish and rice in the harbour, as well as for the procuring beef from Leghorn.

7th Saturday The packet not being sailed with the letters of the 6th. to the Commander-in-chief, Captain Hervey moved for a suspension of the master of the packet and that one of his officers might go, to make the greater dispatch; 'twas *resolved* that the master of the packet should not be employed on this urgent occasion.

Captain Hervey moved that some method be found out to settle a safe channel of correspondence for intelligence; *agreed to*, and left to Captain Hervey to settle it. Captain Hervey took notice of the number of French prisoners now on the island, and moved for their being sent away in some vessel to Gibraltar; *unanimously agreed to*.

Colonel Rufane desired it might be considered how far a fireship might be necessary to guard the entrance of the harbour; *agreed* to be taken into consideration on farther intelligence.

Captain Hervey proposed that all the gun carriages, powder and ammunition be removed from the prizes into the Castle; *agreed*.

Also that all the officers and prisoners now about the town should repair to Bloody Island, and there kept under a guard and certain restrictions; *agreed*.

9th Monday A resolution with regard to a vessel arrived with corn from Marseilles looked upon as a spy.

Resolved, that a provision be made for sending off the prisoners on the first appearance of an enemy's fleet.

Resolved that the corn and fish now in the harbour be placed in the King's magazines in the castle, with several other resolutions relating thereto.

Captain Hervey proposed that a proclamation might be made to call in all seafaring people, and notice given them to attend the Commander-in-chief of His Majesty's ships in the port on any alarm; *agreed*.

11th Captain Hervey laid before the Council the dangerous consequences of letting all the Jews go off the island at this time, as he was informed most of the principal ones had already taken their passage in a vessel bound to Villa-Franca, and that if not prevented, the enemy might be encouraged to attack the island, if they never had intended it, on finding the merchants and people already so alarmed as to desert it; *resolved* thereon to send for some of the principal Jews, and to lay an embargo on all people and vessels.

Resolved to demand 30,000 fascines of the inhabitants, and to have them got in as early as possible by the different Terminos.

12th–16th The Council of War met constantly and came to several resolutions, in which some of its members frequently observed to the Lieutenant-Governor that the inhabitants were very dilatory in anything that depended on them. On examination, Lieutenant-Colonel Jefferies found a great deficiency in the corn magazines, and moved that something might be done to supply them ; *agreed.*

This day the different Terminos made their returns of stock etc. : on the island.

Oxen	5,109	
Cowes	1,056	
Sheep	35,473	
Goats	308	
Piggs	1,340	
Corn	5,077	qrs.
Inhabitants . . about	50,000	
Sea-faring men . . .	298	
Volunteers for the Crown .	21	

This account was by everyone looked upon as far short of what the island contained, except in the number of its volunteers for the Crown on this occasion, which it really exceeded.

Resolved that Captain Hervey should sail for intelligence to Villa-Franca.

Several resolutions with regard to the fortifying the harbour.

[Hervey sailed the 25th.]

March 10th Captain Hervey being returned from Villa-Franca confirmed all the former intelligence, and told the Council of War that it was said by the 15th March the enemy would have fifteen sail of men-of-war ready for the sea, and that it would require some more time for the rest of the expedition to be ready, which is given out is to be accompanied by twenty men-of-war. Captain Hervey gave also a detail of the embarkation intended, as is said, against the island.

Also he acquainted the Lieutenant-Governor that, agreeable to the resolution of the Council of War, he had settled the correspondence with the Consul of Nice for the earliest intelligence being dispatched over here, and had answered for his being paid his expences by the Lieutenant-Governor.

Resolution of the Council with regard to Captain Hervey's vigilance on this occasion.

Captain Hervey observed to the Council that he could not but rely on this intelligence, and desired some effectual methods might be taken to oblige the inhabitants to put in execution their part of what has been thought necessary to be done for the security of the island, and represented that no one step hitherto had been taken for the executive part of all the past resolutions ; *seconded* by Colonels Rufane and Jefferies. Captain Hervey moved that as there were a number of the inhabitants who had been employed about the subterraneans, that those people should be either encouraged to serve voluntarily in the castle, or methods taken early to secure them, as they might become very dangerous if left out, in case of a siege ; *resolved* in consequence thereof.

11*th* Captain Hervey moved for the destruction of the town of St. Philip's, as dangerous to the castle by being a cover to the enemy's approaches, and that the rubbish might choke up the wells ; *agreed* to be necessary, but not to be done till one of the last things.

Some resolutions come to with regard to the Chief Engineer's house, and some mills near the castle. Different resolutions with regard to a boom across the harbour, and fortifying the entrance ; Captain Noel and Captain Hervey ordered to prepare and place the boom. Captain Hervey proposed that the cattle should all be drove in from the out Terminos, excepting only such a number as were sufficient to bring in the fascines and soldiers' heavy baggage when ordered to retire from the out-quarters ; *not agreed to*, tho' owned to be necessary. This ill-timed tenderness to the people most strongly painted, and its consequences represented to the Council of War.

[His speech ; see p. 192.]

12*th* Captain Hervey moved that this island be put under martial law, as the only means to have the island speedily put in such a state of defence as may tend to its security and the honour of His Majesty's arms ; *question not thought proper to be put*, by the General opposing it.

14*th* Captain Hervey delivered to the Council of War a very minute account of every principal inhabitant of the island, what they were reckoned worth at a moderate computation, their possessions, stock, and money, and what they might lend the Crown on this occasion ; the inhabitants called in, according to a resolution of the 12th, and Captain Hervey desired by the Council of War to represent to them the motives of their desired attendance, to set forth the present necessity of raising such a sum as required, and the General's dissatisfaction at such a remissness as was observed thro'out every degree of the inhabitants towards the defence of the island etc: etc:

Resolved that the chief inhabitants shall be granted till the 17th instant to bring in this loan, and to make it as easy to themselves as they please.

17th Captain Hervey proposed to the Council of War again to put the island under martial law ; *opposed* by the General.

Captain Hervey ordered by the Council of War to explain to the Commander-in-chief of His Majesty's ships (now present and returned from Leghorn) the former resolutions and the steps that had been taken for the security of the island. The inhabitants attended and gave in their respective loans, which did not amount to above seven or eight thousand dollars out of thirty demanded. Captain Hervey moved to the Council that this was an indecent and a dangerous trifling with the Crown, and that the most earnest means should be used to learn the motives of such an infamous backwardness on this occasion ; *Resolved* to give the inhabitants till the 22nd to make good the rest of the sum required.

Captain Hervey moved that the Clergy should be summoned on this occasion to use their influence on the people, and to know what their different communities could lend ; *agreed to.*

Captain Hervey moved that the chief magistrates should be ordered to raise such a sum on those conditions, and they to be required to raise it in their own way ; *not agreed to.*

Several other resolutions made.

18th Captain Hervey laid before the Council of War the necessity there was to take into immediate consideration the defence of the harbour-mouth, and proposed two fire vessels, one of each side, to guard the entrance, and that one shall be a sufficient burthen and force to be employed as a fireship on any other service ; *agreed to* ; and *resolved* that the Commodore shall find two such and fit them as he shall judge fittest.[1]

Captain Hervey moved that the prizes and prisoners should be sent immediately to some port of safety, if not to Gibraltar ; *seconded* by Colonel Rufane, but *not agreed to.*

Captain Hervey desired another proclamation to call in all seafaring people to give in their names and places of abode, as well as all those once before mentioned that had been employed in the subterraneans ; *agreed to.* Colonel Rufane moved for the return of fascines brought in ; on examination not near a third was yet delivered in of the number demanded the 11th of last month, tho' care had been taken to provide small vessels to bring them in from the out-parts of the island ; *resolved,* that the Lieutenant-Governor do give his orders for the more effectually putting in execution the resolutions of this Council.

[1] They were named *Proserpine* and *Blast* ; see p. 195.

Resolved to land six guns from the ships at Philipet, and a battery to be raised where the mill stood to rake the entrance of the harbour.

22nd Captain Hervey moved that all the former resolutions should be put in immediate execution, and that every measure should be pursued for the island defence as if the enemy were to be landed tomorrow, and used many pressing arguments for this being agreed to; was *seconded* by Colonel Rufane; but *not agreed to*. Return was made from the clergy of their loan, which amounted to 400 dollars; the magistrates of the four Terminos gave nothing; Captain Hervey moved that the General should call the principal ones together by proclamation, and express once more his dissatisfaction at their behaviour on this occasion; yet all was silent, and *no question put*.

Captain Hervey moved again with many arguments that all former resolutions should be without hesitation or delay put in execution, and that unless that was agreed, that the members of the Council sat useless there. Many other questions were put and resolutions agreed to, too minute to be inserted in the course of these numerous meetings, and few or none put in execution. The General desired a man-of-war might go cruise off the North end of the island for intelligence; the Commodore objected it useless, but would not vote against it; *resolved*, that a man-of-war go off the North end of the island to give the alarm on appearance of the enemy. Captain Hervey moved again that the prizes be sent away, and the King's stores which he had put into one of his own prizes.

Captain Hervey moved that if the prisoners were not sent off the island, at least they should be put all on board an empty vessel, placed in St. Stephen's cove under the cannon of the castle, as they would require too numerous a guard anywhere else for that small garrison to spare, and be too dangerous a reinforcement if suffered to escape to their men-of-war; *agreed to*.

Captain Hervey moved once more for the driving in all the cattle, securing all the magazines of corn and wine, and for the destruction of the town of St. Philip's; opposed by the General as too destructive to the inhabitants, and *no question put upon it*.

The *Phoenix* sailed next morning, the 23rd, for intelligence off the island.

APPENDIX C

HERVEY AND HENRY FOX IN 1756[1]

On the 24th June Henry Fox, then Secretary of State, received Hervey's letter of the 24th May; he did not welcome its contents. The defence of Minorca had been a worrying problem for the ministers, and, believing that the threat of invasion at home was real, they had plumped for concentrating strength in the Channel to the exclusion of adequate measures in the Mediterranean. Although Fox could point to occasions on which he had advised the earlier despatch of Byng with a stronger squadron, and also the earlier despatch of the reinforcements which followed him, he knew that this unheeded advice would avail him but little in the struggle for office which the impending disaster at St. Philip's would precipitate. Byng's despondent despatch from Gibraltar before he sailed for Mahon and La Galissonnière's bombastic description of the battle had both reached London on the 2nd June; Fox's experience of men and the world helped him to guess aright the subsequent behaviour of the English fleet. "We have nothing from them, but I doubt not our first news will be that Byng is returned to Gibraltar and that a Council of War says he did wisely."[2]

Fox had for many years been an intimate friend of Lord and Lady Hervey, and after Lord Hervey's death his widow kept up a frequent correspondence, which is in part preserved at Melbury. This connection made him the sole member of the administration whom Hervey could address on terms of friendship and with any chance of success. His letter[3] arrived the same day as Byng's despatch describing the battle, which he had helped to write.

However cautious I shall ever be of intruding on your time, which I know the public has such a claim to, yet the late action between our fleet and the French's the 20th this month off Mahon I think is an event too important not to take the first opportunity of giving you just a general account of it; and as I have this instant heard a vessel is presently to be dispatched away, I shall not let slip the occasion, tho' I have scarce time to write my letter, much less to dwell on particulars, and therefore hope you'll excuse the incorrectness of it.

He then gave an account of the battle similar to that in the text of his Memoirs,[4] emphasising all the points favourable to the Admiral, and abusing

[1] Unless otherwise stated, all the letters quoted in this appendix are from Melbury.

[2] Fox to Devonshire, 3rd June.

[3] "*Defiance*, off Minorca May 25th 1756."

[4] p. 204.

no-one in the fleet. He included the statement that the French sailed " three feet to our one, that 'twas impossible to close with them again." Except for this exaggeration, the account was unobjectionable; but the latter part of the letter contained criticism of the Ministry, which Hervey could not have expected Fox to welcome.

[The 24th] a Council of War was called after the state and conditions of the fleet was given in, which was laid before the Council, and as 'twas thought impossible with ever so great a victory to relieve Minorca, and not even to land succours where they are invested by 17,000 men, could we have spared the Regiment that is on board for the service of the fleet, and which indeed are very sickly, it was by land and sea unanimously thought highly necessary to go for Gibraltar, as that garrison is threatened after the taking Mahon. I hope with all my heart we shall find stores at Gibraltar from England, and if we have a reinforcement out of six sail, we shall shortly be able to recover the command of the Mediterranean which they have now got possession of to the great detriment, if not destruction, of all our trade; as I believe it will not be thought possible to spare or venture any ships for convoys, while they have a fleet certainly superior to ours in force, and by all accounts were to be reinforced by four sail of the line ready many days since to sail from Toulon. We have many sick and wounded in the fleet, scarce a ship that if we were to begin again but must now go into action some 40, 60 or 80 men less than they did before, when they were all short, and no hospital-ship to put them in. Masts totally disabled, no port to refit of ours within 180 leagues. Everyone here calls out loudly on the manner this fleet was sent and how late, how equipped, no storeships, no stores, no hospital ship, no fireship, nor no tender. The Council of War had liked to have ran into very strong reasons for their resolutions, but the Admiral put a stop by saying to the Rear and other gentlemen he only wanted their sentiments by which he might direct his own, but would not suffer no implication of any reflections on any office of the Government's. So it all ended. We hope to see a reinforcement, and if it was to join us shortly I hope we should yet go back to action.

Fox sent the letter to Lady Hervey.[1]

Dear Madam,—I send you your son's letter. It is private, so I have not shewn it to anybody, because the blaming people here will neither do Mr. Hervey nor them any good. And indeed, dear madam, there is nothing in this whole matter that gives me so much concern as to see the uneasiness our fleet has all along been under that they are but equal to the French, tho' in fact, let them say what they please, they are a little

[1] 25th June.

superior.[1] You will observe that Mr. Hervey was called off before he was near enough to view the mouth of the harbour, so that Byng knows no more of what he lays so much stress upon, the impossibility of succouring Fort St. Philip's, than we do here. Byng is sent for and will be tried for disobedience to orders. Adieu.

Lady Hervey was fearful of the trouble in which her impetuous son might involve himself.

I return you, my dear sir, with a thousand thanks, Augustus' letter which has given me a great deal of pain, as I think even by those accounts every situation was not made the most of. I am heartily vexed at the whole, as an Englishwoman and as a well-wisher to Byng. I am also frightened lest all those who composed the Council of War should receive censure. Dear Sir, I should be glad to see you before I go on my great journey [to Scotland] but how is it possible? . . . The complaint of our fleet that they were only equal to that of the French doesn't seem in my opinion to turn upon the bare equality, but that they are superior in strength whenever they are equal in number. I wish for the sake of England that the new Admirals may do better than Byng, but I wish for Byng's sake that he had done that better. Adieu, my dear, I am vexed and uneasy, but ever with truth and faithfully and affectionately yours.

Saturday noon. Do you know anything of the affairs in Albany;[2] 'tis hard to have such children make one uneasy as can never reward it by making one happy?[3]

Fox replied on the 8th July, first reassuring her about a letter (can it have been a *billet doux*?) which Hervey had written to France, and then giving some worldly advice, not calculated to appeal to one who was defending a dear friend.

Dear Madam,—No other harm can happen to Captain Hervey from his imprudence than from a little ridicule as to his being very fond of the French, and *fort employé de leur donner de ses nouvelles*. It was before war was declared, and there was no harm in his letter. It was an idle thing as well let alone, but can be of no ill consequence to him. I am more afraid that his gratitude to Byng joined to a lively disposition may make him talk imprudently when he finds in how different a light his superiors here look on that Admiral's conduct from that in which his Captains, and par-

[1] A month later Fox had changed his ideas on this point. On the 27th July he wrote to his "jackal", Welbore Ellis, discussing the behaviour of the captains at the Council of War after the battle " . . . The match (in which I think the superiority was at first on their [i.e. the French] side, tho' that is treason to suppose) was no longer equal."

[2] In America, where her youngest son William was serving in the 44th Regiment.

[3] Undated.

ticularly Captain Hervey, represent it. I wish I could advise him to do his own duty, as I dare say he will, well: and neither write nor speak of that of others. But particularly not to write his thoughts on such occasions.

A fortnight later Fox received another letter from Hervey,[1] the text of which was unexceptionable, but the enclosures which came with it clearly indicated that he was unlikely to accept the advice Fox had sent to his mother.

Sir, As I flatter myself you have some time since had my letter of the 18th of this month,[2] which I wrote to you from this place to acquaint you that the fleet was hourly expected and of my being sent to prepare the hospital, I shall not further dwell on the particulars therein, but beg leave, as I promised, to have the honour of enclosing you just a little plan of four different positions of the two fleets the day they engaged. I own it very badly executed, not having really time, but it is exact as to positions,[3] my changing into the *Hampton Court* out of the *Defiance* occasions great hurry, and here, sir, I must once more repeat my thanks and my gratitude for that mark of your favour and protection which I shall ever acknowledge. We are preparing the fleet to return to Minorca with the greatest expedition, but the disabled ships will delay us some days; I wish the increase of our very great number of sick does not still more, tho' I hear the Admirals intends if it is possible to replace the sick with the men out of the frigates. This reinforcement has at least made us equal in number to the French should they be reinforced from Toulon, which I hear they are, tho' so various are our reports here with regard to the motions about Minorca, that I do not think it prudent to venture repeating any to Mr. Fox, on the whole 'tis to be hoped it is not yet entirely lost. I am of opinion if we have sufficient force to keep in the fleet at Toulon that we may yet oblige the enemy to abandon their views on Minorca, still more so if they should not have withdrawn any of their forces before our approach, as in my poor opinion the more they have on that island the better, as such numbers must in many ways distress them in time. Perhaps I may be wrong, but I think I have been long enough this way to know that Minorca cannot supply the numbers it now contains not three months—June, July and August are at best very sickly to the inhabitants. What may it not be supposed to be to newcomers not restrained from the licentious use of liquor, fruit and cucumbers, which that island abounds with and which are so destructive to everyone. These are my hopes, let others produce their doubts and their fears. I am glad the Admiral is hurrying everyone and I'm told will sail the instant

[1] "*Hampton Court* at Gibraltar, June 26th 1756."

[2] Missing; presumably it enclosed the Minutes of the Council of War at Mahon (Appendix B) a copy of which is at Melbury.

[3] Three of them are reproduced in the text; the fourth plan, showing the two fleets after the engagement, is not reproduced.

the crippled ships are in any sort of readiness. At the back of the plan is a list of the two squadrons as they stood when we engaged them—by which you'll see what a superiority from the weight of their ships, metal of their guns and numbers of their men.[1] I hope in God we shall now meet them that you may have no reason to repent having placed me in the *Hampton Court* which I look upon myself obliged to you alone, sir, for . . .

A week after the date of Hervey's letter the *Antelope* anchored in Gibraltar Bay, and Hawke had replaced Byng in command. Fox sent the letter and its enclosures to Lady Hervey.[2]

Dear Madam,—I must acknowledge receipt of a most obliging letter from Captain Hervey at the same time that this (which I here enclose) come to my hands yesterday. I do not blame Mr. Hervey, who is so much obliged to Mr. Byng, but his account is on the face of it so partial that it won't do neither Mr. Byng nor him any service to show it, but the contrary. For example, in the list of ships on each side to show how great the French superiority was, he swells the number and weight of their guns beyond measure, and actually leaves the *Deptford*, a 50-gun ship, out of our line, lessening the number of our guns, too, in a manner that every clerk of the Admiralty could contradict,[3] and indeed his letter and sketch of the action would confirm anybody, and does me, in the universal belief of Byng's ill behaviour. There are many letters in town dated Gibraltar June 26th and they all agree that the whole fleet, his own division as well as West's, cry out against him. I am very sorry for it, and have not, as some of my brother ministers have, the wretched comfort of thinking that his ill conduct will divert the blame. We are, notwithstanding that, and shall be, much blamed. The rage of people increases hourly. I don't deserve blame but that won't save me from it, and though I were to meet with no more than I deserve, that would not alleviate the concern I am under for this great and irretrievable loss, for seeing no good event to set against it, but on the contrary more distress than this country ever yet struggled with, civil war excepted. . . . Pray, dear madam, when you write to Captain Hervey make my compliments and return my thanks and if you think, as I do, that I may as well be excused writing to him on this occasion, excuse me to him. Adieu.

Lady Hervey replied on the 7th August from Scotland, where she was staying with the Murrays at Mellerstain.

[1] The list sent by Hervey is similar to that on p. 204, with the addition of the weight of metal in the opposing fleets. He shows, correctly, that the French carried heavier guns than did the English.

[2] 24th July.

[3] Hervey's figures for the numbers of guns carried by the British ships are correct. It was probably not known at home that ten guns had been landed from Edgcumbe's original squadron to reinforce St. Philip's Castle.

I am sure, my dear sir, I must always acknowledge the receipt of everything that is kind and friendly from you; how gratefully I feel it, I can't and I think it is needless for me to express; were it possible for me to prove it, nothing nor no consideration on earth could or should prevent it. I have wrote to Augustus and have given him the best, indeed the only advice I could give him, which is to make use of nothing but truth in justification of his unhappy friend, as all fallacies and exagerations can only hurt the man and cause he wishes to serve. But not to employ his utmost powers with truth to vindicate his friend is what I can neither advise or wish; on the contrary I would excite him to it, as it is what on like occasion I would do myself at all hazards and perils, and so the best friend I have in the world shall find if ever there is occasion for it, which on *his* account (why should I not plainly say on *yours*) I hope will never happen, but if it should, here it is under my hand, and keep it, I beg of you. I have spirit and courage to make it good, tho' fortune and life itself were both concerned.

These are perilous times, my dear sir, God knows what may happen. The suffering, perhaps even encouraging a mob to declare they will have—or otherwise do themselves—what they call justice, is not only the most wicked, but the most weak and dangerous thing imaginable; if they are supported or allowed to make such insolent illegal declarations who knows whose turn may be next? I have heard a very extraordinary placard afixed up at the Exchange and permitted to remain there for several hours. I think it should warn those people who have it in their power to quell a mob from suffering them to threaten an innocent man, for such should everyone be supposed at least, who is not by *law* proved to be contrary; I am not quite of the opinion you seem to be with regard to this very unfortunate man, and that not from the bias of Augustus's opinion, or his obligations, may have given me, but from some circumstances I cannot write. I fear, be it how it will, this poor man must be the scape-goat. I am sorry for it on his account, I am offended at it for the sake of justice, but I am hurt by it beyond expression as an Englishwoman. I think you are perfectly in the right not to answer Augustus's letter at this time, and so I have told him; if on any other occasion or subject you will sometime or other do him the favour to write two or three lines to him, I know him well enough to be sure it would oblige him extremely. He is *un peu fier*, but very grateful in his temper, and where he is attached, thoroughly and warmly so. He is very uneasy lest he should lose his ship and the opportunity of serving, if there is an action in the Mediterranean this year, by his being sent for home as an evidence; and on the other hand as he thinks he can be a material one, he is very earnest to do his friend that piece of service. In short he is under the greatest anxiety and concern imaginable. He earnestly wishes to perform some *action d'éclat*; but if he must return as an evidence hopes it may be in his own ship, and the rest of the evidence with him if desired, that he may not lose her as soon as he has got her. . . .

Adieu! may you meet with no more blame than you deserve and if possible with all the rewards and distinctions you merit; my best wishes and best services are devoted to you. . . .

Fox did not challenge her defence of her son's conduct.

I will send Captain Hervey's letter, and as you have so obligingly mentioned me in it I cannot let it go without a word of my own avowing what your Ladyship says of me in regard to him. A ship is already gone to fetch the witnesses desired, of whom he is one, and I understand the Captains required as witnesses do not lose their ships as they are to be commanded by officers appointed to the command of them during the absence of the Captains. The Mob, dear madam, is not excited against Byng. The greatest care has been taken at least that they should not even get a sight of him. . . .[1]

A month later Fox wrote to Lady Hervey a paragraph which shows that the opposing interests of the politician and of the sailor were irreconcilable. The former was a minister trying to retain power, even if that end should require the sacrifice to injustice of the Government's chosen admiral; the latter was defending a dear friend and patron, who had been inadequately equipped and scandalously treated.

I see no difficulty that Captain Hervey can be under. He will be upon oath and will give true evidence. There is no room for friendship for giving evidence, and nobody will blame his doing Mr. Byng all the service he can. If the event should ruin Mr. Byng, that will grieve Mr. Hervey and be distressful, but Mr. Hervey's character as an officer or a man of courage can not on this occasion be complicated with Mr. Byng's. . . .[2]

Four months later when the trial was on at Portsmouth, Lady Hervey wrote to her son, describing a meeting with Fox;[3] it could properly confirm Hervey in his view that Fox was the "conscious and concealed persecutor" of the Admiral.

It is just a week since I have either heard from or wrote to my dear Boy, but I cannot forbear telling you how very very agreeably I have pased these last two days, in hearing the most pleasing the most grateful to my ears commendations of my dear Augustus. Lady Stafford was the first who told me that she heard that you had spoke or rather given in your evidence with a grace and an eloquence which was admired by all who heard you; at Lady George Sackville's several people made me

[1] 17th August. [2] 14th September.
[3] 13th January 1757; letter at Ickworth.

compliments upon it. Yesterday I went to see poor Felton[1] who amidst all his sufferings (which are really exquisite) hearing Mrs. Hervey and I talking of the same subject, said he had heard from different people that it was impossible for anything to be better, that the whole evidence (your's I mean) was the clearest, the best connected and the most guarded imaginable; but last night Mr. Fox, who came to me at 8 o'clock and stayed with me till near 11, said it was the most extraordinary thing imaginable that one could not hear anything whatever without it being represented in two different lights, quite black or quite white, that yesterday morning he had been told by one who had assisted at the trial that it went extremely ill for Mr. Byng, and two hours after he heard by another man who had also been present several days that it went extremely well; he then corrected himself and said there is, however, one thing in which all agree, which is that Mr. Hervey's evidence was as fine and as masterly a thing as ever was heard—a clearness and a perspicuity ran through the whole, not an improper or unnecessary word—indeed, Madam, said he, Mr. Hervey has most extraordinary good parts. I said I had long thought so and that I wished when parts were so wanted and so rare, that they would make use of them where they were. . . .

Adieu dear, dear Boy. I long to know truly if everything goes as we wish for; there is no getting at any truth here. . . .

The truth is that Fox was justified in trying to divert much of the blame for the loss of Minorca onto Byng for his unenterprising behaviour off Mahon—provided he did not exceed the bounds of fairness. The mutilation of the Admiral's despatch and the tacit, if not active, encouragement of the mob were unworthy incidents in this attempt to make the Admiral scapegoat for all the sins of the ministry; but it was Fox's conduct after the finding and sentence of the Court-Martial which can in no way be excused. The love of office and the knowledge that those who advocated leniency were flying in the face of royal and popular favour, were too strong for him; he acquiesced at the unjust execution, and that "fixed" Hervey's opinion of him.

[1] Felton Hervey, the Captain's uncle; see Introduction p. xiv.

APPENDIX D.

HORACE WALPOLE'S QUERIES

Horace Walpole was bitterly opposed in politics to Newcastle, Fox, Hardwicke and Anson, and in his *Memoirs of the Reign of George II* (Vol. II, p. 288), before describing the events leading up to Byng's execution, he is careful to make plain his attitude towards the Admiral " lest prejudice against the persecutors, or for the persecuted, should be suspected of having influenced my narrative."

" I can appeal to God that I never spoke to Mr. Byng in my life, nor had the most distant acquaintance with any one of his family. The man I never saw but in the street, or in the House of Commons, and there I thought his carriage haughty and disgusting. From reports, I had formed a mean opinion of his understanding ; and from the clamours of the world, I was carried away with the multitude in believing he had not done his duty ; and in thinking his behaviour under *his* circumstances weak and arrogant. I never interested myself enough about him to inquire whether this opinion was well or ill founded. When his pamphlet[1] appeared, I read it, and found he had been cruelly and scandalously treated. I knew enough not to wonder at this conduct in *some* of his persecutors—yet it concerned not me ; and I thought no more about it till the sentence, and the behaviour of his Judges which accompanied it, struck me with astonishment ! I could not conceive, how men could acquit honourably and condemn to death with the same breath ! How men could feel so much, and be so insensible at the same instant ; and from the prejudice of education which had told me that the law of England understood that its ministers of Justice should always be Counsel *for* the prisoner, I could not comprehend how the members of the Court-Martial came to think that a small corner of a law ought to preponderate for rigour, against a whole body of the same law which they understood directed them to mercy ; and I was still more startled to hear men urge that their consciences were bound by an oath, which their consciences told them would lead them to murder."

The *Queries* which Hervey got published in the *London Chronicle* on 8–10th February 1757 gave expression to these sentiments. The MS is among his papers, and is in Walpole's hand ; across the top of the page Hervey has written " These are not mine but Mr. Horace Walpole's sent to me, and which I printed." They are devoid of that vicious cynicism which Walpole's detractors find so distasteful. In an eloquent plea for humanity and clemency he steers clear of political mud-slinging and personal abuse, and confines himself to the injustice of carrying out the sentence.

[1] Which printed the Admiral's despatch in full for the first time.—Ed.

QUERIES

ADDRESSED TO EVERY ENGLISHMAN'S OWN FEELING

Is the death of any one man of such consequence, that to obtain it would be worth while to break thro' the known practice, and overturn the settled customs of all our courts of judicature?

Lenity is the established spirit of the laws of *England*: *new* and *ambiguous* terms are never interpreted *against* a prisoner. In doubtful cases the judge always directs a jury to find *for* the prisoner: and even if he is condemned, if any favourable circumstances appear for him, it is customary for the court to recommend him to mercy; and it is most unheard of to execute a prisoner so recommended.

Admiral Byng was not only most earnestly recommended to mercy by his judges, but they declared that they only found him guilty by the harshness and obscurity of a *New Military Law*.

Who will advise the throne of mercy in the tenderest of all cases to contradict it's usual compassion?

Who would wish to have a criminal executed, by interpreting an obscure and severe law in the worst sense?

Who wishes to establish a precedent for setting aside the recommendation of judges and juries?

What case can ever hereafter be pleaded as hard if Admiral Byng is put to death?

When can *any* criminal hope for so favourable a case, as to have his judge declare that he condemns him against his conscience?

If the conscience of a judge is disregarded, is not the next step, to expect that judges should not regard their consciences?

If mercy does not preponderate in doubtful cases, what advantages have the laws of England over the despotic maxims of Turkey?

Does not, whoever demands the death of Admiral Byng in the present circumstances, give his approbation to interpreting *military* law in the worst sense? Does not he subject himself, his friends and his posterity to the worst of precedents? And do not the people court arbitrary power, if they countenance the utmost rigour of a *new* law, under which two[1] admirals have declared it impossible for them to serve?

If Admiral *Byng* should be executed, and yet this dreadful Twelfth

[1] Printed as "several Admirals"; the two are, of course, West and Forbes.

Article of *War* should hereafter be repealed, will it not prove the hardship of his fate ?[1]

When this very law was proposed, it was urged that in a hard or doubtful case his M——y would have the power of pardoning. Can that case be clear or not hard, in which the judges have declared that they pronounced sentence against their consciences ?[2]

If an eminent person of the law has declared that the very sentence is illegal, will it not be a hard case, to put a man to death against such an opinion ?

Who can avoid hoping that a very hard precedent will not be introduced under the longest and mildest reign since the conquest ?

[1] In 1779, after Keppel's court-martial, the Article *was* amended to permit the court to impose a sentence alternative to death, if they thought fit. 19 Geo. III, cap. 17.

[2] See p. 78.

INDEX

INDEX

Naval officers are mostly shown in the ranks which they held when Hervey wrote about them. The figures in parentheses immediately after the rank indicate the date of their seniority; Hervey's rank as a captain dated from 1747.

An asterisk denotes Hervey's more particular lady-friends.

Hervey is referred to as " AH ".